TRANSPARENCY MA

to accompany

SYSTEMS ANALYSIS AND DESIGN METHODS

Third Edition

Jeffrey L. Whitten
Lonnie D. Bentley
Victor M. Barlow
All of Purdue University

IRWIN
Burr Ridge, Illinois
Boston, Massachusetts
Sydney, Australia

©Richard D. Irwin, Inc., 1986, 1989, and 1994

All rights reserved. The contents, or parts thereof, may be reproduced for classroom use with *Systems Analysis and Design Methods,* Third Edition, by Whitten, Bentley, and Barlow, provided such reproductions bear copyright notice and the number reproduced does not exceed the number of students using the text, but may not be reproduced in any form for any other purpose without written permission of the publisher.

Printed in the United States of America.

ISBN 0-256-09365-2

1 2 3 4 5 6 7 8 9 0 WCB 1 0 9 8 7 6 5 4

SADM3
Transparency Guide

#	SADM3 Black & White Transparency Masters FIGURE	DESCRIPTION	TEXT PAGE
1	Figure 1.1	Job Description for a Systems Analyst	p. 10
2	Figure 1.3	Organization of the Information Systems Function	p. 14
3	Figure 1.4	People with Whom the Analyst Must Work	p. 18
4	Figure 2.1	The People Building Block of Information Systems	p. 41
5	Figure 2.2	Different Types of System Users	p. 43
6	Figure 2.4	A View of Data Suitable for System Owners	p. 49
7	Figure 2.5	A View of Data Suitable for System Users	p. 50
8	Figure 2.6	A View of Data Suitable for System Designers	p. 51
9	Figure 2.7	A View of Data Suitable for System Builders	p. 52
10	Figure 2.9	A System Owner's View of Activities	p. 54
11	Figure 2.13	A View of Activities Suitable for System Builders	p. 64
12	Figure 2.15	A View of Networks Suitable for System Owners	p. 67
13	Figure 2.17	A View of Networks Suitable for System Designers	p. 71
14	Figure 3.2	Systems Entropy Occurs Sometime During the Systems Support Phase	p. 96
15	Figure 3.3	Principles of Systems Development	p. 97
16	Figure 3.4	The PIECES Framework	p. 99
17	Figure 4.1	IS Dimensions Emphasized by Today's Structured Techniques	p. 144
18	Figure 4.2	Structured Programming Concepts	p. 146
19	Figure 4.3	The End Product of Structured Design	p. 148
20	Figure 4.4	An End Product of Structured Analysis	p. 150
21	Figure 4.5	An End-Product of Data Modeling	p. 153
22	Figure 5.2	A Life Cycle-Based Framework for CASE Tools	p. 171
23	Figure 5.3	CASE Tools for Systems Planning	p. 172
24	Figure 5.4	A Typical CASE Tool for Systems Planning	p. 173
25	Figure 5.5	CASE Tools for Systems Analysis and Design	p. 174
26	Figure 5.6	Typical CASE Tools for Systems Analysis and Design	p. 175
27	Figure 5.7	CASE Tools for Systems Design and Implementation	p. 177
28	Figure 5.8	An Application Programmer's Workbench	p. 178
29	Figure 5.9	CASE Tools for Systems Support	p. 180
30	Figure 5.10	Reverse Engineering	p. 182
31	Figure 5.17	Data Integration of File Transfer	p. 192
32	Figure 5.18	Data Integration through a Data Link	p. 193
33	Figure 5.19	Cost Justification of CASE	p. 200
34	Figure 5.20	A Development Center's Organization	p. 202
35	Figure 6.1	Systems Planning	p. 214
36	Figure 6.2	Critical Success Factor Hierarchy	p. 215
37	Figure 6.3	Value Chain Analysis	p. 217
38	Figure 6.5	Context Model	p. 222
39	Figure 6.6	An Outline for a Planning Project Charter	p. 224
40	Figure 6.8	Association Matrices	p. 226
41	Figure 6.10	Organization Charts	p. 230
42	Figure 6.11	Decomposition Diagram	p. 231
43	Figure 6.12	A Subject Data Model	p. 232
44	Figure 6.13	An Outline for an Information Architecture and Plan	p. 237

#	FIGURE	DESCRIPTION	PAGE
45	Figure 6 . 16	Data Flow Diagrams	p. 244
46	Figure 7 . 4	Request for System Services	p. 258
47	Figure 7 . 5	Sample Questions for Survey Phase Interview	p. 259
48	Figure 7 . 6	Context Model	p. 260
49	Figure 7 . 7	Problem/Opportunity Survey Matrix	p. 261
50	Figure 7 . 8	An Outline for a Project Feasibility Assessment	p. 263
51	Figure 7 . 12	A Problem/Opportunity/Objective/Constraint Matrix	p. 276
52	Figure 7 . 13	An Outline for a Business Problem Statement	p. 278
53	Figure 7 . 16	Data Model Diagrams	p. 283
54	Figure 7 . 17	Data Flow Diagrams	p. 284
55	Figure 7 . 18	Connectivity Diagrams	p. 285
56	Figure 7 . 19	A Hard Copy Requirements Statement	p. 290
57	Figure 8 . 1	Types of System Models	p. 305
58	Figure 8 . 3	An Artistic Data Model	p. 307
59	Figure 8 . 4	An Entity Relationship Diagram as a Data Model	p. 309
60	Figure 8 . 6	Examples of Entities	p. 311
61	Figure 8 . 7	Data Attributes That Describe an Entity	p. 313
62	Figure 8 . 8	Entity Supertypes and Subtypes	p. 314
63	Figure 8 . 9	Multiple Relationships between the Same Entities	p. 315
64	Figure 8 . 11	Alternative Notations for Relationships That Are Described by Data Attributes	p. 318
65	Figure 8 . 12	Relationships between Occurrences of the Same Entity	p. 319
66	Figure 8 . 13	N-Ary Relationships	p. 320
67	Figure 8 . 14	Rules Governing Relationships	p. 320
68	Figure 8 . 15	A Chen-Style Data Model	p. 322
69	Figure 8 . 16	A Martin-Style Data Model	p. 323
70	Figure 8 . 17	A Bachman-Style Data Model	p. 324
71	Figure 8 . 18	A Simpler Bachman-Style Data Model	p. 326
72	Figure 8 . 19	CASE Tools for Data Modeling	p. 328
73	Figure 8 . 20	SoundStage Member Services Data Entities	p. 334
74	Figure 8 . 21	SoundStage Data Entity Identifiers	p. 335
75	Figure 8 . 22	Relationship Matrix	p. 335
76	Figure 8 . 23	The SoundStage Essential Data Model	p. 337
77	Figure 8 . 24	Forms Sampling	p. 339
78	Figure 8 . 25	Fully Attributed Entities	p. 341
79	Figure 9 . 1	Types of Systems Models	p. 349
80	Figure 9 . 4	DeMarco and/or Yourdon DFD	p. 354
81	Figure 9 . 5	Common DFD Errors	p. 356
82	Figure 9 . 6	Eliminating Routing Processes	p. 357
83	Figure 9 . 7	The Data Flow Packet Concept	p. 358
84	Figure 9 . 8	Diverging Data Flows	p. 359
85	Figure 9 . 10	Subset of a Data Model	p. 362
86	Figure 9 . 11	Data Store Guidelines	p. 363
87	Figure 9 . 12	CASE Tool for DFDs	p. 364
88	Figure 9 . 13	A Context Diagram	p. 369
89	Figure 9 . 14	The Expansion Approach to Drawing DFDs	p. 371
90	Figure 9 . 15	The Explosion Approach to Drawing DFDs	p. 372
91	Figure 9 . 16	Decomposition Diagram	p. 374
	Figure 9 . 17	Decomposition Diagram (concluded)	p. 375
92	Figure 9 . 18	Data Store Decomposition	p. 377
93	Figure 9 . 19	An Overview Data Flow Diagram	p. 379-380

#	FIGURE	DESCRIPTION	PAGE
94	Figure 9 . 22	An Alternative Overview Data Flow Diagram	p. 380
95	Figure 9 . 20	A Middle-Level Data Flow Diagram	p. 381
96	Figure 9 . 21	Another Middle-Level DFD for Membership	p. 382
97	Figure 9 . 22	Another Middle-Level DFD for Order Processing	p. 383
98	Figure 9 . 23	Another Middle-Level DFD	p. 384
99	Figure 9 . 24	A Simple Primitive-Level DFD	p. 385
100	Figure 9 . 25	Primitive DFD for Automatically Shipping a Dated Order	p. 386
101	Figure 9 . 26	Primitive DFD for Filling a Member's Order Response	p. 387
102	Figure 9 . 27	Primitive DFD for Filling a Special or Bonus Order	p. 388
103	Figure 9 . 28	Primitive DFD for Renewal Subscription Order	p. 390
104	Figure 9 . 28	Primitive DFD for Referral Subscription Order	p. 391
105	Figure 9 . 28	Primitive DFD for the Membership Reporting Subsystem	p. 389
106	Figure 9 . 28	Primitive DFD for Data Maintenance	p. 392
107	Figure 9 . 29	A Level-Zero DFD Using the Gane and Sarson Expansion Approach	p. 393
108	Figure 9 . 30	A Level-One DFD Using the Gane and Sarson Expansion Approach	p. 394-395
109	Figure 10 . 2	Centralized Computing with Time-Sharing	p. 405
110	Figure 10 . 3	Distributed Computing	p. 406
111	Figure 10 . 4	Client/Server Computing	p. 408
112	Figure 11 . 1	Sample Project Repository Entry	p. 427
113	Figure 11 . 2	The Organization of a Project Repository	p. 430
114	Figure 11 . 3	The Sequence Data Structure	p. 431
115	Figure 11 . 4	The Exclusive-or Selection Data Structure	p. 432
116	Figure 11 . 5	The Inclusive-or Selection Data Structure	p. 432
117	Figure 11 . 6	A Common Misuse of the Selection Data Structure	p. 433
118	Figure 11 . 7	The Repetition Data Structure	p. 433
119	Figure 11 . 8	A Nested Repeating Data Structure	p. 434
120	Figure 11 . 9	Optional Data Attributes in a Data Structure	p. 435
121	Figure 11 . 10	Common Data Structures	p. 435
122	Figure 11 . 11	A Decision Table for Specifying a Store's Check-Cashing Policy	p. 438
123	Figure 11 . 12	A Decision Table for Solving the Poker Chip Problem	p. 440
124	Figure 11 . 13	Entering All Possible Rules into a Decision Table	p. 442
125	Figure 11 . 14	Defining the Actions for Each Rule in a Decision Table	p. 443
126	Figure 11 . 15	Simplifying a Decision Table	p. 444
127	Figure 11 . 16	Simplified Decision Table for the Credit Union Dividend Policy	p. 445
128	Figure 11 . 17	A Sample Structured English Description of a Business Procedure	p. 446
129	Figure 11 . 18	A Sample Action Diagram Description of a Business Procedure	p. 447
130	Figure 11 . 19	A Sample Tight English Description of a Business Procedure	p. 447
131	Figure 11 . 20	The Case and If-Then-Otherwise Constructs in Structured English	p. 448
132	Figure 11 . 21	The Repetition Construct of Structured English	p. 450
133	Figure 11 . 22	Project Repository Entry for a Data Entity from a Data Model	p. 452
134	Figure 11 . 23	Project Repository Entry for a Data Flow from a Process Model	p. 454
135	Figure 11 . 24	Project Repository Entry for a Data Store from a Process Model	p. 455

#	FIGURE	DESCRIPTION	PAGE
136	Figure 11 . 25	Project Repository Entry for a Record	p. 457
137	Figure 11 . 26	Project Repository Entry for a Data Attribute	p. 458
138	Figure 11 . 27	Project Repository Entry for a Table of Codes	p. 461
139	Figure 11 . 28	Project Repository Entry for a Process Appearing on a Process Model	p. 462
140	Figure 11 . 29	Project Repository Entry for a Decision Table	p. 463
141	Figure 11 . 30	Project Repository Entry for a Location	p. 464
142	Figure 12 . 3	Partially Completed Candidate Matrix	p. 478
143	Figure 12 . 4	Partially Completed Feasibility Matrix	p. 479
144	Figure 12 . 5	Sample Rankings Matrix	p. 480
145	Figure 12 . 7	Request for Proposals (RFP)	p. 483
146	Figure 13 . 1	Data Entities and Attributes for SoundStage Entertainment Club	p. 508
147	Figure 13 . 3	Transformation of the MEMBER Entity into 1NF	p. 512
148	Figure 13 . 4	Transformation of the BACKORDER Entity into 1NF	p. 513
149	Figure 13 . 5	Analysis and Transformation of the ORDERED PRODUCT Entity into 2NF	p. 515
150	Figure 13 . 7	Analysis and Transformation of Entities into 3NF	p. 517
151	Figure 13 . 9	Further Simplification through Inspection	p. 520
152	Figure 13 . 10	Final Entity Relationship Data Model	p. 521
153	Figure 13 . 11	Final Mapping of Data Attributes to Data Entities	p. 522
154	Figure 13 . 12	Sample Table for Recording Event Analysis	p. 526
155	Figure 13 . 13	Partially Completed Event Analysis Table	p. 527
156	Figure 13 . 14	Sample CASE Tool Entry for Event Analysis	p. 529
157	Figure 13 . 15	Revised DFD for PROMOTION Subsystem	p. 531
158	Figure 14 . 1	Point-to-Point Network	p. 540
159	Figure 14 . 2	Bus Network	p. 541
160	Figure 14 . 3	Star Network	p. 542
161	Figure 14 . 4	Hierarchical Network	p. 543
162	Figure 14 . 5	Ring Network	p. 544
163	Figure 14 . 6	Diverging Data Flows	p. 551
164	Figure 14 . 10	A Person/Machine Boundary	p. 560
165	Figure 14 . 11	A Manual Design Unit	p. 561
166	Figure 14 . 12	Analyzing Response-Time Requirements	p. 562
167	Figure 14 . 13	An On-Line Design Unit	p. 563
168	Figure 14 . 14	A Network Topology DFD	p. 565
169	Figure 14 . 15	A Network Topology DFD	p. 566
170	Figure 14 . 16	Distributed Data Stores	p. 567
171	Figure 14 . 17	Distributed Processes	p. 568
172	Figure 14 . 18	A Final Design Unit DFD	p. 569
173	Figure 15 . 2	Sample Attribute Repository Description	p. 583
174	Figure 15 . 3	Fixed-Length versus Variable-Length Records	p. 584
175	Figure 15 . 4	Sample Repository Entry for the ORDERS FILE	p. 585
176	Figure 15 . 5	Alternative Sequential File Organizations of Records	p. 588
177	Figure 15 . 6	Indexed File Organization	p. 589
178	Figure 15 . 9	Relational Data Structures	p. 594
179	Figure 15 . 10	Partitioned Entity Relationship Data Model for SoundStage	p. 597
180	Figure 15 . 11	Preliminary Attribute Content of the ORDERS FILE	p. 598
181	Figure 15 . 12	Implementing Relationships through Attributes	p. 600
182	Figure 15 . 13	Final Attribute Contents of the ORDERS FILE	p. 601
183	Figure 15 . 14	Typical CASE Repository Report	p. 602

#	FIGURE	DESCRIPTION	PAGE
184	Figure 15.15	Detailed Logical Requirements and File Design Specifications for the ORDERS FILE	p. 603
185	Figure 15.16	Distributed Data Model for SoundStage	p. 606
186	Figure 15.17	A Relational Database Schema for SoundStage	p. 608
187	Figure 15.18	Project Repository Entry for a Table (Part 1)	p. 610
188	Figure 15.19	Project Repository Entry for a Table (Part 2)	p. 610
189	Figure 16.1	Typical External Turnaround Document	p. 630
190	Figure 16.2	Sample Internal Outputs	p. 631
191	Figure 16.3	Alternative Input Procedures for Batch Input Media	p. 633
192	Figure 16.4	Keying from Source Documents	p. 637
193	Figure 16.5	Modulus 11 Self-Checking-Digit Technique	p. 639
194	Figure 16.6	A Design Unit Data Flow Diagram for SoundStage Inputs	p. 641
195	Figure 16.7	Description of a Typical Input	p. 641
196	Figure 16.8	Attribute Repository Entry for the Contents of MEMBER ORDER RESPONSE	p. 642
197	Figure 16.9	Source Document Design Zones	p. 643
198	Figure 16.10	Display Layout Chart for On-Line MEMBER ORDER RESPONSE	p. 646
199	Figure 16.11	Display Layout Chart for On-Line MEMBER ORDER RESPONSE Fields to be Input	p. 648
200	Figure 16.12	Specifications for Display Attributes and Error Messages for MEMBER ORDER RESPONSE Input Screen	p. 649
201	Figure 16.13	Alternative Graphic Design for On-Line MEMBER ORDER RESPONSE	p. 650
202	Figure 16.14	Sample Input Record Layout for Batch MEMBER ORDER RESPONSE Input	p. 651
203	Figure 16.15	Sample Input Record Layout for Multiple Input Records	p. 652
204	Figure 16.16	Design Specifications for ORDER TO BE FILLED	p. 655
205	Figure 16.17	Attribute Details of ORDER TO BE FILLED Output	p. 655
206	Figure 16.18	Sample Attribute Screen	p. 657
207	Figure 16.19	Sample Prototypes Generated from a Spreadsheet	p. 658
208	Figure 16.20	Prototyped Output Screen from a CASE Tool	p. 659
209	Figure 16.21	Printer Spacing Chart for ORDER TO BE FILLED	p. 661
210	Figure 16.22	Display Layout Chart	p. 662-663
211	Figure 17.1	A Typical Example of a GUI from Microsoft Windows	p. 675
212	Figure 17.2	Radio Buttons and Check Boxes in a GUI	p. 676
213	Figure 17.3	Screen Zones	p. 678
214	Figure 17.4	Sample Zones for a Screen	p. 679
215	Figure 17.5	Classic Hierarchical Menu Dialogue	p. 682
216	Figure 17.6	Alternative Pull-Down and Pop-Up Menu Dialogue	p. 683
217	Figure 17.7	Sample State Transition Diagram for Documenting Dialogue	p. 685
218	Figure 17.8	State Transition Diagram Conventions	p. 686
219	Figure 17.9	State Transition Diagram for SoundStage Member Service Project	p. 687-688
220	Figure 17.10	Display Layout Chart for the MEMBER SERVICES SYSTEM MENU Screen	p. 691
221	Figure 17.11	Display Layout Chart for the ORDER PROCESSING SUBSYSTEM MENU Screen	p. 692
222	Figure 17.12	Display Layout Chart for the ORDER TRANSACTIONS MENU Screen	p. 694

#	FIGURE	DESCRIPTION	PAGE
223	Figure 17.13	Display Layout Chart for MEMBER ORDER ENTRY HELP Screen	p. 695
224	Figure 17.14	Sample Help Messages for the Member Order Help Screen	p. 696
225	Figure 18.2	Warnier/Orr Notation	p. 704
226	Figure 18.4	A De Facto Standard Structure Chart for Most Programs	p. 708
227	Figure 18.5	Primitive Functions Performed by INITIATE and TERMINATE PROCESSING Modules	p. 708
228	Figure 18.6	Transaction Centers for a Simple Program	p. 709
229	Figure 18.7	On-Line Transaction Centers	p. 710
230	Figure 18.8	Primitive Process	p. 711
231	Figure 18.9	Factoring MAIN PROCESSING into Cohesive Primitives	p. 712
232	Figure 18.10	Data Structure Factoring	p. 712
233	Figure 18.11	Pseudocode	p. 715
234	Figure 18.12	Data Flow Diagram for PROCESS MEMBER ORDERS	p. 716
235	Figure 18.13	Structure Chart for PROCESS MEMBER ORDERS	p. 717
236	Figure 18.14	Structured English	p. 718
237	Figure 19.4	A Program Development Life Cycle	p. 733
238	Figure 19.7	An Outline for a Training Manual	p. 739
239	Figure A.1	PERT Notation	p. 772
240	Figure A.2	Project Planning Table	p. 774
241	Figure A.3	Completed PERT Chart	p. 774
242	Figure A.4	Sample PERT Chart for an SDLC	p. 777
243	Figure A.5	Simple Gantt Chart for an SDLC	p. 778
244	Figure A.6	Progress Reporting with Gantt Charts	p. 779
245	Figure A.7	Management Expectations Matrix	p. 781
246	Figure A.8	Management Expectations for the American Moon Landing Project	p. 782
247	Figure A.9	An Initial Management Expectations Matrix	p. 784
248	Figure A.10	Adjusting Resources in a Management Expectations Matrix	p. 785
249	Figure A.11	Priority Migration in a Management Expectations Matrix	p. 786
250	Figure B.1	Sample Interview Guide	p. 803
251	Figure C.2	Costs for a Proposed Systems Solution	p. 820
252	Figure C.3	Payback Analysis for a Project	p. 824
253	Figure C.4	Partial Table for Present Value of a Dollar	p. 825
254	Figure C.5	Net Present Value Analysis for a Project	p. 827
255	Figure C.6	Sample Blank Feasibility Analysis	p. 828
256	Figure C.7	Sample Candidate System Matrix	p. 829
257	Figure C.8	Sample Blank Feasibility Comparison Matrix	p. 830
258	Figure C.9	Sample Feasibility Analysis Matrix	p. 831
259	Figure D.1	Typical Outline and Time Allocation for an Oral Presentation	p. 843
260	Figure D.2	Guidelines for Visual Aids	p. 844
261	Figure D.3	Typical Project Walkthrough Form	p. 848-849
262	Figure D.4	Formats for Written Reports	p. 852
263	Figure D.5	Secondary Elements for a Written Report	p. 853
264	Figure D.6	Steps in Writing a Report	p. 854

Transparency Masters

Job Description for a Systems Analyst

TM-1

The job description for a systems analyst will vary from firm to firm. This description is representative of a systems analyst.

JOB TITLE:	Systems analyst (multiple-job levels)
REPORTS TO:	Systems development team manager or assistant director of systems development
DESCRIPTION:	A systems analyst shall be responsible for studying the problems and needs set forth by this organization to determine how computer hardware, applications software, files and databases, networks, people, and procedures can best solve these problems and improve business and information systems.
RESPONSIBILITIES:	1. Evaluates projects for feasibility. 2. Estimates personnel requirements, budgets, and schedules for systems development and maintenance projects. 3. Performs interviews and other fact gathering. 4. Documents and analyzes current system operations. 5. Defines user requirements for improving or replacing systems. 6. Identifies potential applications of computer technology that may fulfill requirements. 7. Evaluates applications of computer technology for feasibility. 8. Recommends new systems and technical solutions to end users and management. 9. Identifies potential hardware and software vendors, when appropriate. 10. Recommends and selects hardware and software purchases (subject to approval). 11. Designs system inputs, outputs, on-line dialogue, flow, and procedures. 12. Designs files and databases (subject to approval by Data Administration). 13. Writes, tests, and/or supervises applications software development. 14. Trains users to work with new systems and versions. 15. Converts operations to new systems or versions. 16. Supports operational applications.
EXTERNAL CONTACTS:	1. Assigned end users of mainframe computers and applications. 2. Assigned owners (end user management) of mainframe computers and applications. 3. Data Administration Center personnel. 4. Network Administration Center personnel. 5. Information Center personnel. 6. Operations Center personnel. 7. Methodology/CASE expert and staff. 8. Computer hardware and software vendors. 9. Other systems analysis and development managers.
MINIMUM QUALIFICATIONS:	Bachelor or Masters Degree in Computer Information Systems or related field. Programming experience preferred. Prior experience with business applications considered helpful. Prior training or experience in systems analysis and design, preferably structured methods, preferred. Good communications skills—oral and written—are mandatory.
TRAINING REQUIREMENTS:	Analysts must complete or demonstrate equivalent backgrounds in the following in-hours training courses: STRADIS Methodology and Standards, Joint Application Design (JAD) Techniques, Systems Application Architecture (SAA) Standards, Fundamentals, DB2 Database Design Techniques, CSP Prototyping Techniques, Excelerator/IS Computer Aided Design Techniques, Project Management Techniques, Microcomputer Software Tools, and Interpersonal and Communications Skills for Systems Analysis.

JOB LEVELS:	Initial assignments are based on programming experience and training results. The following job levels are defined:
	    Programmer/analyst: 30% analysis/design—70% programming
	    Analyst/programmer: 50% analysis/design—50% programming
	    Analyst: 70% analysis/design—30% programming
	    Senior analyst: 30% management—60% analysis/design and 10% programming
	    Lead analyst: 100% analysis/design or consulting

©Richard D. Irwin, Inc., 1994

Organization of the Information Systems Function

Every information systems shop develops its own unique structure; however, this structure is fairly typical of a progressive shop.

TM–2

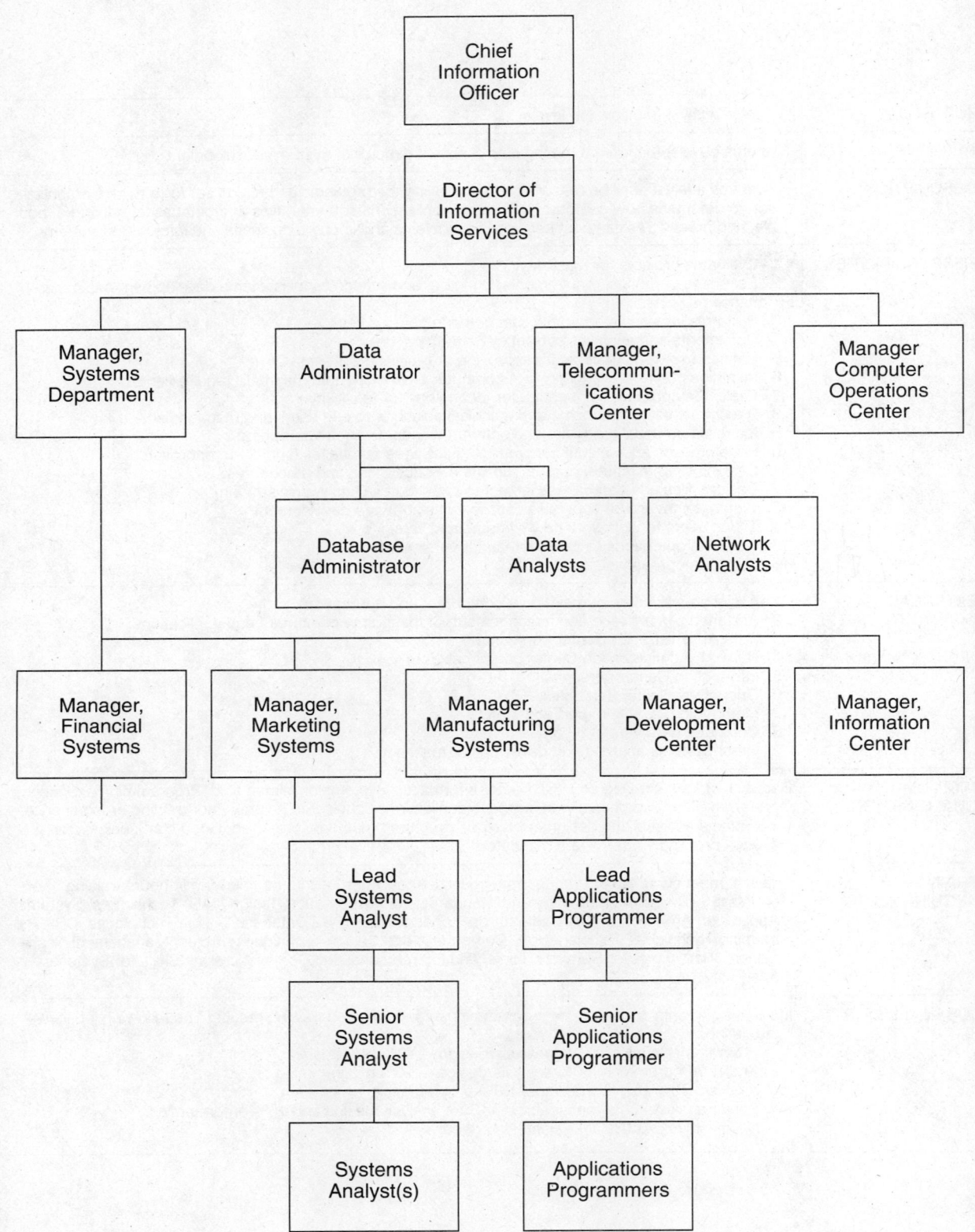

©Richard D. Irwin, Inc., 1994

People with Whom the Analyst Must Work

As facilitators of systems development, the analyst must work with many types of people, both technical and nontechnical.

TM-3

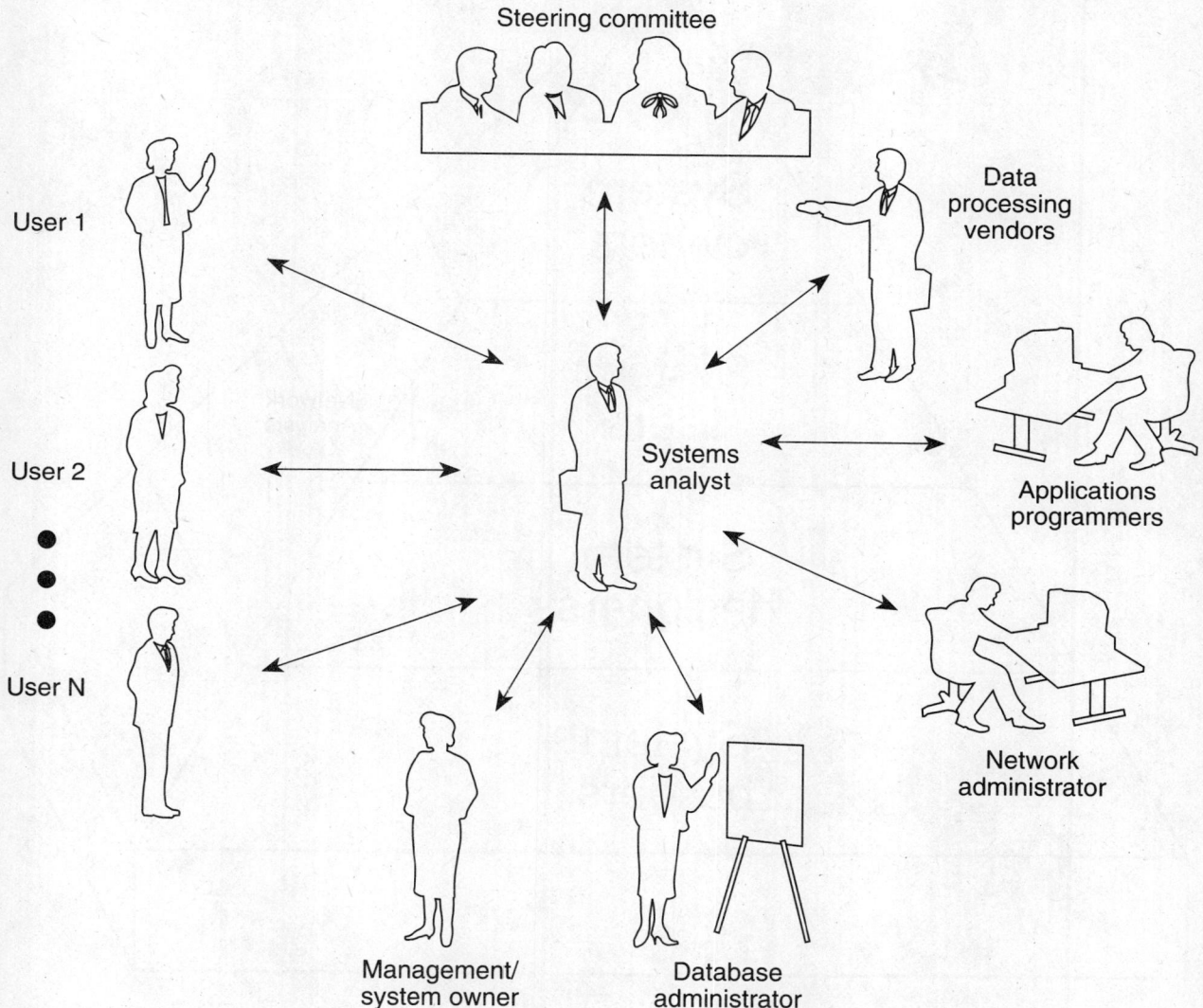

The People Building Block of Information Systems
This face of your pyramid model identifies the players in the information systems game. They are classified according to their development roles.

TM–4

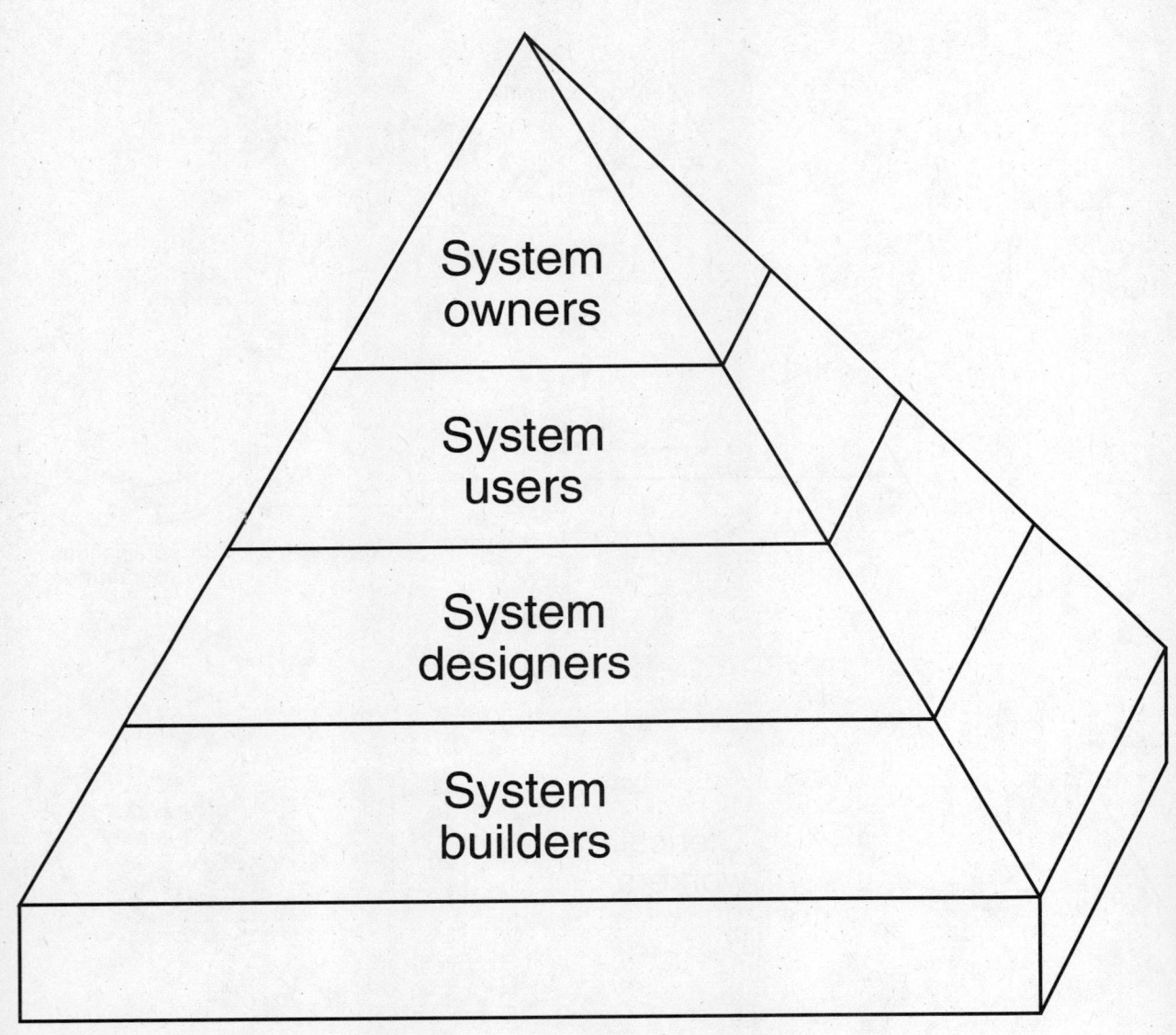

©Richard D. Irwin, Inc., 1994

Different Types of System Users
This alternate view of the PEOPLE face of your pyramid represents how system users view themselves. Most system users fall into one of the five groups shown on the pyramid.

TM–5

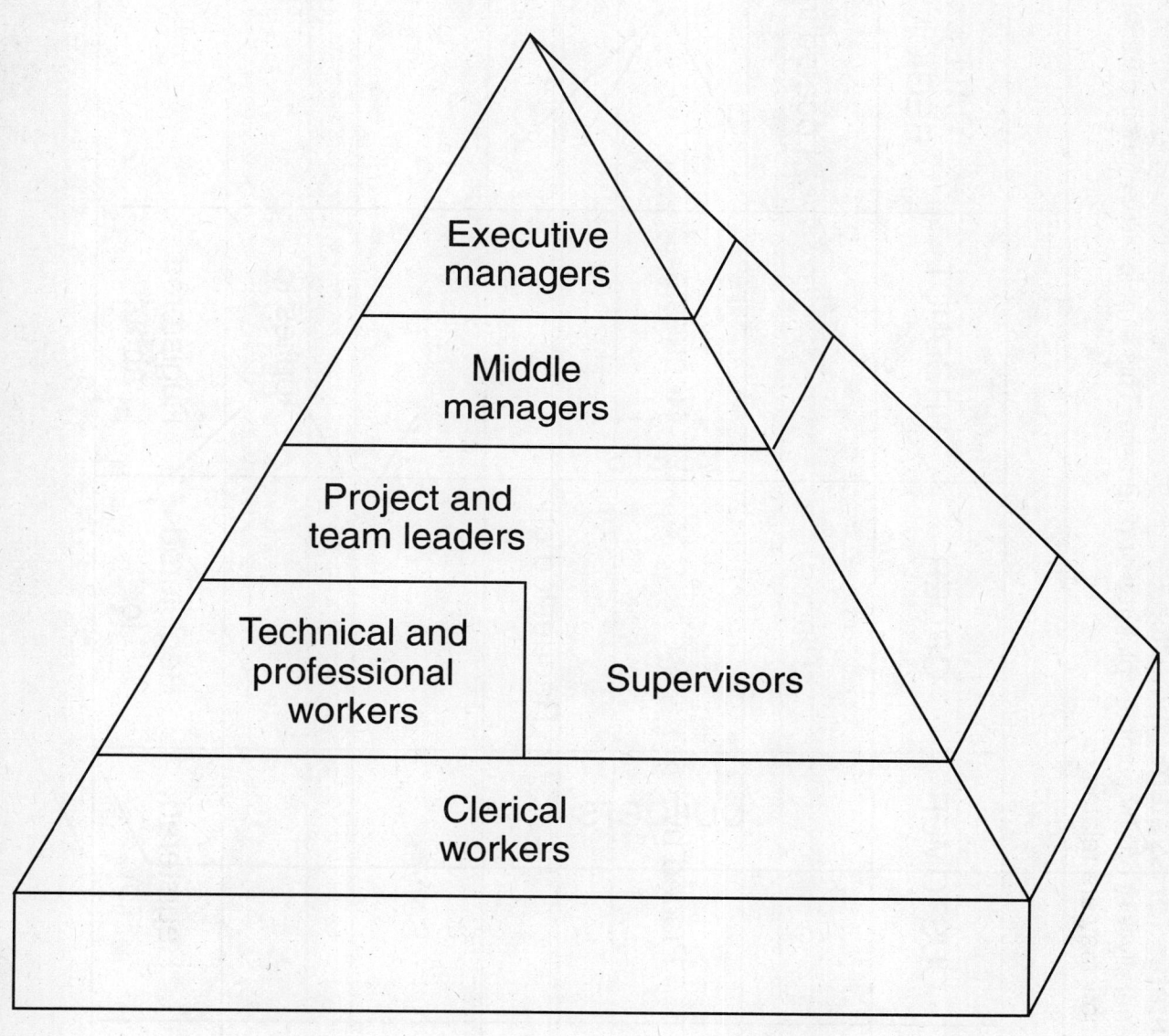

©Richard D. Irwin, Inc., 1994

A View of Data Suitable for System Owners

System owners are generally "put off" by complex pictures or diagrams. This simple view of their data focuses on business entities and how they are related.

TM–6

Entity	CUSTOMER	ORDER	PRODUCT	SALES REGION	FORECAST
CUSTOMER		Places		Located in	
ORDER	Placed by		Requests		
PRODUCT		Requested on			Has
SALES REGION	Serves				
FORECAST			Applies to		
COMPLAINT	Registered by	Registered for	Registered about		

©Richard D. Irwin, Inc., 1994

A View of Data Suitable for System Users
System users can generally understand relatively simple diagrams of data if they are properly presented and explained.

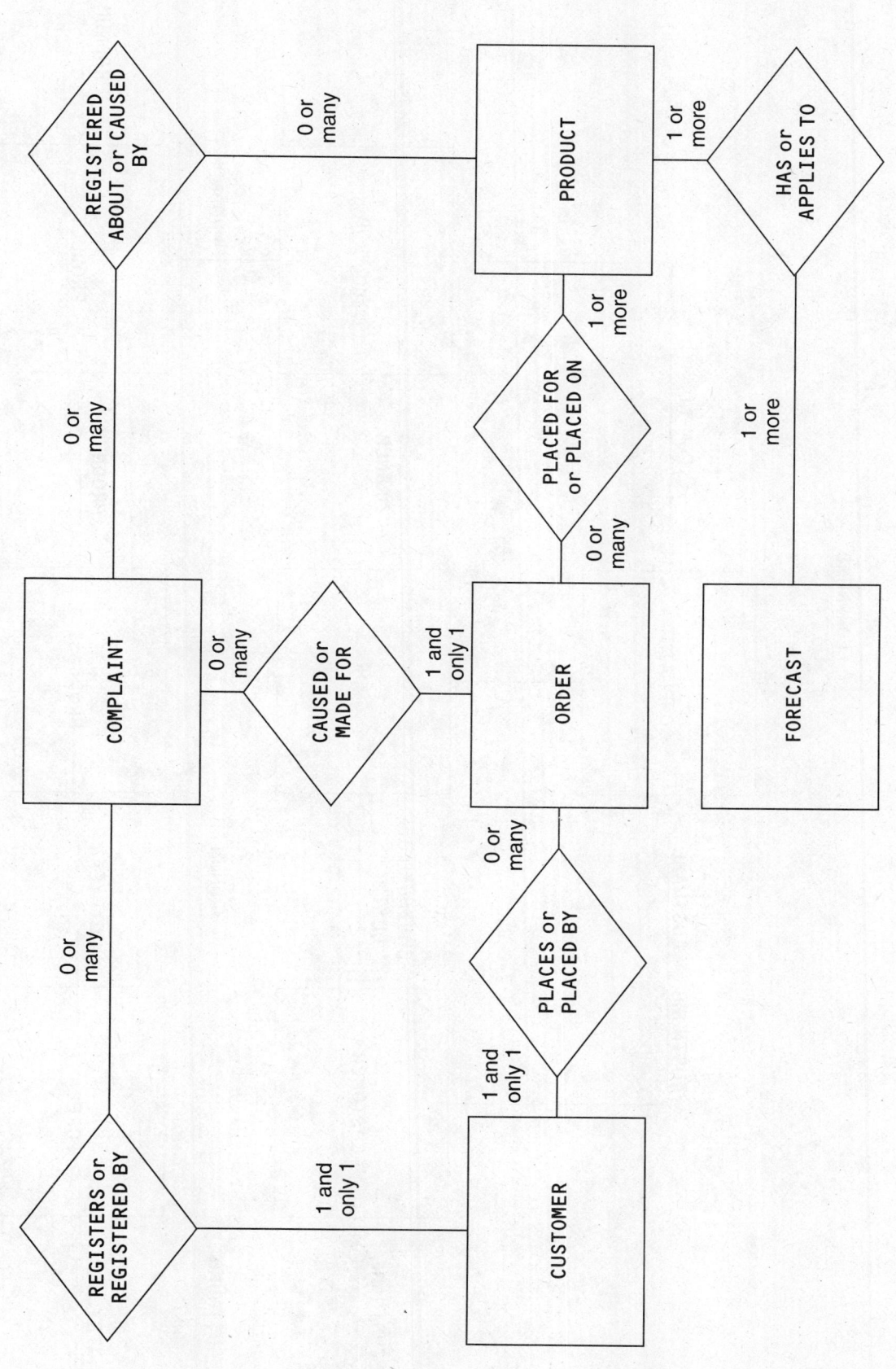

TM-7

© Richard D. Irwin, Inc., 1994

A View of Data Suitable for System Designers
System designers usually illustrate data in somewhat greater technical detail than system owners or users.

TM-8

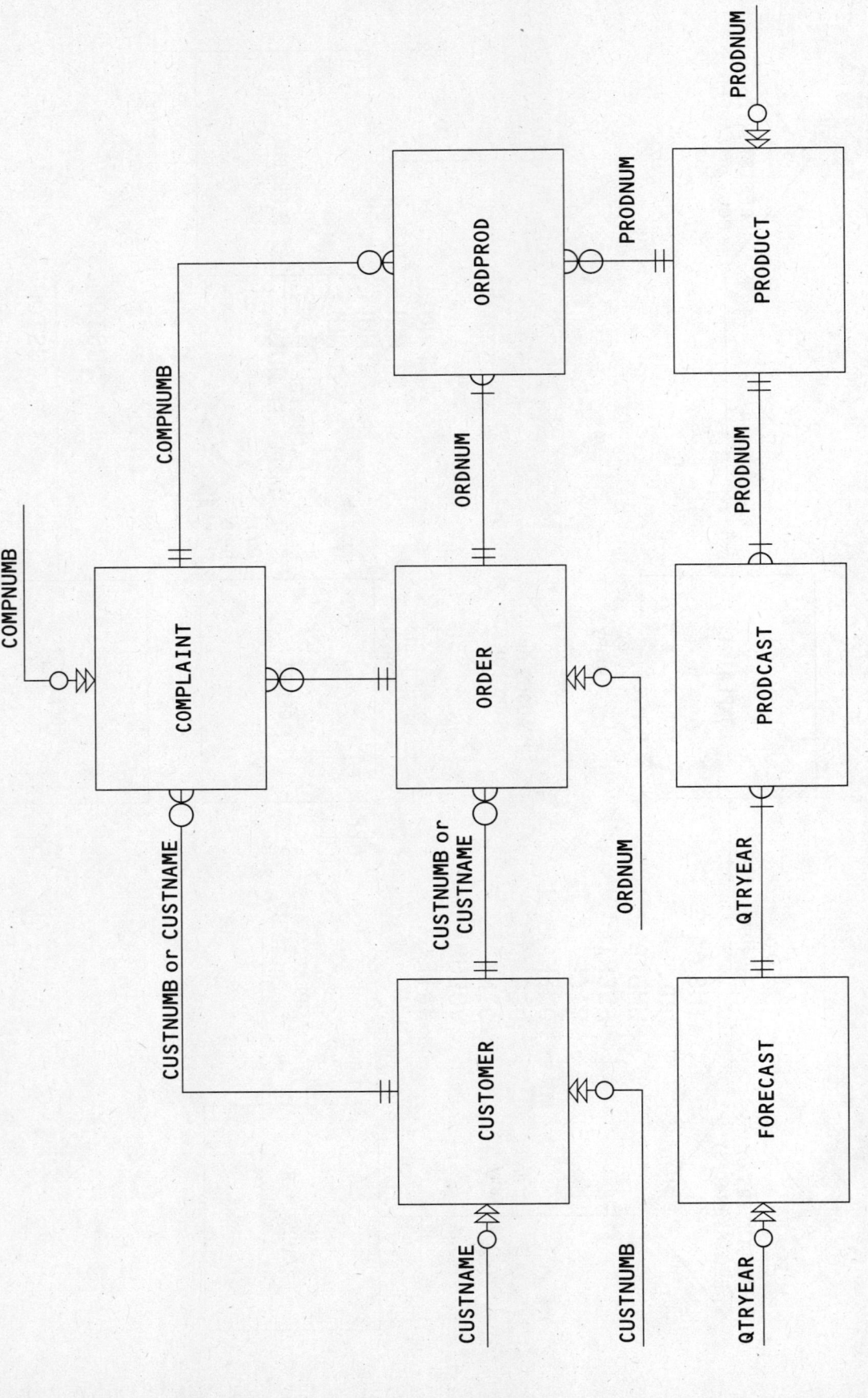

© Richard D. Irwin, Inc., 1994

A View of Data Suitable for System Builders

System builders must use precise languages to describe data to a computer system.

```
DATA DIVISION.
FILE SECTION.
FD  PRODUCT-FILE
    RECORD CONTAINS 64 CHARACTERS.
01  PRODUCT-RECORD.
    05 PRODUCT-NUMBER       PIC 9(6).
    05 PRODUCT-DESCRIPTION  PIC X(30).
    05 PRODUCT-PRICE        PIC 9(3)V99.
    05 QUANTITY-ON-HAND     PIC 9(6).
    05 QTY-ON-ORDER         PIC 9(6).
    05 REORDER-POINT        PIC 9(6).
    05 DISCOUNT-VOLUME      PIC 999.
    05 DISCOUNT-RATE        PIC V99.
```

```
CREATE TABLE CUSTOMER
    (CUSTNUMB  CHAR (10) NOT NULL,
     CUSTNAME  CHAR (32) NOT NULL,
     CUSTADDR  CHAR (20) NOT NULL,
     CUSTCITY  CHAR (10) NOT NULL,
     CUSTST    CHAR (2) NOT NULL,
     CUSTZIP   CHAR (9) NOT NULL,
     CUSTAREA  CHAR (3),
     CUSTPHN   CHAR (7),
     CUSTBAL   DECIMAL (7,2),
     CUSTRATG  CHAR (1),
     CUSTLIMT  SMALLINT)
CREATE INDEX CNUMBIDX ON CUSTOMER (CUSTNUMB)

CREATE INDEX CNAMEIDX ON CUSTOMER (CUSTNAME)
```

A System Owner's View of Activities

System owners usually see business and information systems in terms of functions—void of details such as inputs, outputs, and procedures.

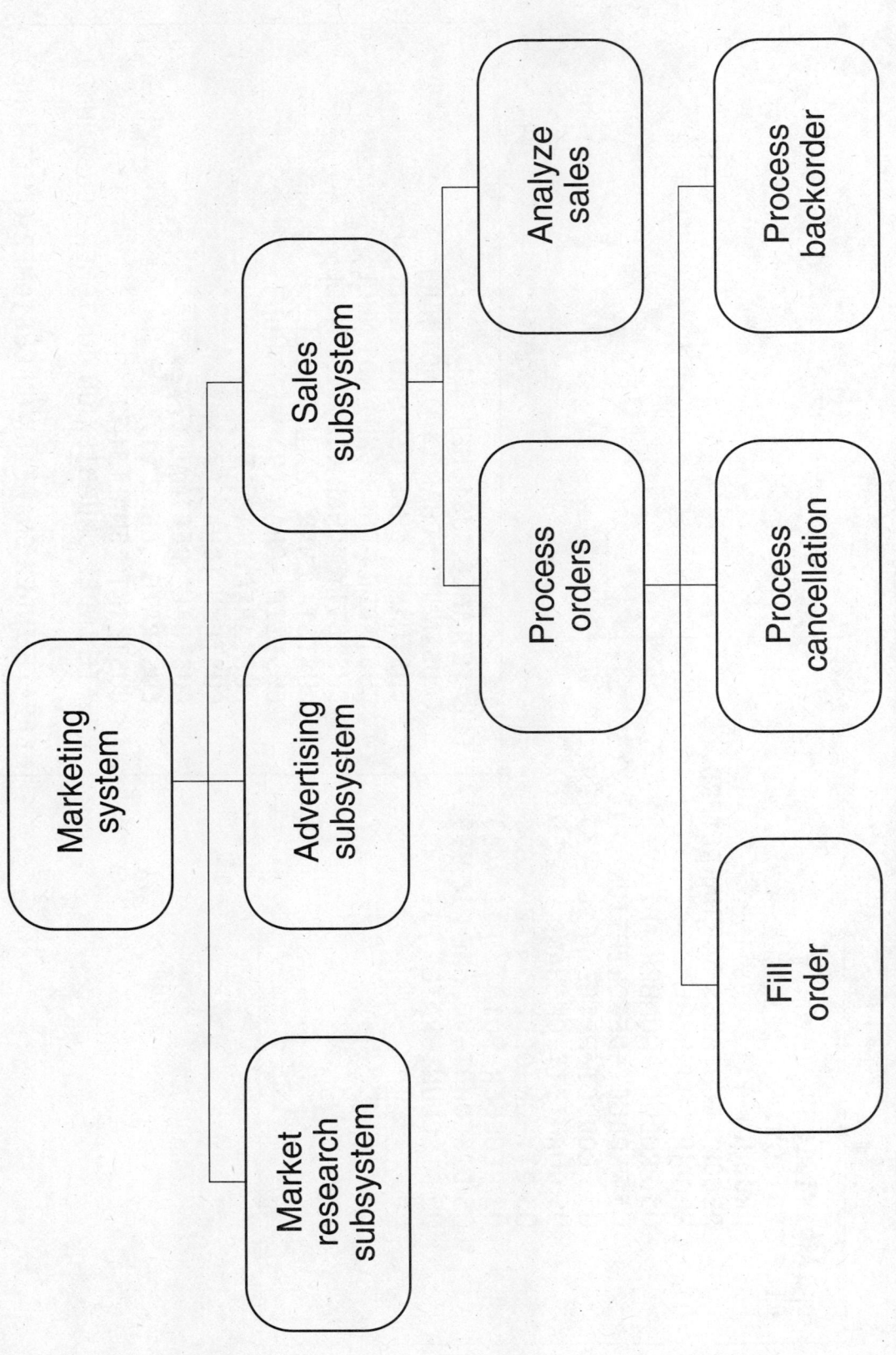

©Richard D. Irwin, Inc., 1994

TM–10

A View of Activities Suitable for System Builders

System builders use precise computer languages to describe processes and activities to a computer system.

```
PROCEDURE DIVISION.
A000-CREATE-SALES-REPORT.
    OPEN INPUT SALES-INPUT-FILE
        OUTPUT SALES-REPORT-FILE.
    WRITE SALES-REPORT-LINE FROM FIRST-HEADING-LINE AFTER ADVANCING TO-
        TOP-OF-PAGE.
    WRITE SALES-REPORT-LINE FROM SECOND-HEADING-LINE AFTER ADVANCING 1
        LINES.
    MOVE SPACE-TWO-LINES TO PROPER-SPACING.
    READ SALES-INPUT-FILE
        AT END
            MOVE 'NO ' TO ARE-THERE-MORE-RECORDS.
    PERFORM B010-PROCESS-SALES-RECORD
        UNTIL THERE-ARE-NO-MORE-RECORDS.
    CLOSE SALES-INPUT-FILE
        SALES-REPORT-FILE.
    STOP RUN.
. . .
```

```
TABLE FILE PRODUCT
PRINT PRODNUMBER AND PRODDESCRIP AND
PRODUCTPRICE AND DISCOUNTVOL AND
DISCOUNTRATE
HEADING
"PRODUCT PRICE LIST REPORT"
END
```

TM–11

©Richard D. Irwin, Inc., 1994

A View of Networks Suitable for System Owners

System owners tend to view networks in terms of business operating locations on a simple map.

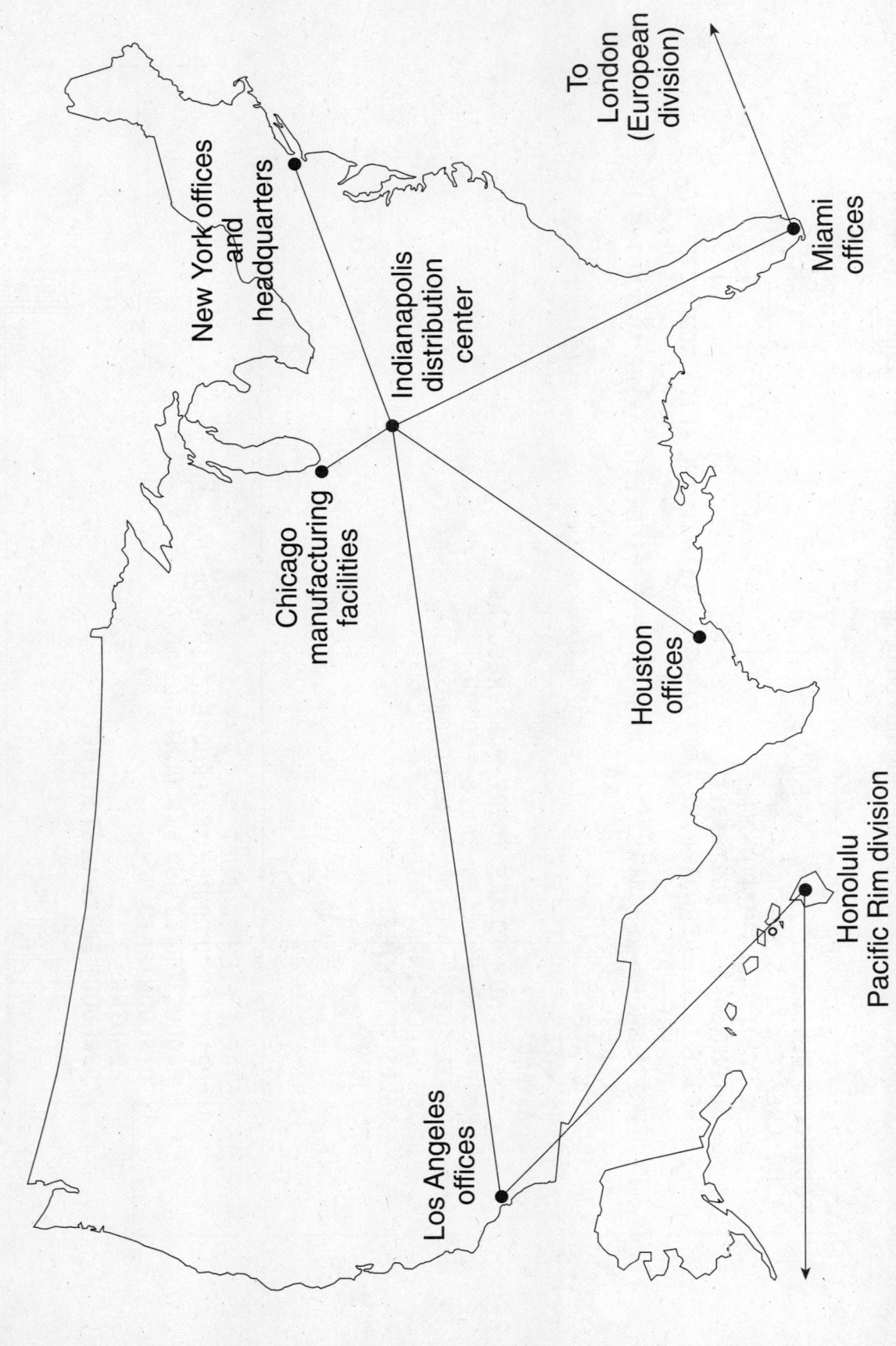

A View of Networks Suitable for System Designers
Designers view networks in technical terms.

TM–13

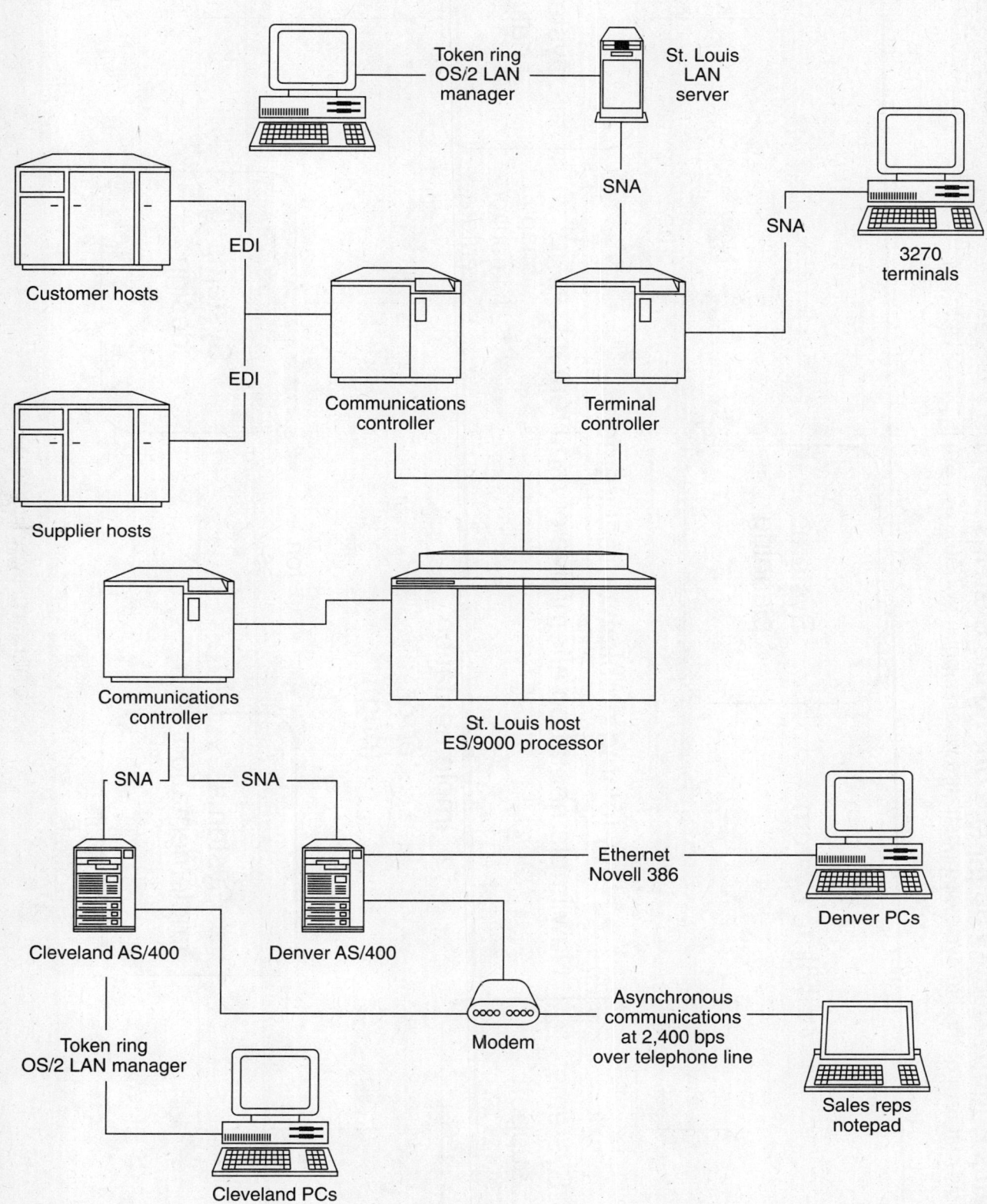

© Richard D. Irwin, Inc., 1994

Systems Entropy Occurs Sometime During the Systems Support Phase

This flow diagram of the life cycle demonstrates what happens when a system is placed into operation.

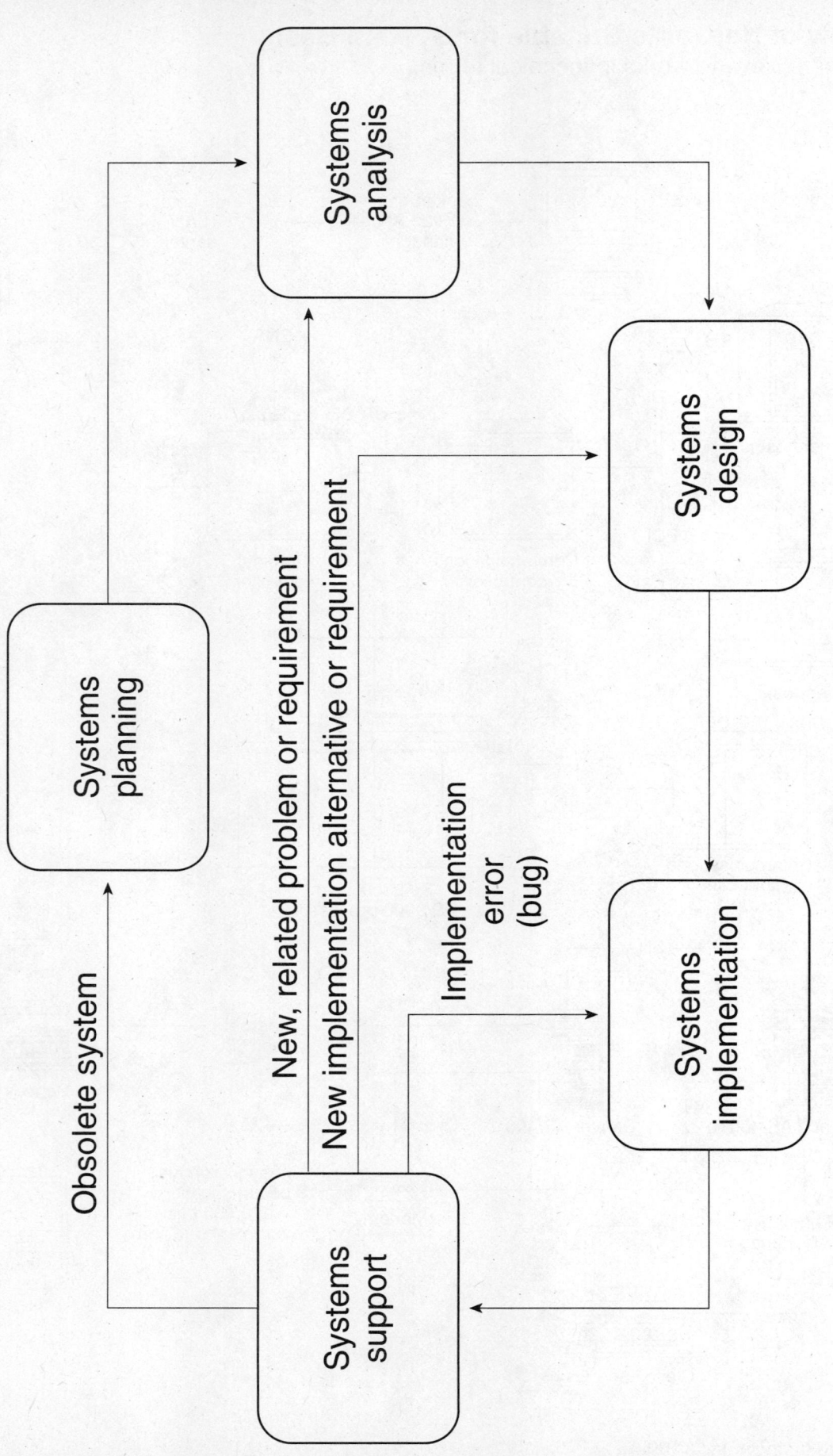

TM-14

© Richard D. Irwin, Inc., 1994

Principles of Systems Development
These eight principles should underlie any version of a systems development life cycle.

- Get the user involved.
- Use a problem-solving approach.
- Establish phases and activities.
- Establish standards for consistent development and documentation.
- Justify systems as capital investments.
- Don't be afraid to cancel or revise scope.
- Divide and conquer.
- Design systems for growth and change.

© Richard D. Irwin, Inc., 1994

The PIECES Framework

The PIECES framework can be used to group problems, opportunities, and directives.

TM–16

The PIECES Problem-Solving Framework and Checklist

The following checklist for problem, opportunity, and directive identification uses Wetherbe's PIECES framework. Note that the categories of PIECES are not mutually exclusive; some possible problems show up in multiple lists. Also, the list of possible problems is not exhaustive. The PIECES framework is equally suited to analyzing both manual and computerized systems and applications.

PERFORMANCE Problems, Opportunities, and Directives
  A. Throughput—the amount of work performed over some period of time.
  B. Response time—the average delay between a transaction or request and a response to that transaction or request.

INFORMATION (and Data) Problems, Opportunities, and Directives
  A. Outputs
    1. Lack of any information
    2. Lack of necessary information
    3. Lack of relevant information
    4. Too much information—"information overload"
    5. Information that is not in a useful format
    6. Information that is not accurate
    7. Information that is difficult to produce
    8. Information is not timely to its subsequent use
  B. Inputs
    1. Data is not captured
    2. Data is not captured in time to be useful
    3. Data is not accurately captured—contains errors
    4. Data is difficult to capture
    5. Data is captured redundantly—same data captured more than once
    6. Too much data is captured
    7. Illegal data is captured
  C. Stored data
    1. Data is stored redundantly in multiple files and/or databases
    2. Stored data is not accurate (may be related to #1)
    3. Data is not secure to accident or vandalism
    4. Data is not well organized
    5. Data is not flexible—not easy to meet new information needs from stored data
    6. Data is not accessible

ECONOMICS Problems, Opportunities, and Directives
  A. Costs are unknown
  B. Costs are untraceable to source
  C. Costs are too high

CONTROL (and Security) Problems, Opportunities, and Directives
  A. Too little security or control
    1. Input data is not adequately edited
    2. Crimes are (or can be) committed against data
       a. Fraud
       b. Embezzlement
    3. Ethics are breached on data or information—refers to data or information getting to unauthorized people
    4. Redundantly stored data is inconsistent in different files or databases
    5. Data privacy regulations or guidelines are being (or can be) violated
    6. Processing errors are occurring (either by people, machines, or software)
    7. Decision-making errors are occurring
  B. Too much control or security
    1. Bureaucratic red tape slows the system
    2. Controls inconvenience customers or employees
    3. Excessive controls cause processing delays

EFFICIENCY Problems, Opportunities, and Directives
  A. People, machines, or computers waste time
    1. Data is redundantly input or copied
    2. Data is redundantly processed
    3. Information is redundantly generated
  B. People, machines, or computers waste materials and supplies
  C. Effort required for tasks is excessive
  D. Materials required for tasks is excessive

SERVICE Problems, Opportunities, and Directives
  A. The system produces inaccurate results
  B. The system produces inconsistent results
  C. The system produces unreliable results
  D. The system is not easy to learn
  E. The system is not easy to use
  F. The system is awkward to use
  G. The system is inflexible to new or exceptional situations
  H. The system is inflexible to change
  I. The system is incompatible with other systems
  J. The system is not coordinated with other systems

© Richard D. Irwin, Inc., 1994

IS Dimensions Emphasized by Today's Structured Techniques TM–17

One basis for classifying the structured techniques is the systems dimension(s) that they "most" emphasize.

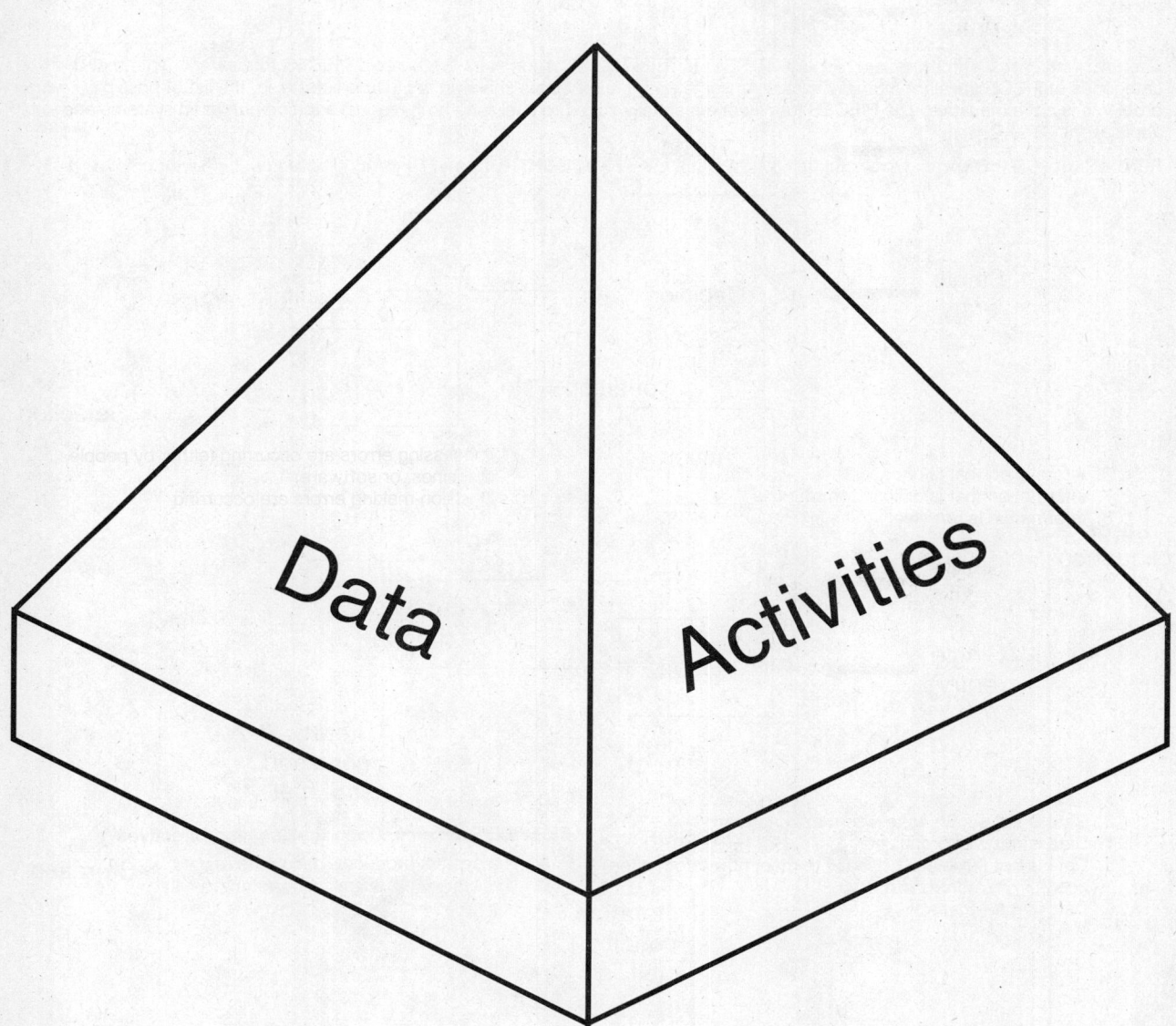

Structured Programming Concepts

This flowchart demonstrates the basic concepts behind structured programming, restricted control structures, and single-entry, single-exit flow.

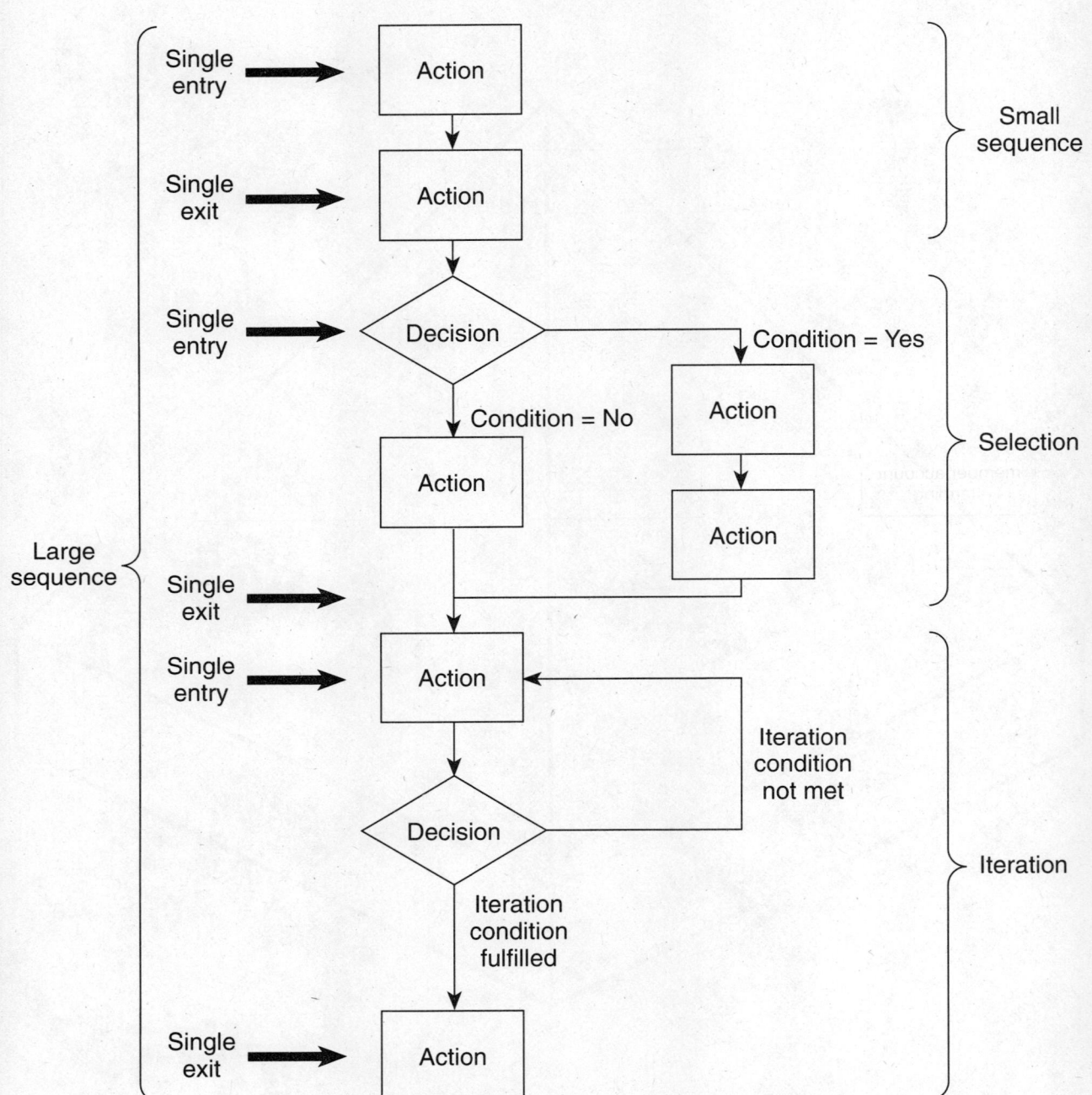

The End Product of Structured Design
This structure chart is typical of the process models that characterize techniques like Yourdon/Constantine structured design.

TM–19

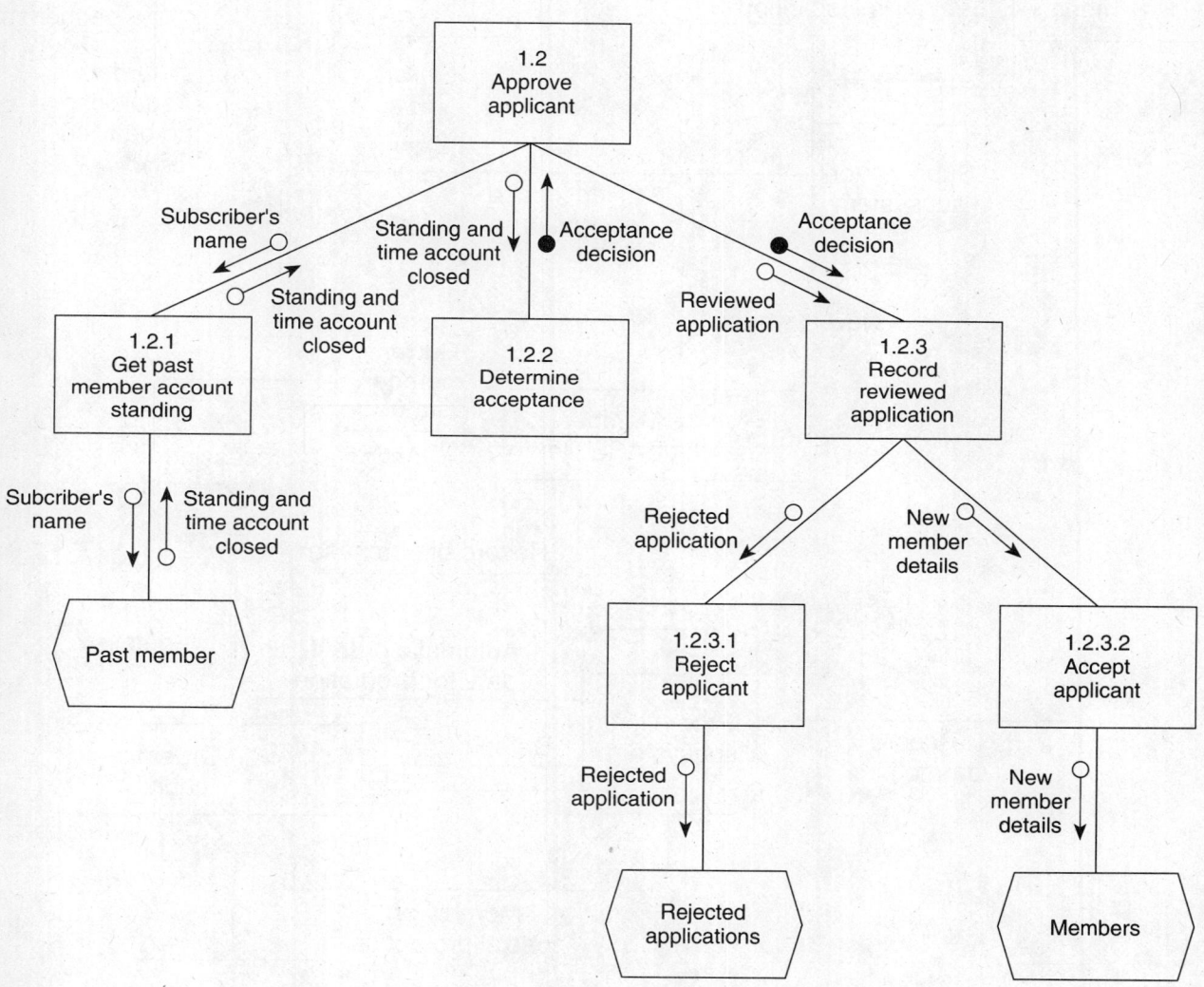

©Richard D. Irwin, Inc., 1994

An End Product of Structured Analysis

This data flow diagram is typical of the process models that characterize methodologies like structured analysis.

TM–20

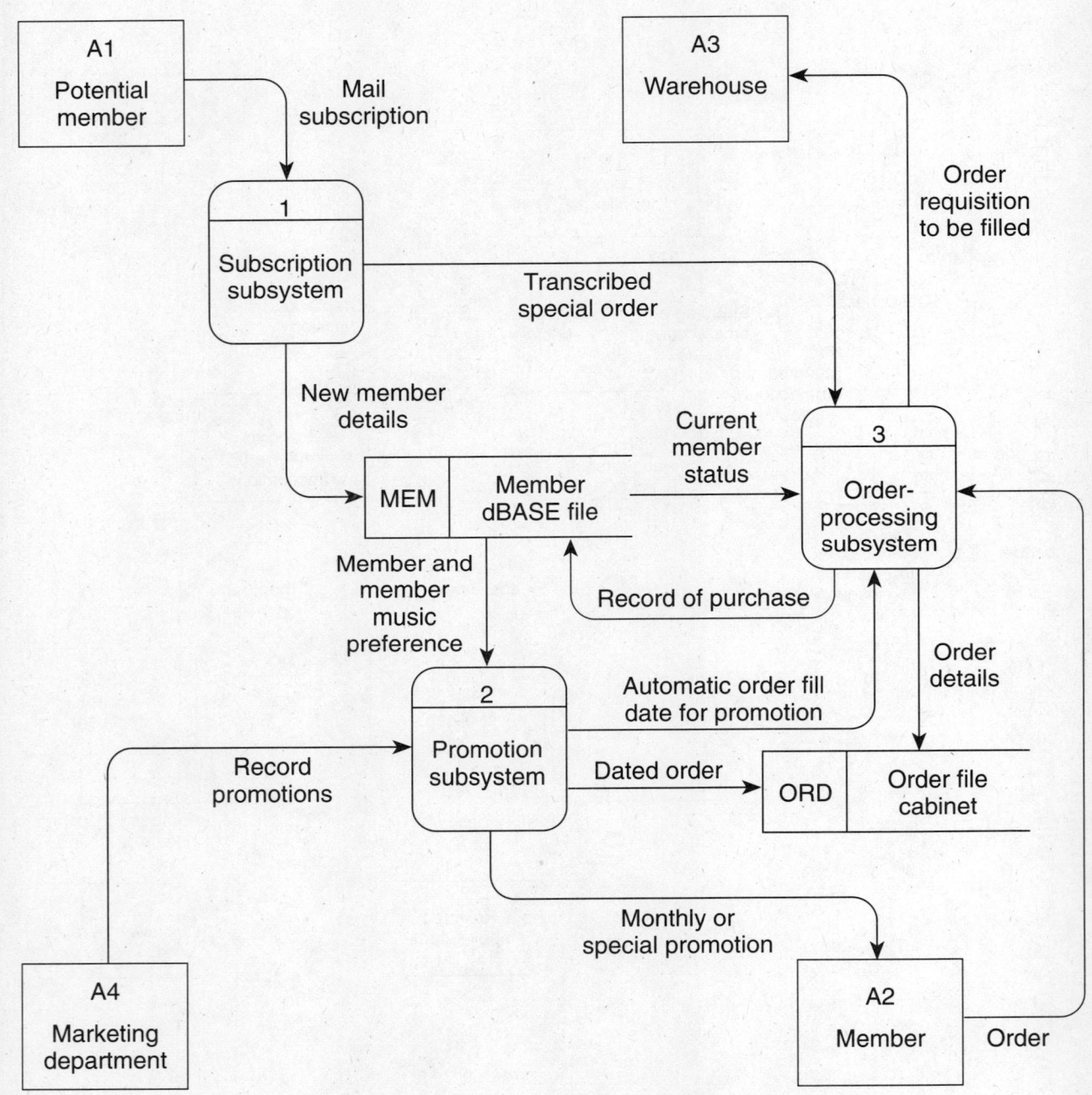

©Richard D. Irwin, Inc., 1994

An End-Product of Data Modeling

This model, called an *entity-relationship-attribute (ERA) diagram*, is typical of the data models that result from data-modeling techniques.

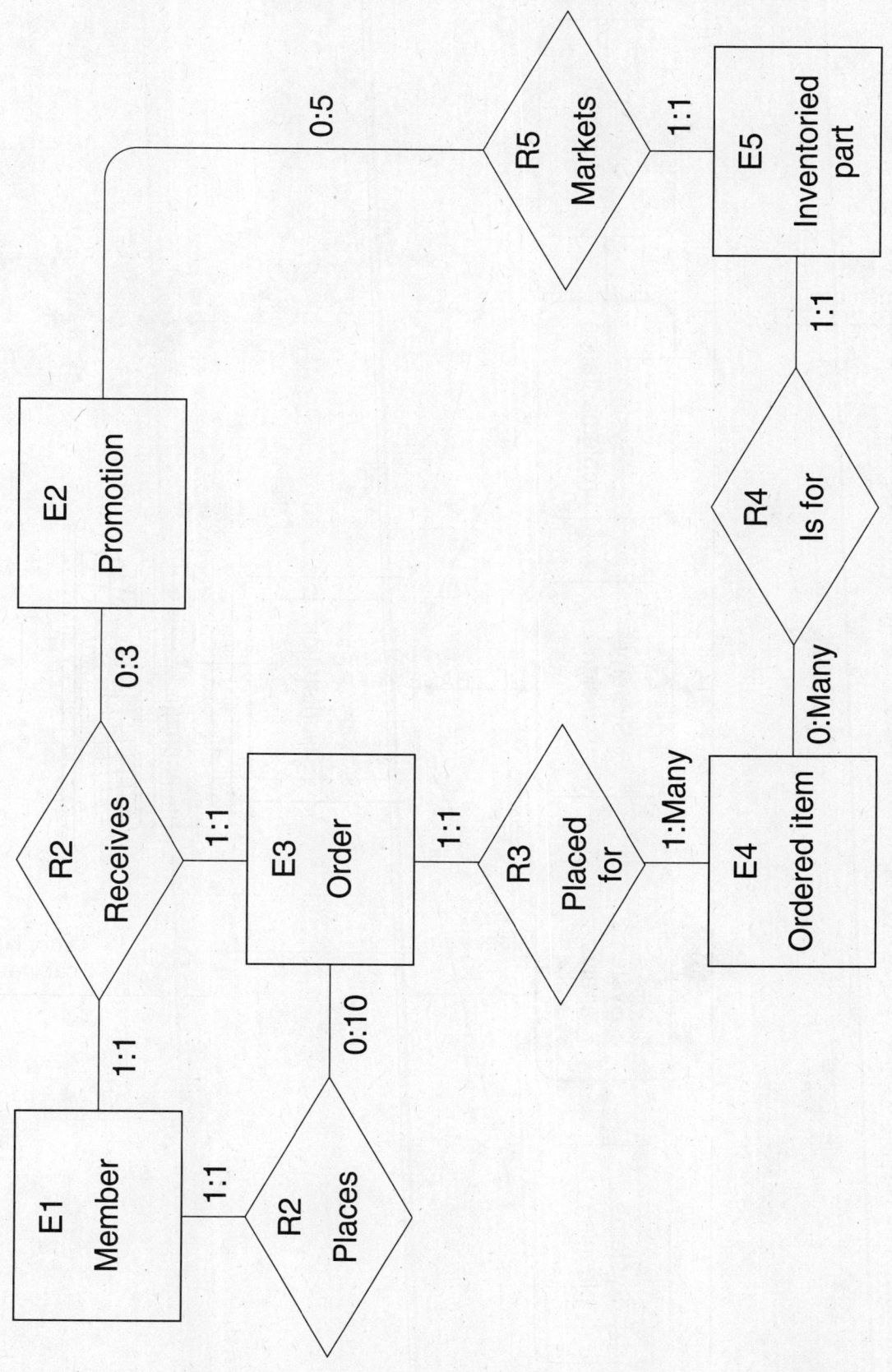

TM–21

© Richard D. Irwin, Inc., 1994

A Life Cycle–Based Framework for CASE Tools
CASE tools can be classified according to the phases in which they automate or assist developers.

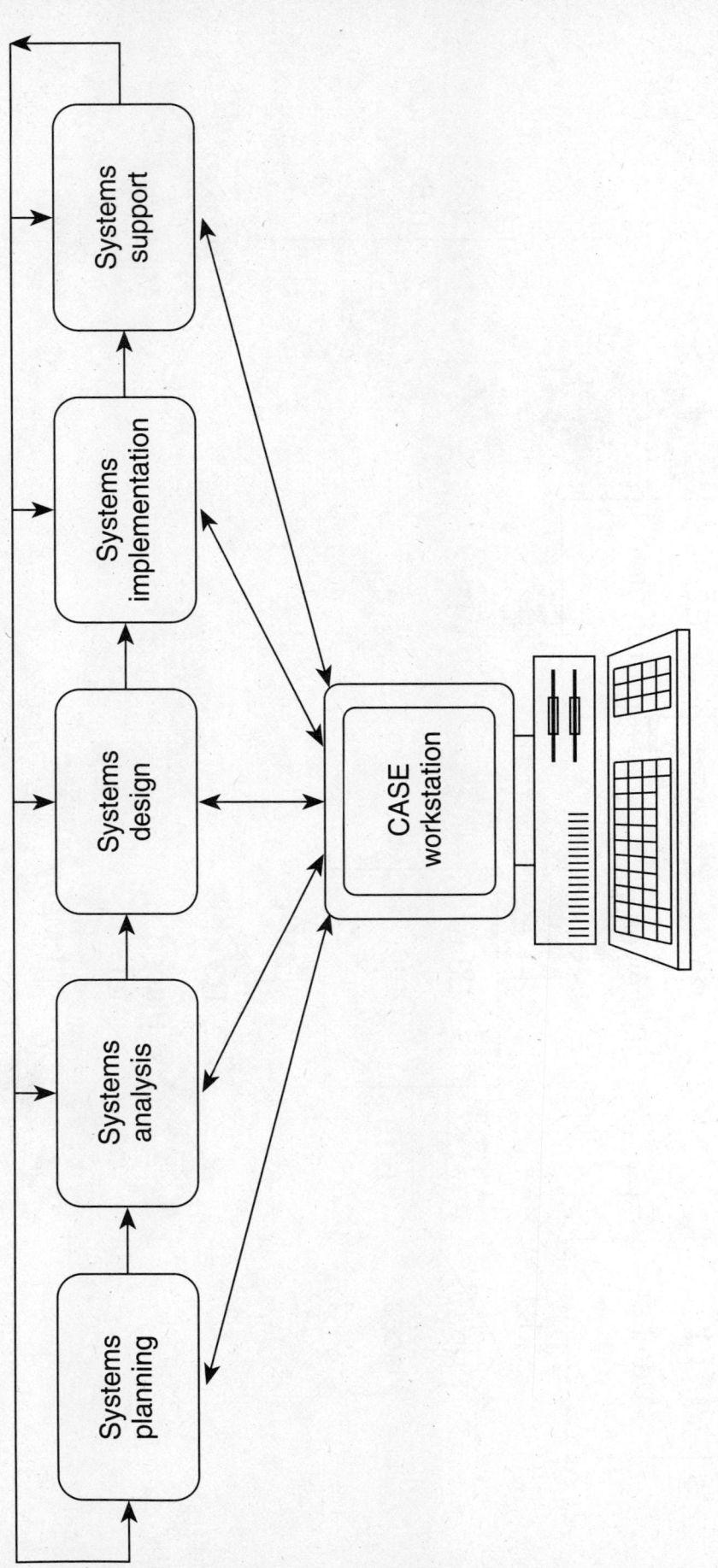

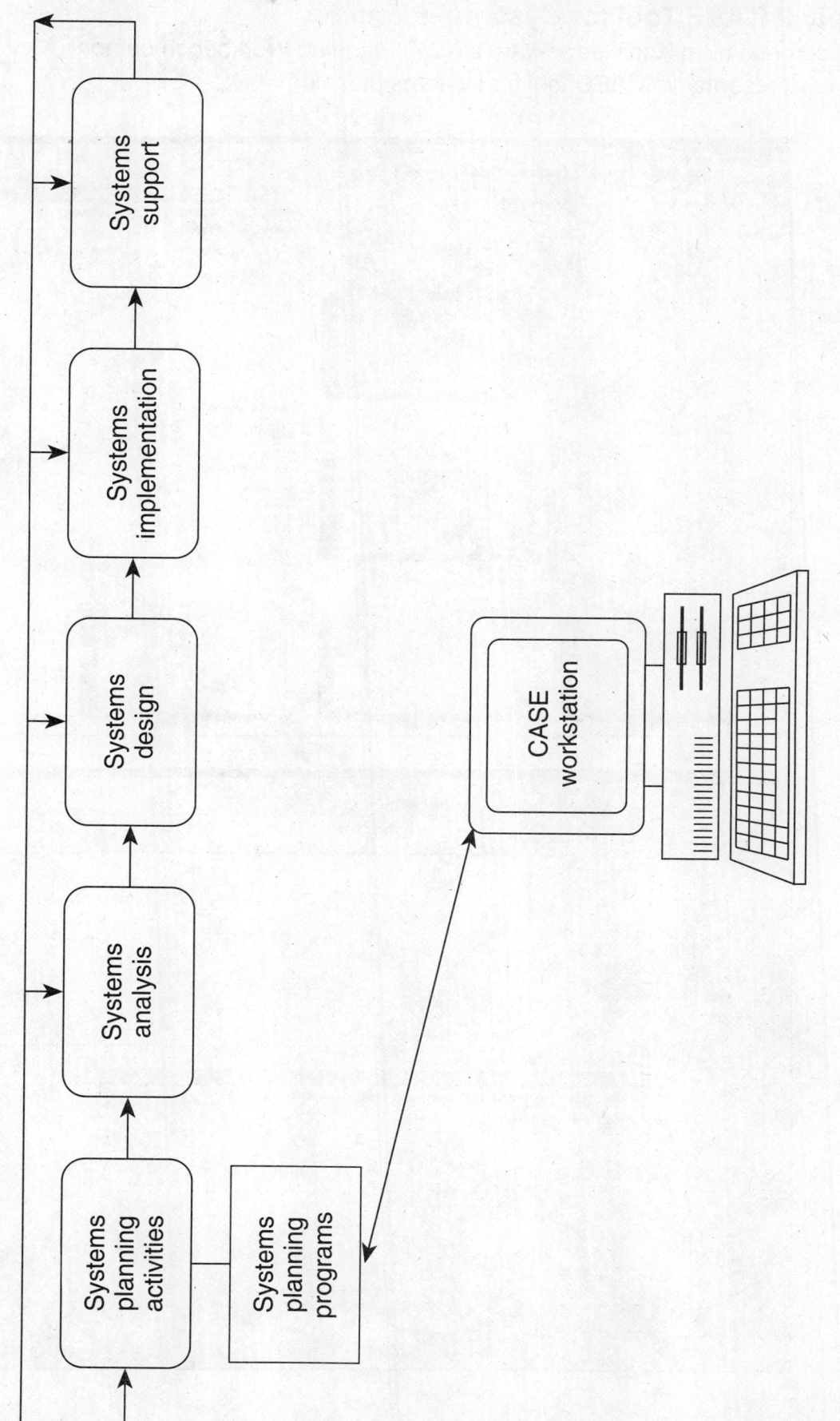

A Typical CASE Tool for Systems Planning

These screens from KnowledgeWare's ADW Planning Workbench demonstrate a representative CASE tool for systems planning.

TM–24

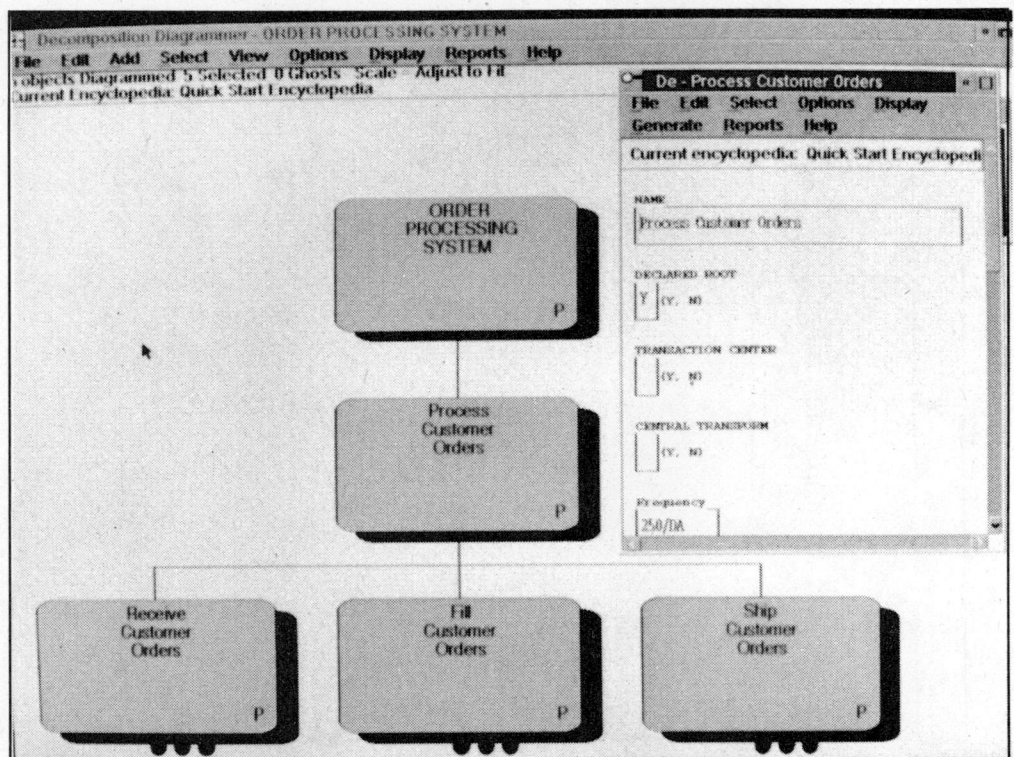

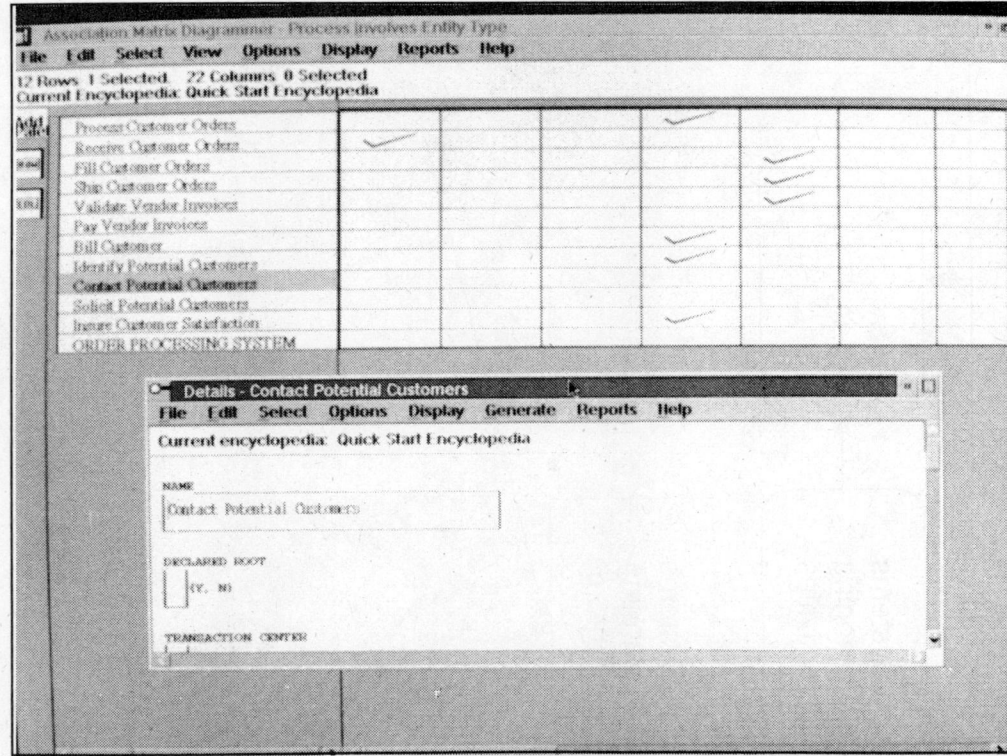

© Richard D. Irwin, Inc., 1994

CASE Tools for Systems Analysis and Design
We now add systems analysis and design tools to our CASE tool kit.

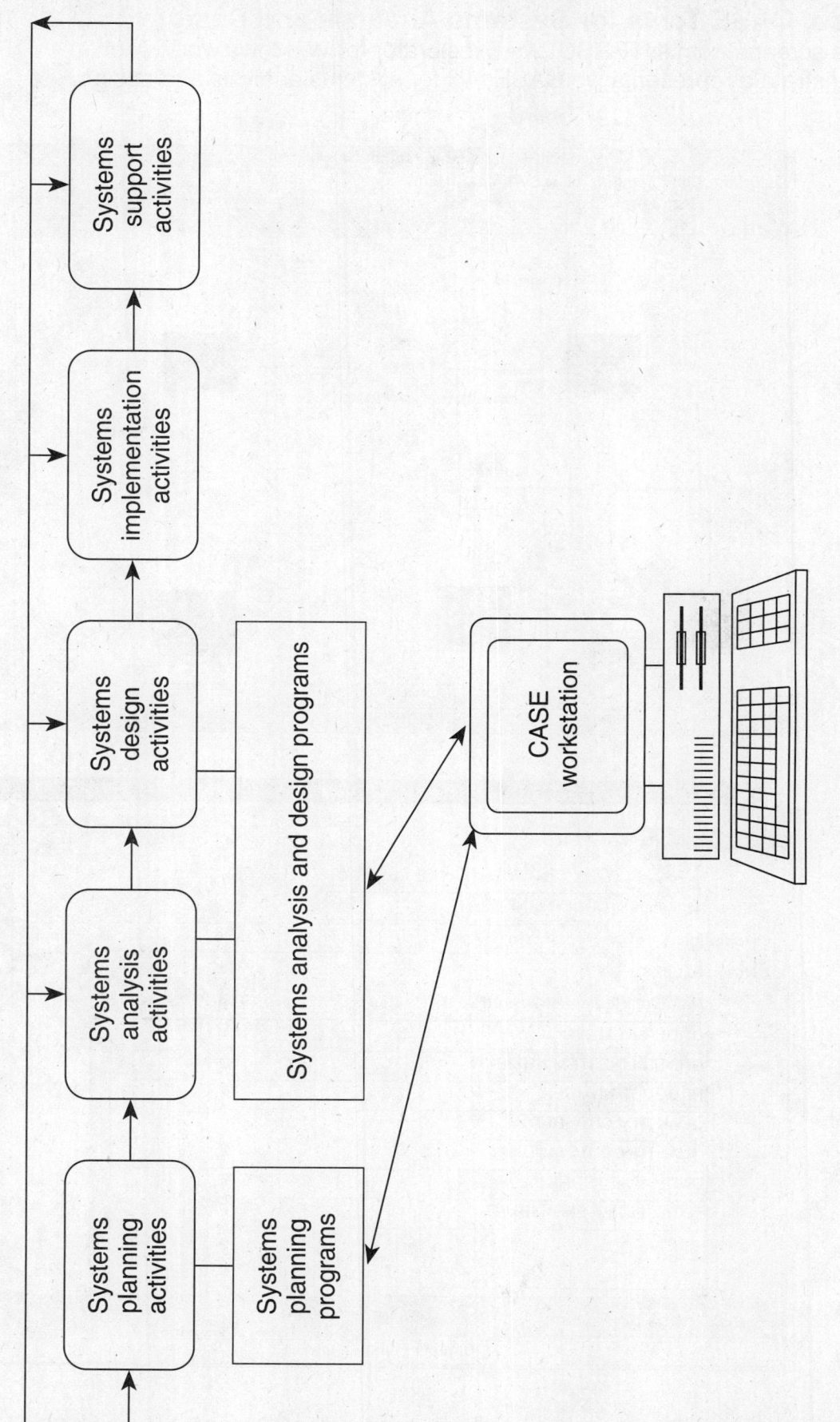

Typical CASE Tools for Systems Analysis and Design

TM–26

These screens from INTERSOLV's Excelerator for Windows workbench demonstrate a representative CASE tool for systems analysis and design.

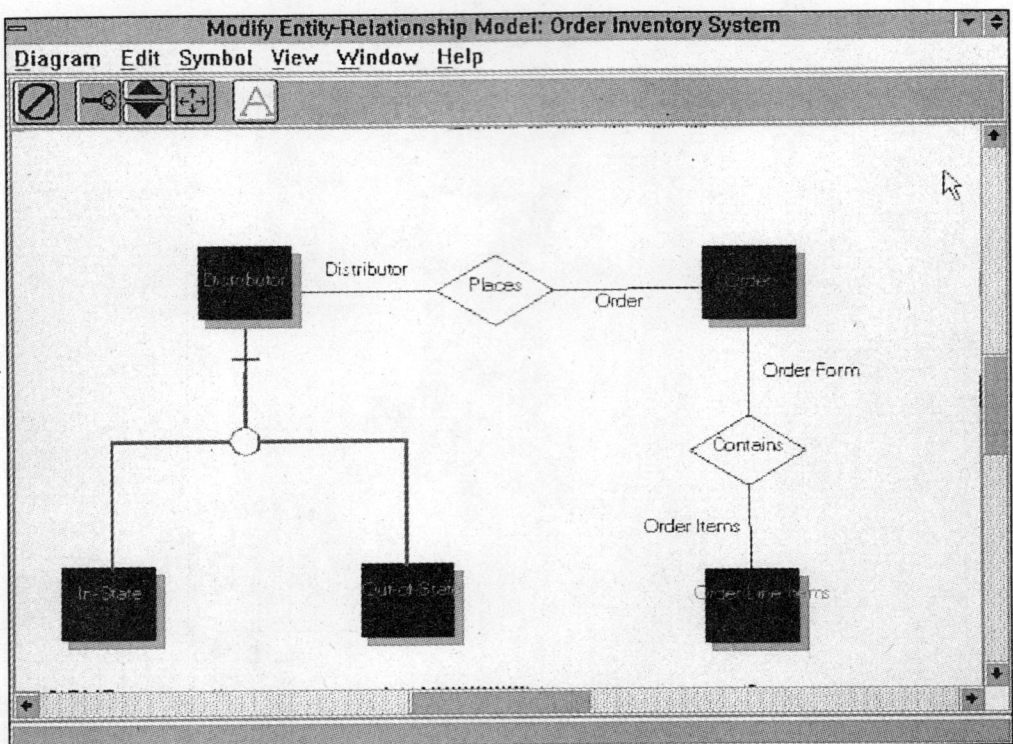

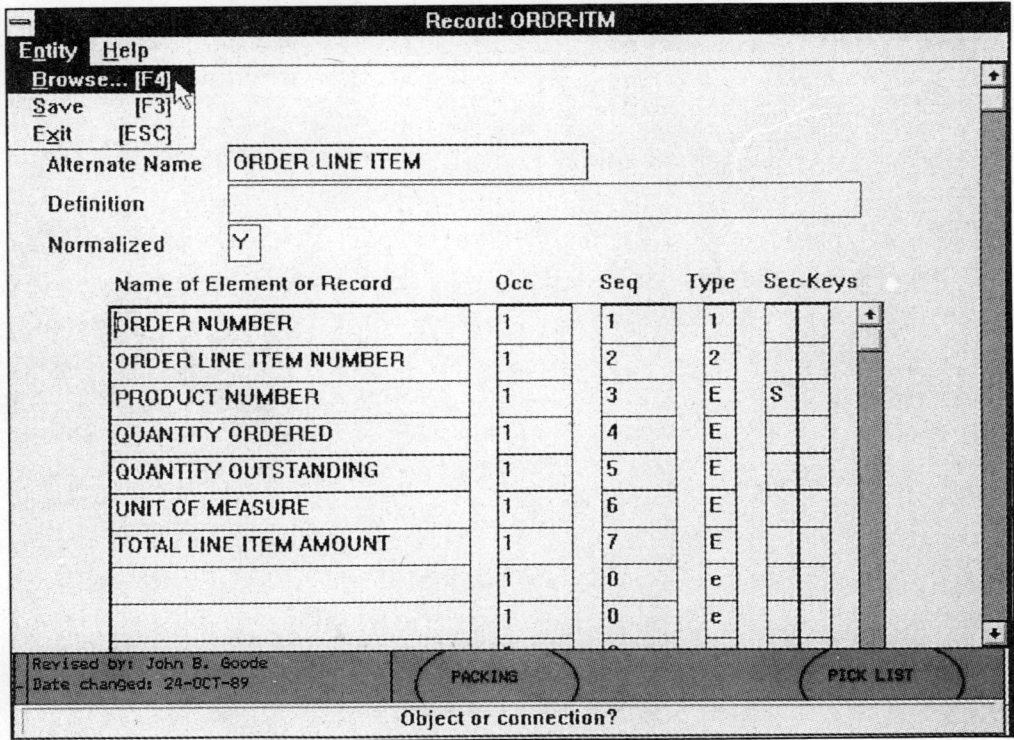

© Richard D. Irwin, Inc., 1994

CASE Tools for Systems Design and Implementation

The next tools we'll add to our CASE tool kit are for detailed systems design and implementation.

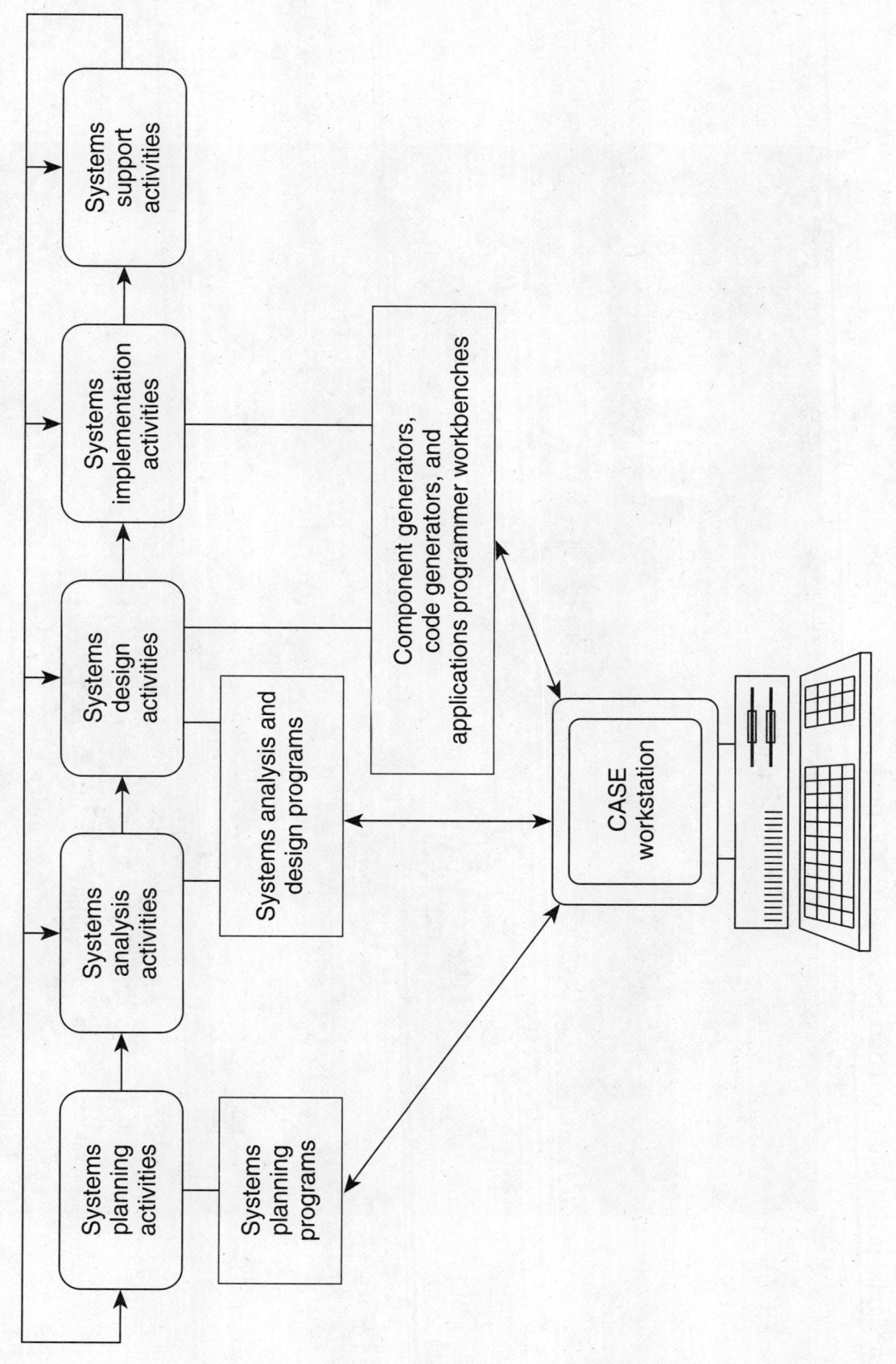

An Application Programmer's Workbench

This screen, from Micro Focus's COBOL Programmer's Workbench demonstrates its ANIMATOR feature that simplifies and enhances testing and debugging of COBOL programs.

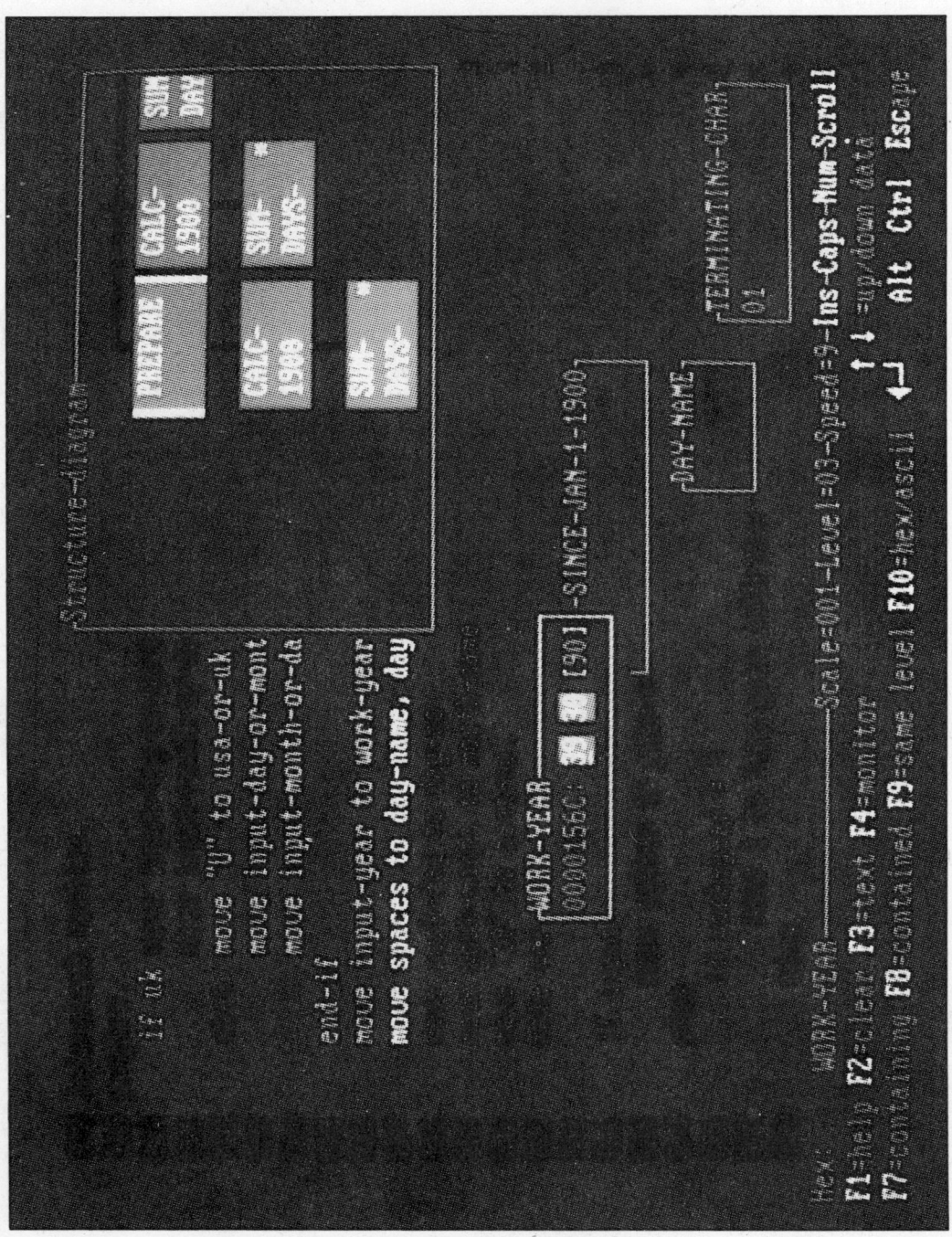

TM–28

© Richard D. Irwin, Inc., 1994

CASE Tools for Systems Support

The next tools we'll add to our CASE tool kit are for maintenance and reengineering of current systems.

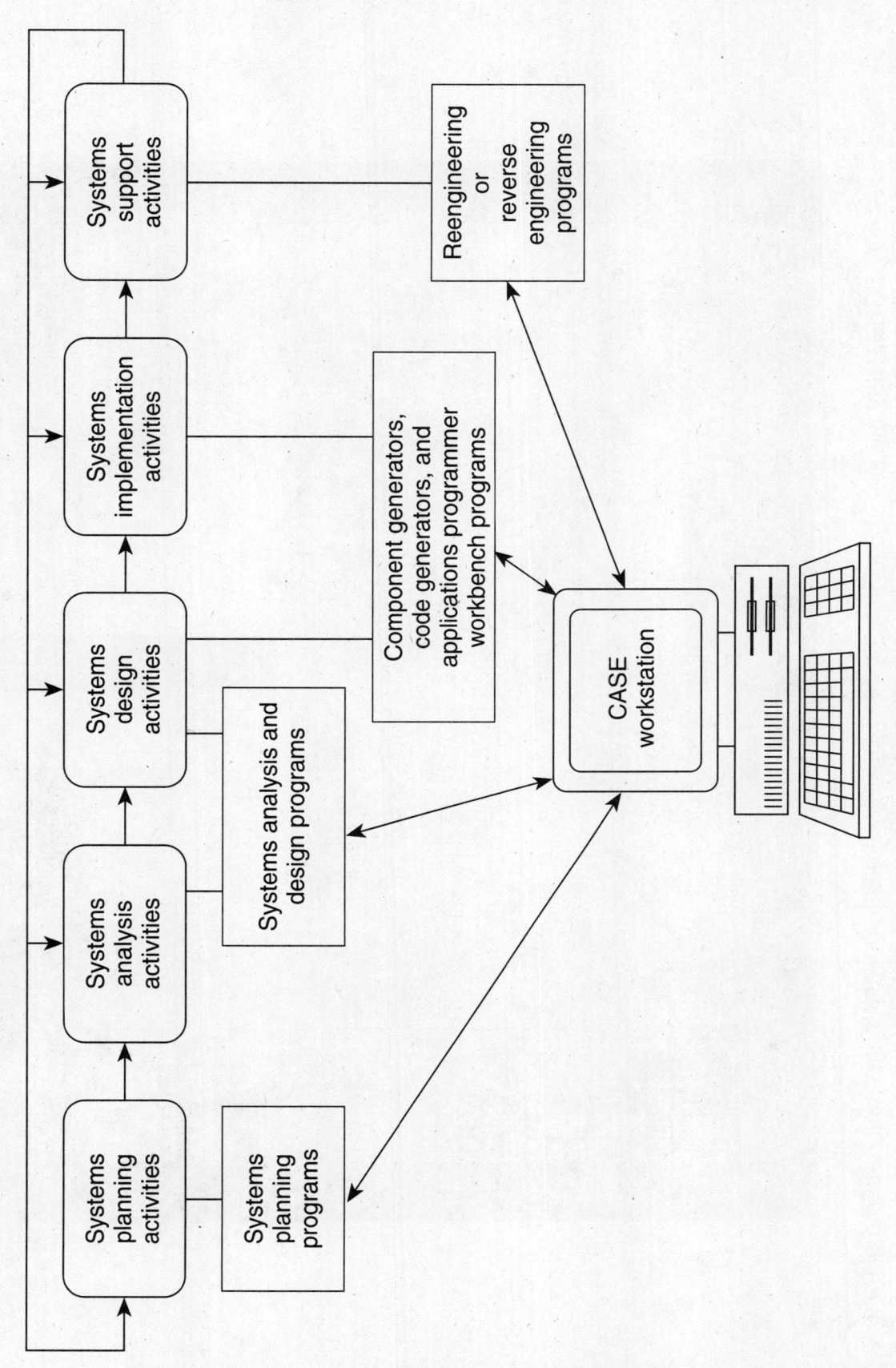

TM-29

© Richard D. Irwin, Inc., 1994

Reverse Engineering

This screen from INTERSOLV's Excelerator for Design Recovery demonstrates a graphical system model created from a COBOL program that was downloaded into this reverse engineering tool. (Courtesy of INTERSOLV, Inc.)

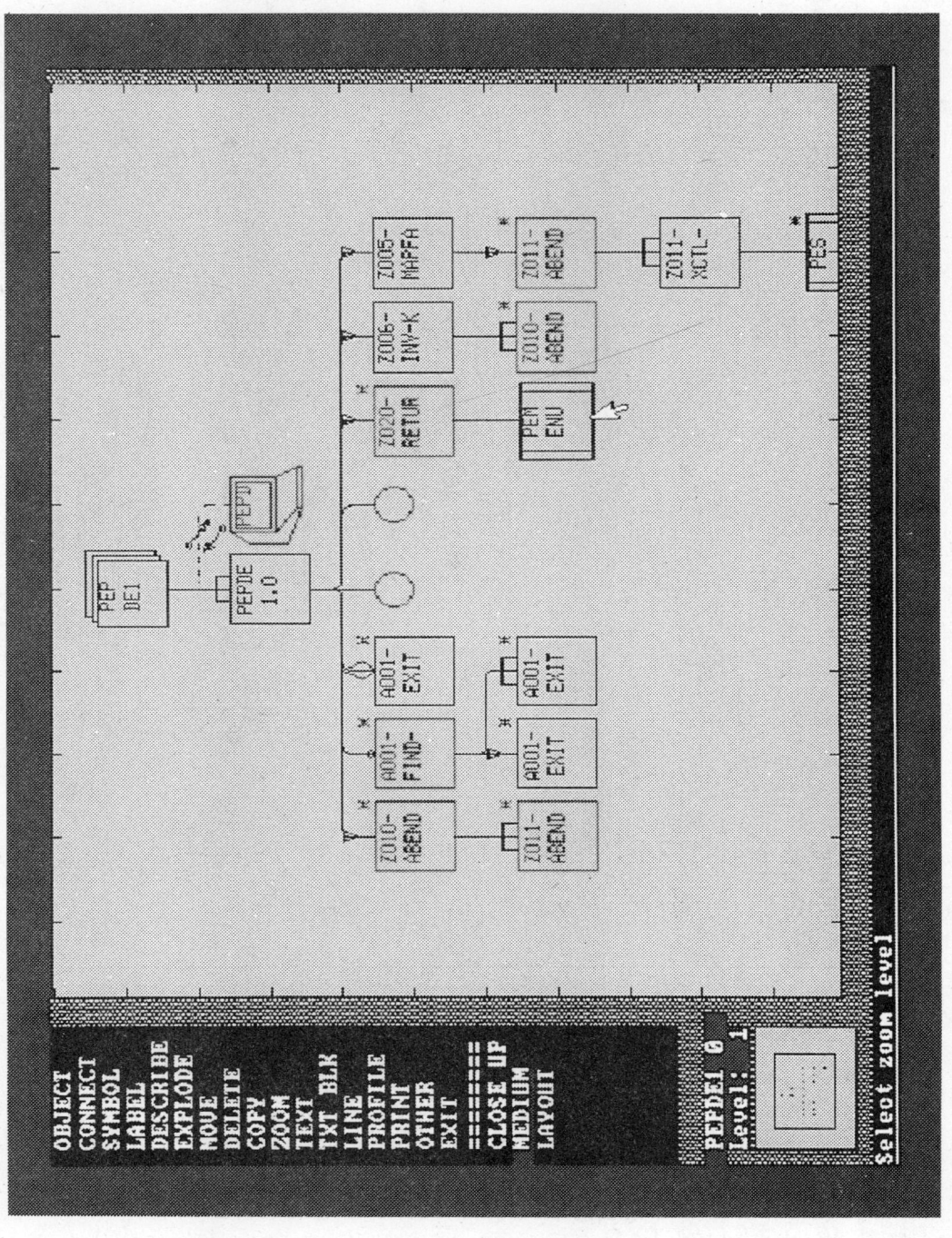

© Richard D. Irwin, Inc., 1994

Data Integration by File Transfer

The most common way for two different vendors to exchange data between their tools is to build in a file transfer facility.

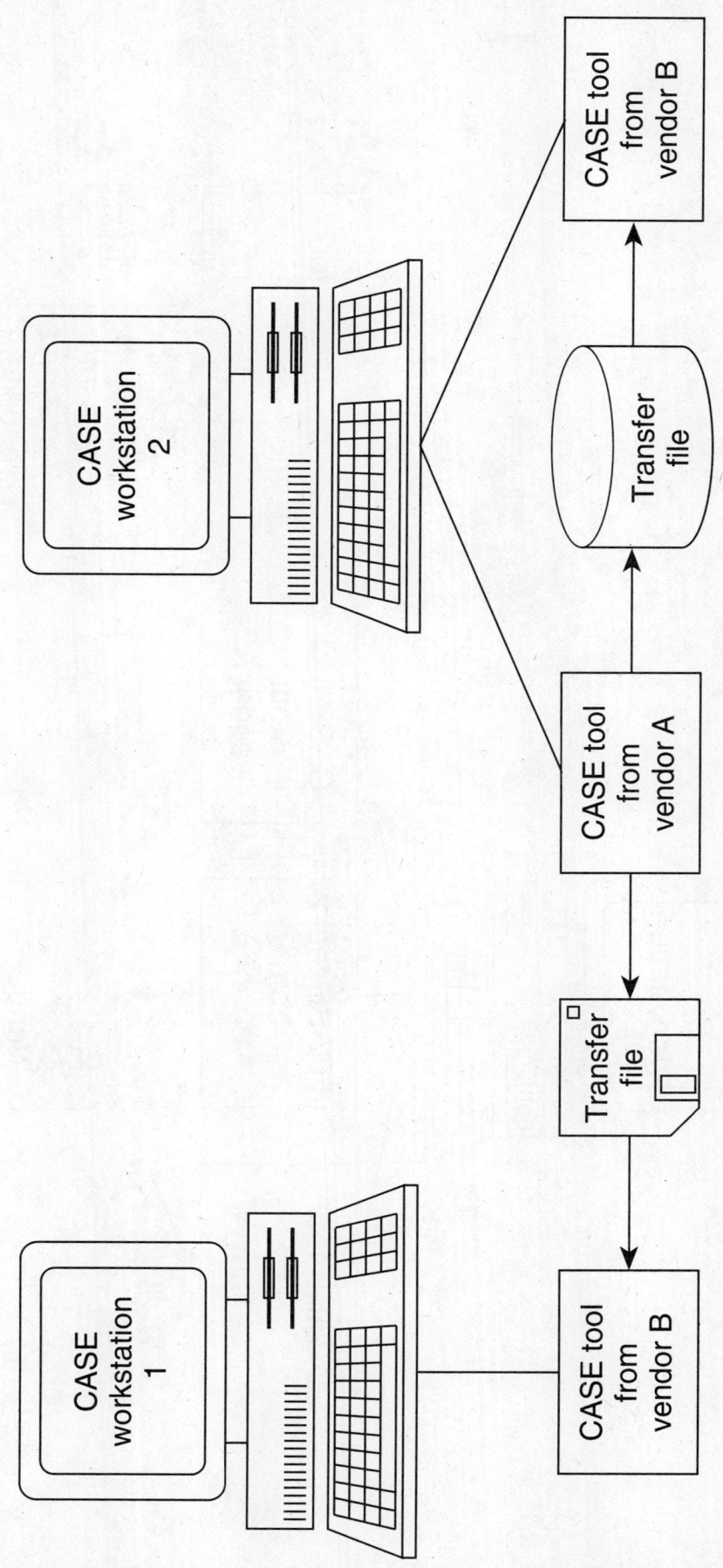

Data Integration through a Data Link

A data link occurs when one vendor "taps" into another vendor's proprietary repository to use or update the data in that repository.

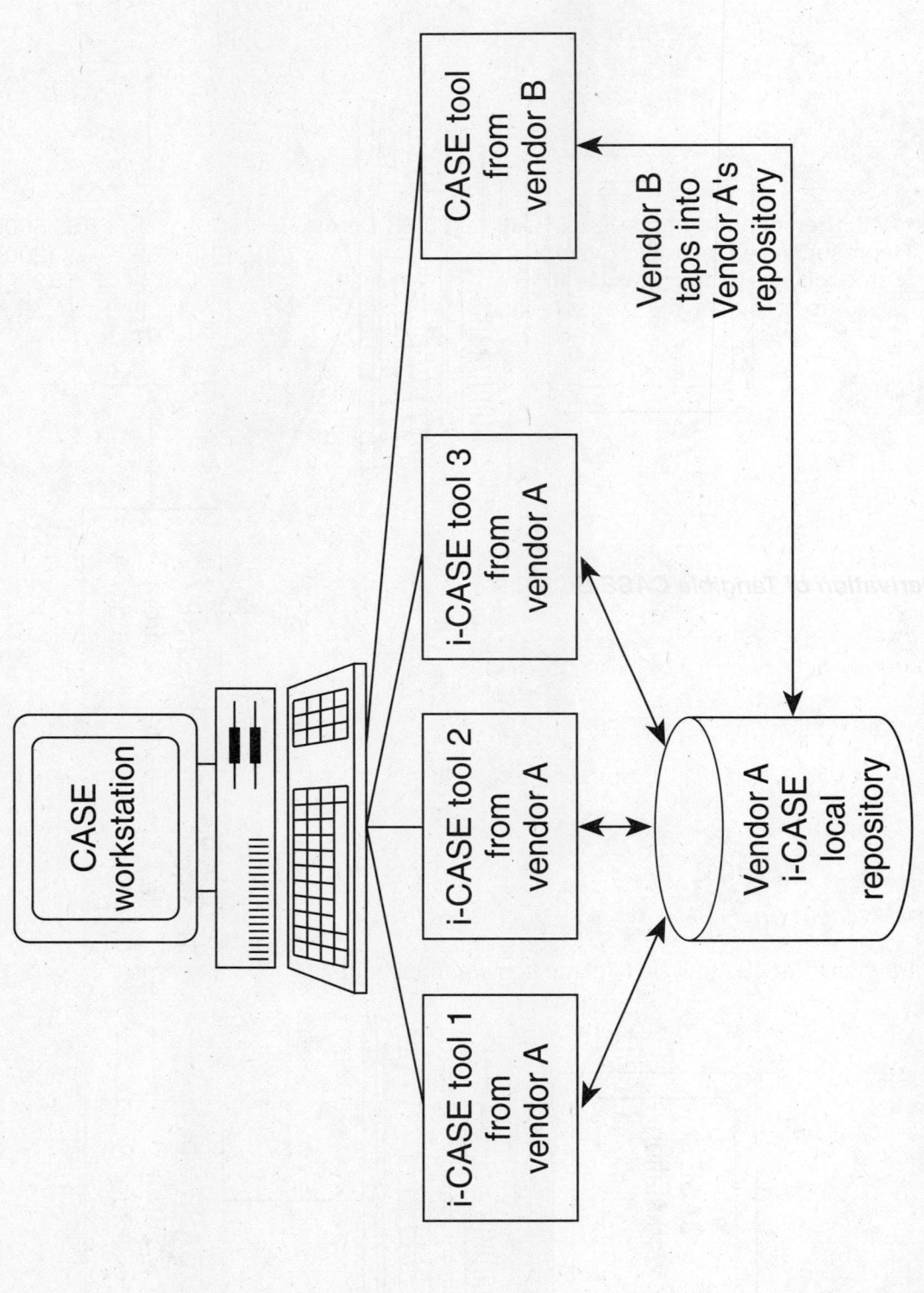

TM–32

© Richard D. Irwin, Inc., 1994

Cost Justification of CASE

This spreadsheet printout provides a simple cost/benefit analysis for CASE.

TM–33

CASE Costs and Benefits

Costs of CASE

80486 Personal Computer 2MB RAM & 200MB Disk	($3,500)
Representative Operating System	(200)
Memory Upgrade from 2MB to 8MB	(300)
High Resolution Graphics Adapter and Display	(1,500)
Mouse	(100)
CASE Software (budget for two tools)	(12,000)
Training on the Two CASE Tools (with travel & lodging)	(3,000)
Four Years Extended Maintenance on CASE Software	(4,000)
Total Costs	**($20,600)**

Derivation of Tangible CASE Benefits

Annual cost of a Systems Analyst (underestimated)		30,000
Overhead for Analyst (e.g., pension, insurance, vacation, etc.)		15,000
Total Annual Employee Cost		$45,000
Estimated Productivity Enhancement (underestimated)	15%	
Annual Productivity		6,750
Total Productivity Benefits (over 5 years)		**$33,750**

Cost/Benefit Analysis

Payback Period Analysis (lifetime costs/annual benefits)	3.1 years
Net Present Value Analysis	
Time Adjusted Benefits (discounted at 10%)	$25,583
Time Adjusted Costs (again, discounted at 10%)	($13,431)
Net Present Value (positive number indicates GOOD investment)	$12,152

©Richard D. Irwin, Inc., 1994

A Development Center's Organization
A development center provides support services for information systems developers.

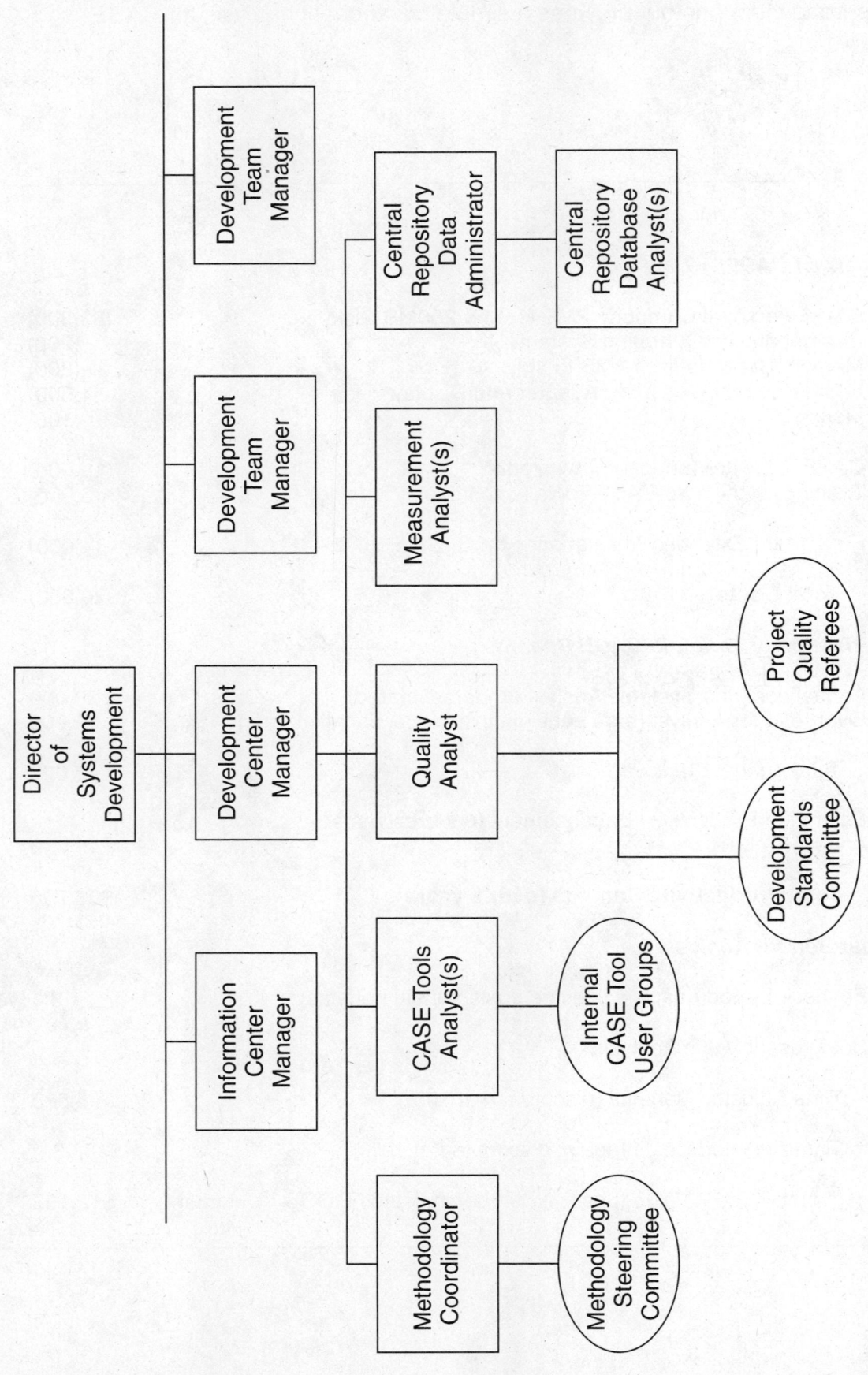

TM-34

©Richard D. Irwin, Inc., 1994

Systems Planning

The three phases of systems planning were introduced in Chapter 3. Planning information and results are recorded in a repository for later use in application development projects.

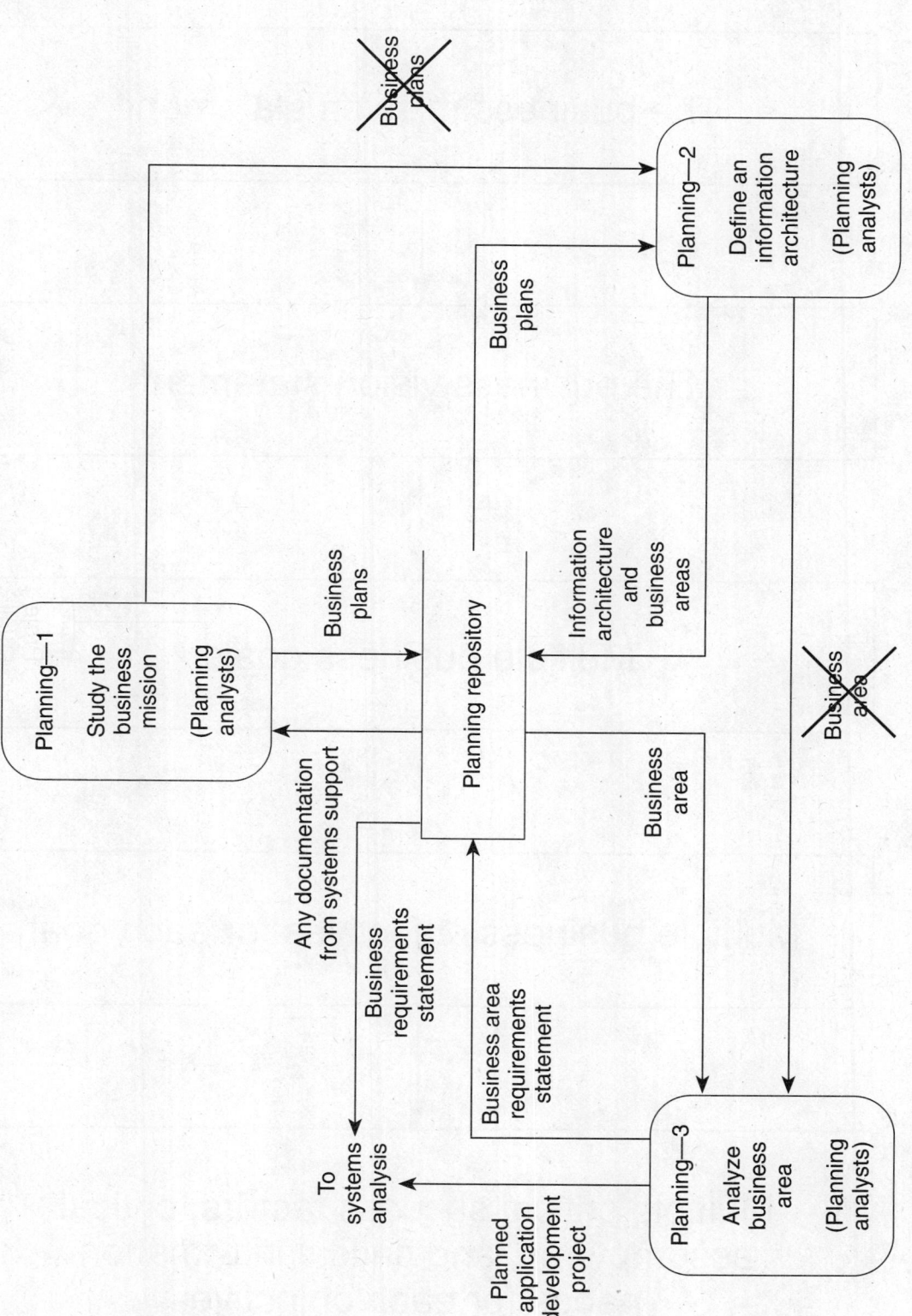

TM–35

© Richard D. Irwin, Inc., 1994

Critical Success Factor Hierarchy TM–36
Information engineering advocates frequently employ the technique of critical success factor (CSF) analysis to measure business performance.

```
┌─────────────────────────────────────────────────────┐
│          The business mission statement             │
└─────────────────────────────────────────────────────┘
                          │
                          ▼
┌─────────────────────────────────────────────────────┐
│          The business vision statement              │
└─────────────────────────────────────────────────────┘
                          │
                          ▼
┌─────────────────────────────────────────────────────┐
│              Multiple business goals                │
└─────────────────────────────────────────────────────┘
                          │
                          ▼
┌─────────────────────────────────────────────────────┐
│     Multiple business objectives for each goal      │
└─────────────────────────────────────────────────────┘
                          │
                          ▼
┌─────────────────────────────────────────────────────┐
│   Multiple critical success factors, critical       │
│   assumptions, and critical information             │
│          needs for each objective                   │
└─────────────────────────────────────────────────────┘
```

©Richard D. Irwin, Inc., 1994

Value Chain Analysis

TM–37

Porter's value chain analysis can be useful in understanding which activities return the most value to a business. This is a value chain diagram for an airline company.

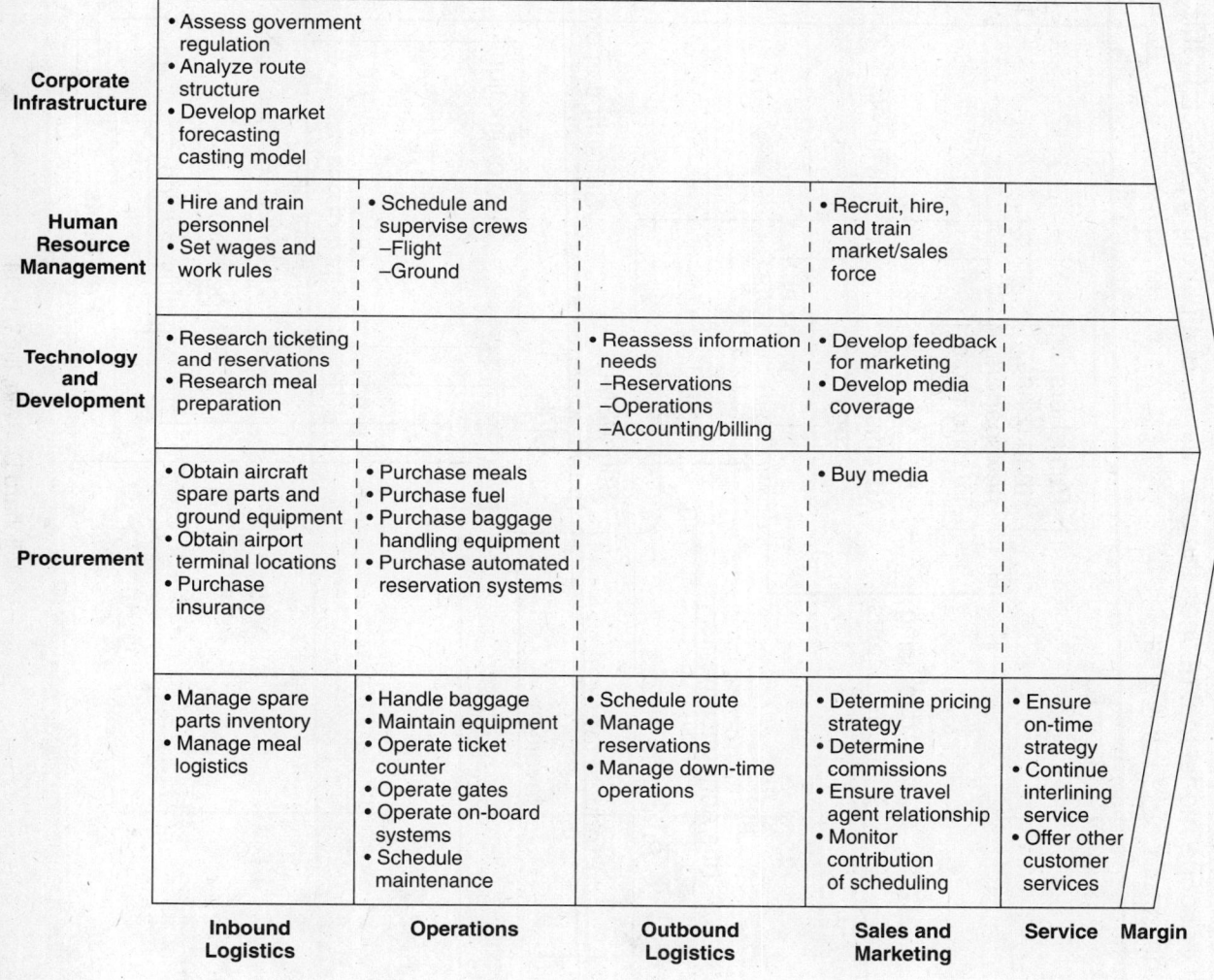

	Inbound Logistics	Operations	Outbound Logistics	Sales and Marketing	Service
Corporate Infrastructure	• Assess government regulation • Analyze route structure • Develop market forecasting casting model				
Human Resource Management	• Hire and train personnel • Set wages and work rules	• Schedule and supervise crews —Flight —Ground		• Recruit, hire, and train market/sales force	
Technology and Development	• Research ticketing and reservations • Research meal preparation		• Reassess information needs —Reservations —Operations —Accounting/billing	• Develop feedback for marketing • Develop media coverage	
Procurement	• Obtain aircraft spare parts and ground equipment • Obtain airport terminal locations • Purchase insurance	• Purchase meals • Purchase fuel • Purchase baggage handling equipment • Purchase automated reservation systems		• Buy media	
	• Manage spare parts inventory • Manage meal logistics	• Handle baggage • Maintain equipment • Operate ticket counter • Operate gates • Operate on-board systems • Schedule maintenance	• Schedule route • Manage reservations • Manage down-time operations	• Determine pricing strategy • Determine commissions • Ensure travel agent relationship • Monitor contribution of scheduling	• Ensure on-time strategy • Continue interlining service • Offer other customer services

Margin

©Richard D. Irwin, Inc., 1994

Context Model

This diagram is a context or scope model that defines the boundaries of a planning project. In this case, the model depicts the business as the center of the universe.

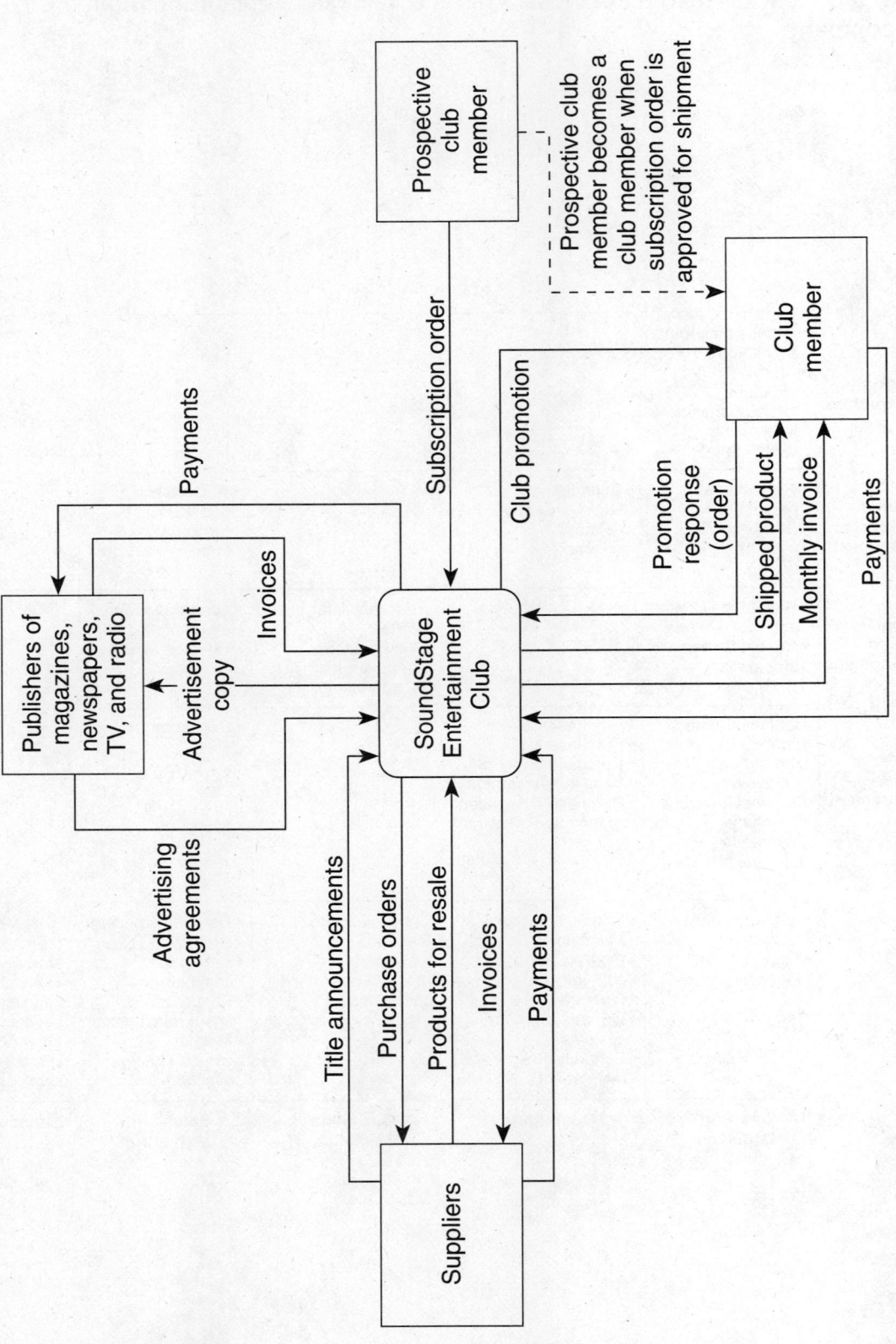

An Outline for a Planning Project Charter   TM-39
This outline is typical of a planning project charter.

Cover letter from executive sponsor serves as letter of authority.

I. Executive summary (maximum: 1-2 pages).
II. Background information (maximum: 1-2 pages).
    A. Purpose of the planning project.
    B. Scope of the planning project.
    C. Expectations of the planning project.
    D. Brief explanation of report contents.
III. Findings of the study phase (2-3 pages).
    A. Business mission and vision.
    B. Competitive analysis (if completed).
    C. Value chain analysis (if completed).
    D. Critical success factors analysis.
        1. Business goals.
        2. Business objectives.
        3. Critical success factors.
        4. Critical assumptions.
        5. Critical information needs.
    E. Problems and opportunities.
IV. Definition phase plan.
    A. A framework for information architecture.
    B. The plan.
        1. Phase objectives.
        2. The planning team.
        3. Activities and deliverables.
        4. Detailed schedule.
        5. Budget.
V. Appendixes (if necessary).

Association Matrices

TM–40

A matrix is the perfect tool for analyzing or comparing any two objects or ideas to learn their relationships. Two examples are presented to demonstrate the diversity of the tool.

A. Function-to-Organization Unit Association Matrix

Business Function \ Organization Unit	Research and Development	Warehouse	Production	Sales	Accounting
Marketing	S			P	S
Product Engineering	P		S	S	S
Process Engineering	P	S	S		S
Inventory Control		P	S		S
Cost Accounting	S	S	S		P

P = Organization unit has primary responsibility for this business function.
S = Organization unit plays some role in this business function.

B. Data-to-Function Association Matrix

Business Function \ Data Subject or "Data Entity"	Customer	Order	Product	Production Lot	Production Process
Marketing	CRUD	CRUD	CRUD		
Product Engineering			RU		R
Process Engineering			R		CRUD
Inventory Control			RU		R
Cost Accounting			RU	R	RU

C = The business function can create instances of this data subject in a database.
R = The business function can read instances of this data subject in a database.
U = The business function can update (change) instances of this data subject in a database.
D = The business function can delete (archive) instances of this data subject in a database.

© Richard D. Irwin, Inc., 1994

Organization Charts

Organization charts model the reporting relationships in the business.

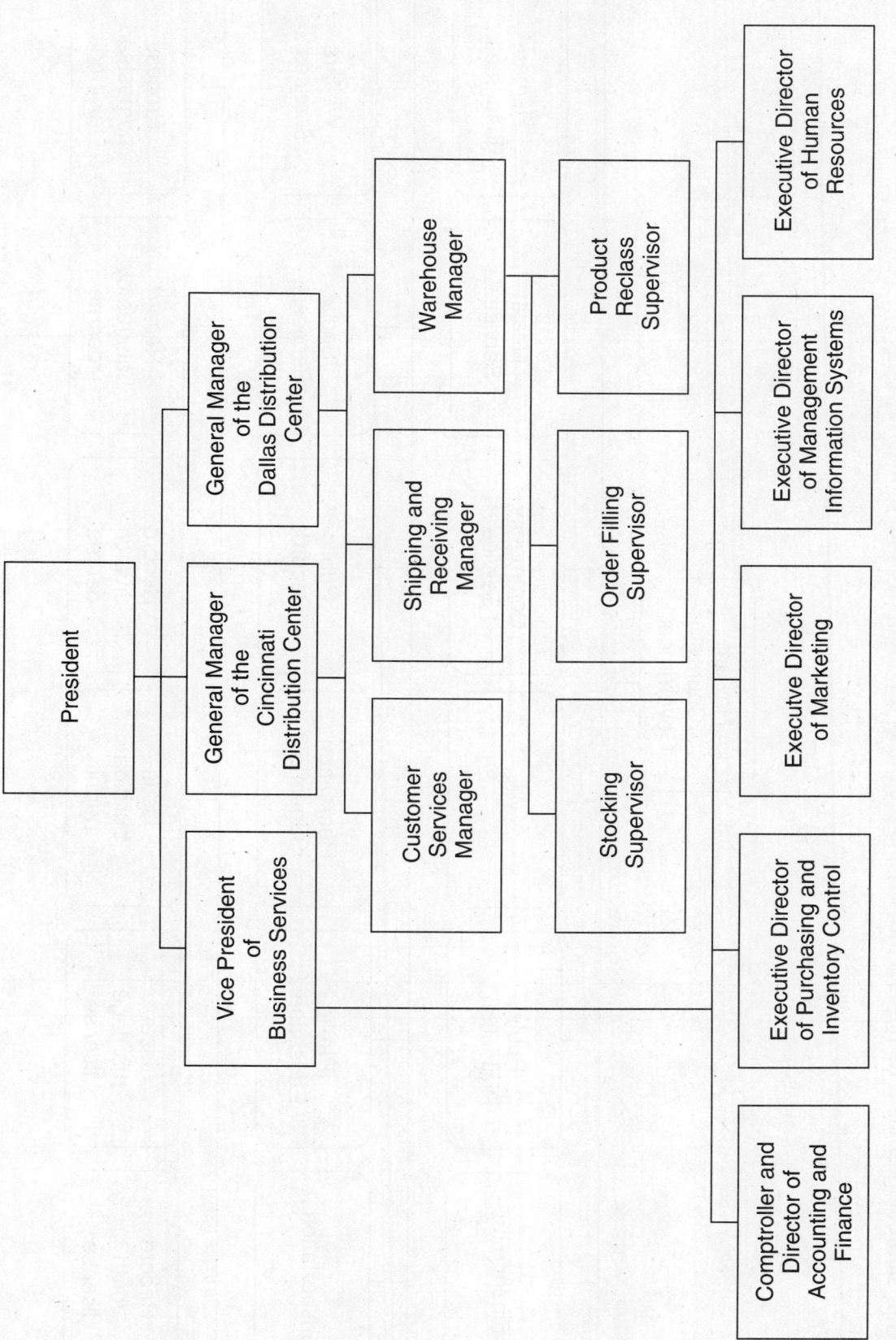

Decomposition Diagram
A decomposition diagram is a useful tool that breaks factors of an enterprise into functions and processes.

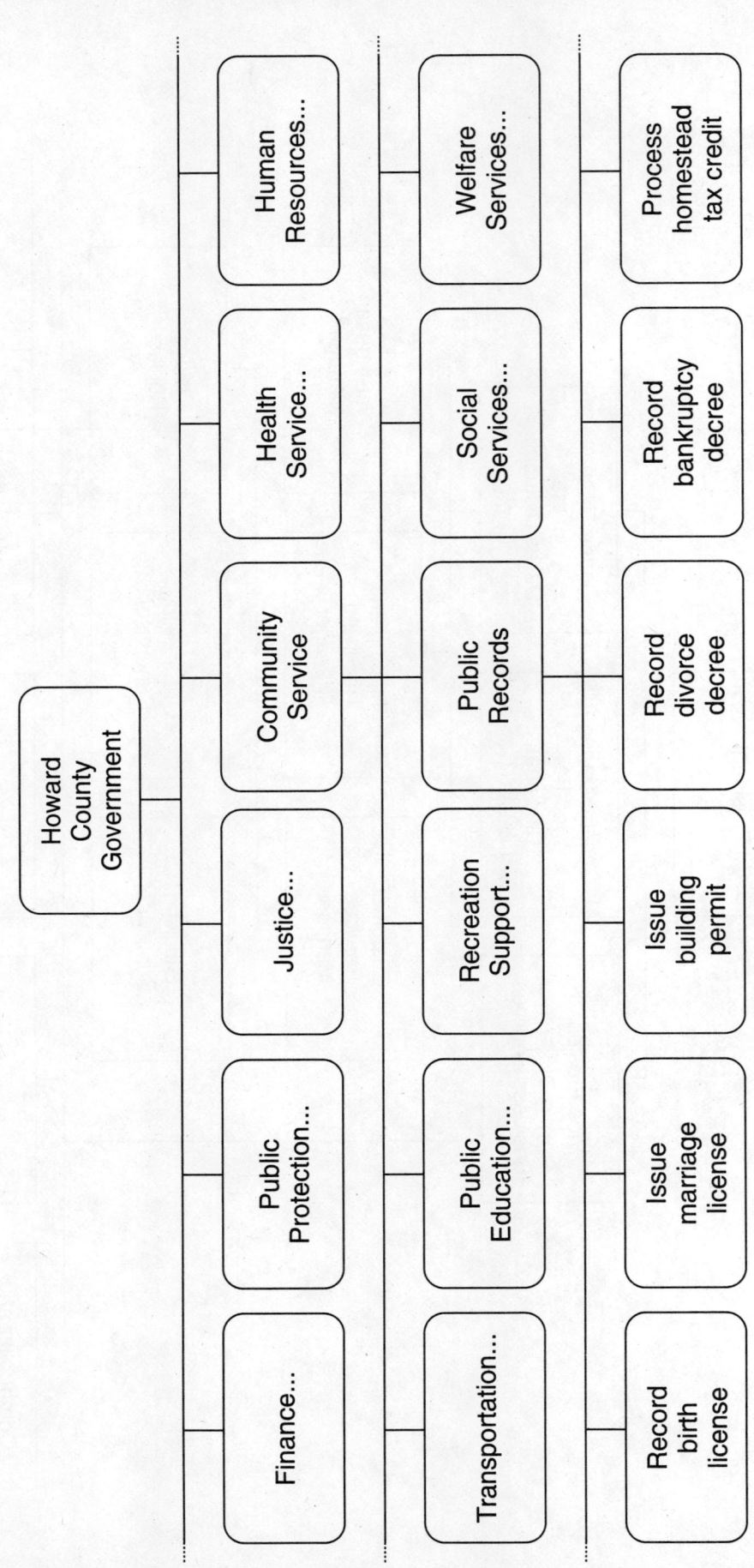

TM-42

© Richard D. Irwin, Inc., 1994

A Subject Data Model
A subject data model is an important tool for defining information needs and shared data requirements.

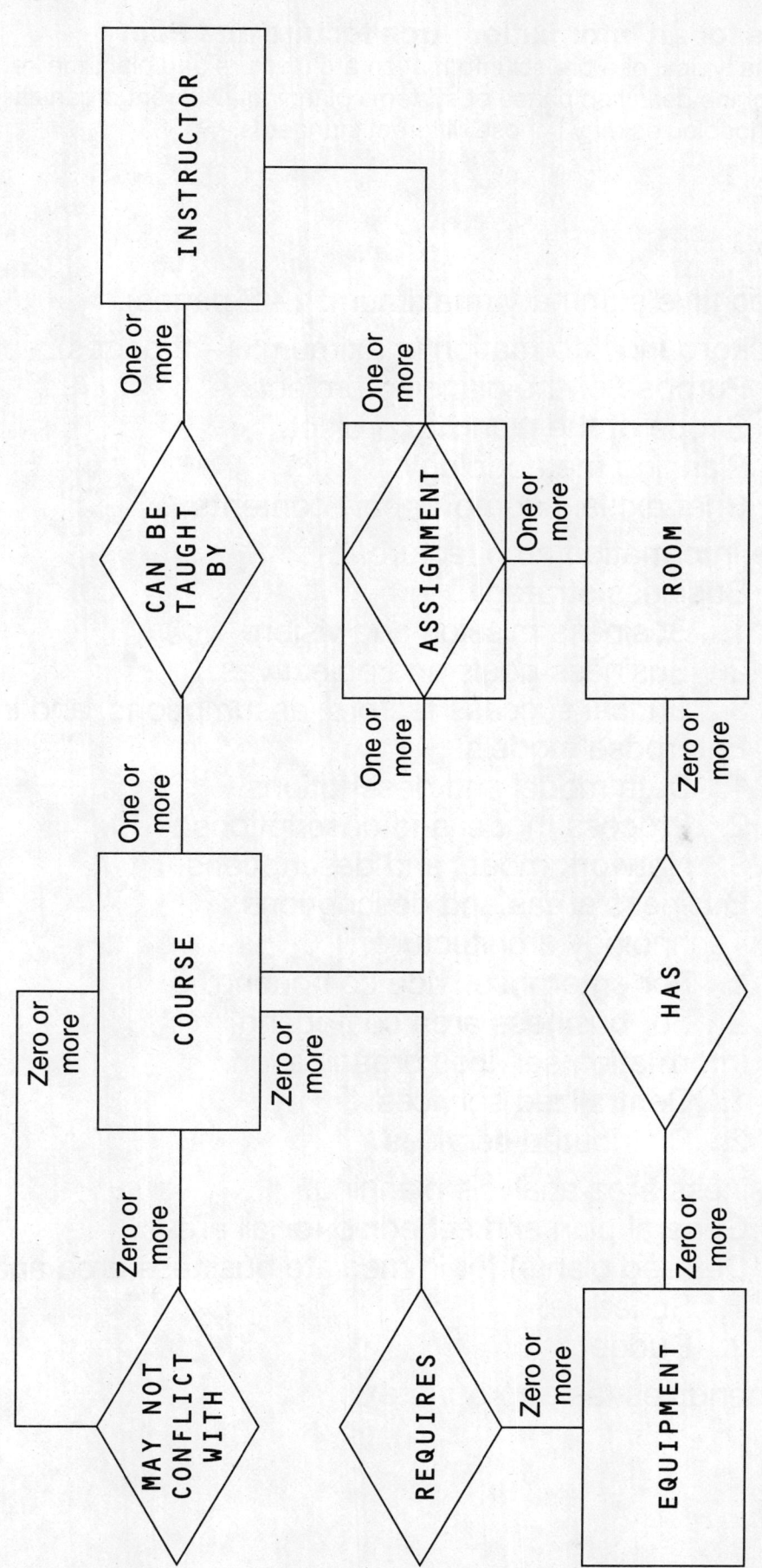

TM–43

© Richard D. Irwin, Inc., 1994

An Outline for an Information Architecture and Plan TM–44

This outline is typical of a project information architecture and plan, the key deliverable of the definition phase of systems planning. Different organizations or methodologies may impose different standards.

I. Executive summary (maximum: 1–2 pages).
II. Background information (maximum: 1–2 pages).
    A. Purpose of the planning project.
    B. Scope of the planning project.
    C. Planning methodology.
    D. Brief explanation of report contents.
III. The information architecture.
    A. Business strategy.
        1. Business mission and vision.
        2. Business goals and objectives.
        3. Critical success factors, assumptions, and information.
    B. Enterprise models.
        1. Data model and descriptions.
        2. Process model and descriptions.
        3. Network model and descriptions.
    C. Business areas and descriptions.
    D. Technology architecture.
        1. For enterprise-wide computing.
        2. For business area computing.
    E. Information services organization.
        1. Centralized services.
        2. Distributed services.
IV. Business area analysis planning.
    A. General plan and schedule for all areas.
    B. Detailed plan(s) for immediate business area analysis.
        1. Schedule.
        2. Budget.
V. Appendixes (as appropriate).

© Richard D. Irwin, Inc., 1994

Data Flow Diagrams

A data flow diagram is a useful tool that tracks the flow of data through business processes.

TM-45

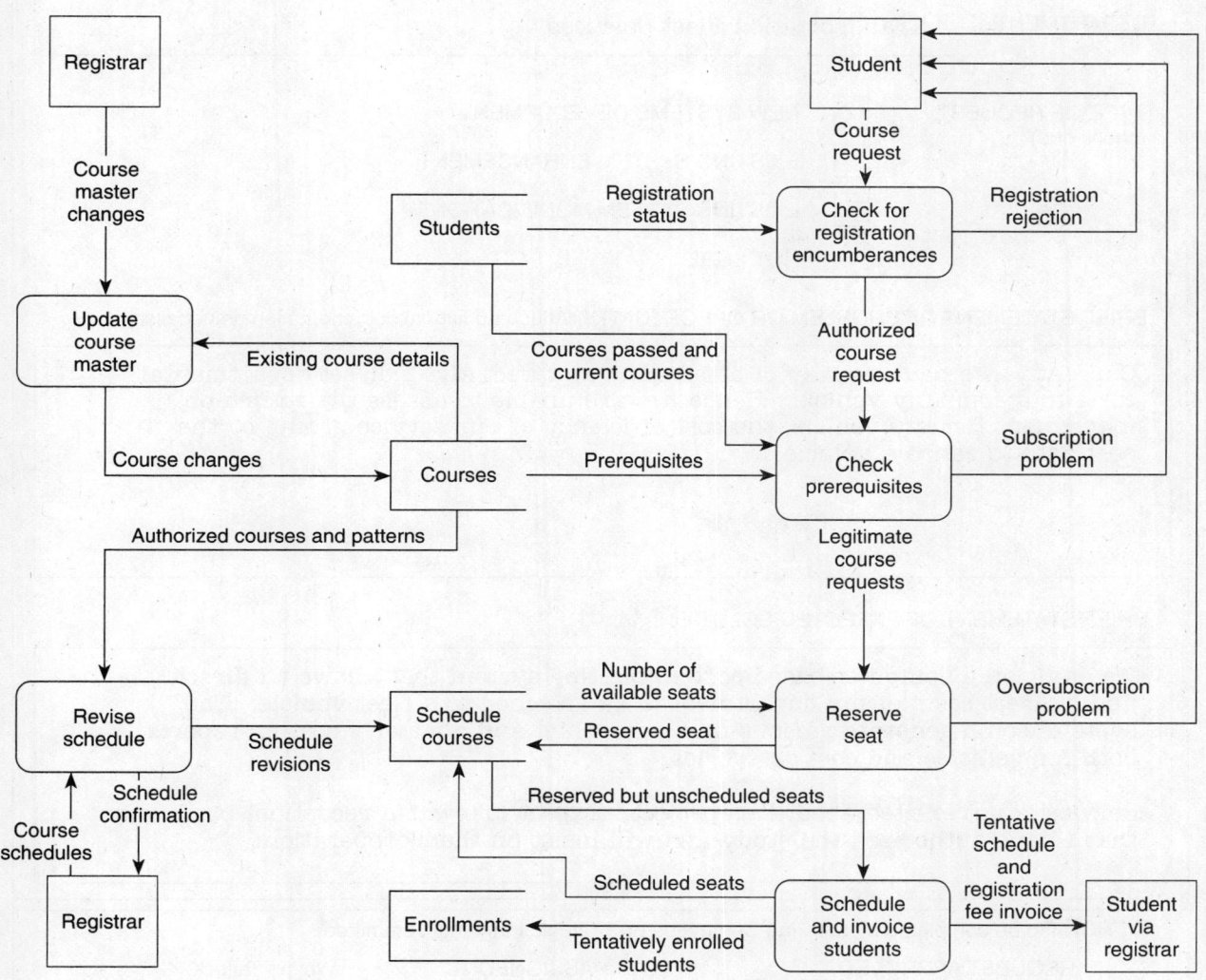

© Richard D. Irwin, Inc., 1994

Request for System Services

In some organizations a project request must be submitted on a standard request form.

TM–46

FORM IS-100-A.RFSS

Request for System Services

SUBMITTED BY: Barbara Rushin **Date:** July 25, 1993

DEPARTMENT: Transportation Fleet Services

TYPE OF REQUEST: (check one)
- [x] NEW SYSTEMS DEVELOPMENT
- [ ] EXISTING SYSTEM ENHANCEMENT
- [ ] EXISTING SYSTEM MODIFICATION
- [ ] NOT SURE

BRIEF STATEMENT OF PROBLEM OR OPPORTUNITY (Attach additional documentation as necessary):

Currently, we have no way of attributing all direct and indirect departmental costs to a company vehicle. Hence, we are unable to assess the return on investment for any vehicle, the cost efficiency of our service group, or the best date to retire a vehicle.

BRIEF STATEMENT OF EXPECTED SOLUTION:

We envision a computer-based cost-accounting system that allows all direct and indirect costs of my department to be assigned to a fleet vehicle. The system would generate various daily, monthly, and quarterly costing reports, both for vehicles and cost categories.

Service is not excited about this project. Expect lukewarm reception, but know that I have authorized the study and will insist on their cooperation.

ACTION (To be completed by Steering Committee or Strategic Planning Committee)

- [x] REQUEST APPROVED: ASSIGNED TO: Wayne Tatlock
                              START DATE: ASAP
                              BUDGET: $30,000
- [ ] REQUEST DELAYED: BACKLOGGED UNTIL: _____
- [ ] REQUEST REJECTED

Susan S. Bodkin   *ISS Steering Committee*   *August 15, 1993*
Signature   Representing   Date

LAST REVISED: October 1992

© Richard D. Irwin, Inc., 1994

Sample Questions for Survey Phase Interview

These questions, organized around information system building blocks, are representative of those asked in a first interview for a project.

About PEOPLE
- Who would be the end-users (*direct users*) of any system that we might build?
- Would anyone be indirectly affected by the system (*indirect users*)?
- Who developed the existing system?
- What people or political problems, opportunities, or directives triggered this project request?
- How will management and users feel about this project if it is approved for application development?
- How do the managers and users feel about working with computers and computer professionals?

About DATA
- What are the key inputs to this system?
- What are the key outputs from this system?
- Is any data currently being captured and stored in computer files and/or databases?

About ACTIVITIES
- What is the purpose or mission of this business area?
- What are the goals and objectives of this business area?
- Has any of this system been computerized (possibly by end-users with personal computers)?

About NETWORKS
- Will this project provide support for multiple locations? If so, where are they?
- How do the locations currently communicate?
- Are any computer networks currently in use?

© Richard D. Irwin, Inc., 1994

Context Model

This diagram is a context or scoping model that defines the boundaries of a system project. In this case the model depicts the activity view of the system.

TM-48

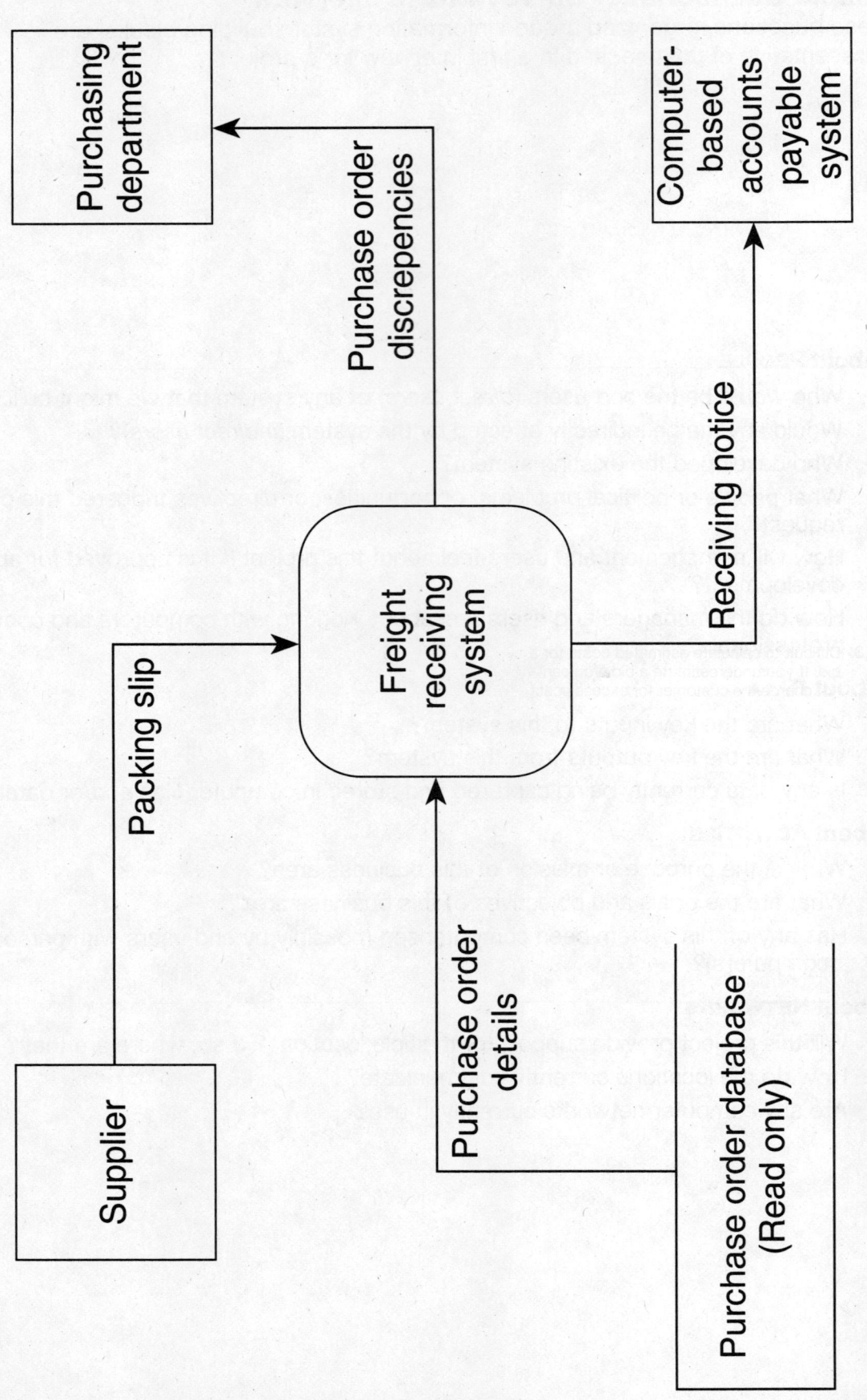

© Richard D. Irwin, Inc., 1994

Problem/Opportunity Survey Matrix

TM–49

This simple template allows analysts to document the classification of problems and opportunities.

Problem/Opportunity	Urgency?	Visibility?	Annual Benefits?	Priority?	Solution
1. Response time to bid on sporting events is excessive. We lose a lot of possible contracts.	Fix within six months	High	$250,000	2	New development
2. Number of potential events is growing faster than our ability to bid on those events. The opportunity to bid on additional, profitable events exists.	Fix within one year	Medium	$125,000	6	New development
3. Difficult to calculate estimated costs for a bid. If you underestimate a bid, you cannot charge the customer for excess costs.	Fix within three months	High	$50,000	4	Enhancement, then new development
4. There is no historical database on which to base future estimates.	Fix within six months	Low	$20,000	5	New development
5. We have recently purchased a competitor; however, we have since discovered fundamental incompatibilities between our respective event-scheduling data and systems.	Need immediate fix, if possible	High	$75,000	1	Quick fix, then new development
6. We have overbooked vehicles and equipment for events and subsequently incurred costly rental expenses to legally cover obligations.	Need within six months	High	$2,500	3	Leave well enough alone
7. We have occasionally booked events only to discover that we didn't have the "properly skilled" staff matched to the obligations.	Need within two years	Medium	$10,000	7	New development

©Richard D. Irwin, Inc., 1994

An Outline for Project Feasibility Assessment TM–50
This outline is typical of a project feasibility assessment or initial study report.

I. Executive summary (maximum: 1 page).
   A. Summary of recommendation.
   B. Brief statement of anticipated benefits.
   C. Brief explanation of report contents.
II. Background information (maximum: 1–2 pages).
   A. Brief description of project request.
   B. Brief explanation of summary phase activities completed.
III. Findings (2–3 pages).
   A. Problems and analysis.
   B. Opportunities and analysis.
   C. Directives and implications.
IV. Detailed recommendation.
   A. Narrative recommendation (1 page).
      1. Quick fixes (as necessary).
      2. Enhancements (as necessary).
      3. New systems development (as necessary).
   B. Project scope (0–3 pages).
      1. Process context model (optional).
      2. Data context model (optional).
      3. Network context model (optional).
   C. Project plan (3–4 pages).
      1. Initial project objectives.
      2. Initial master plan and assumptions.
      3. Detailed plan for study phase.
   D. Appendices (if necessary).

© Richard D. Irwin, Inc., 1994

A Problem/Opportunity/Objective/Constraint Matrix

TM−51

This template provides a vehicle for recording and analyzing problems and opportunities, and recording new system objectives.

Problem/Opportunity	Causes and/or Effects	System Objectives	System Constraint
1. Problem: Response time to bid on sporting events is excessive. 2. Opportunity: Number of potential events is expected to grow faster than the company's ability to bid on those events. 3. Problem: Difficult to calculate costs for a bid. 4. Problem/opportunity: No historical database on which to base future estimates.	**Causes:** There is no historical database of actual costs incurred for any type of event. There is currently no way to estimate revenue from advertisers. Resource requirements and availability data are inconsistent and unreliable. All estimates are made manually, using a variety of individual methods; therefore, if one estimator gets behind schedule, he can't pass off the estimate to another estimator. **Effects:** The company loses $150,000 per year due to inability to bid within specified deadlines. The company also loses the opportunity to bid on approximately $125,000 worth of events per year. The company loses $60,000 per year in contracts because of its tendency to overbid on most events to avoid absorbing excess costs.	1. Standardize the method and rules for estimation by December 1, 1993. 2. Create appropriate databases for estimation factors (e.g., costs, revenues, and resources) by March 1, 1994. 3. Reduce time required for any estimate from two weeks to two days by May 1, 1994.	1. There is a maximum budget for the entire project (meaning all system objectives for all problems and opportunities) of $150,000.
5. Problem: Fundamental incompatibilities between the company's and recently acquired competitor's current event-scheduling data and systems.	**Causes:** Traditional business line has been "sporting events." Acquisition of Eventron, Inc., adds new types of events such as "the performing arts" and "political" events to the agenda. **Effects:** It is feared that the company's bidding and scheduling problems may infect the successful business as acquired. The loss potential exceeds $900,000 per year of standing or repeat contracts.	1. Standardize the method and rules for estimation by December 1, 1993. 2. Preserve existing databases for appropriate estimation factors (e.g., costs, revenues, and resources) by December 1, 1993. 3. Retain the current system's ability to bid on its unique events within five working days.	1. Many of Eventron's contracts cover the same event over several years. The system must retain the ability to work within defacto contract standards for certain types of events. 2. The new, merged system must run on the same Apple Macintosh computers and AppleTalk LAN.

©Richard D. Irwin, Inc., 1994

An Outline for a Business Problem Statement

This outline is typical of a project feasibility assessment or detailed study report.

I. Executive summary (maximum: 2 pages).
   A. Summary of recommendation.
   B. Summary of problems, opportunities, and constraints.
   C. Brief statement of objectives for a new system.
   D. Brief explanation of report contents.

II. Description of study phase activities and methods (2–3 pages).
   A. Interviews/JAD sessions conducted.
   B. Samples collected.
   C. Surveys conducted.
   D. Observations performed.

III. Overview of current system (5–7 pages).
   A. Strategic planning implications (if appropriate).
   B. Models of current system.
      1. Organization chart.
      2. Data model(s).
      3. Process model(s).
      4. Network model(s).

IV. Cause/effect analysis of current system (5–10 pages).
   A. Performance analysis.
   B. Information and data analysis.
   C. Efficiency analysis.
   D. Control and security analysis.
   E. Economic analysis.
   F. Service analysis.

V. Detailed recommendations.
   A. Proposed objectives for new system (2–3 pages).
      1. Prioritized list of objectives.
      2. List of constraints.
   B. Proposed project scope (1–2 pages).
   C. Proposed project plan (2–4 pages).
      1. Overall project plan and schedule.
      2. Detailed plan and schedule for definition phase.

VI. Appendices (if necessary).

© Richard D. Irwin, Inc., 1994

Data Model Diagrams

Data model diagrams (also called entity-relationship diagrams) are a favorite tool for modeling the data requirements for a new system.

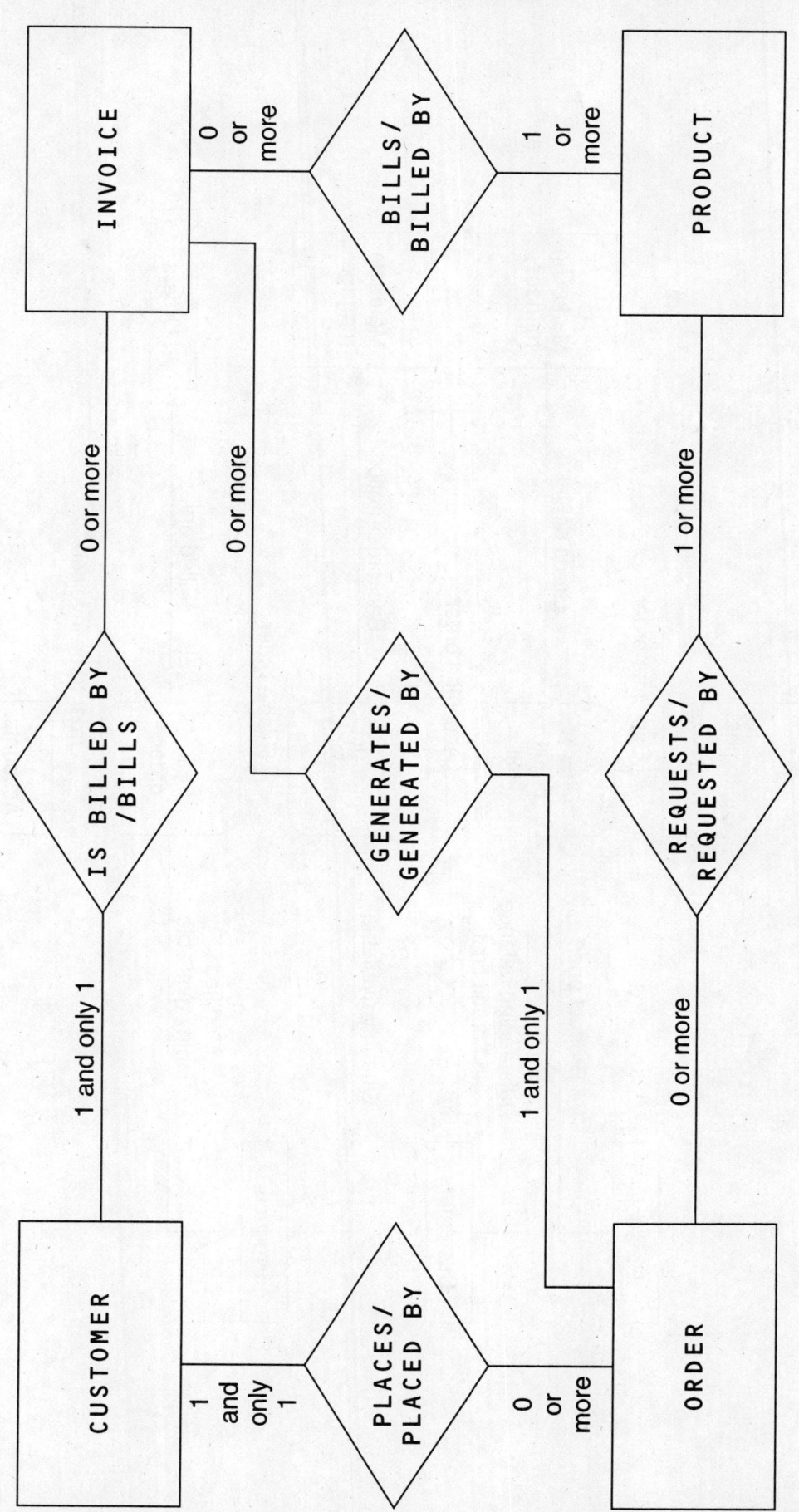

TM–53

© Richard D. Irwin, Inc., 1994

Data Flow Diagrams

Data flow diagrams are a favorite tool for documenting process or activity requirements for a new system.

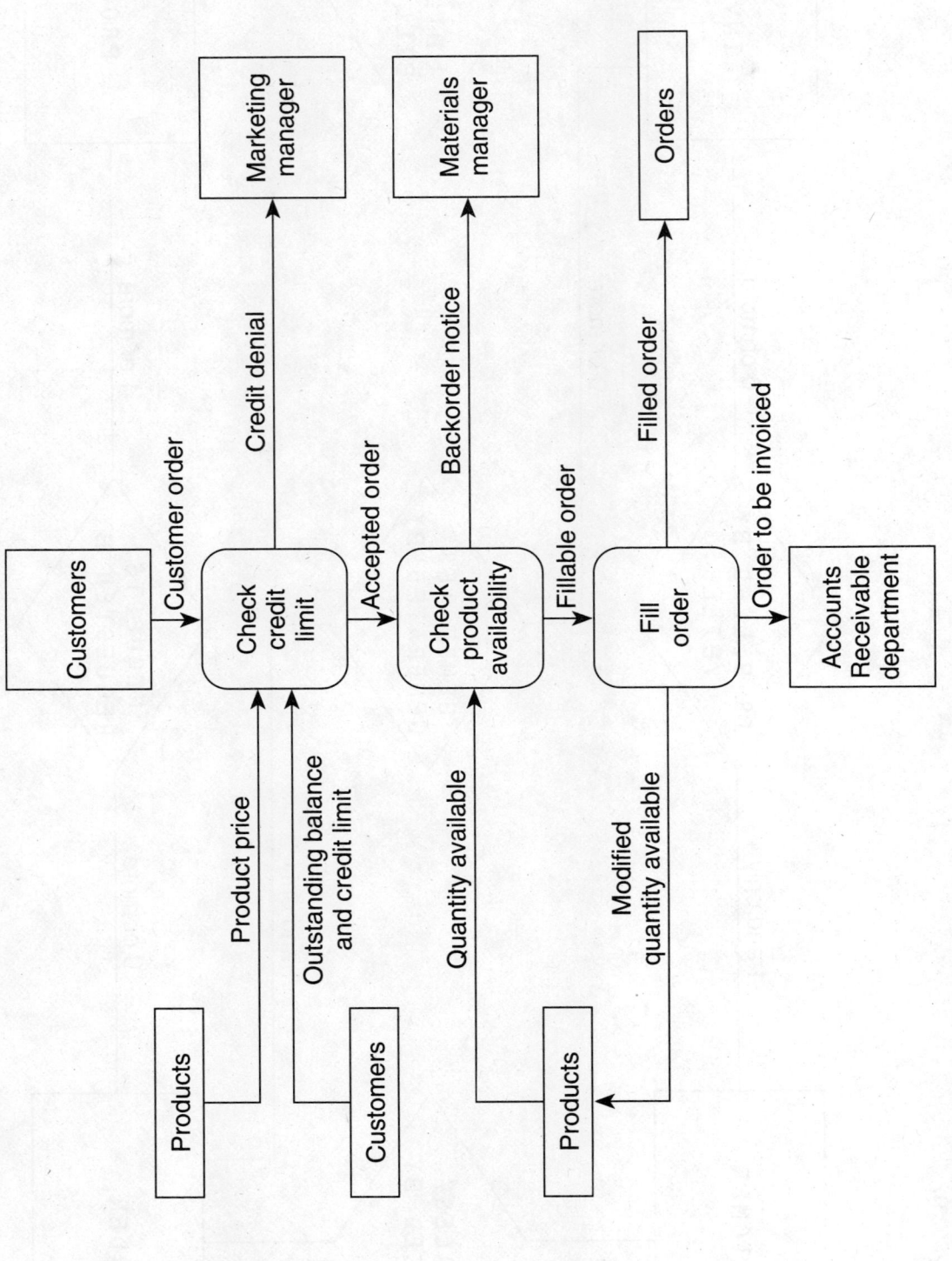

Connectivity Diagrams

Connectivity diagrams are useful for depicting geographic locations where data and processing may become important.

TM–55

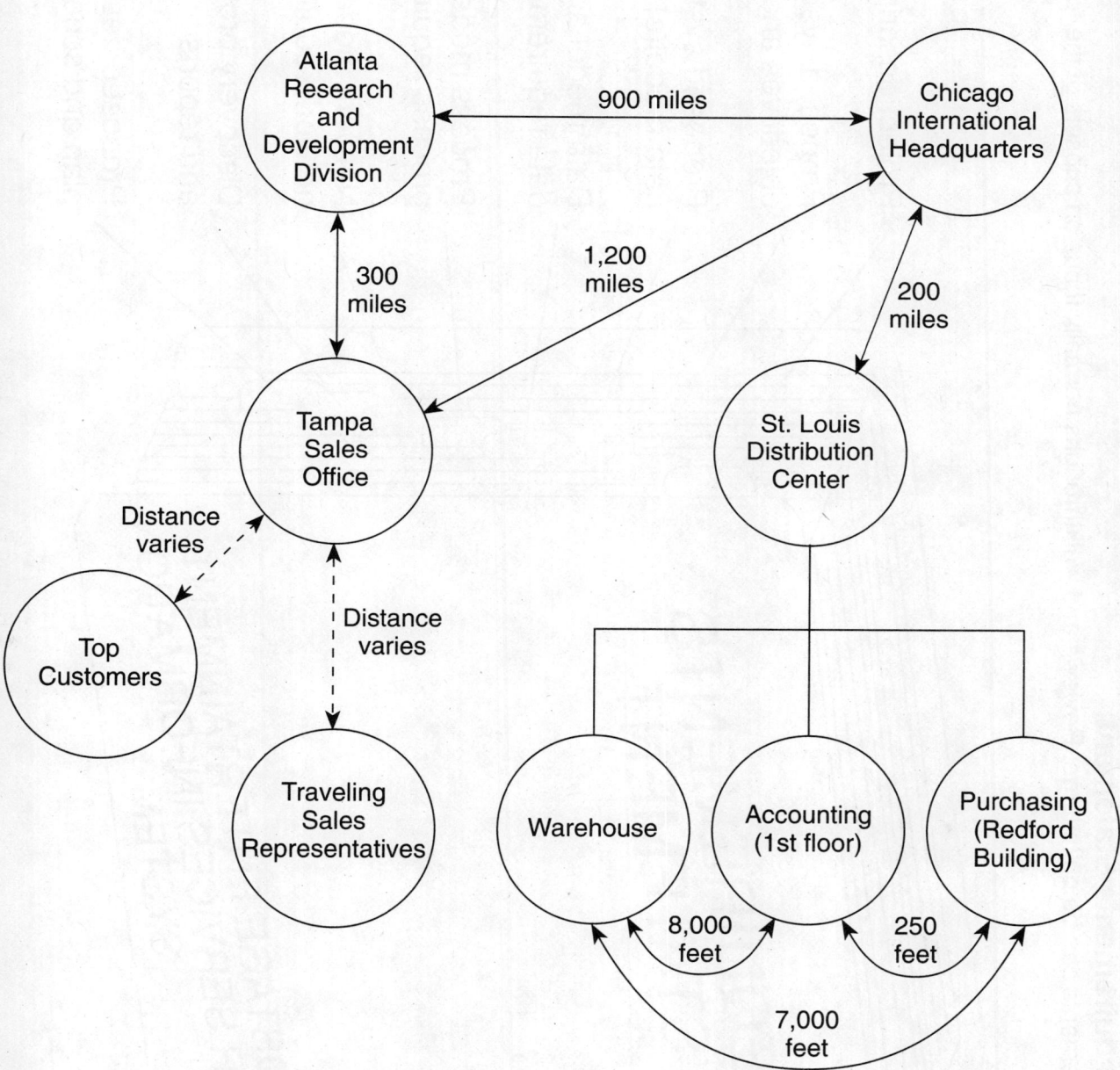

©Richard D. Irwin, Inc., 1994

A Hard Copy Requirements Statement

Requirements statements can be quite large. Reviews and walkthroughs normally focus on subsets of the total documentation.

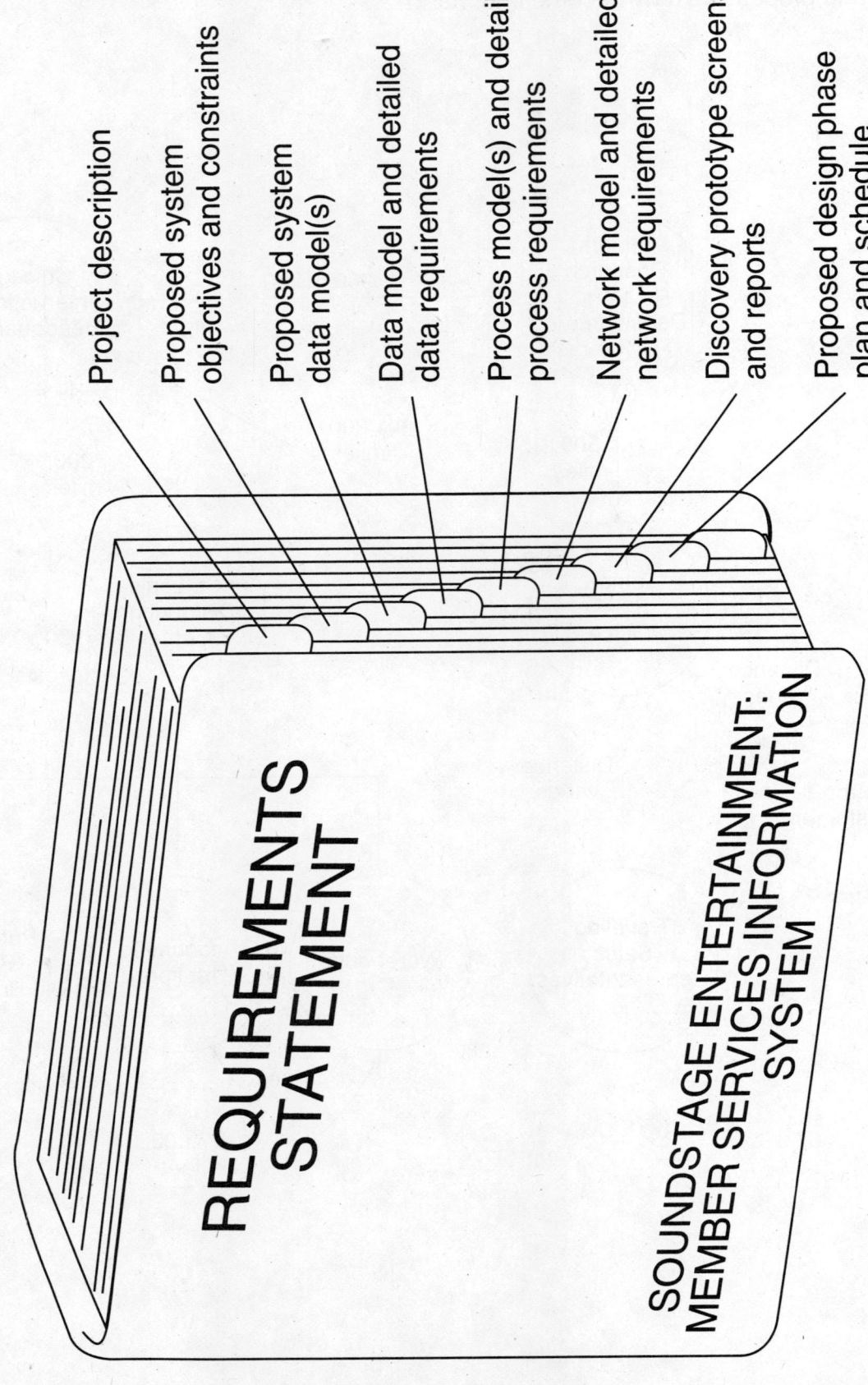

Types of System Models

Most system models depict either a current or proposed system. Most system models "should" also depict either the essential or implementation of a system.

Models	Essential System (Describes "What"; Also Known as the Logical System)	Implementation System (Describes "What" plus "How"; Also Known as the Physical System)
Current System (Existing System)	An essential model of the current system depicts those aspects of the current system that are essential to the business and that should be retained—no matter how we choose to implement the system.	An implementation model of the current system depicts how the current system is physically implemented (inclusive of technology). By default, the implementation model includes all of the essential aspects of the current system.
Proposed System (Target System)	An essential model of the proposed system depicts the business and user requirements for the system—regardless of how that system might be implemented.	An implementation model of the proposed system depicts how the proposed system will be physically implemented (inclusive of technology). By default, the implementation model must include all of the essential aspects of the proposed system.

© Richard D. Irwin, Inc., 1994

An Artistic Data Model
A data model depicts things about which a business stores data and the relationships between those things.

TM-58

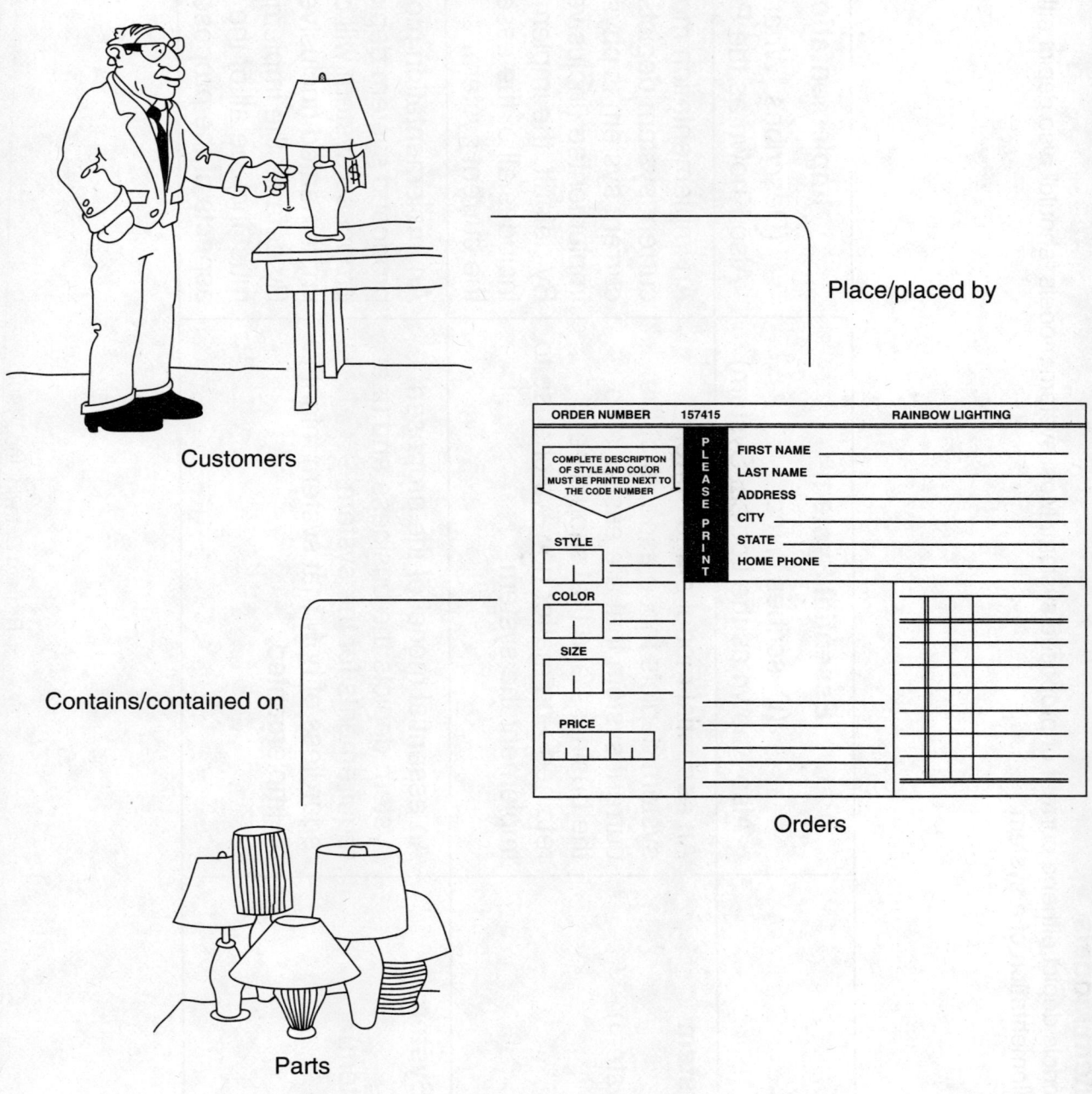

© Richard D. Irwin, Inc., 1994

An Entity Relationship Diagram as a Data Model

One of the most popular data modeling tools is Peter Chen's entity relationship diagram. Entities (rectangles) are described by data attributes, which in this example are written inside the rectangles. Relationships are depicted by diamonds that are connected to the rectangles.

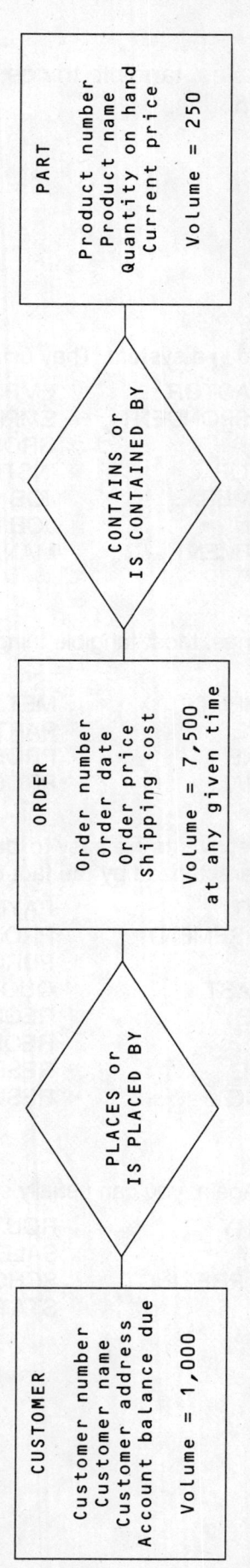

© Richard D. Irwin, Inc., 1994

TM-59

Examples of Entities

TM-60

Entities mostly correspond to roles, tangible things, events, and locations. They are named with singular nouns.

Entities that describe roles played in a system. They usually represent people or organizations.

ACCOUNT	CONTRACTOR	EMPLOYEE	OFFICE
AGENCY	CORRESPONDENT	EMPLOYER	OFFICER
ANIMAL	CLIENT	GROUP	SALESPERSON
APPLICANT	CREDITOR	INSTRUCTOR	STUDENT
BORROWER	CUSTOMER	JOB OPENING	SUPPLIER
CHAPTER	DIVISION	JOB POSITION	TEAM
CHILD	DEPARTMENT	MANAGER	VENDOR
CLASS			

Entities that describe tangible things. Most tangible things are easy to identify because you can see and touch them.

BOOK	EQUIPMENT	METAL	SERVICE
CHEMICAL	ISOTOPE	PART	SUBSTANCE
COURSE	MACHINE	PRODUCT	VEHICLE
DISK	MATERIAL	PROGRAM	

Entities that describe events. Most events are easy to identify because the business records data on forms and in files. Events are characterized by the fact that they happen and have duration.

AGREEMENT	DEPOSIT	PAYMENT	SEMESTER
APPLICATION	DISBURSEMENT	PROJECT	SHIPMENT
APPOINTMENT	FLIGHT	PURCHASE ORDER	STEP
ASSIGNMENT	FORECAST	QUOTE	TASK
BACKORDER	INVOICE	REGISTRATION	TEST
BUDGET	JOB	REQUISITION	TIME BUCKET
CLAIM	LICENSE	RESERVATION	WORK ORDER
CONTRACT	MEETING	RESUME	
DEFECT RETURN			

Entities that describe locations. Again, you can usually see locations.

BRANCH	COUNTRY	ROUTE	STORAGE BIN
BUILDING	COUNTY	SALES REGION	VOTER PRECINCT
CAMPUS	POLICE PRECINCT	SCHOOL ZONE	WAREHOUSE ZONE
CITY	ROOM	STATE	

© Richard D. Irwin, Inc., 1994

Data Attributes that Describe an Entity

Every entity is described by two or more data attributes. When implemented as a simple table, as shown here, the attributes (columns) take on values for each occurrence (row) of the entity.

Entity definition: **PART** — Identifier: **PART NUMBER** — Data attributes: PART DESCRIPTION, UNIT OF MEASURE, QUANTITY ON HAND, QUANTITY ON ORDER, UNIT COST

PART NUMBER	PART DESCRIPTION	UNIT OF MEASURE	QUANTITY ON HAND	QUANTITY ON ORDER	UNIT COST
567M	¾-inch lug nut	Dozen	43	20	8.98
567P	1-inch lug nut	Dozen	0	100	9.98
568A	¼-inch fitted nut	Each	134	0	5.98
...					
689	½-inch hose	Foot	90	0	3.98
690	¾-inch hose	Foot	7	100	4.39
691	1-inch hose	Foot	66	0	5.98
...					
745	½-inch hose clamp	Each	107	0	.98
746	¾-inch hose clamp	Each	21	20	.98
747	1-inch hose clamp	Each	0	30	1.98
...					

Entity implementation — One occurrence of the entity

© Richard D. Irwin, Inc., 1994

TM–61

Entity Supertypes and Subtypes

In this ERD, EMPLOYEE is an entity supertype whose occurrences can be grouped into two entity subtypes: SALARIED EMPLOYEE and HOURLY EMPLOYEE.

TM-62

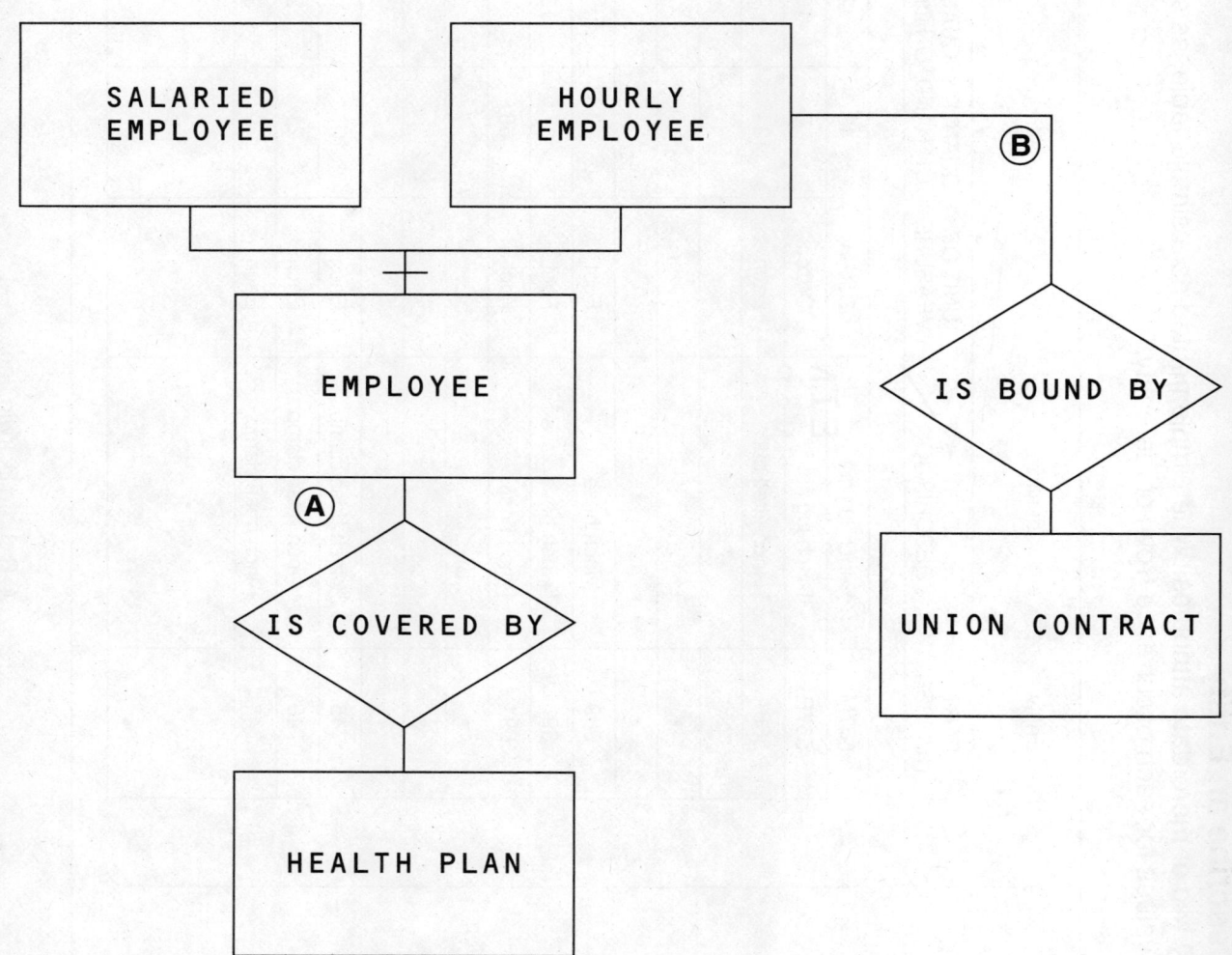

Multiple Relationships between the Same Entities

Any pair of entities may participate in multiple relationships, each having its own meaning.

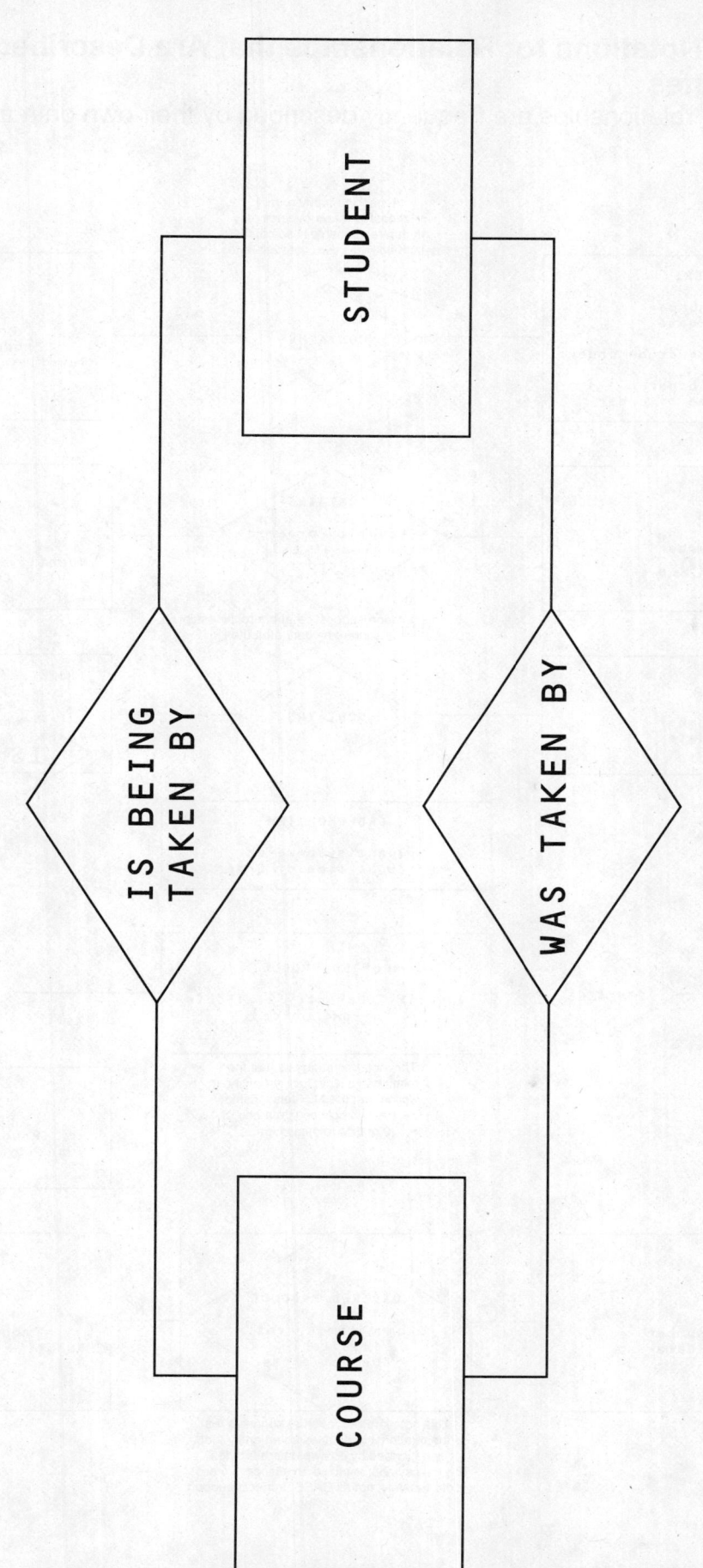

Alternative Notations for Relationships that Are Described by Data Attributes   TM–64

Many-to-many relationships are frequently described by their own data attributes.

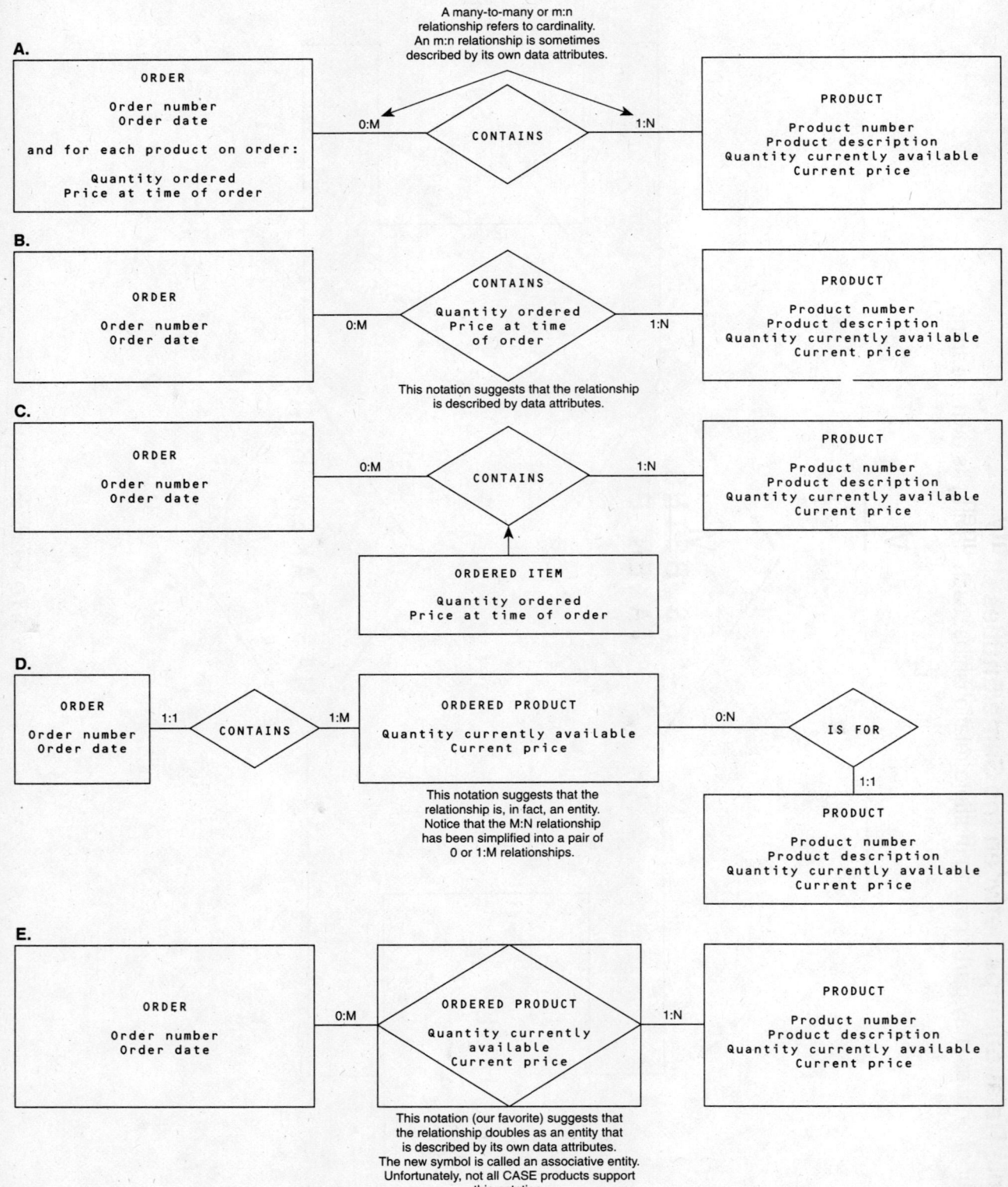

© Richard D. Irwin, Inc., 1994

Relationships between Occurrences of the Same Entity

Sometimes an entity's occurrences can be related to different occurrences of the same entity.

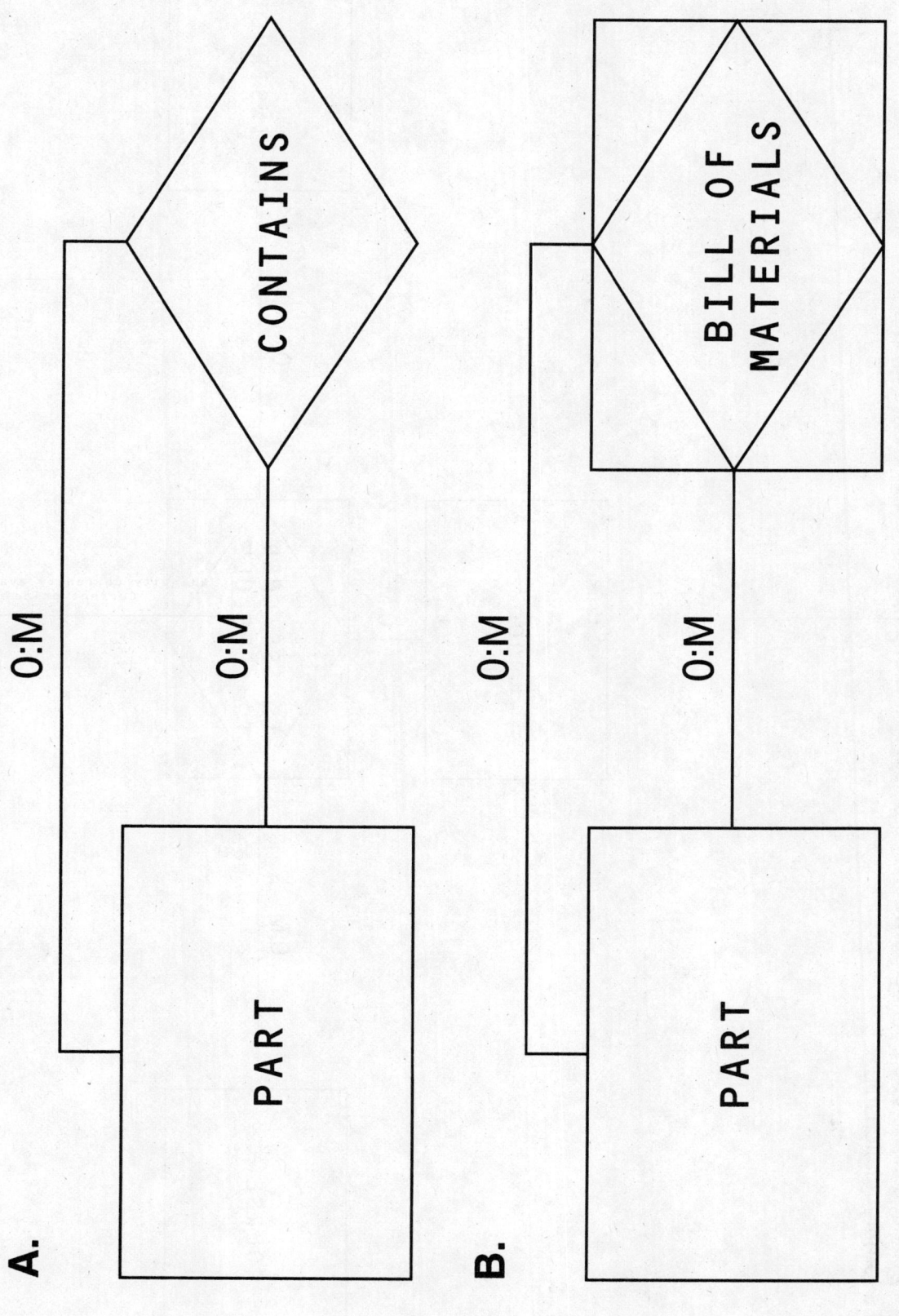

N-Ary Relationships

An N-Ary relationship is one defined between N entities. In this example N = 3—thus, we have what is commonly called a ternary relationship.

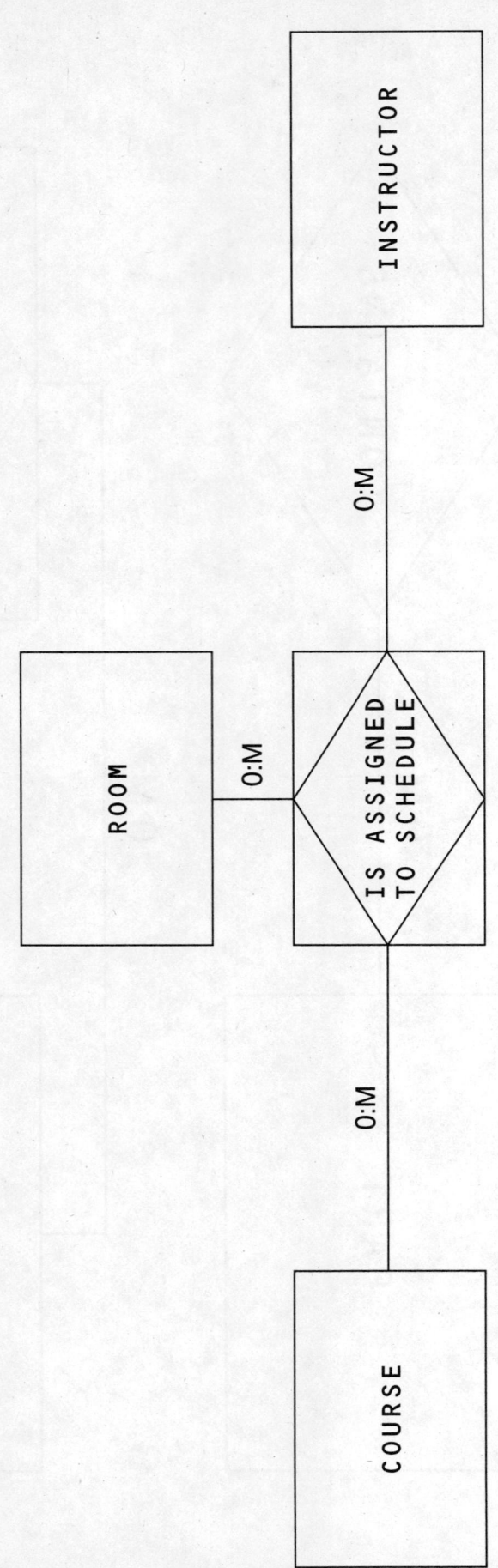

Rules Governing Relationships
Some relationships must occur together. Others must not occur together.

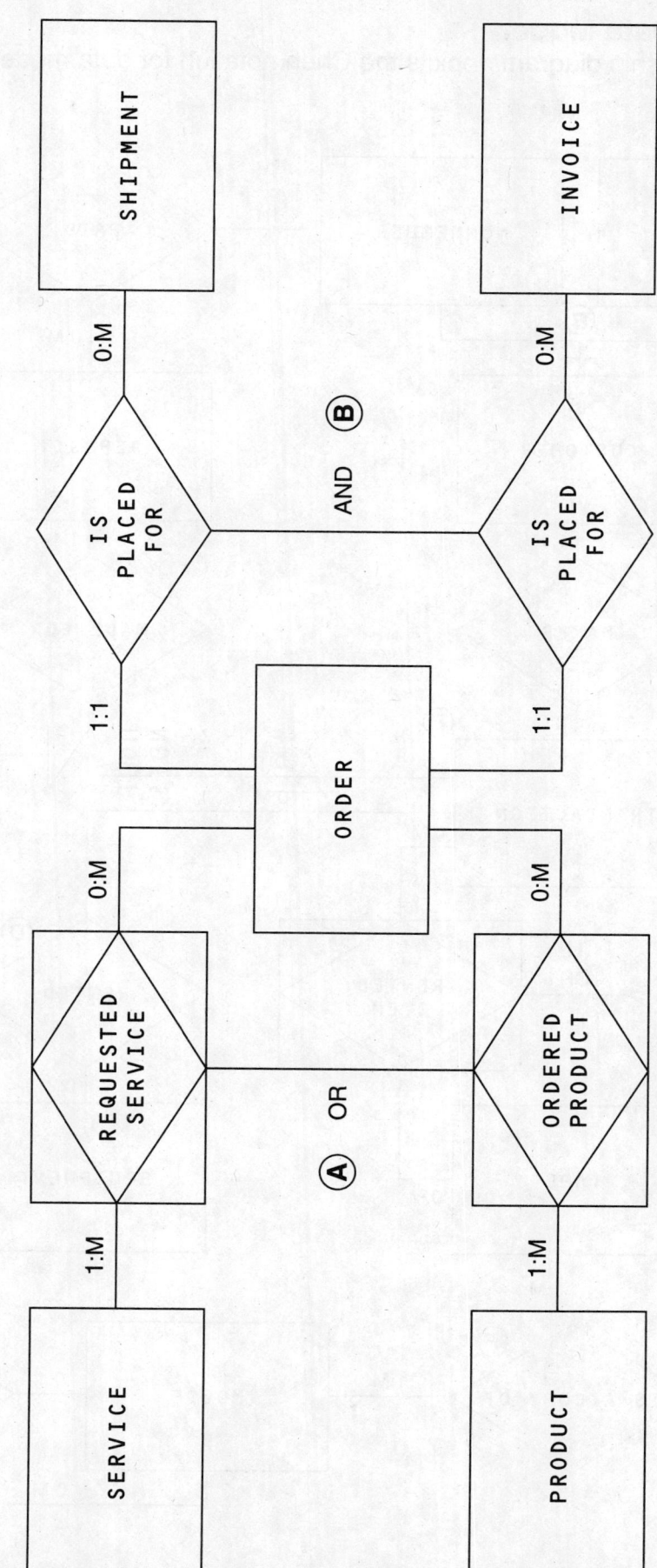

A Chen-Style Data Model
This entity relationship diagram depicts the Chen notation for data modeling.

TM-68

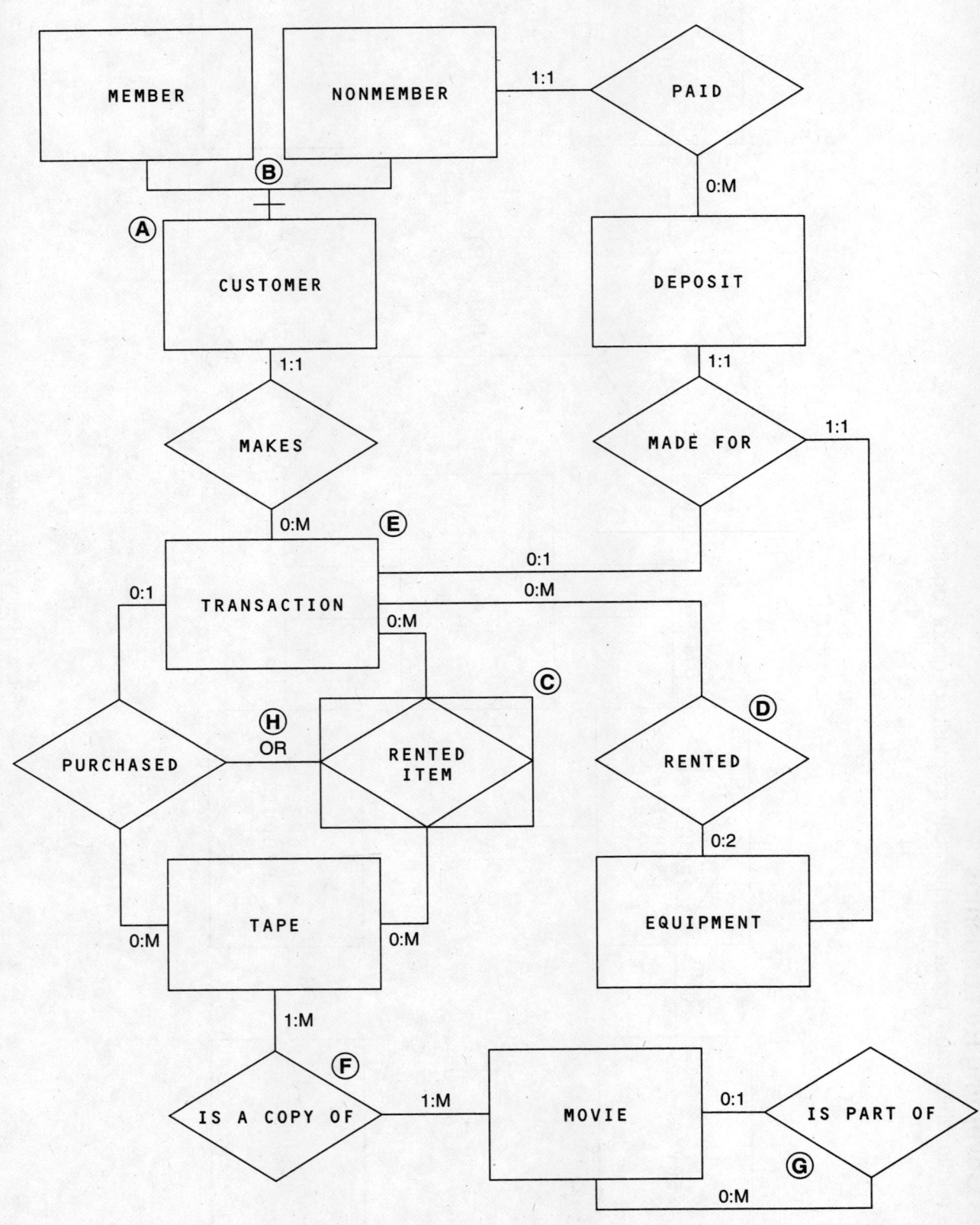

©Richard D. Irwin, Inc., 1994

A Martin-Style Data Model

This entity relationship diagram depicts the Martin notation for data modeling.

TM-69

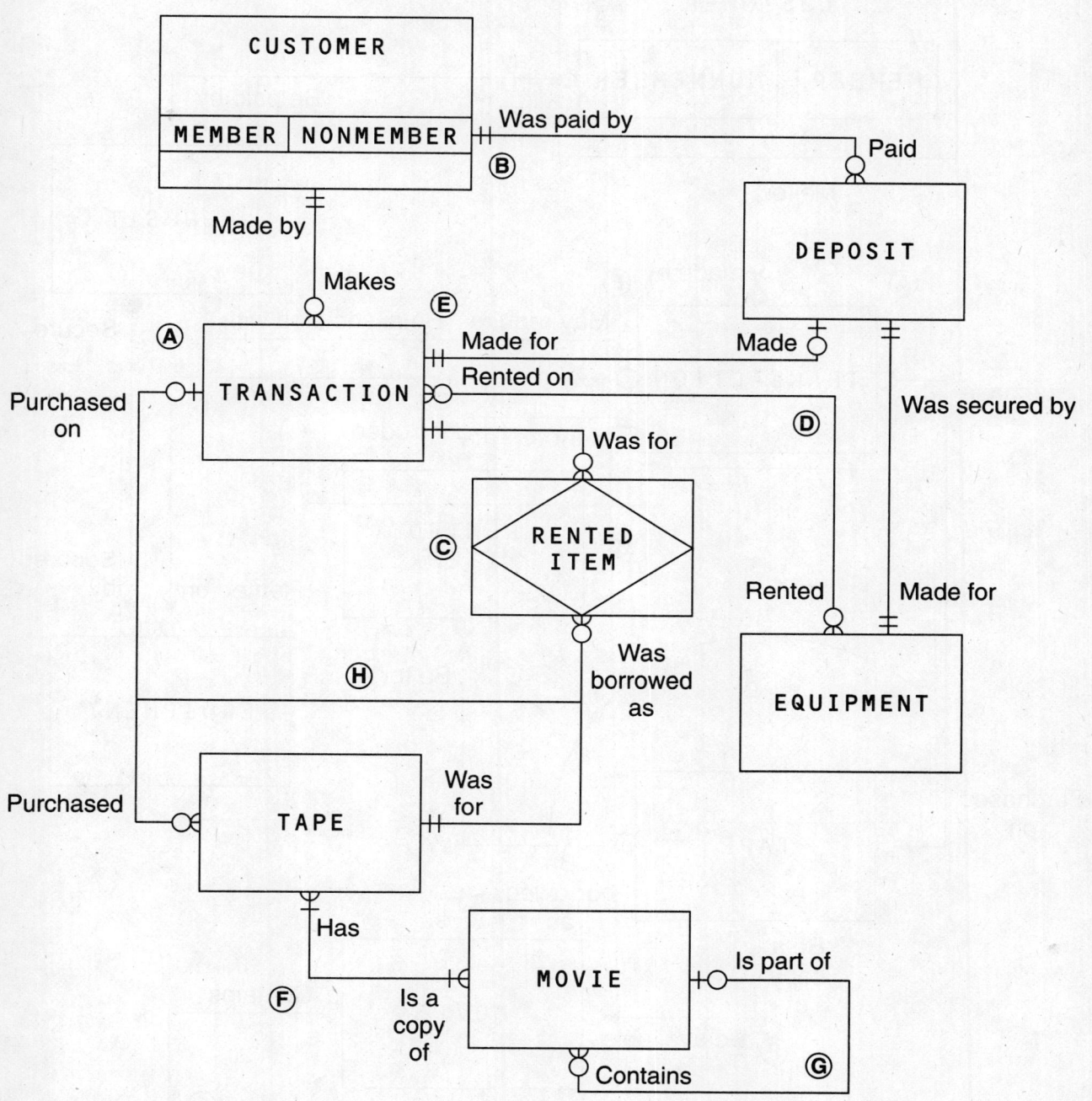

© Richard D. Irwin, Inc., 1994

A Bachman-Style Data Model

This entity relationship diagram depicts the Bachman notation for data modeling.

TM-70

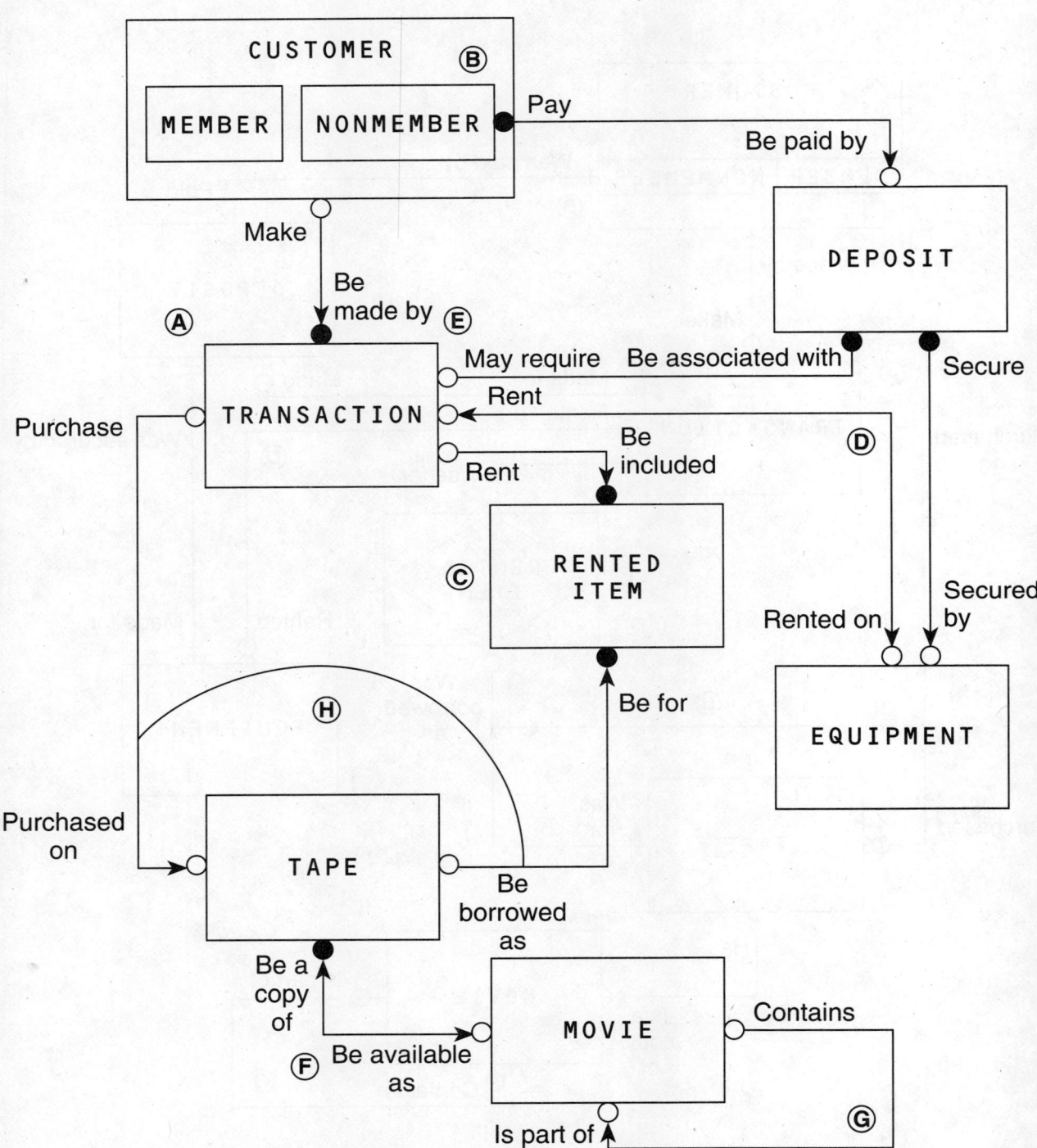

© Richard D. Irwin, Inc., 1994

A Simpler Bachman-Style Data Model

TM–71

This entity relationship diagram depicts an earlier and simpler Bachman notation for data modeling.

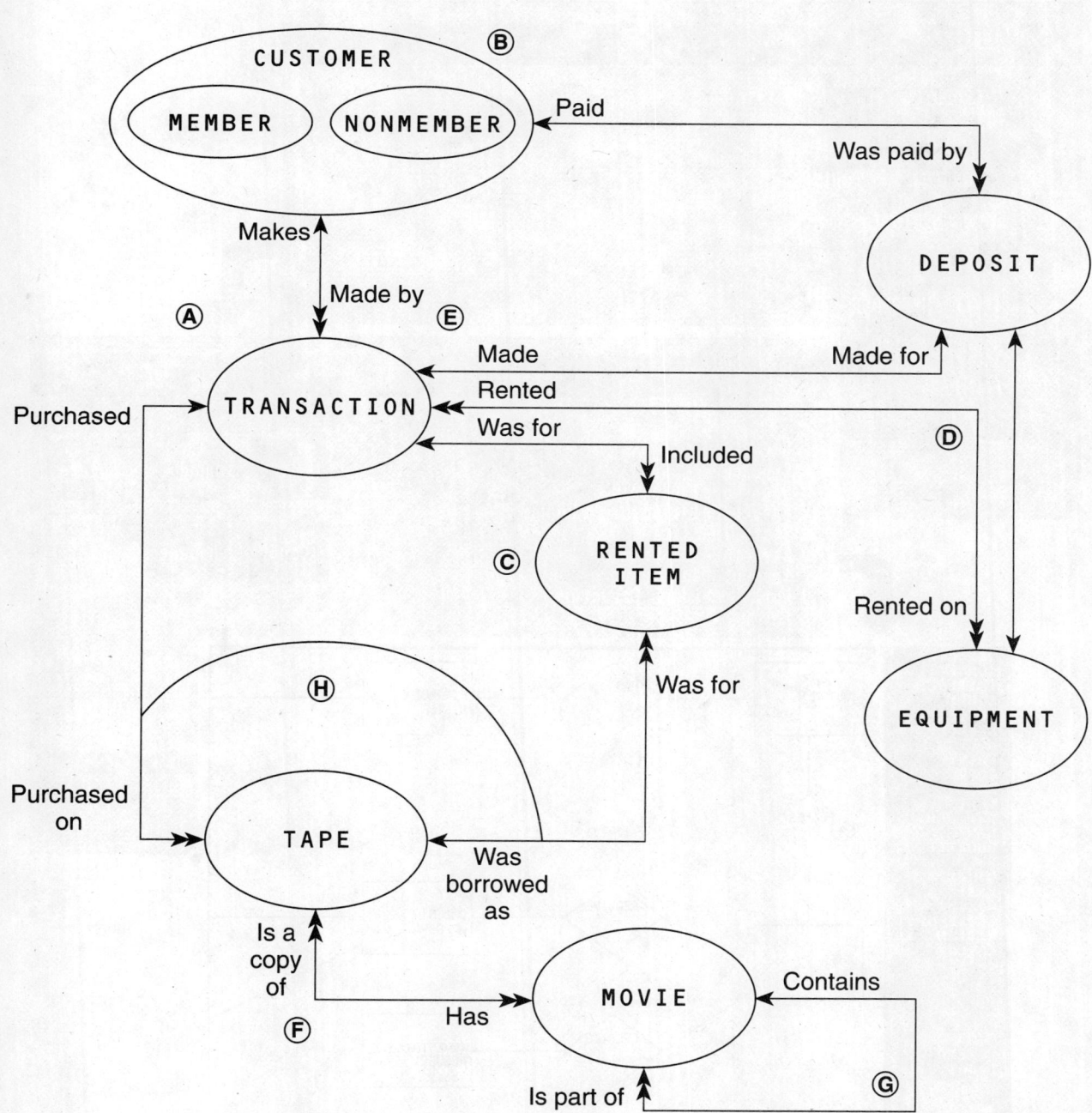

©Richard D. Irwin, Inc., 1994

CASE Tools for Data Modeling

TM-72

This sequence of screens demonstrates a popular CASE tool's usefulness in drawing data models. (Screens were captured from INTERSOLV's Excelerator/IS.)

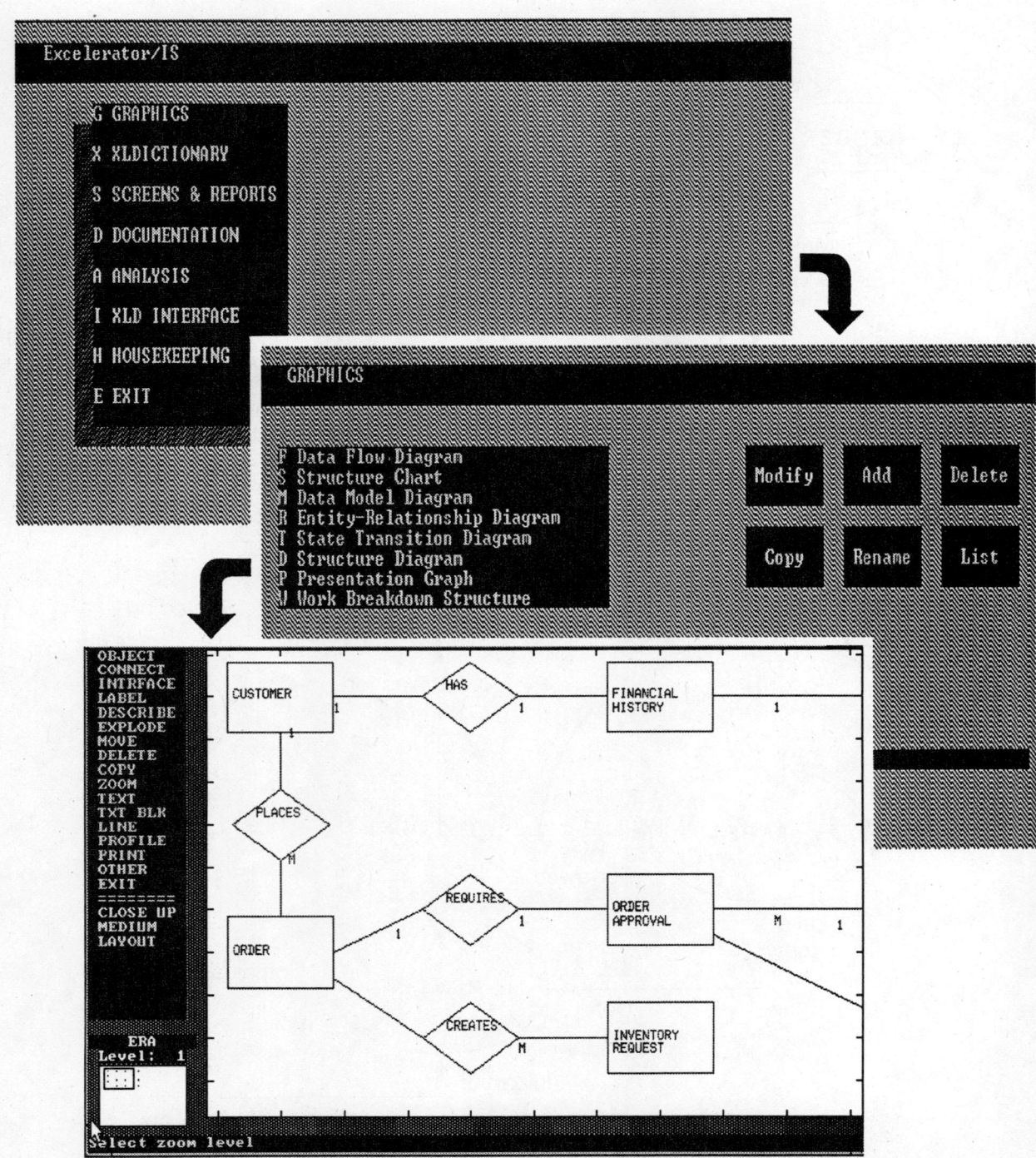

© Richard D. Irwin, Inc., 1994

SoundStage Member Services Data Entities

Data entity definitions are recorded in a project repository.

AGREEMENT: A contract whereby a member agrees to purchase a certain number of products within a certain time period. After fulfilling that agreement, the member will receive bonus credits, as specified in the agreement, for each additional purchase.

BACKORDER: An order or partial order created in response to SoundStage's inability to fill a member's order due to lack of stock.

CLUB: A SoundStage membership group to which members can belong. Examples include the Compact Disc Club and the VHS Videotape Club.

MEMBER: A member of one or more clubs.

ORDER: An automatic, dated order generated in response to a monthly promotion. The order may be approved, revised, or canceled via the member's response. If not canceled or revised by a specified date, the order is normally shipped.

PRODUCT: Audio, video, or other entertainment merchandise sold to members through the club.

PROMOTION: Monthly or quarterly events whereby automatic, dated orders are created for all members in a club. The promotion specifies a "Selection of the Month" that will automatically be filled unless it is canceled or revised by the member within a specified time period.

© Richard D. Irwin, Inc., 1994

SoundStage Data Entity Identifiers

Data entity occurrences must be uniquely identifiable by an attribute or some combination of attributes.

AGREEMENT: <u>AGREEMENTS NUMBER SUFFIX</u>

BACKORDER: <u>ORDER NUMBER</u> + <u>BACKORDER DATE</u>

CLUB: <u>CLUB NAME</u>

MEMBER: <u>MEMBER NUMBER</u> or <u>MEMBER NAME</u>

ORDER: <u>ORDER NUMBER</u>

PRODUCT: <u>PRODUCT NUMBER</u> + <u>MEDIA CODE</u>

PROMOTION: <u>CLUB NAME</u> + <u>PROMOTION DATE</u>

Relationship Matrix

Relationships can sometimes be defined using a simple entity-to-entity matrix. Some CASE tools support such a matrix and can generate an ERD from such a matrix.

ENTITY	MEMBER	CLUB	AGREEMENT	PROMOTION	ORDER	PRODUCT	BACKORDER
MEMBER		ENROLLED IN one or more	IS BOUND TO one or more		MUST RESPOND TO zero or more –and– RESPONDED TO zero or more		
CLUB	ENROLLS zero or more		ESTABLISHES one or more	SPONSORS zero or more			
AGREEMENT	BINDS zero or more	ESTABLISHED FOR one and only one					
PROMOTION		SPONSORED BY one and only one			GENERATES one or more	PROMOTES one or more	
ORDER	AWAITS RESPONSE FROM one and only one –and– RESPONDED TO BY one and only one			GENERATED BY one and only one		REQUESTED one or more	GENERATES zero or one
PRODUCT				PROMOTED BY zero or more	REQUESTED BY zero or more		CONTAINED ON zero or more
BACKORDER					GENERATED FOR one and only one	CONTAINS one or more	

© Richard D. Irwin, Inc., 1994

The SoundStage Essential Data Model

These are the entities and relationships about which SoundStage wants to store data.

TM-76

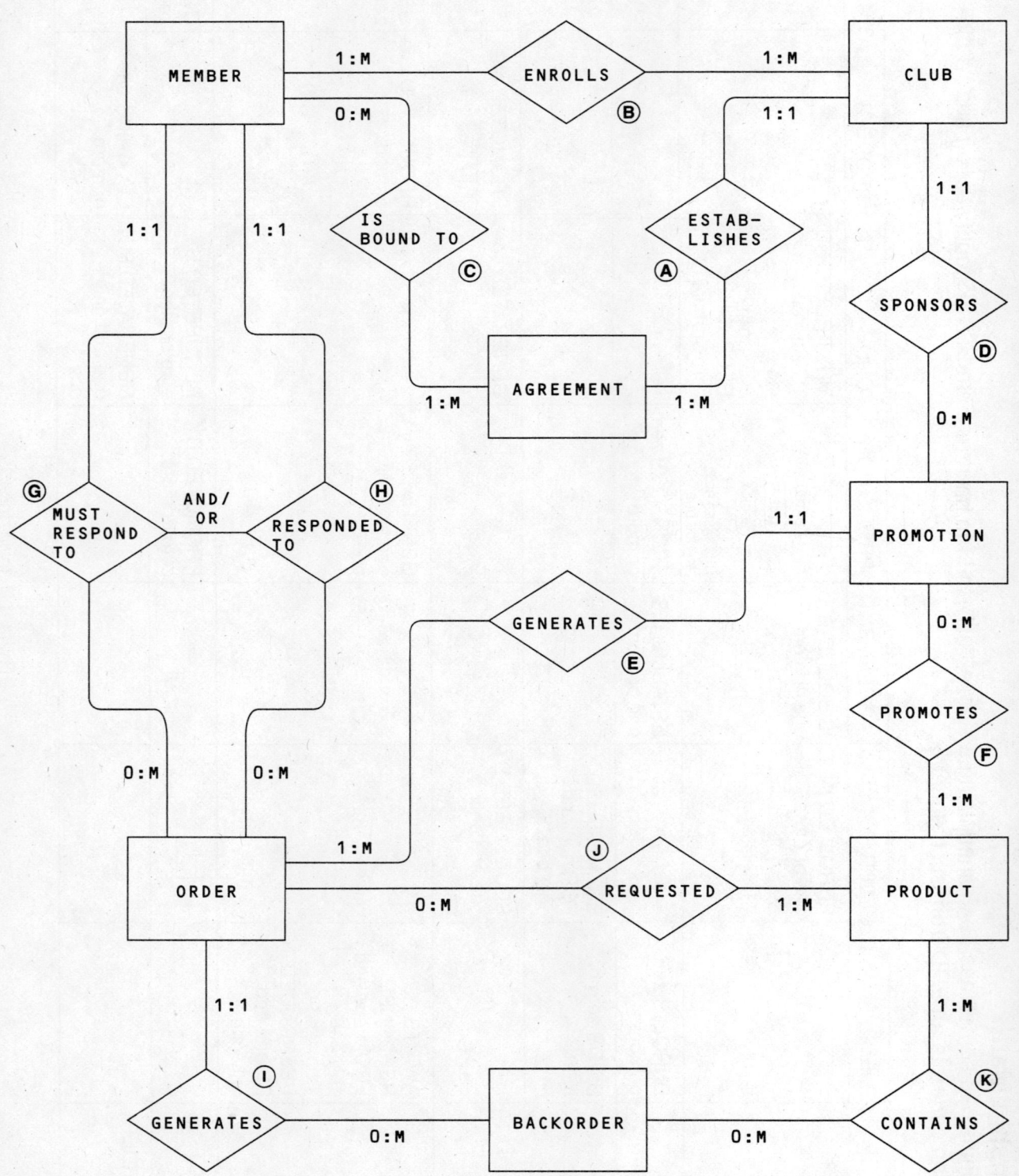

© Richard D. Irwin, Inc., 1994

Forms Sampling

Data attributes can be gleaned from sample forms and files. This form has been marked to identify data attributes.

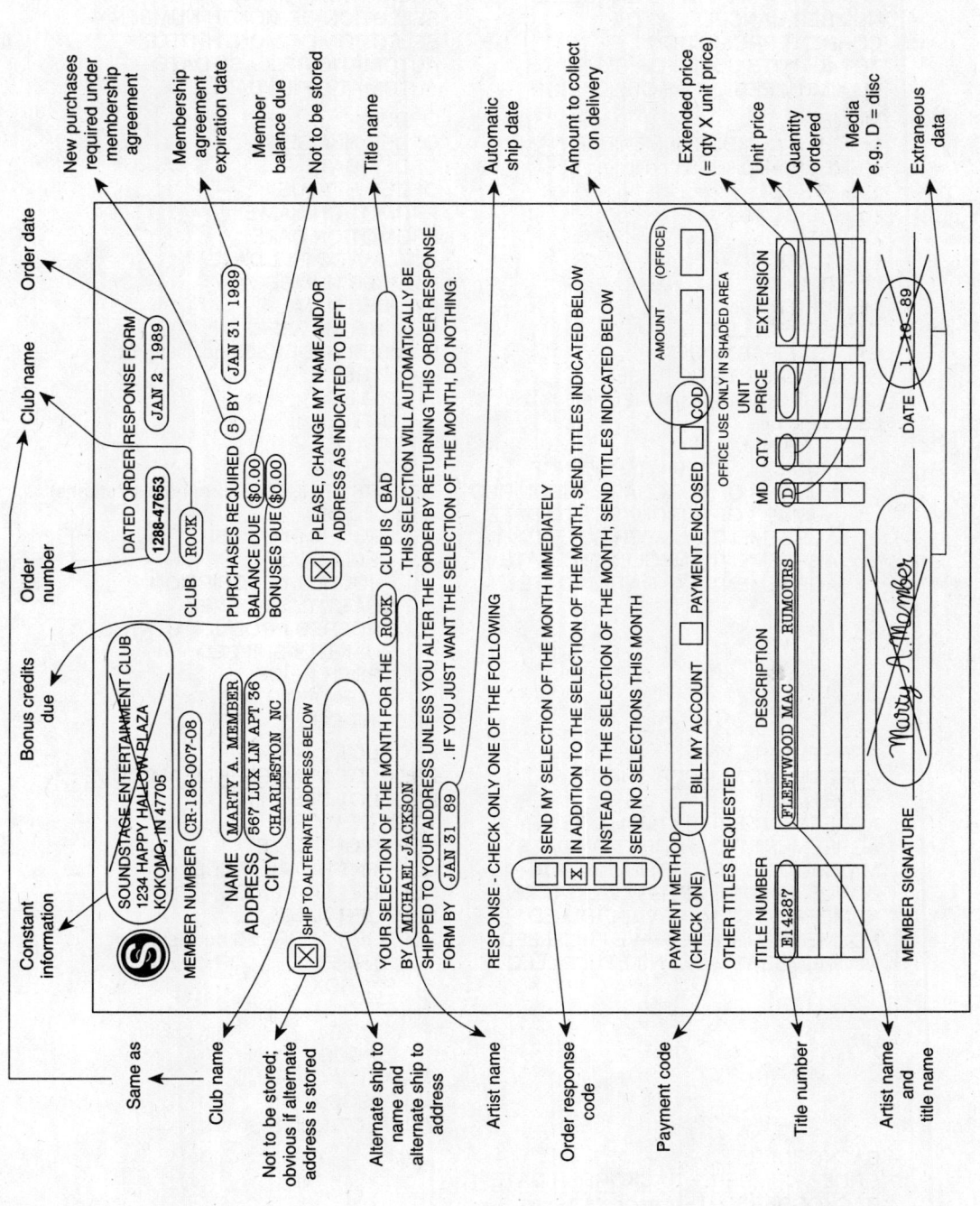

Fully Attributed Entities

Notice that each attribute is recorded in one and only one entity.

TM-78

CLUB:
CLUB NAME
NUMBER OF MEMBERS ENROLLED
NUMBER CANCELED YTD
CURRENT PROMOTION
TOTAL UNITS SOLD FOR CLUB
MAXIMUM PERIOD OF OBLIGATION

MEMBER:
MEMBER NUMBER or MEMBER NAME
MEMBER ADDRESS consisting of:
    STREET
    P.O.BOX
    CITY
    STATE
    ZIPCODE
MEMBER PHONE
DATE ENROLLED
BALANCE PAST DUE
BONUS CREDITS NOT USED
CLUB GROUP (repeats 1-n times)
consisting of:
    CLUB NAME
    MUSICAL/MOVIE PREFERENCE
    NUMBER OF PURCHASES REQUIRED
    NUMBER OF PURCHASES TO DATE
    AGREEMENT NUMBER SUFFIX
    AGREEMENT ENROLLMENT DATE
    AGREEMENT EXPIRATION DATE

AGREEMENT:
AGREEMENT NUMBER SUFFIX
CLUB NAME
AGREEMENT EXPIRATION DATE
AGREEMENT PLAN CREATION DATE
MAXIMUM PERIOD OF OBLIGATION
BONUS CREDITS AFTER OBLIGATION
NUMBER OF MEMBERS ENROLLED
NO. MEMBERS WHO HAVE FULFILLED
NO. MEMBERS HAVE NOT FULFILLED

BACKORDER:
ORDER NUMBER + BACKORDER DATE
BACKORDERED ITEM (repeats 1-n times)
consisting of:
    PRODUCT NUMBER
    MEDIA CODE
    PRODUCT DESCRPTION
    QUANTITY BACKORDERED

PROMOTION:
CLUB NAME + PROMOTION DATE
PROMOTION TYPE
SELECTION OF MONTH NUMBER
SELECTION OF MONTH TITLE
AUTOMATIC RELEASE DATE
AUTOMATIC FILL DATE

ORDER:
ORDER NUMBER
ORDER DATE
ORDER STATUS
PROMOTION NAME
PROMOTION DATE
AUTOMATIC FILL DATE
MEMBER NUMBER
MEMBER NAME
FORMER MEMBER?
MEMBER ADDRESS consisting of:
    STREET
    P.O.BOX
    CITY
    STATE
    ZIPCODE
ORDERED PRODUCT (repeats 1-n times)
consisting of:
    PRODUCT NUMBER
    MEDIA CODE
    PRODUCT DESCRIPTION
    QUANTITY ORDERED
    ORDERED PRODUCT STATUS
    QUANTITY SHIPPED
    ORDER PRICE
    EXTENDED PRICE
AMOUNT DUE

PRODUCT:
PRODUCT NUMBER + MEDIA CODE
PRODUCT DESCRIPTION
TITLE OF WORK
COPYRIGHT DATE
CURRENT RETAIL PRICE
CURRENT LIST PRICE
SUPPLIER NAME
SUPPLIER ADDRESS consisting of:
    STREET
    P.O.BOX
    CITY
    STATE
    ZIPCODE
QUANTITY ON HAND
UNITS SOLD
VALUE OF UNITS SOLD

© Richard D. Irwin, Inc., 1994

Types of System Models

Most system models depict either a current or proposed system. Most system models "should" also depict either the essential or implementation of a system.

Models	Essential System (Describes "What", Also Known as the Logical System)	Implementation System (Describes "What" plus "How", Also Known as the Physical System)
Current System (Existing System)	An essential model of the current system depicts those aspects of the current system that are essential to the business and that should be retained—no matter how we choose to implement the system.	An implementation model of the current system depicts how the current system is physically implemented (inclusive of technology). By default, the implementation model includes all of the essential aspects of the current system.
Proposed System (Target System)	An essential model of the proposed system depicts the business and user requirements for the system—regardless of how that system might be implemented.	An implementation model of the proposed system depicts how the proposed system will be physically implemented (inclusive of technology). By default, the implementation model must include all of the essential requirements of the proposed system.

© Richard D. Irwin, Inc., 1994

DeMarco and/or Yourdon DFD
This DFD demonstrates the DeMarco or Yourdon symbol set.

TM–80

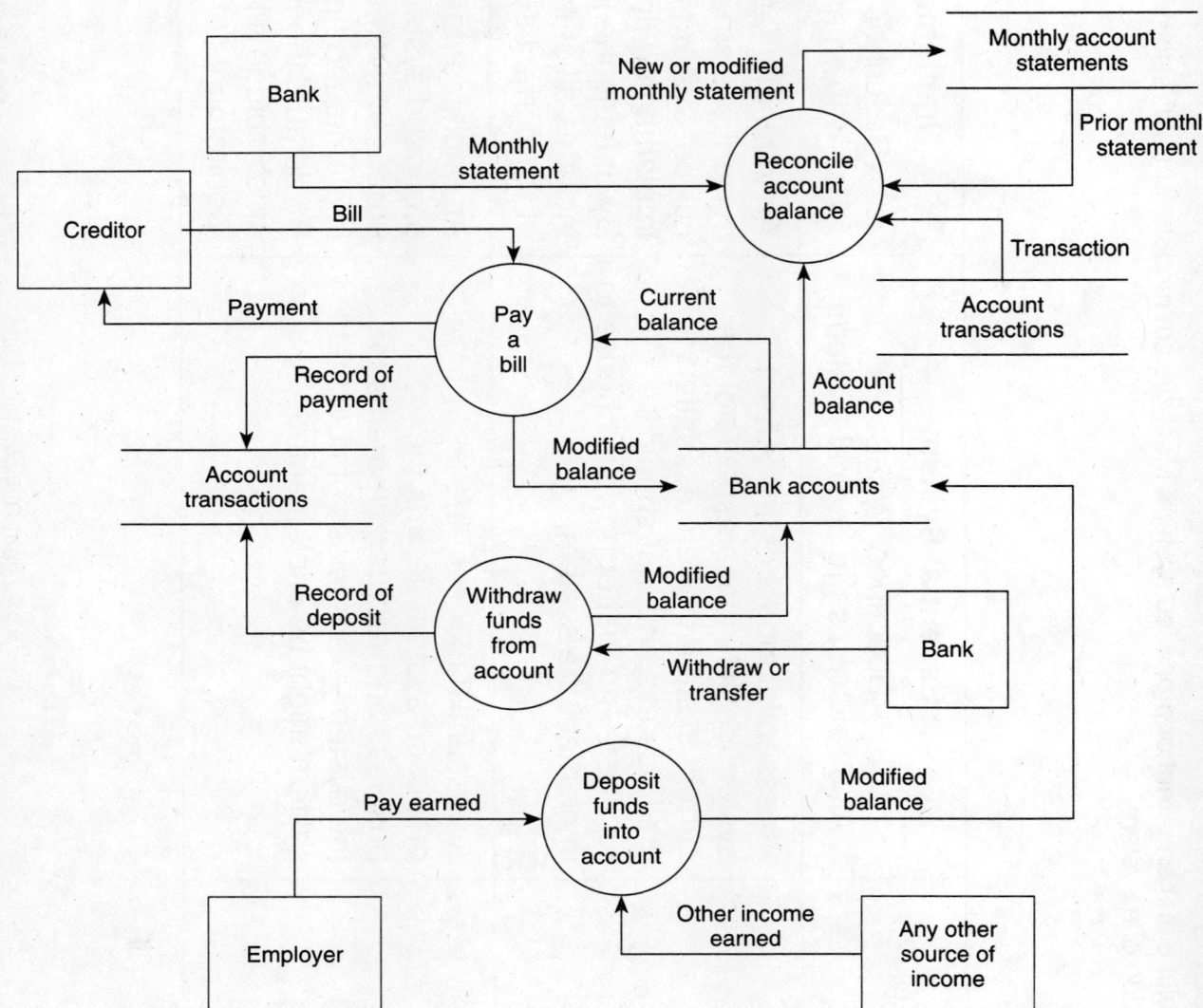

Common DFD Errors

TM–81

Process 1 has inputs but produces no outputs. This is called a *black hole*.
Process 2 produces outputs but receives no inputs. This is called a *miracle*.
Process 3 has inputs and outputs; however, the inputs are not sufficient to produce the outputs. This is called a *gray hole*.

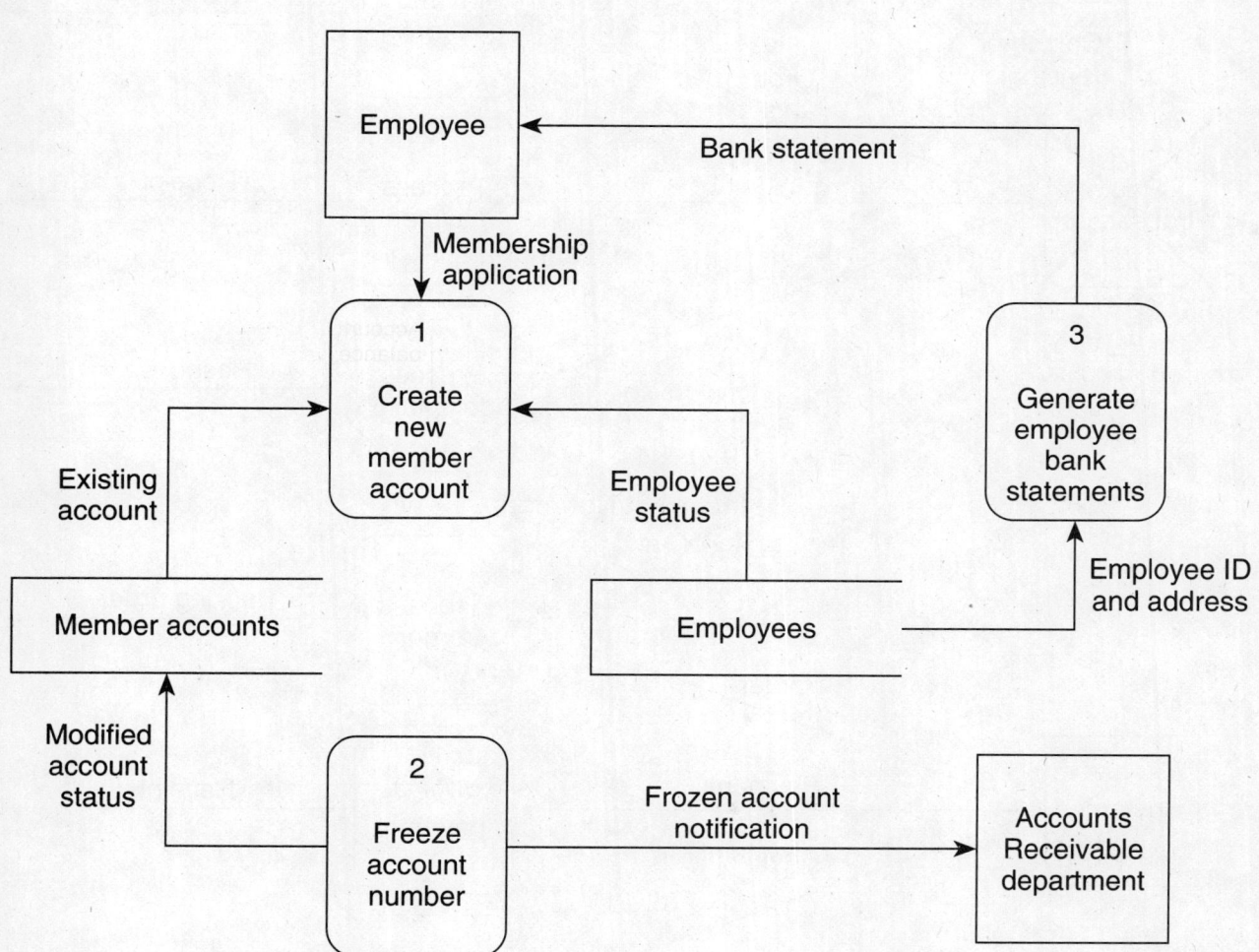

©Richard D. Irwin, Inc., 1994

Eliminating Routing Processes

Processes that do not change or make decisions using incoming data should be eliminated. This also eliminates duplicated data flow names.

TM-82

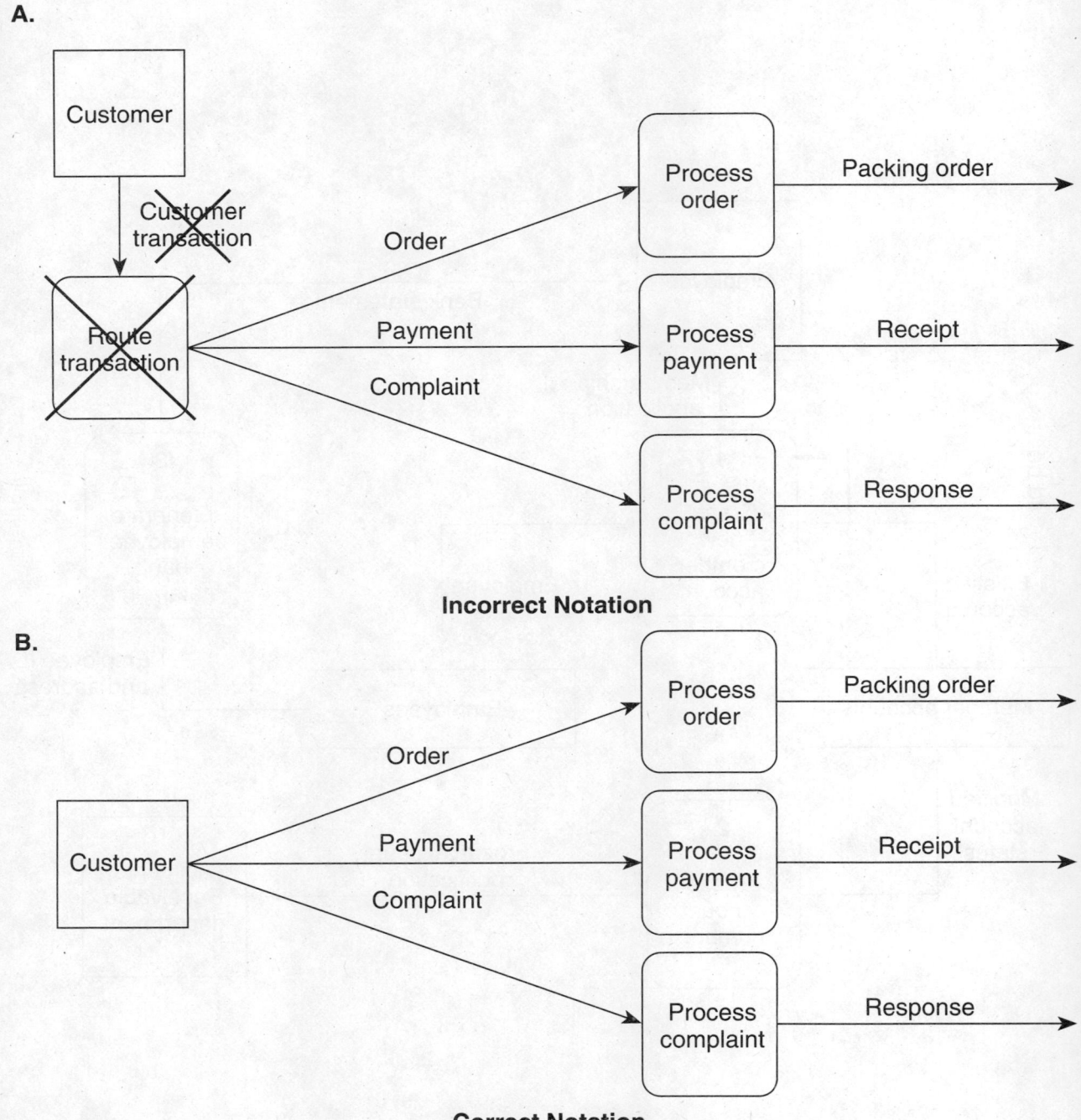

The Data Flow Packet Concept
If two or more separate data flows always travel together, they should be shown as a single data flow.

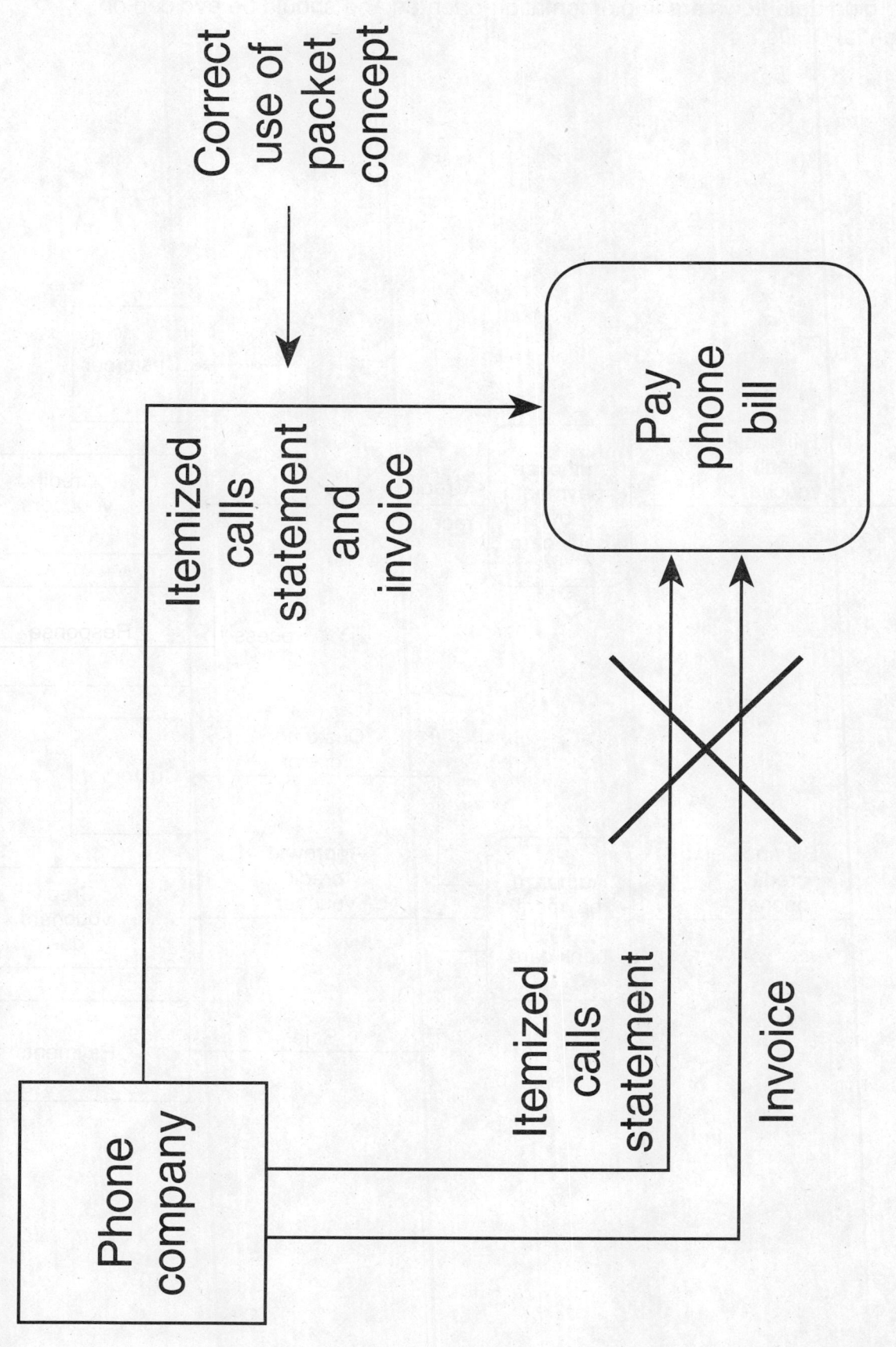

TM–83

© Richard D. Irwin, Inc., 1994

Diverging Data Flows

Diverging data flows are implementation-oriented and should be avoided on essential DFDs.

TM–84

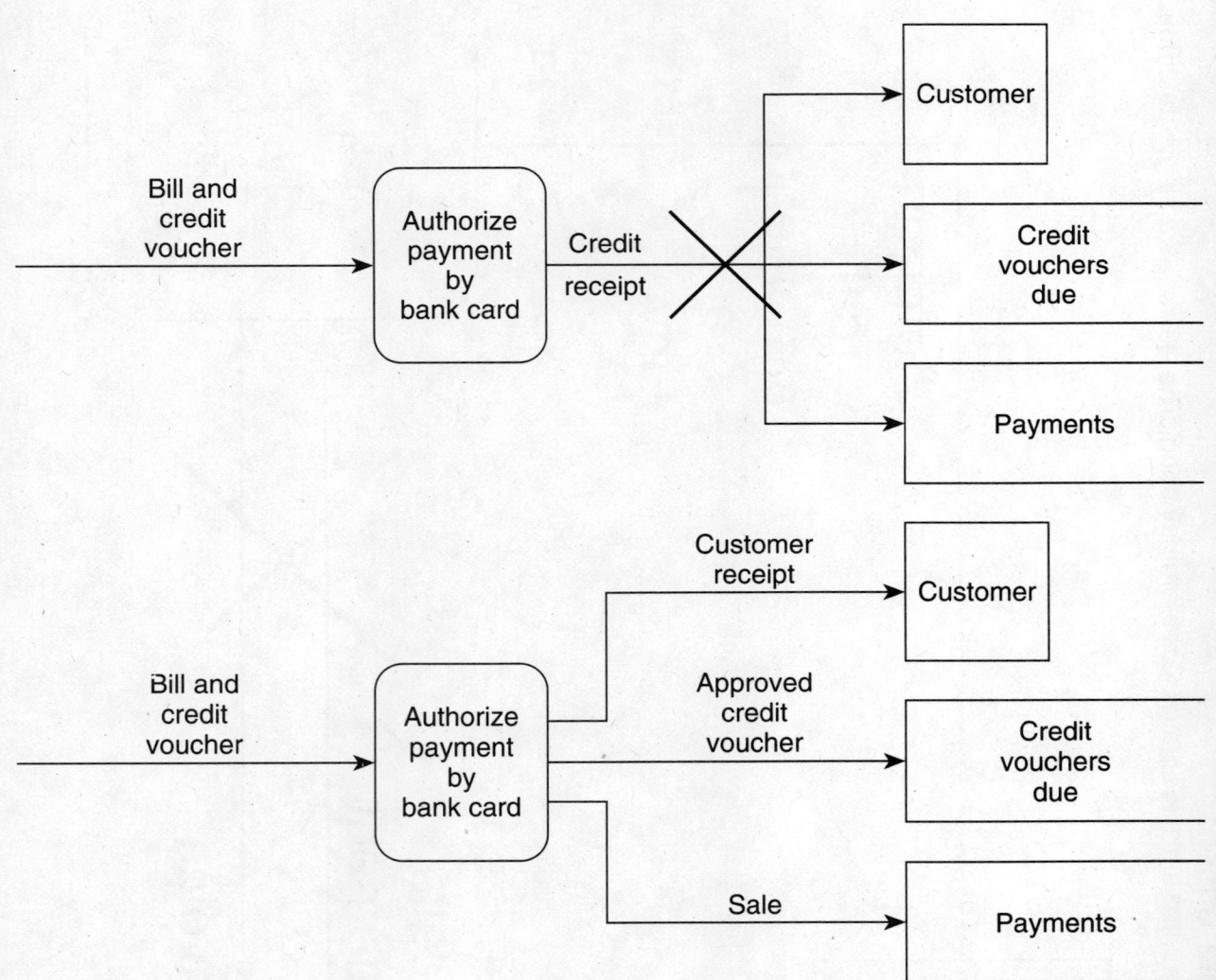

© Richard D. Irwin, Inc., 1994

Subset of a Data Model

Data modeling, covered in Chapter 8, is linked to process modeling. The entities in this typical data model correspond to data stores on the process model.

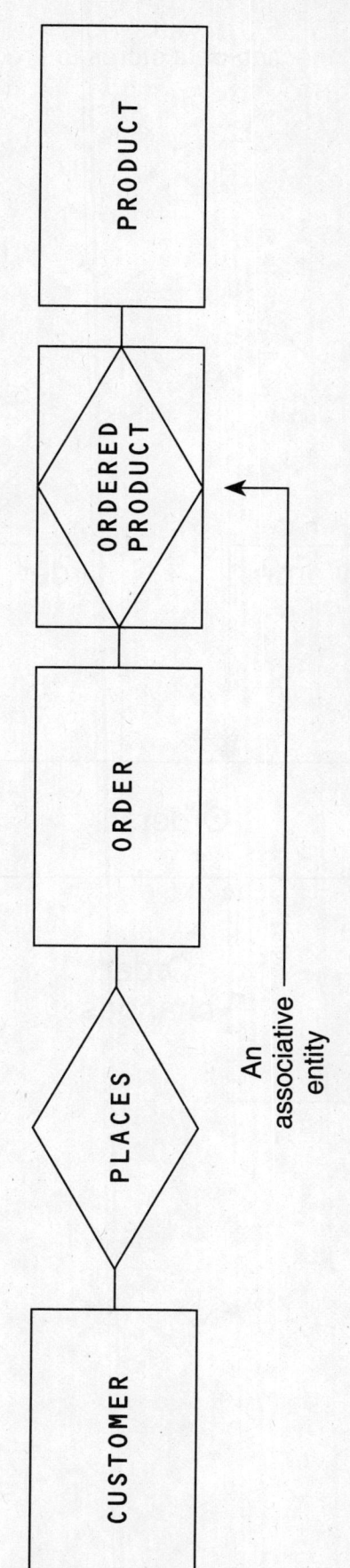

© Richard D. Irwin, Inc., 1994

TM–85

Data Store Guidelines
Use these guidelines when connecting data stores to processes.

TM–86

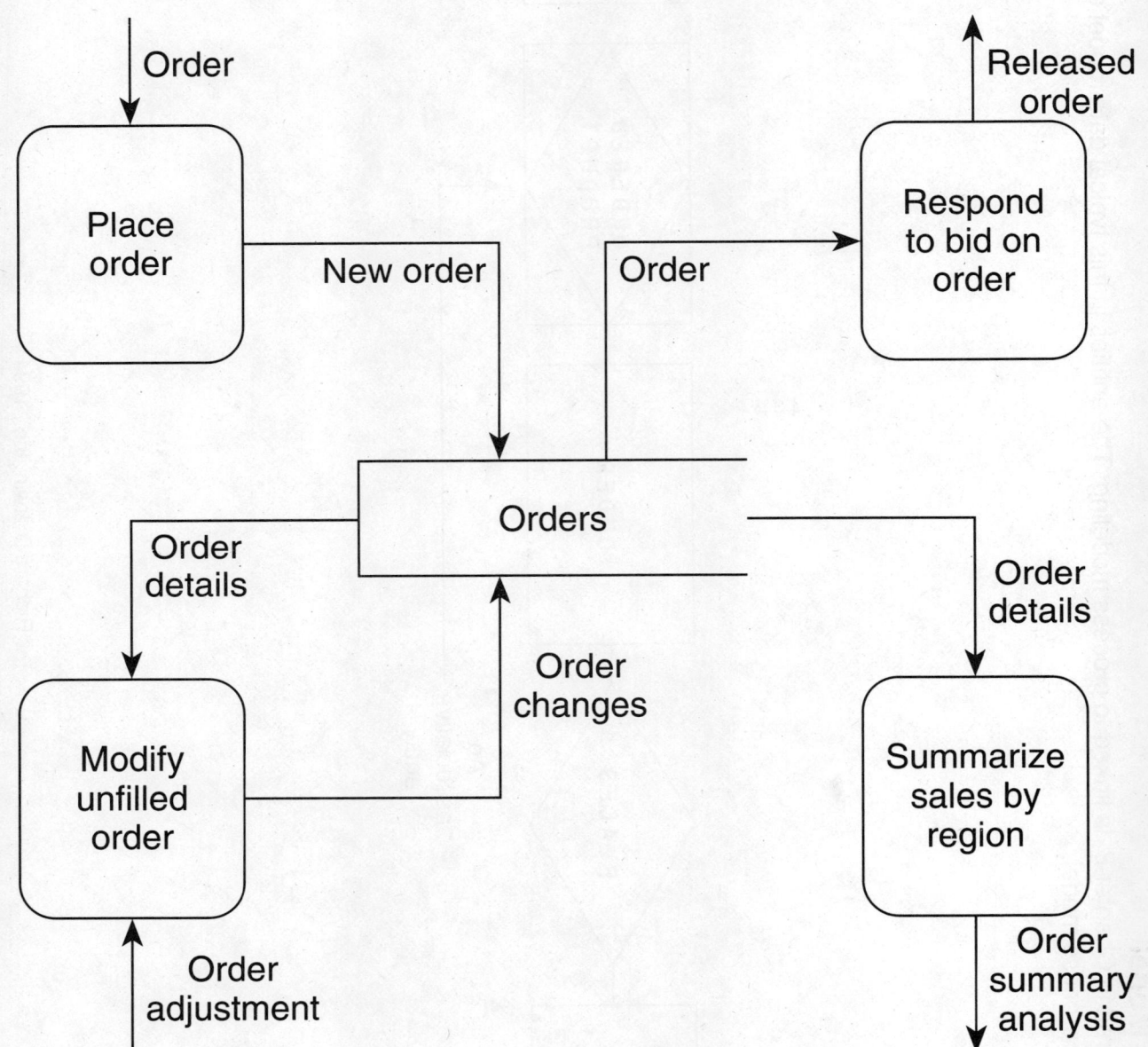

CASE Tool for DFDs
Data flow diagrams can be drawn with most upper-case tools.

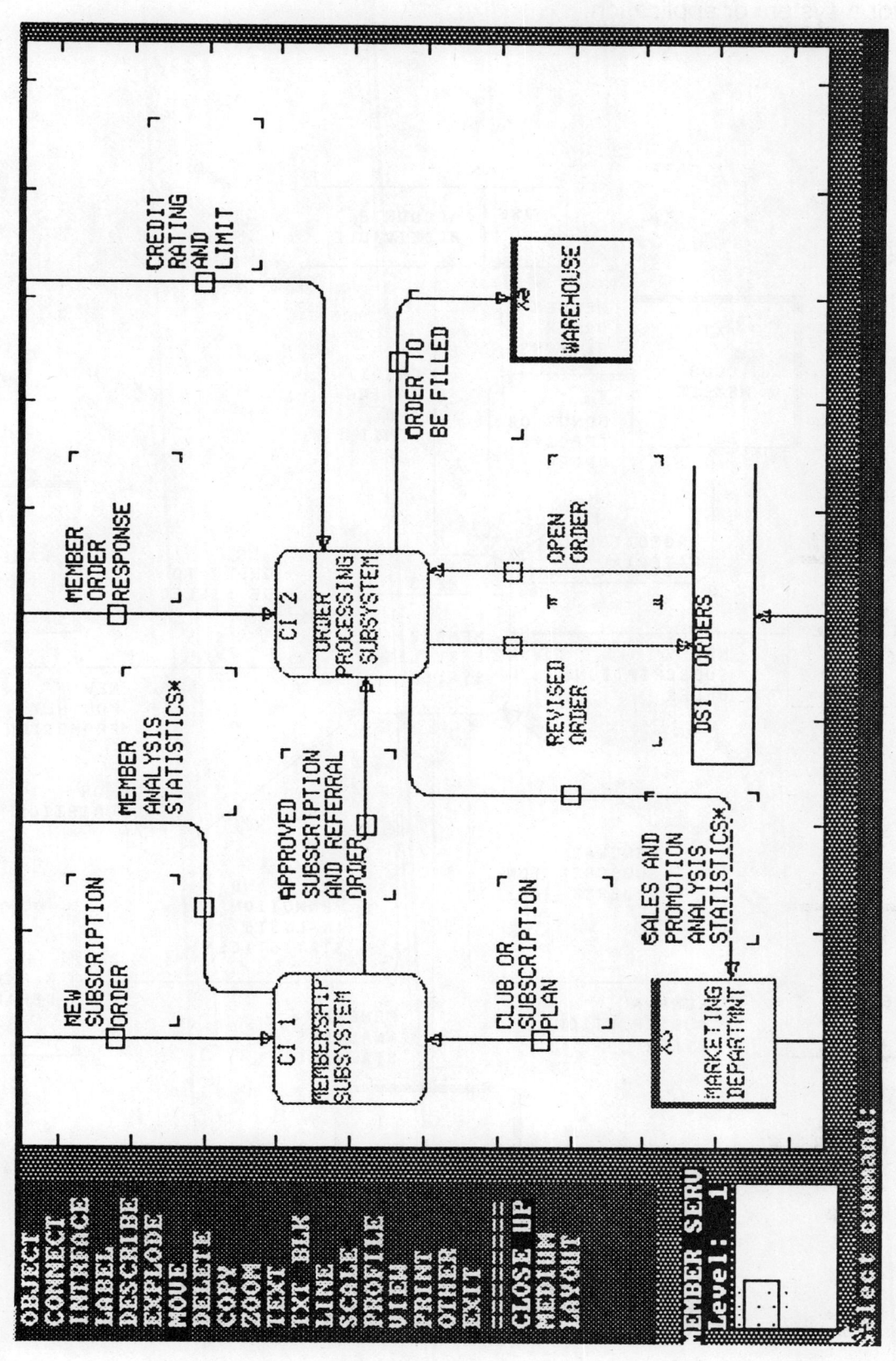

A Context Diagram

The context (data flow) diagram is the most general process model you can draw for a system or application.

TM-88

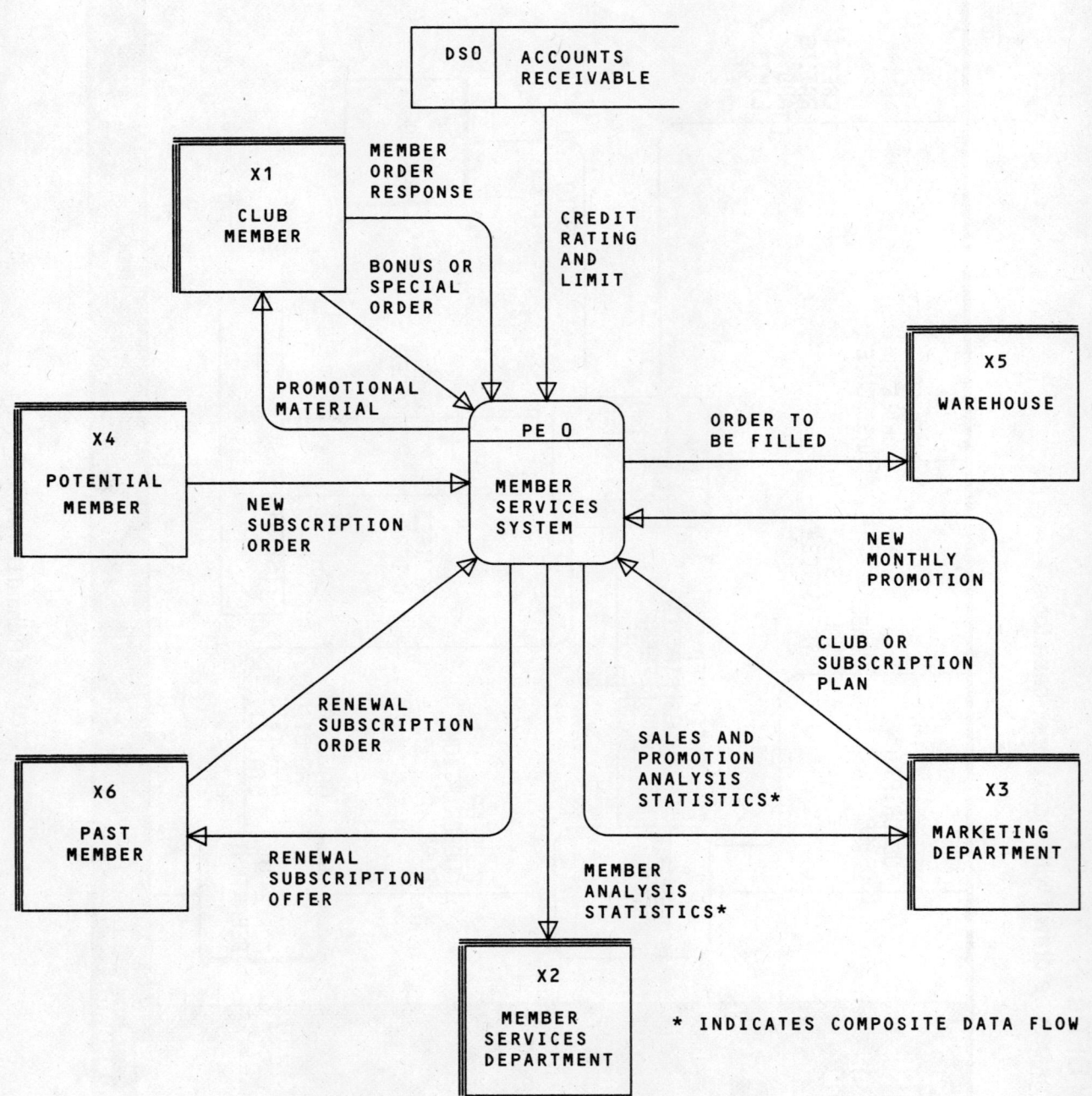

* INDICATES COMPOSITE DATA FLOW

©Richard D. Irwin, Inc., 1994

The Expansion Approach to Drawing DFDs

As suggested by Gane and Sarson, this diagramming technique requires the analyst to draw two DFDs—one overview DFD and a detailed DFD.

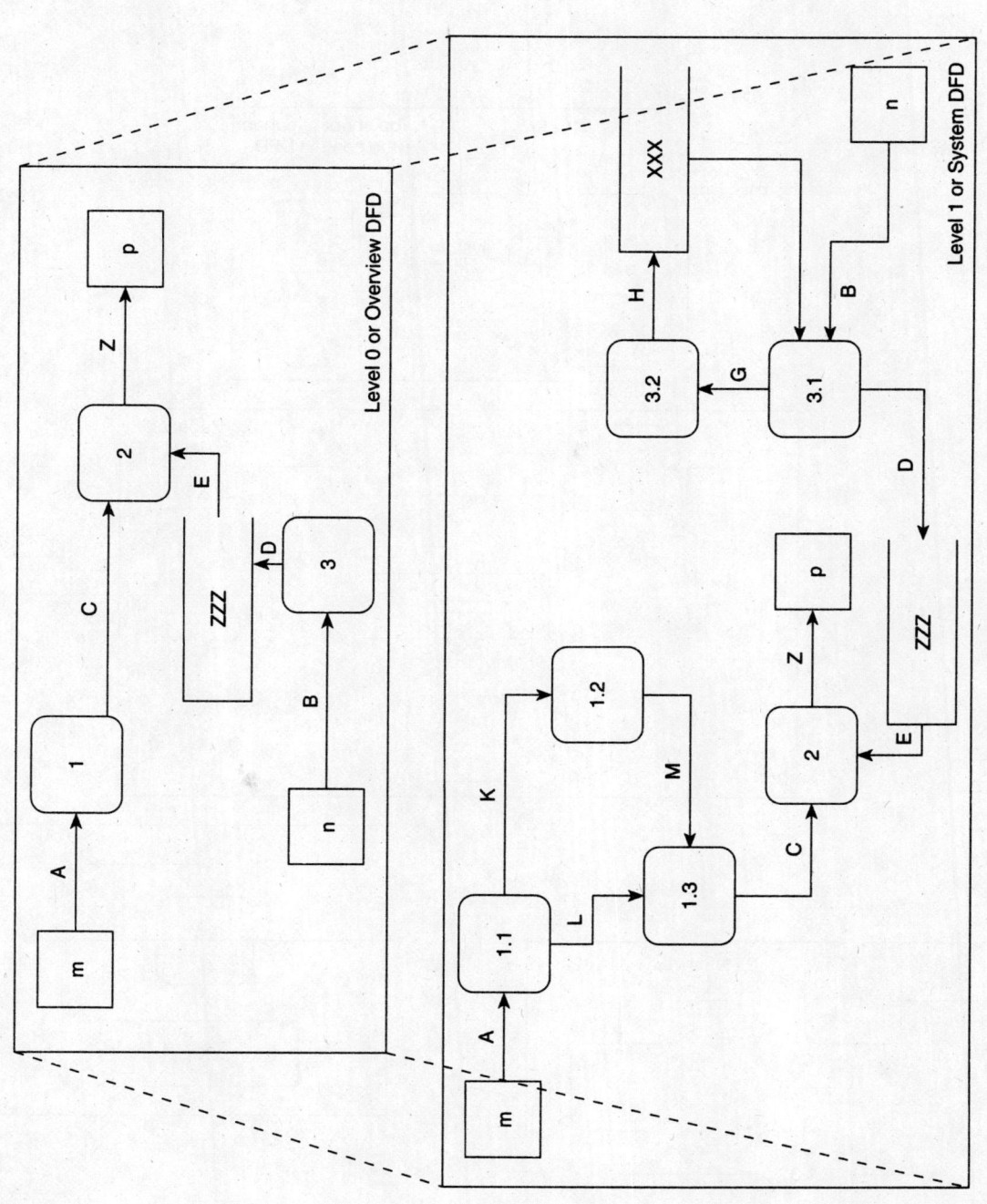

© Richard D. Irwin, Inc., 1994

TM–89

The Explosion Approach to Drawing DFDs
As suggested by DeMarco and others, this diagramming technique requires the analyst to draw multiple DFDs, each one exploding from a single process on another diagram, until the system is completely modeled.

TM – 90

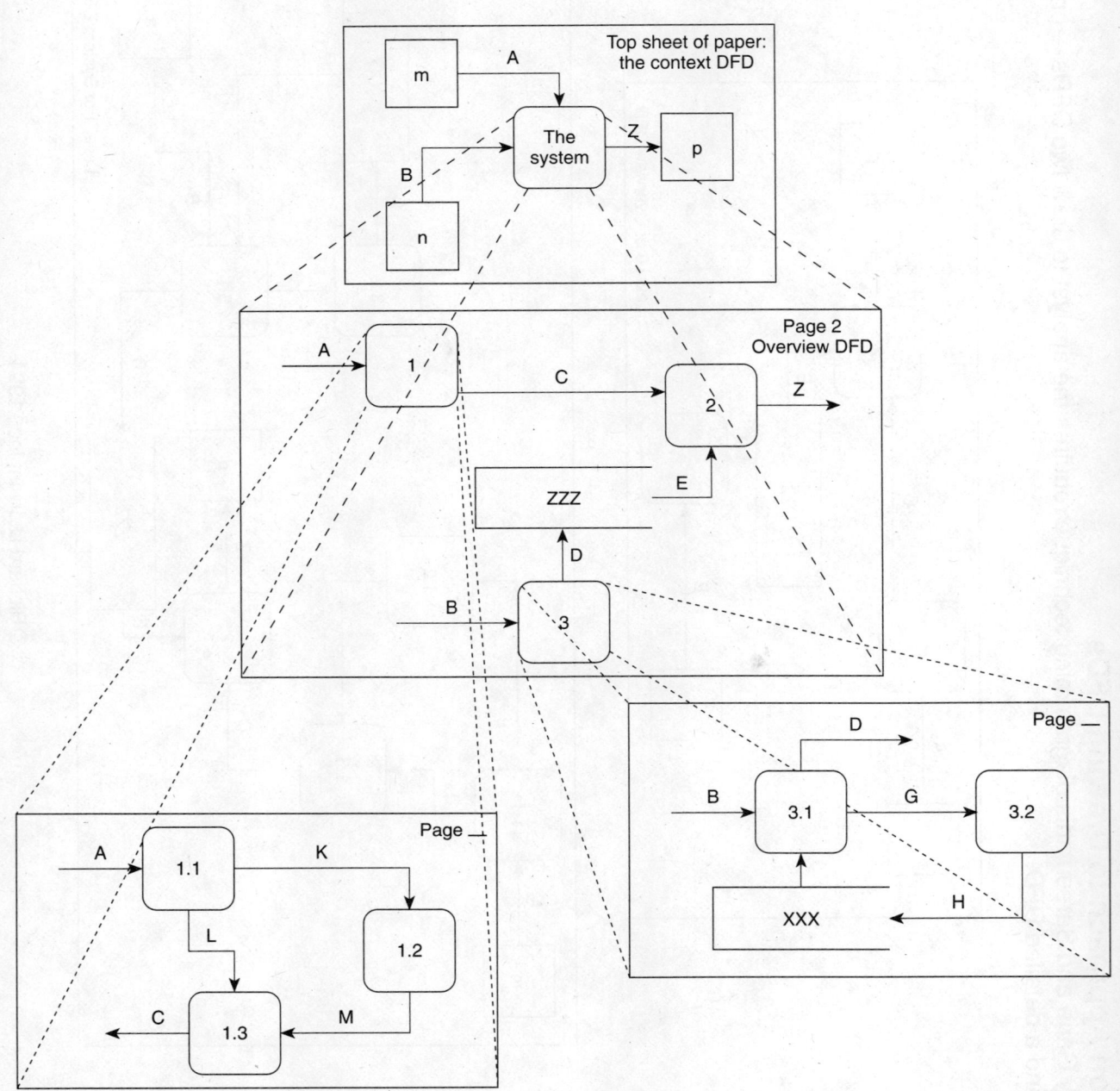

Decomposition Diagram

This is the first page of the decomposition diagram for our SoundStage project.

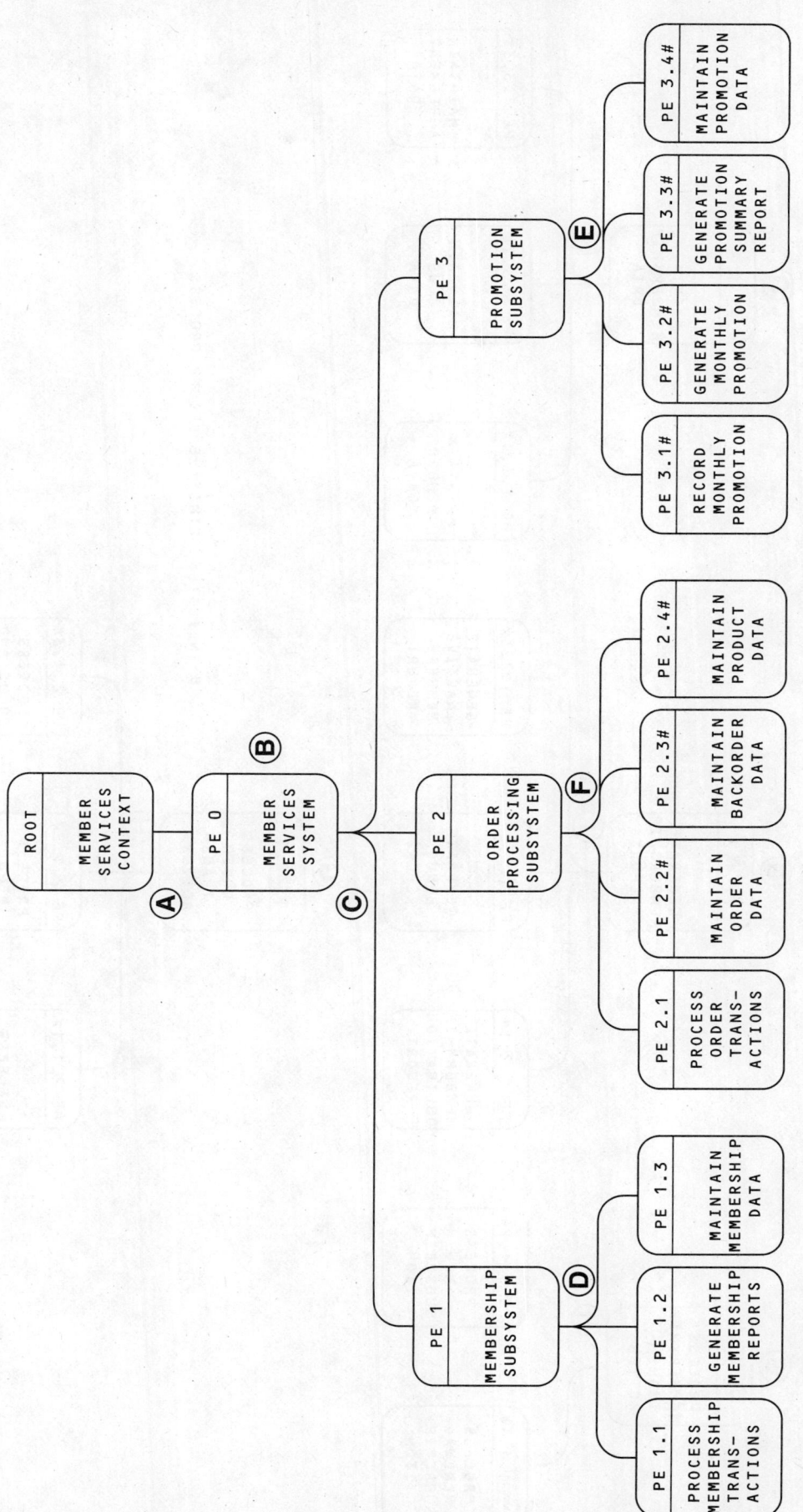

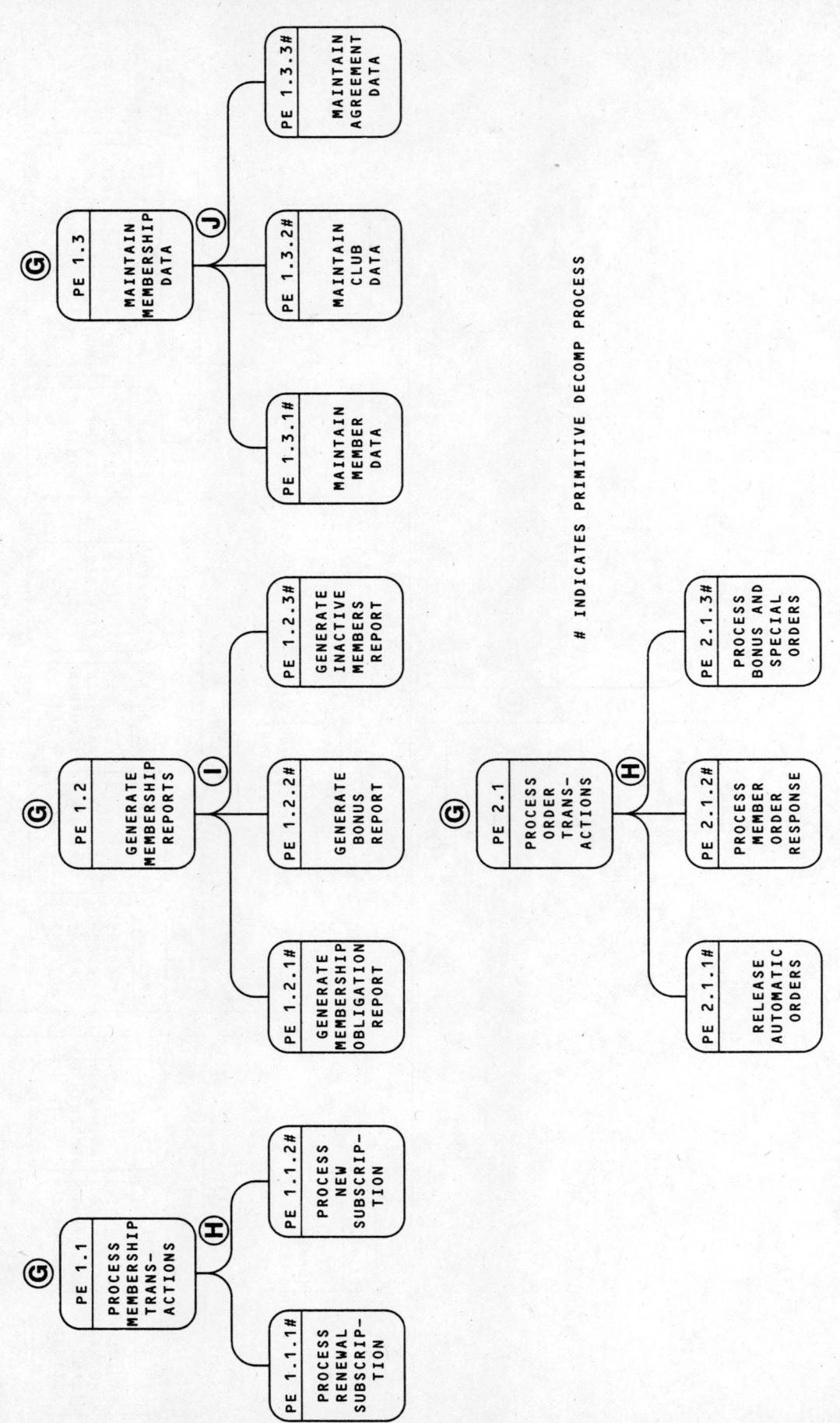

Data Store Decomposition

This decomposition diagram depicts the data stores to be used in our diagrams.

TM-92

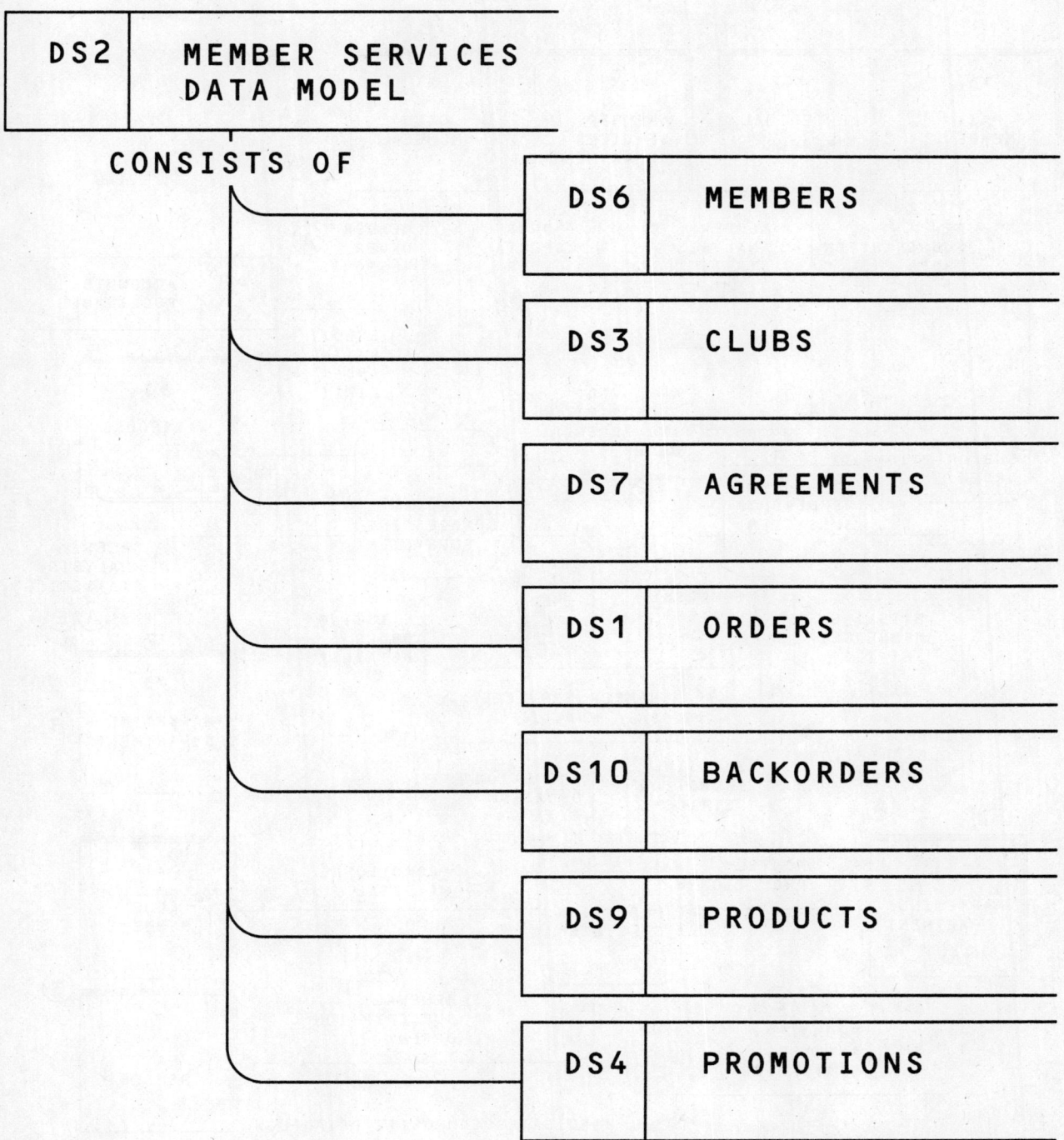

An Overview Data Flow Diagram

TM-93

An overview data flow diagram shows the interaction between key subsystems and/or functions.

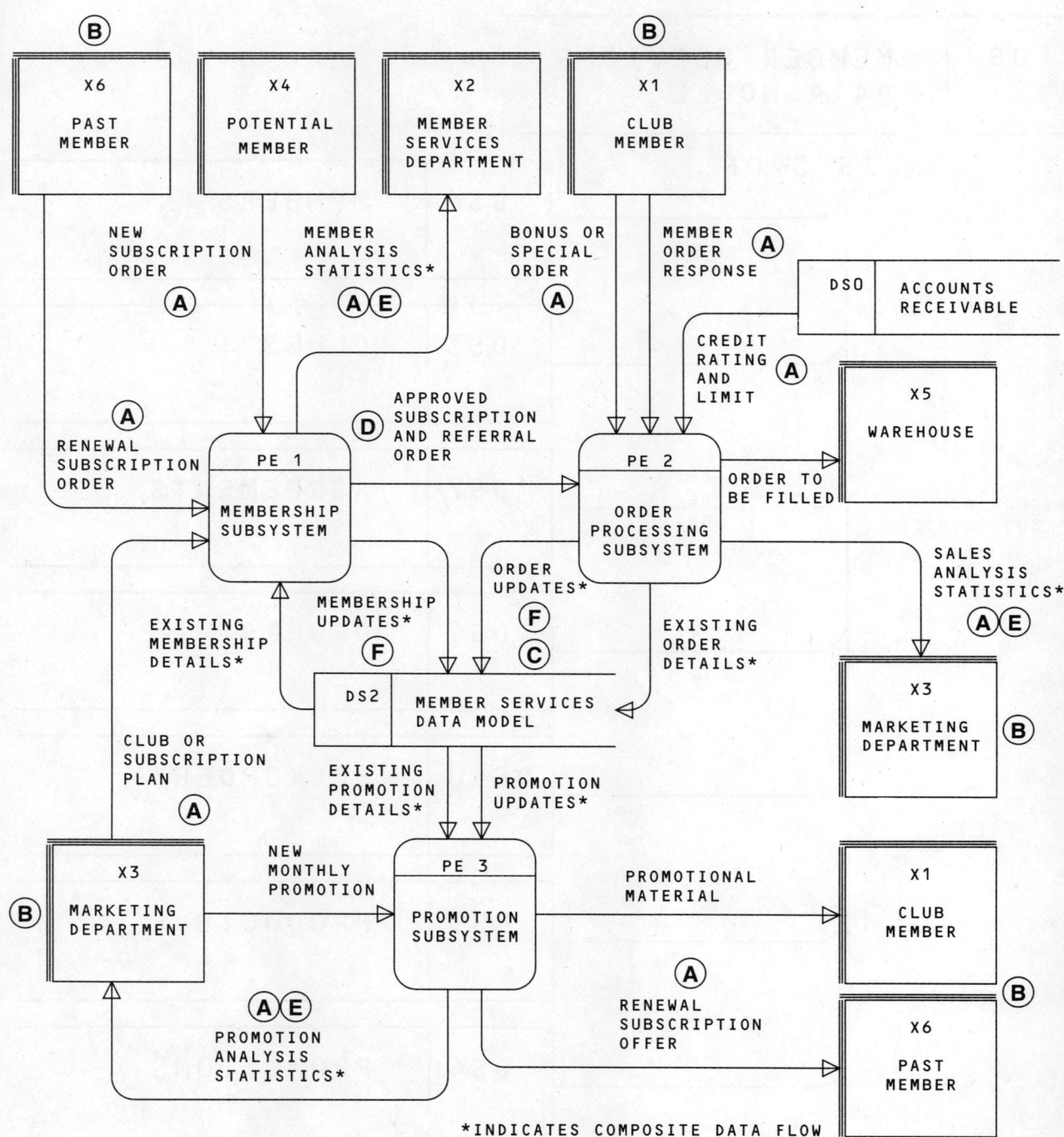

© Richard D. Irwin, Inc., 1994

An Alternative Overview Data Flow Diagram TM-94

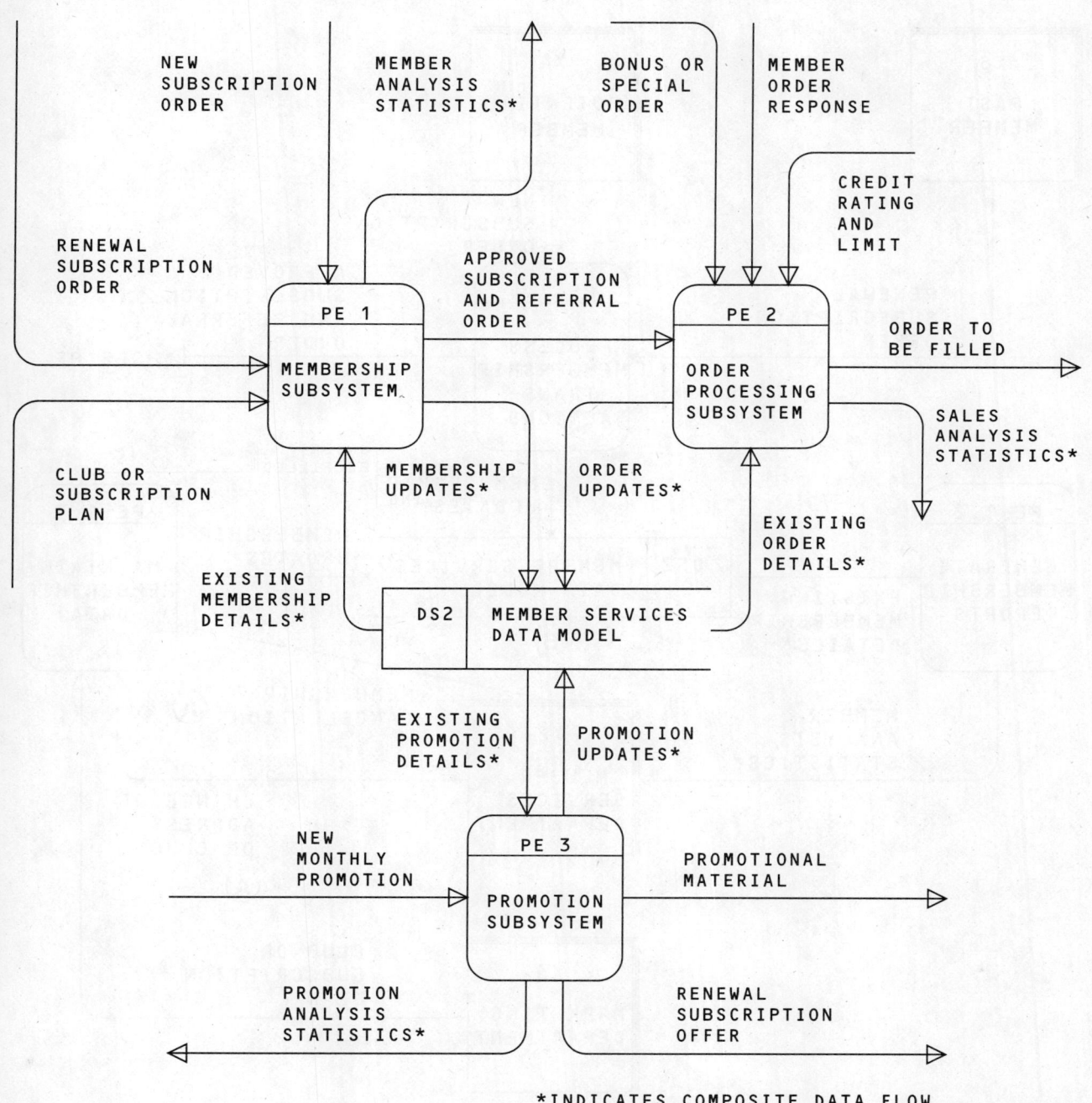

*INDICATES COMPOSITE DATA FLOW

©Richard D. Irwin, Inc., 1994

A Middle-Level Data Flow Diagram

A middle-level diagram consists of processes that will still be exploded to reveal more detail.

TM-95

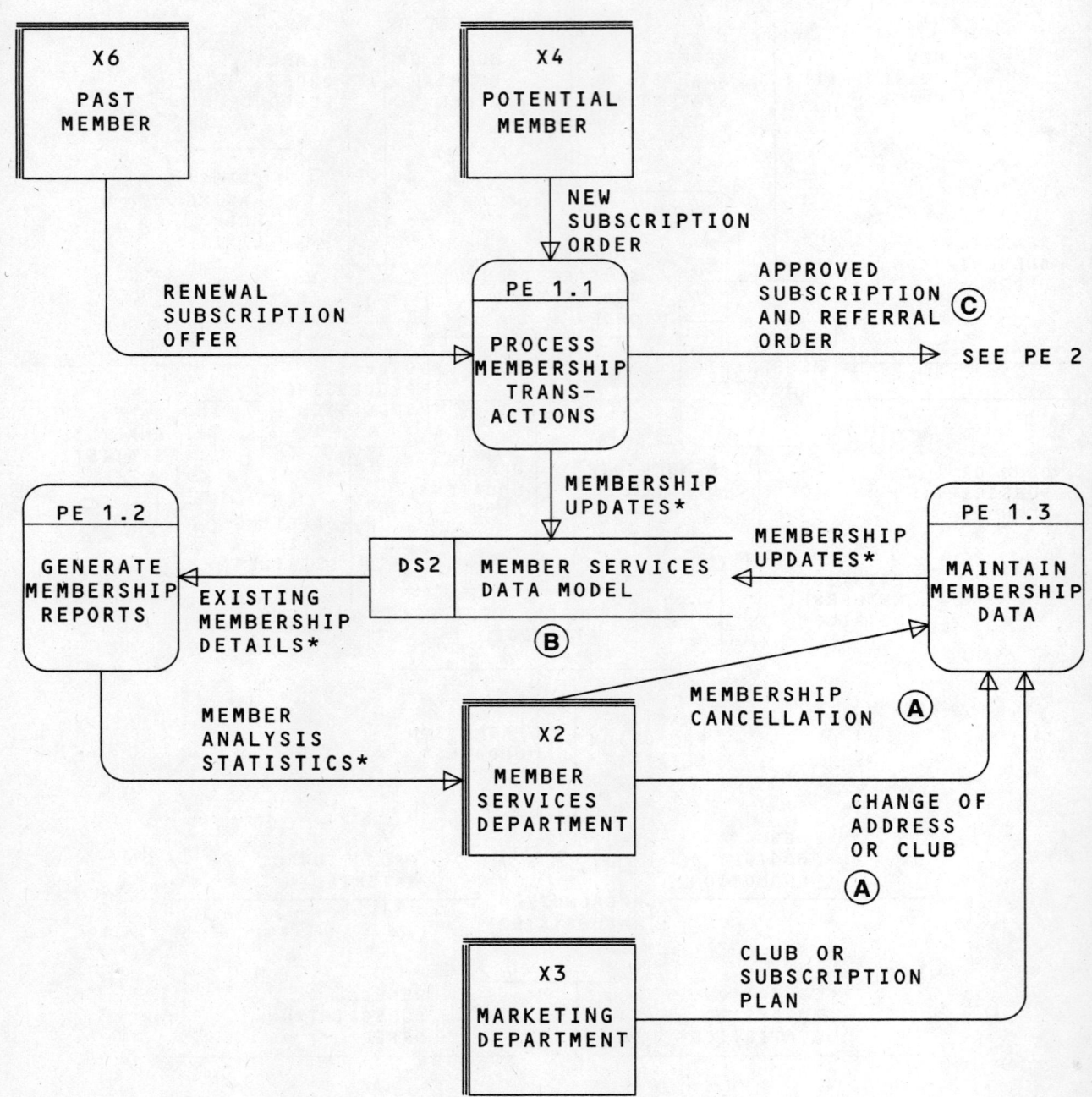

© Richard D. Irwin, Inc., 1994

Another Middle-Level DFD for Membership

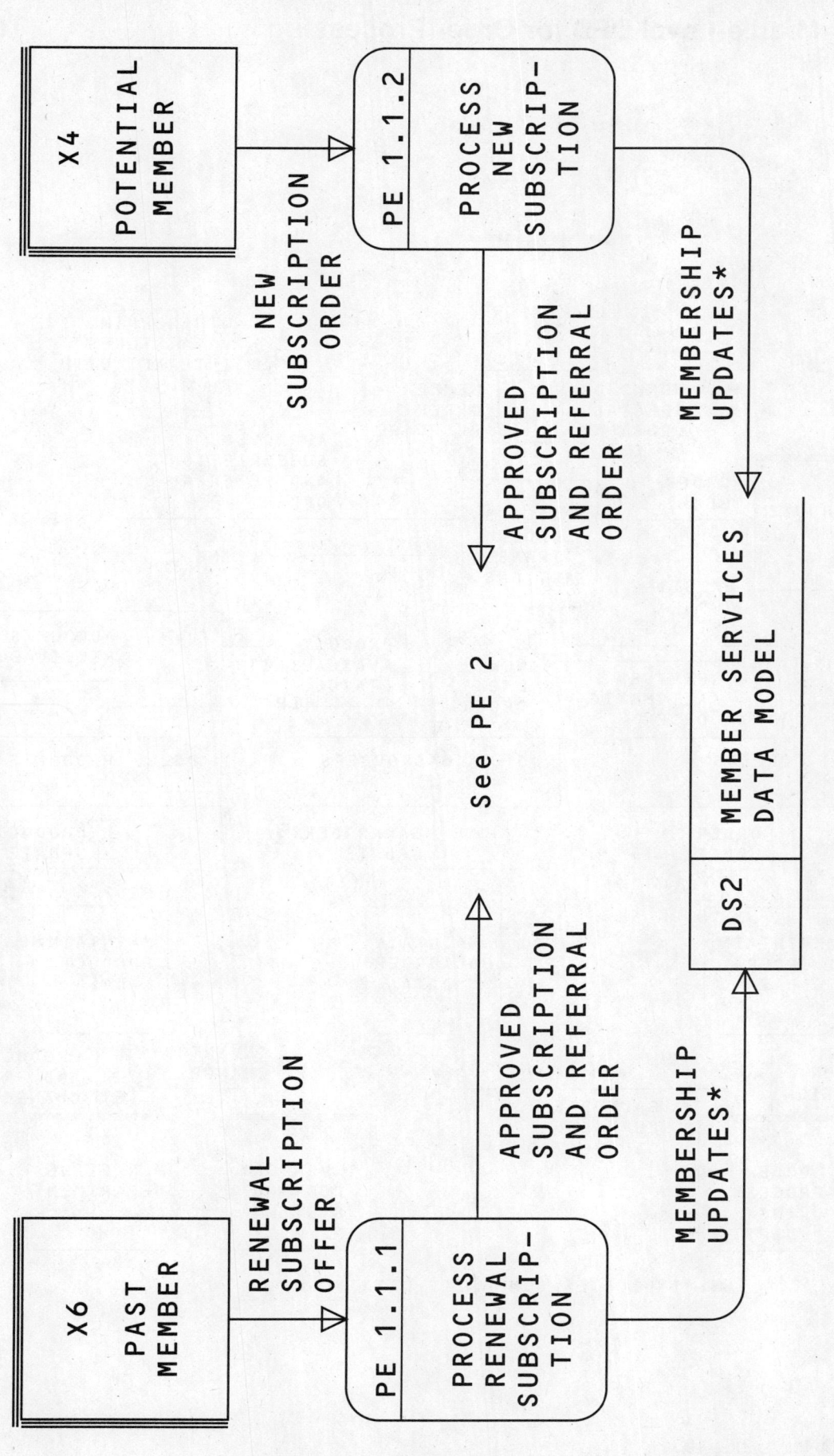

Another Middle-Level DFD for Order Processing

TM-97

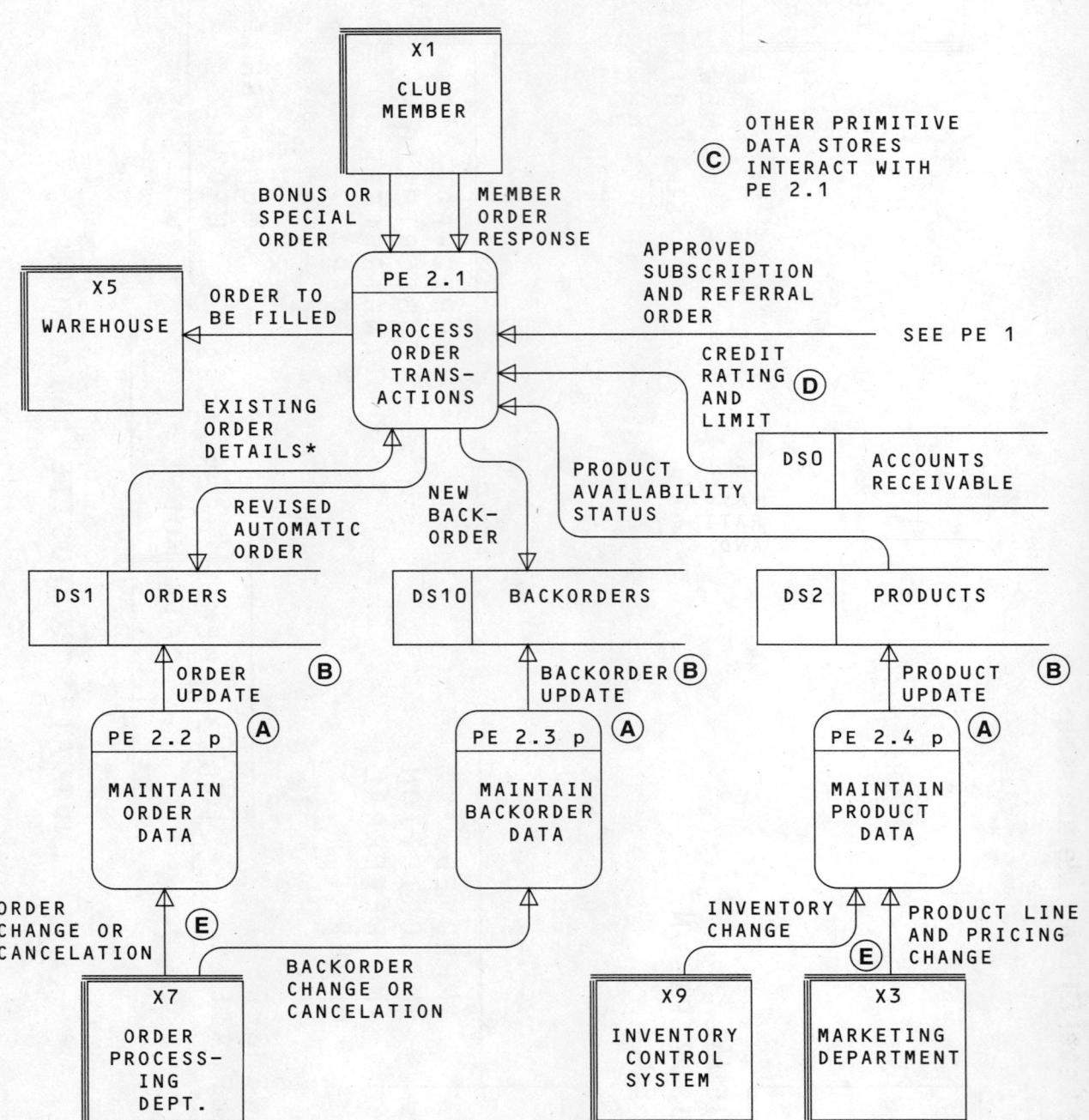

*INDICATES COMPOSITE DATA FLOW

© Richard D. Irwin, Inc., 1994

Another Middle-Level DFD TM–98

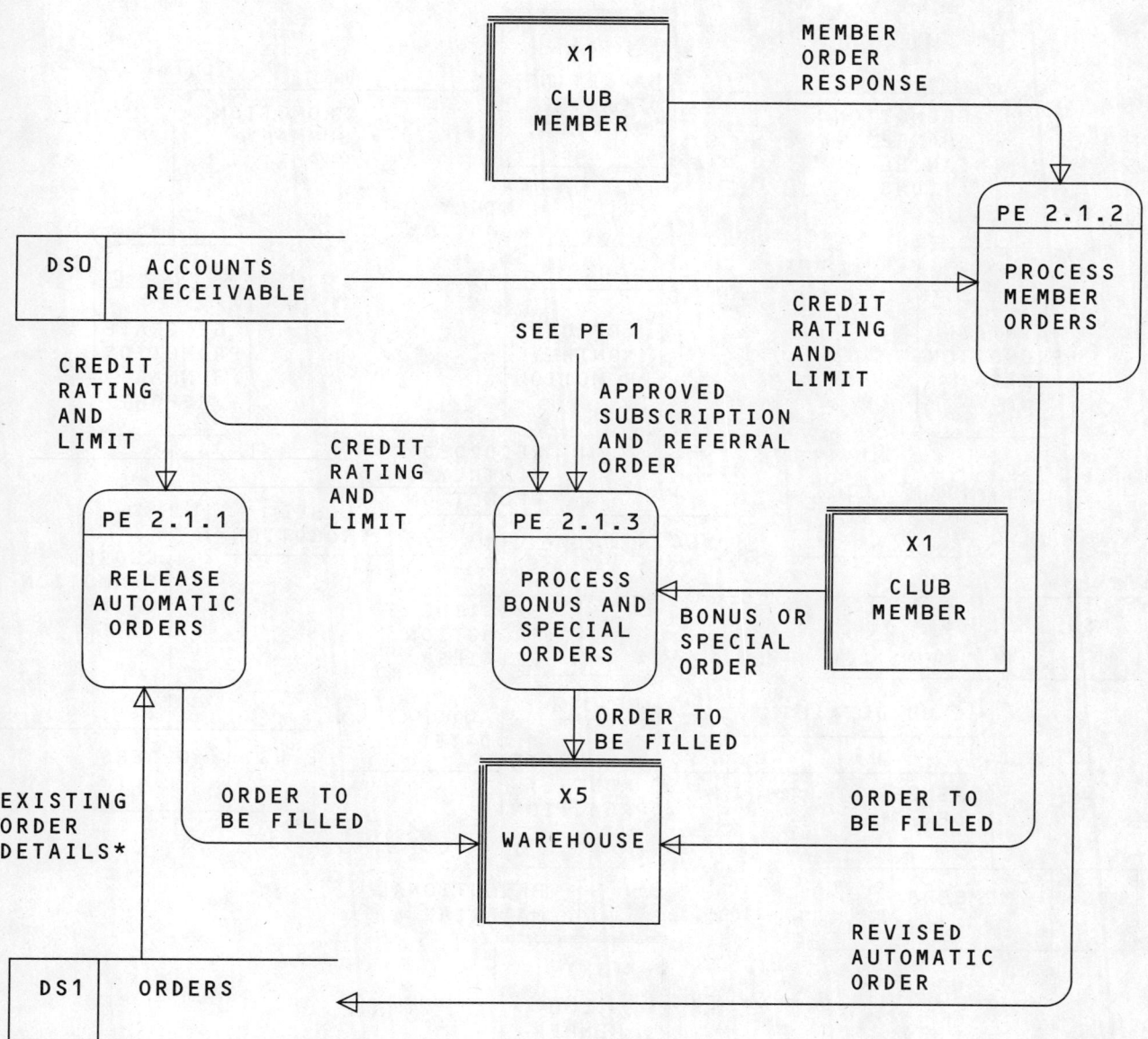

*INDICATES COMPOSITE DATA FLOW

©Richard D. Irwin, Inc., 1994

A Simple Primitive-Level DFD

A primitive-level DFD contains some processes (marked by letter "p") that do not further explode.

TM-99

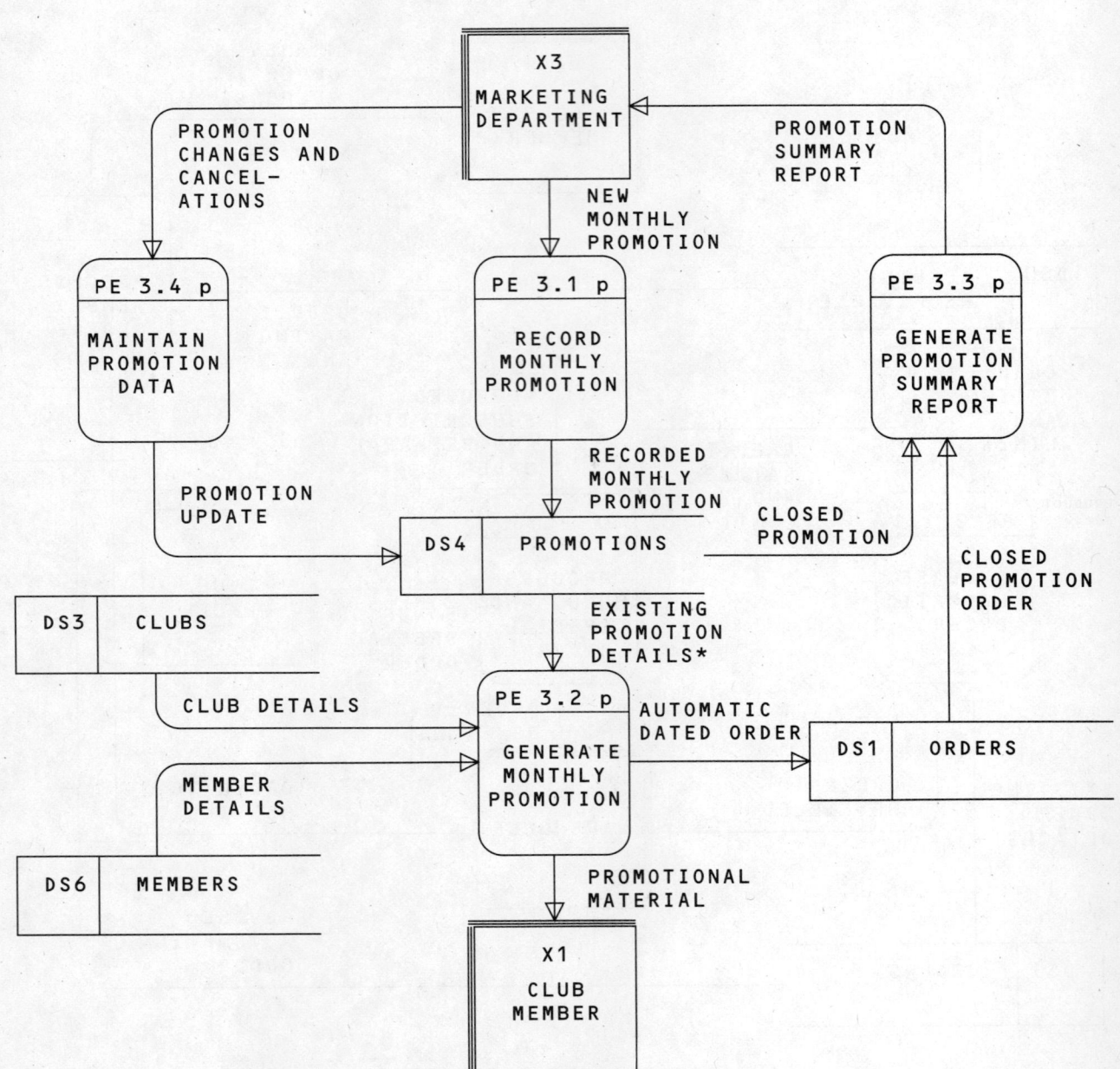

©Richard D. Irwin, Inc., 1994

Primitive DFD for Automatically Shipping a Dated Order

TM-100

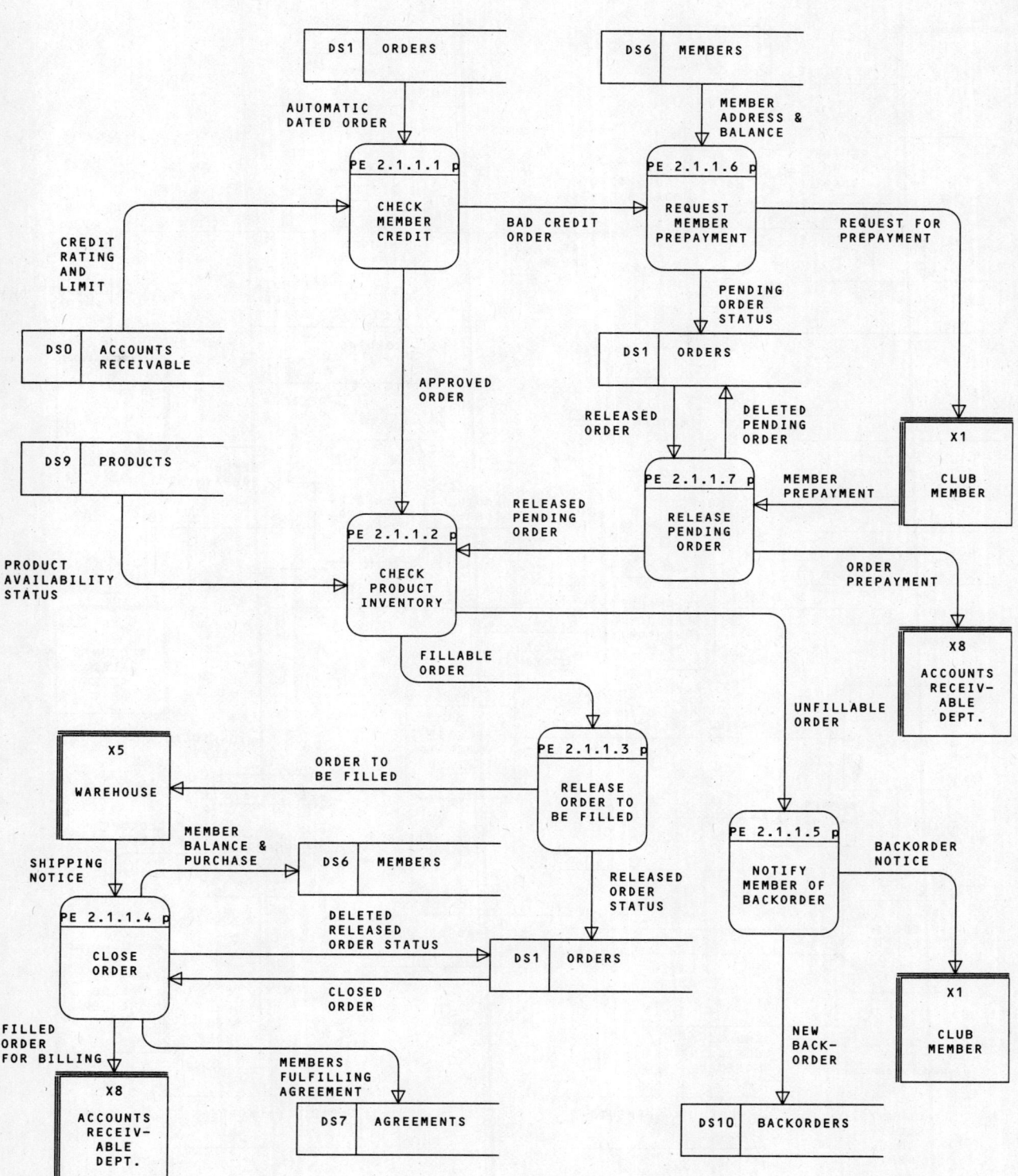

©Richard D. Irwin, Inc., 1994

Primitive DFD for Filling a Member's Order Response

TM-101

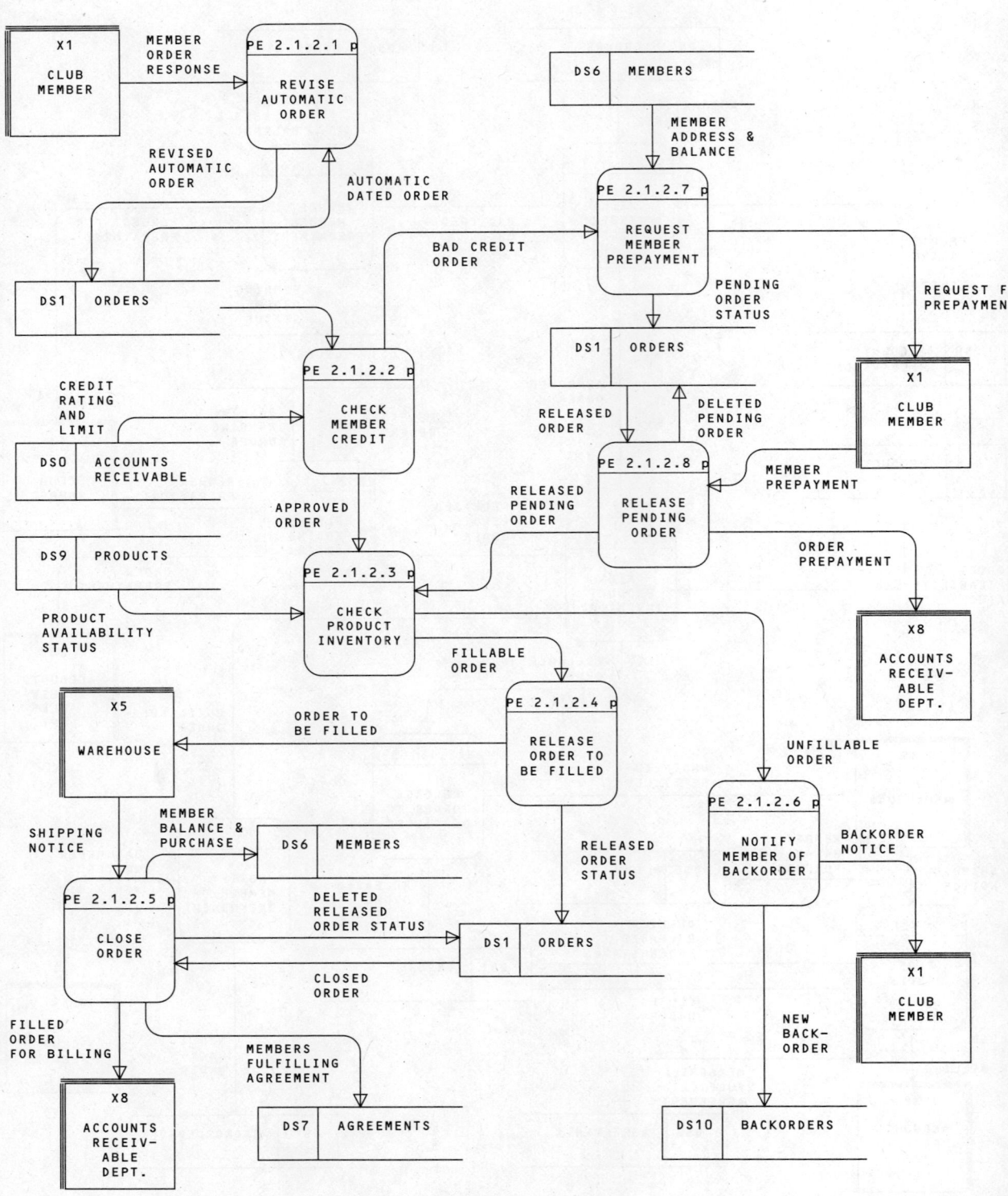

© Richard D. Irwin, Inc., 1994

Primitive DFD for Filling a Special or Bonus Order   TM-102

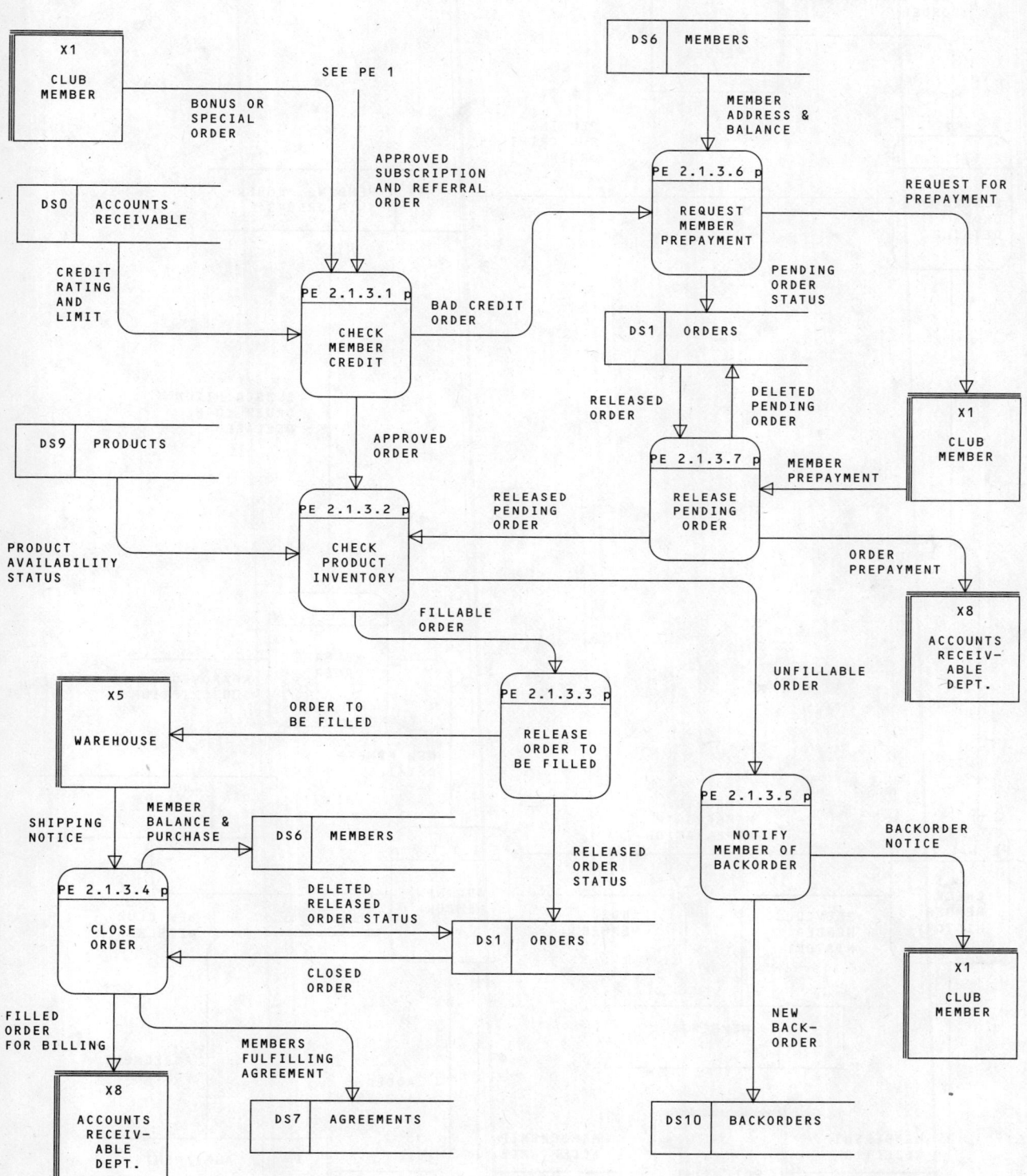

Primitive DFD for Renewal Subscription Order

TM-103

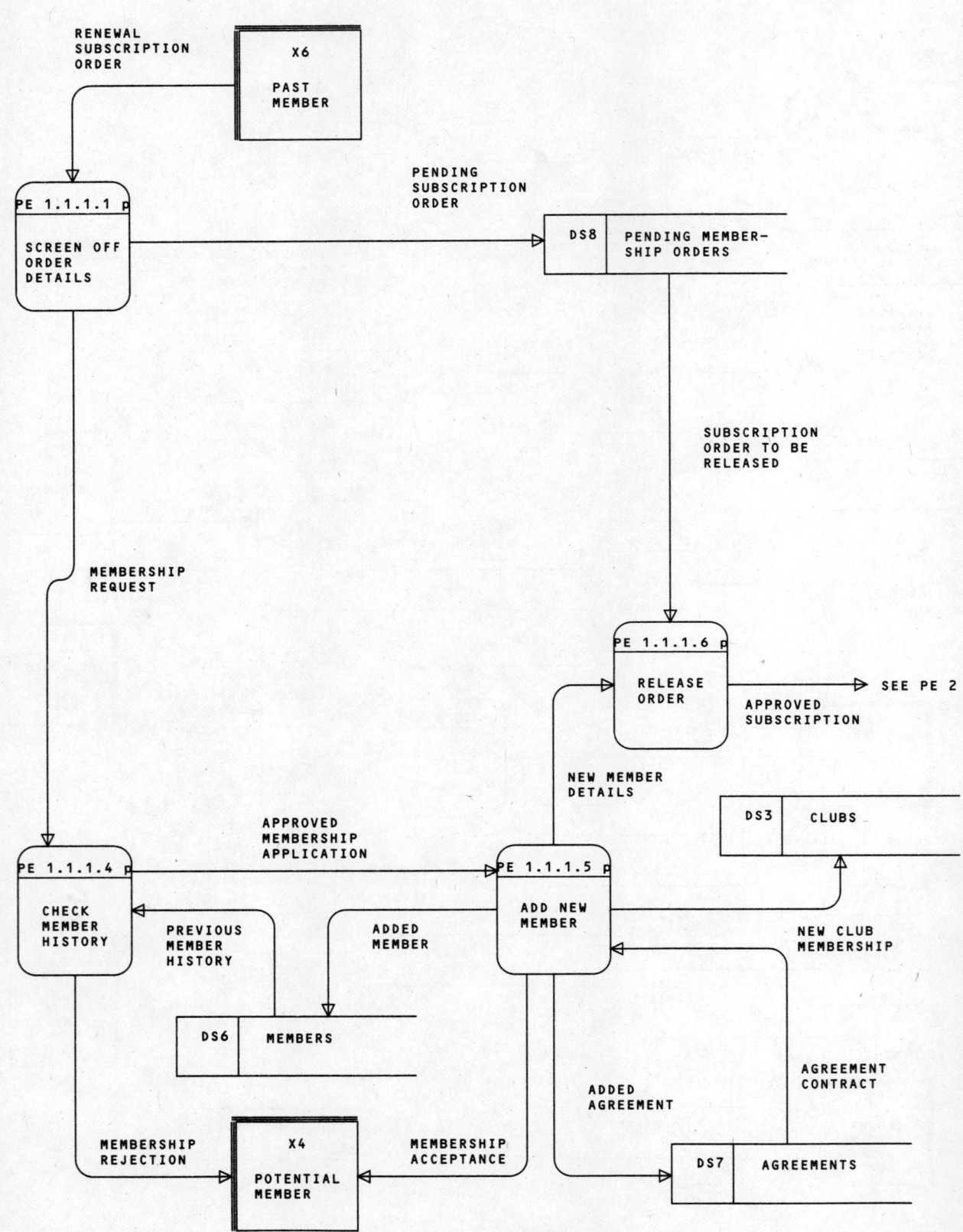

© Richard D. Irwin, Inc., 1994

Primitive DFD for Referral Subscription Order

TM-104

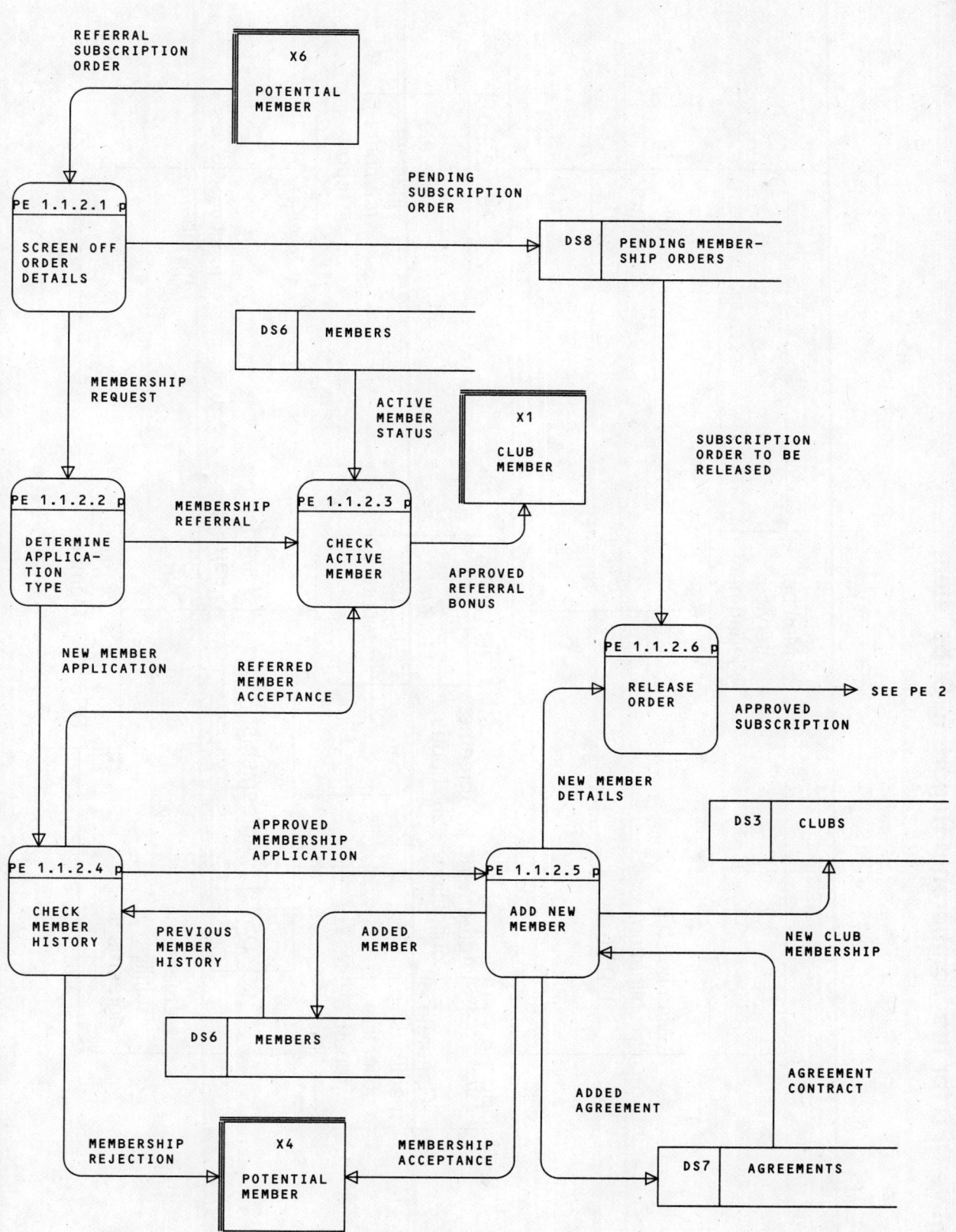

© Richard D. Irwin, Inc., 1994

Primitive DFD for the Membership Reporting Subsystem

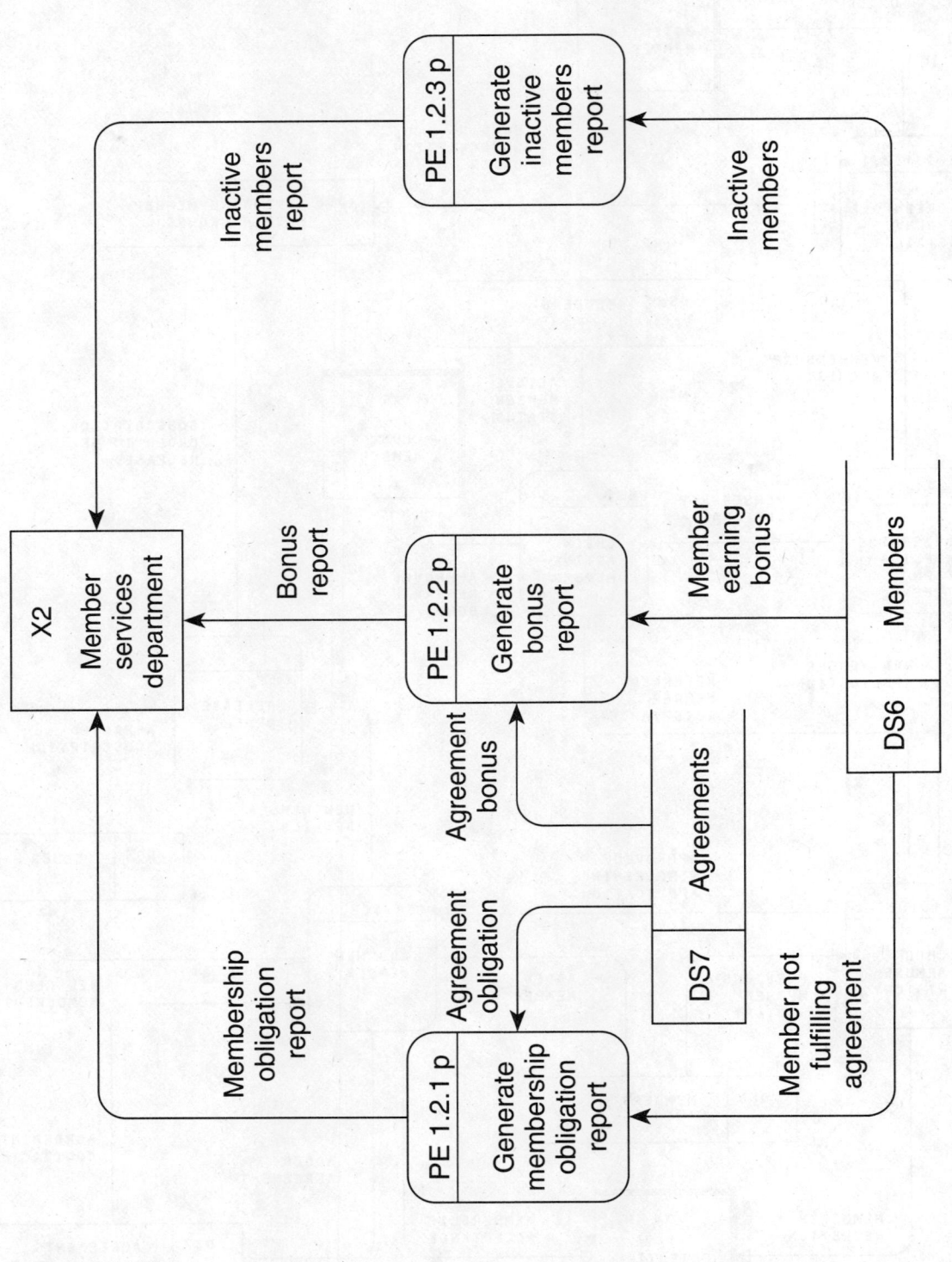

TM-105

© Richard D. Irwin, Inc., 1994

Primitive DFD for Data Maintenance

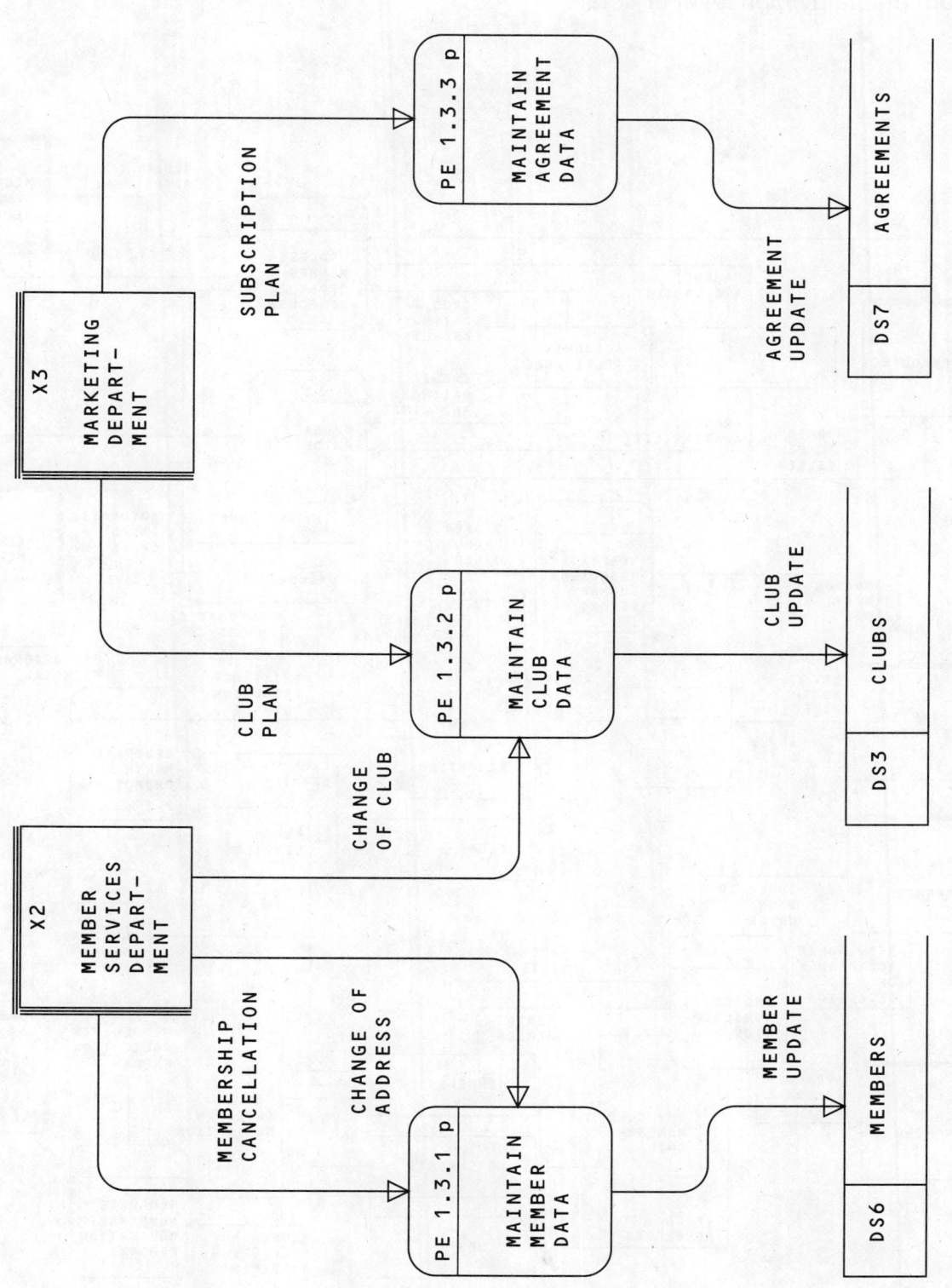

A Level-Zero DFD Using the Gane and Sarson Expansion Approach

TM-107

The expansion approach begins with a single DFD that models the entire system at a fairly high level of detail.

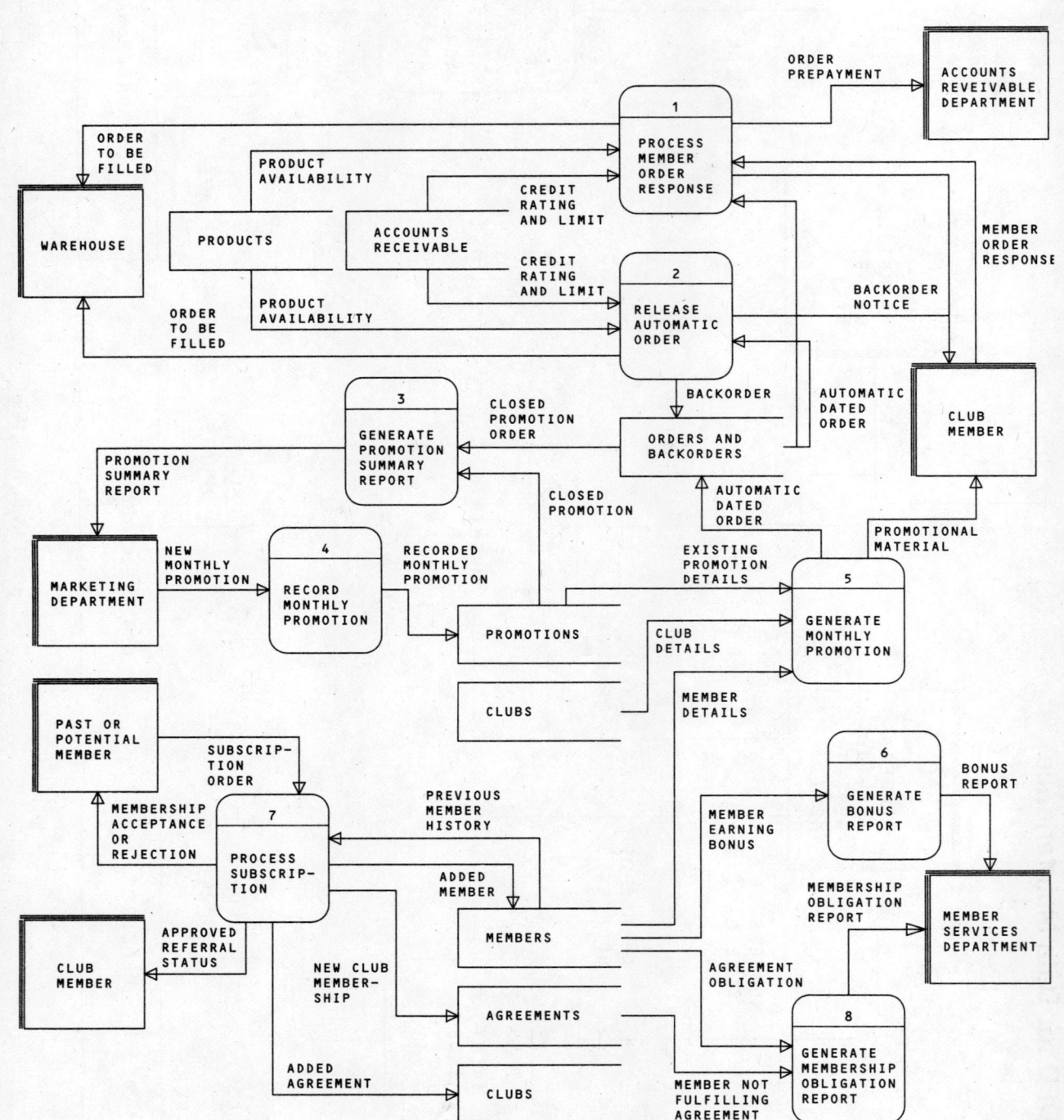

© Richard D. Irwin, Inc., 1994

A Level-One DFD Using the Gane and Sarson Expansion Approach

TM-108

The expansion approach concludes with an expanded view of the level-zero DFD—once again, a single DFD.

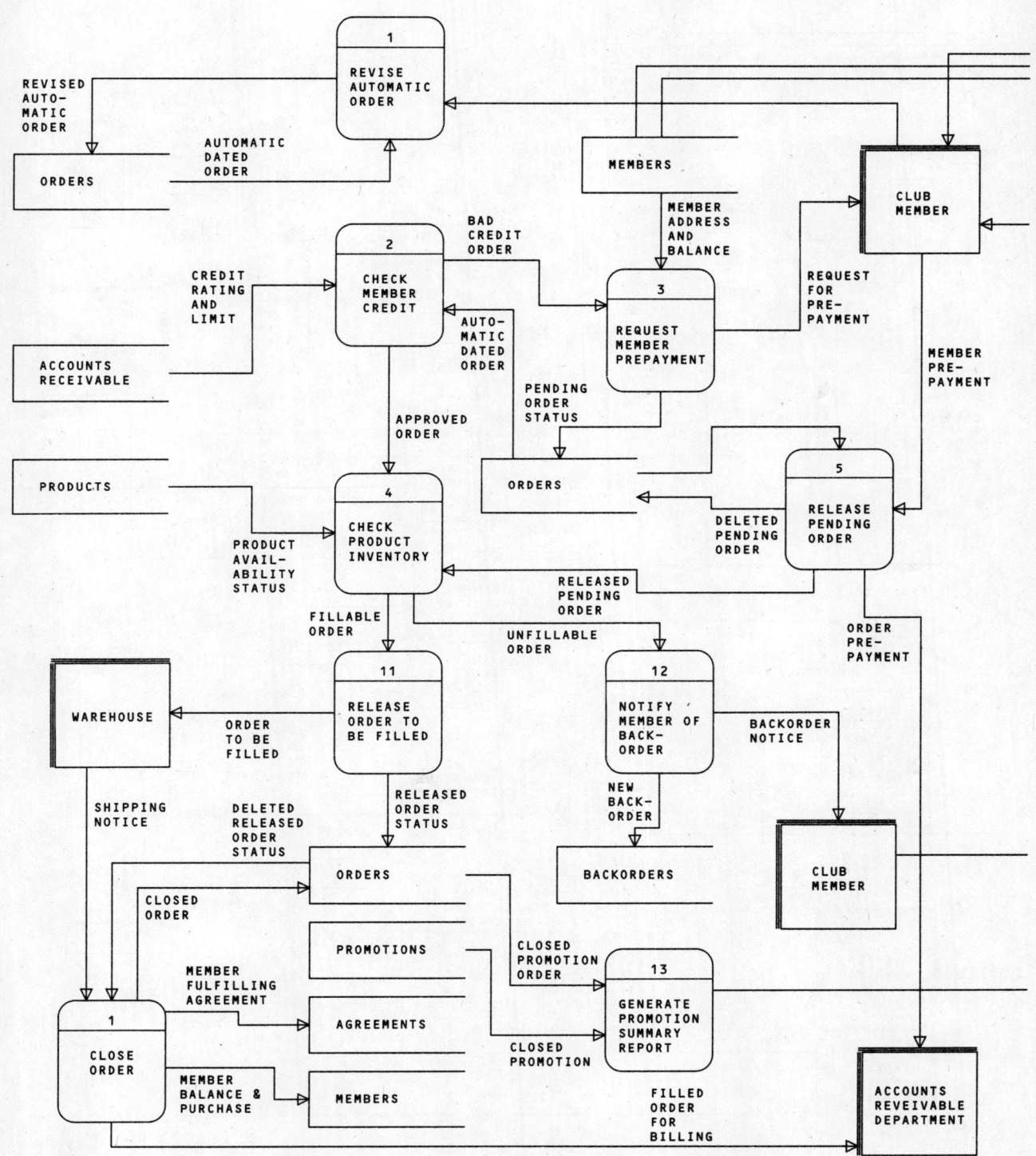

© Richard D. Irwin, Inc., 1994

TM-108
(concl)

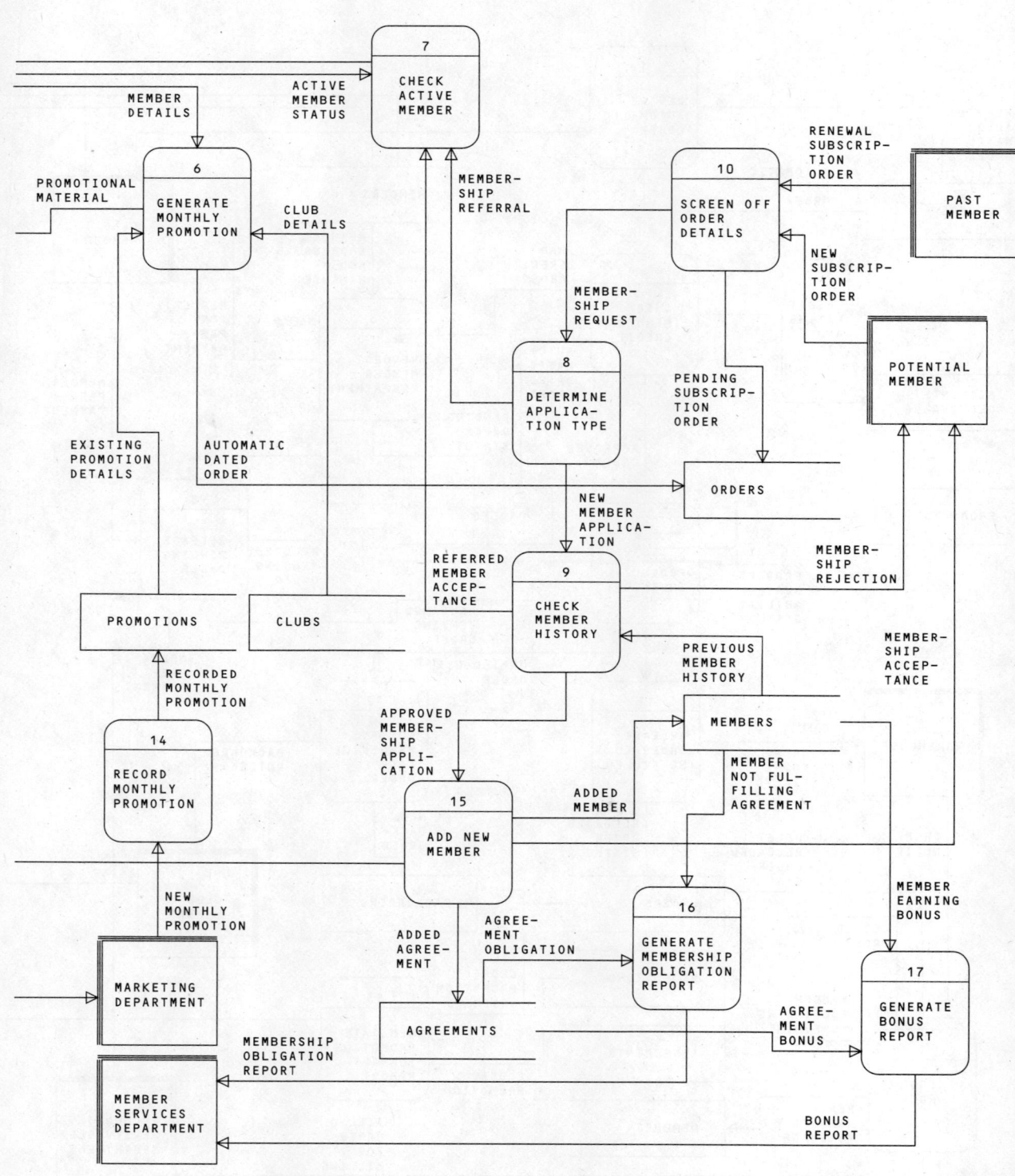

©Richard D. Irwin, Inc., 1994

Centralized Computing with Time-Sharing
Today, most existing information systems applications use centralized computing with time-sharing.

TM–109

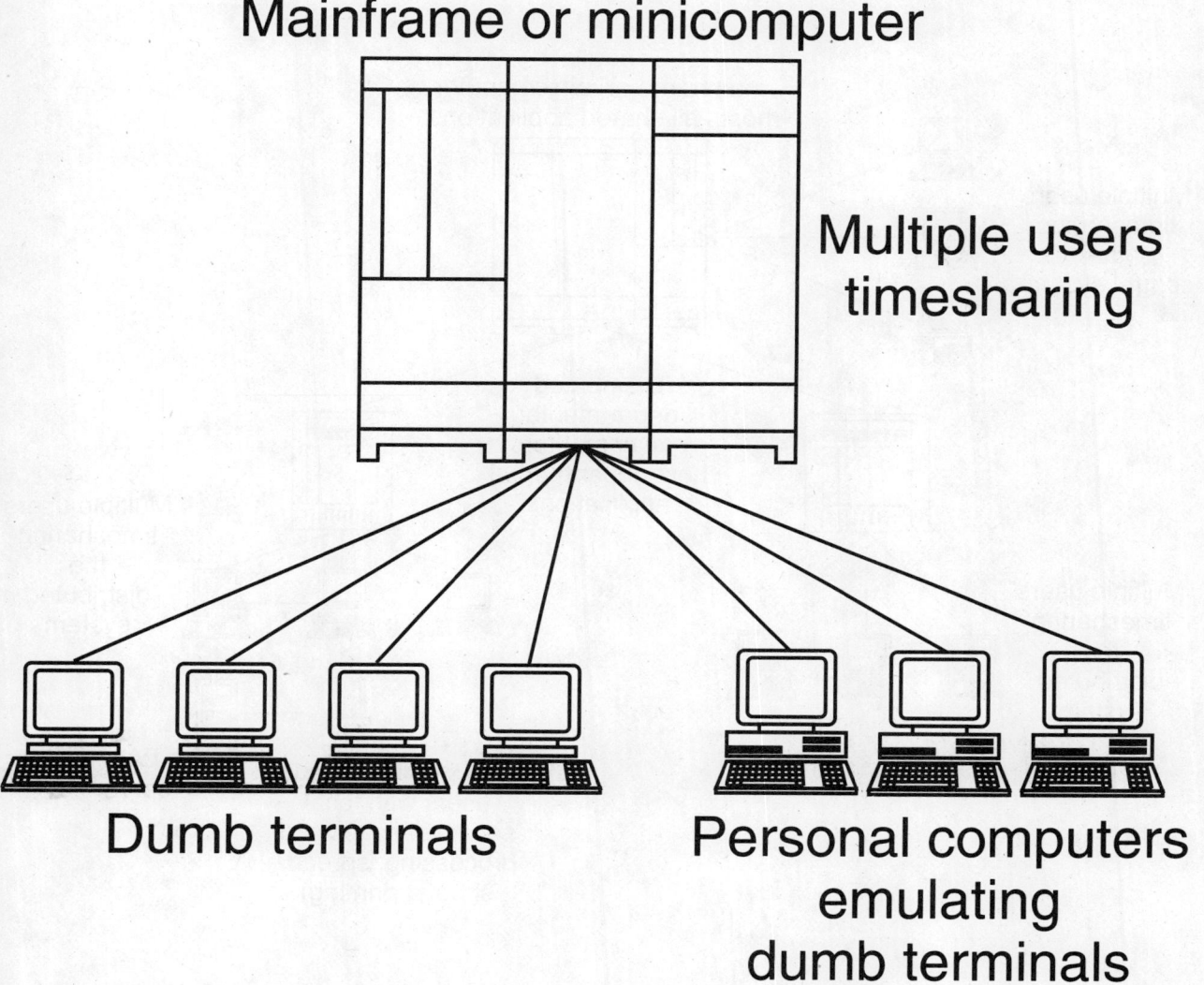

Distributed Computing

Distributed computing reallocates application processes to a network of timesharing computers.

TM–110

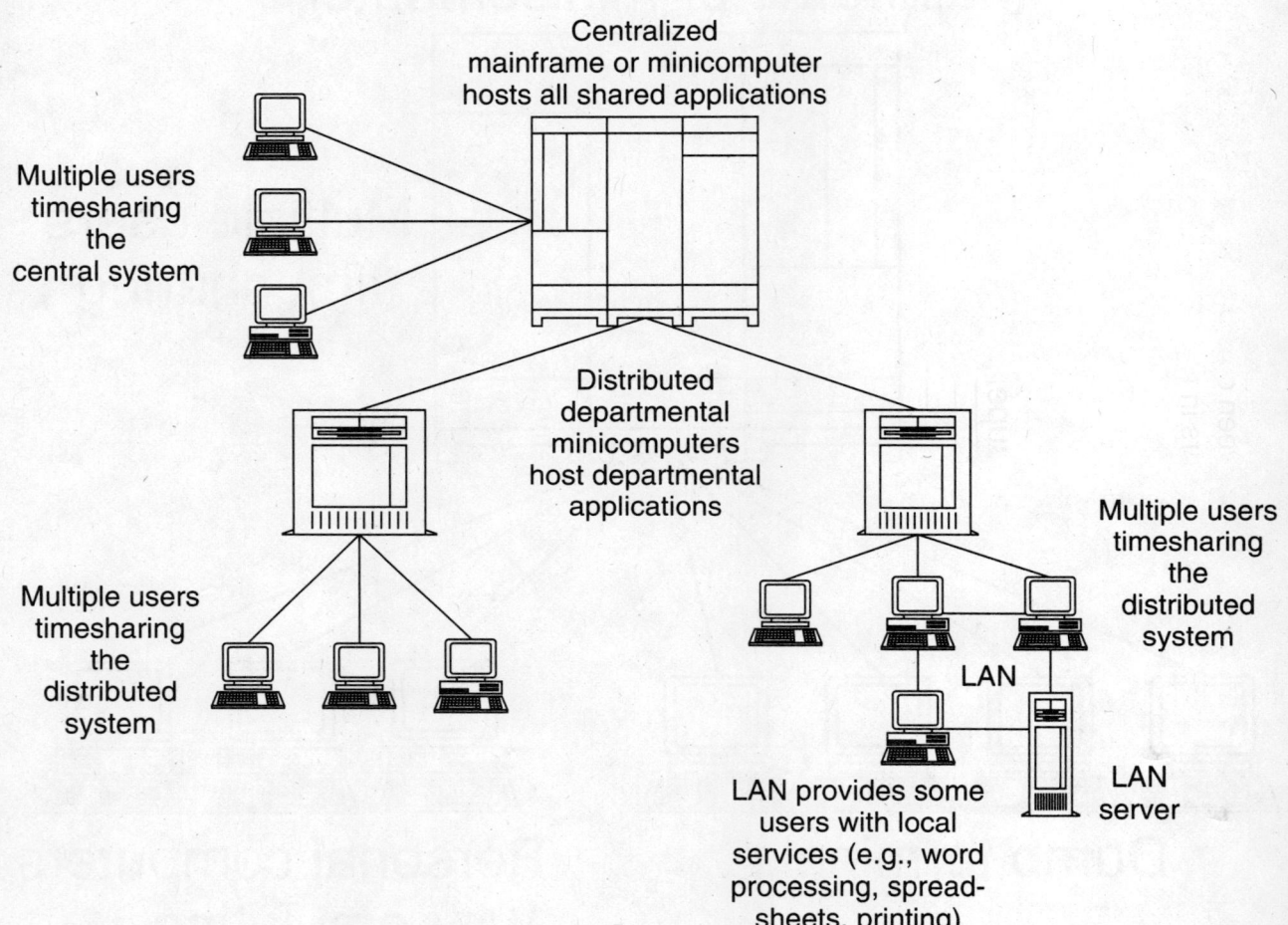

© Richard D. Irwin, Inc., 1994

Client/Server Computing

In a client/server network, processing workloads are shared between client workstations (PCs) and task-specific servers. Notice that mainframes and minicomputers can be servers in the client/server network.

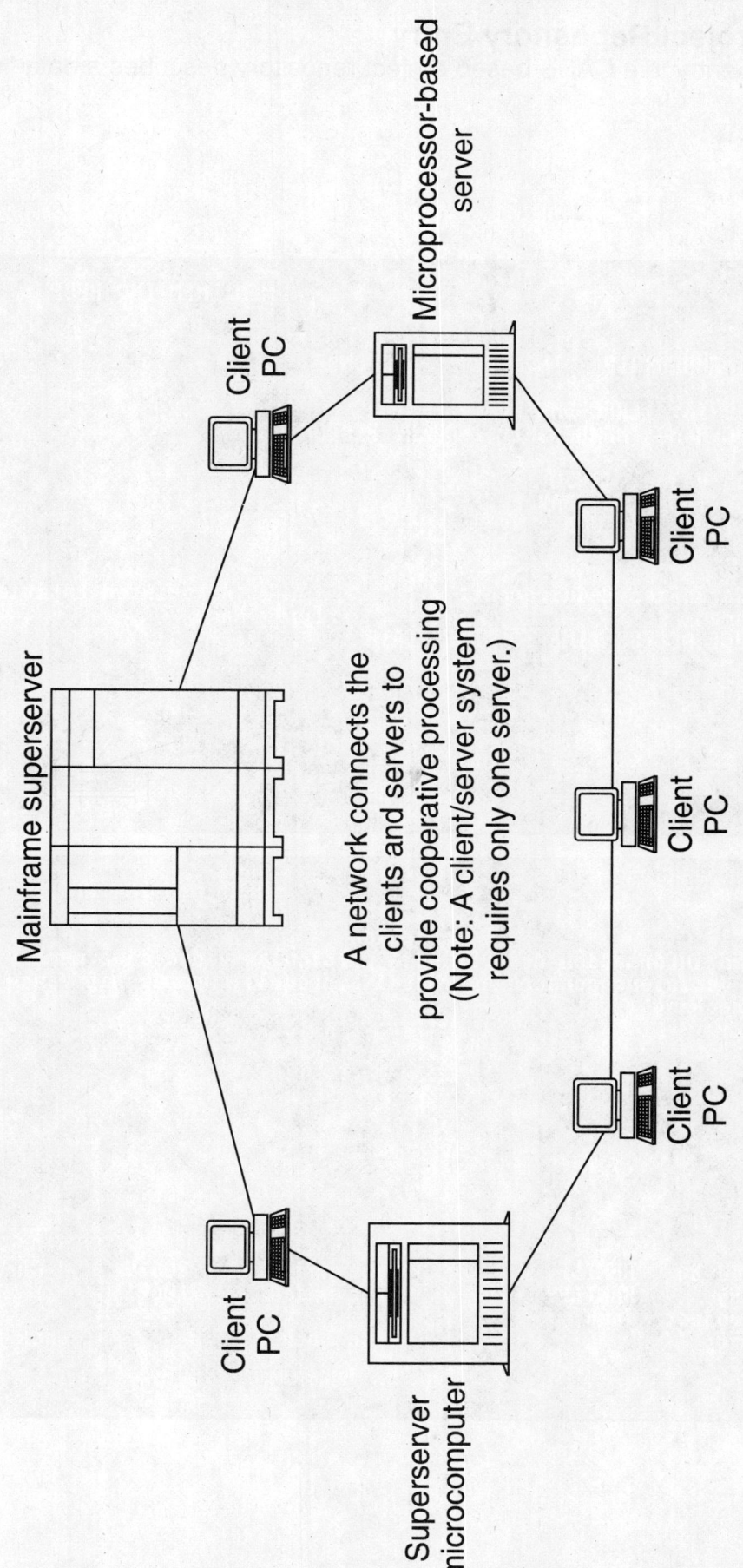

© Richard D. Irwin, Inc., 1994

Sample Project Repository Entry

This sample entry in a CASE-based project repository describes a data flow.

TM–112

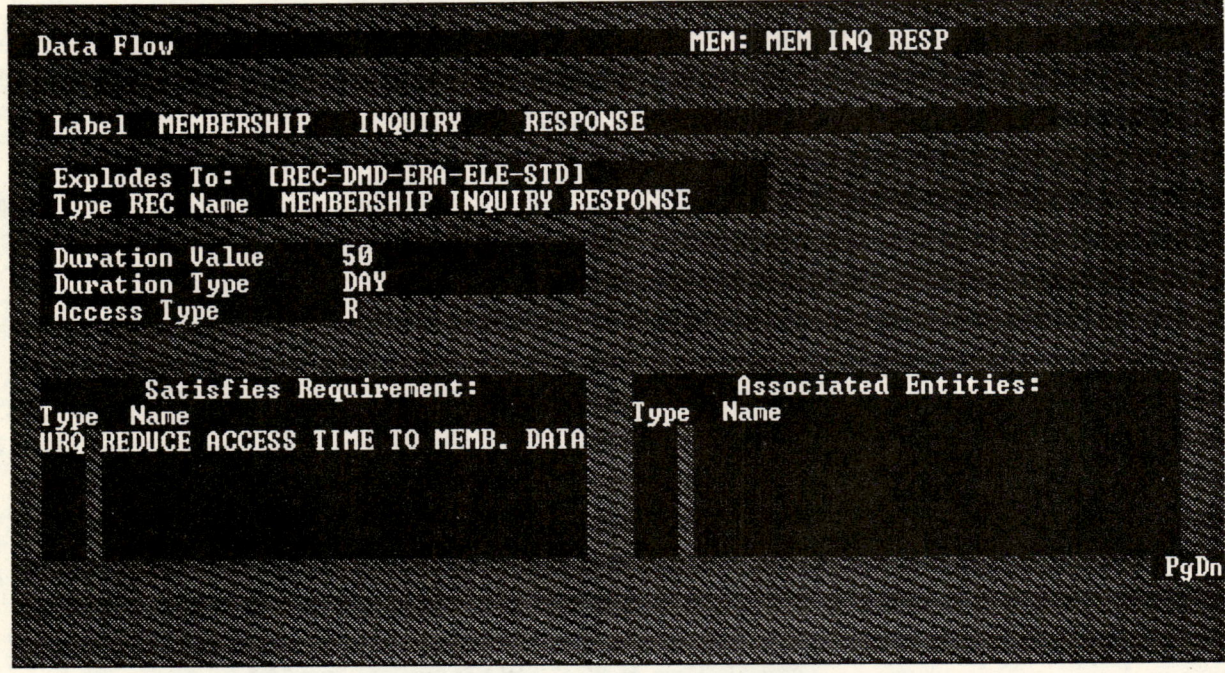
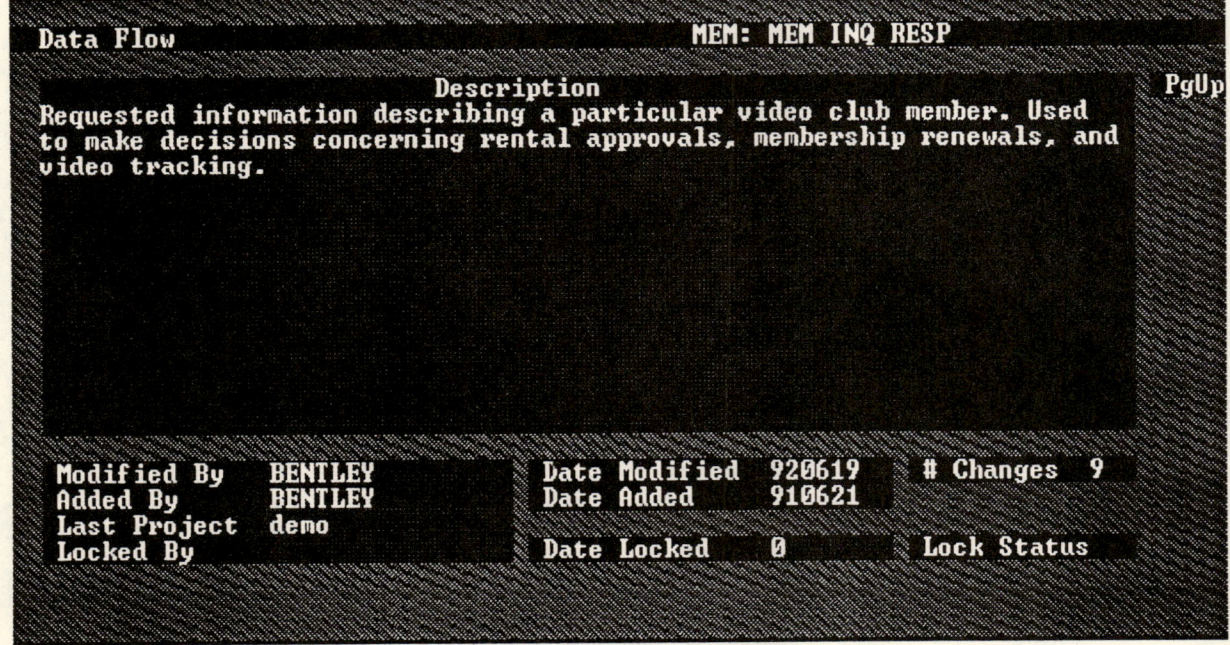

© Richard D. Irwin, Inc., 1994

The Organization of a Project Repository
Although many project repositories are maintained on computers, the contents are usually printed for reference.

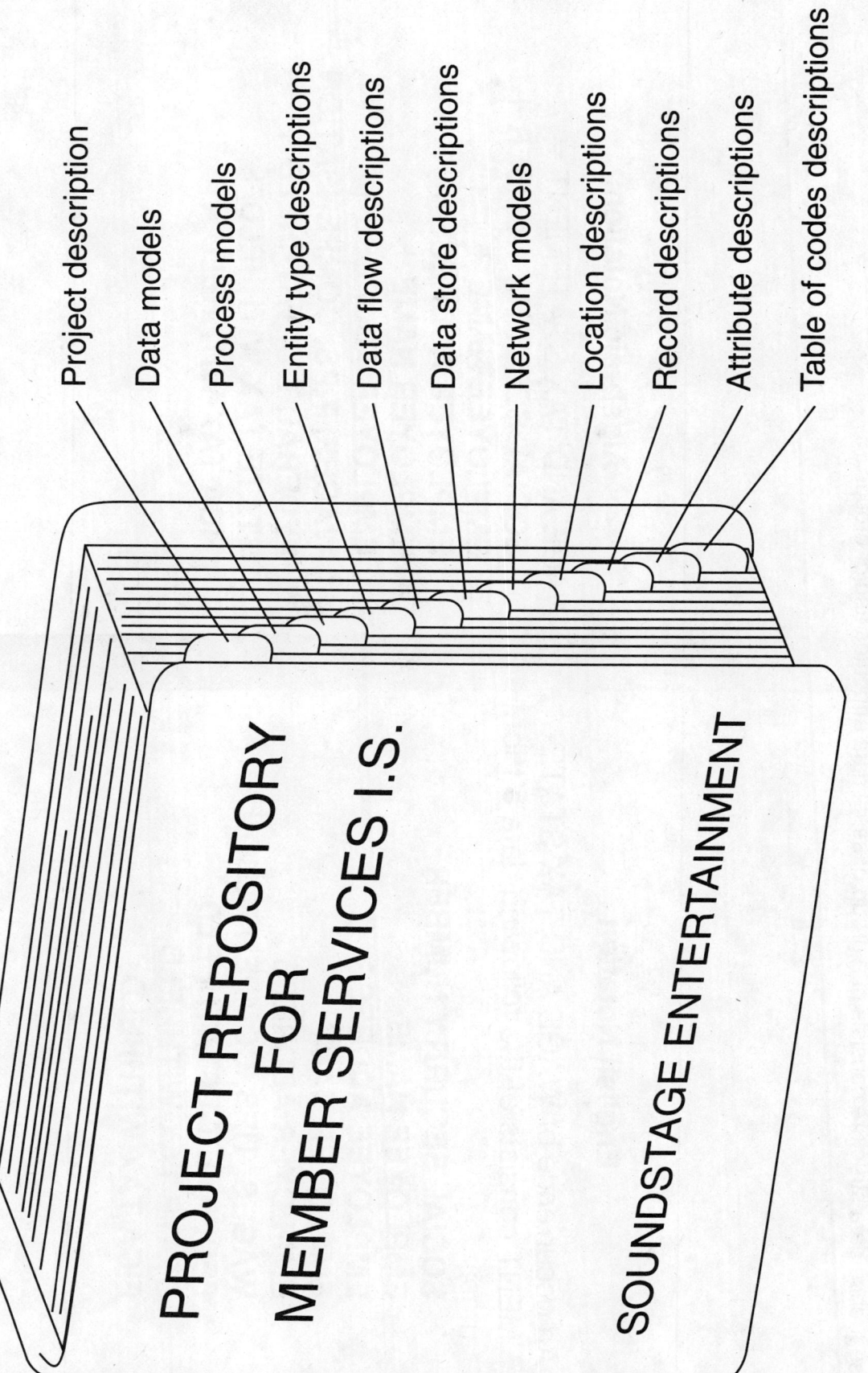

The Sequence Data Structure
The sequence data structure consists of a group of serial data attributes and/or groups.

English Notation

An occurrence of WAGE AND TAX STATEMENT consists of the following data attributes:

**SOCIAL SECURITY NUMBER
EMPLOYEE NAME
EMPLOYEE ADDRESS
EMPLOYER NAME
EMPLOYER ADDRESS
WAGES, TIPS, COMPENSATION
FEDERAL TAX WITHHELD
STATE TAX WITHHELD
FICA TAX WITHHELD**

Algebraic Notation

WAGE AND TAX STATEMENT =
SOCIAL SECURITY NUMBER +
EMPLOYEE NAME +
EMPLOYEE ADDRESS +
EMPLOYER NAME +
EMPLOYER ADDRESS +
WAGES, TIPS, COMPENSATION +
FEDERAL TAX WITHHELD +
STATE TAX WITHHELD +
FICA TAX WITHHELD

© Richard D. Irwin, Inc., 1994

The Exclusive-or Selection Data Structure
The exclusive-or selection data structure describes a group of data attributes from which one and only one may assume a value for the overall data structure.

English Notation

An ORDER consists of the following data attributes:
ORDER DATE
Only one of the following attributes:
SOCIAL SECURITY NUMBER
CUSTOMER ACCOUNT NUMBER

Algebraic Notation

ORDER =
ORDER DATE +
[SOCIAL SECURITY NUMBER,
CUSTOMER ACCOUNT NUMBER]

TM-115

© Richard D. Irwin, Inc., 1994

The Inclusive-or Selection Data Structure

The inclusive-or selection data structure describes a group of data attributes from which one or more may assume a value for the overall data structure.

English Notation

A TRAVEL EXPENSE VOUCHER consists of the following data attributes:
  EMPLOYEE ID NUMBER
  EMPLOYEE NAME
  DATE TRIP STARTED
  DATE TRIP COMPLETED
  PURPOSE OF TRIP
  MILES TRAVELED
  MILEAGE CHARGE
One or more of the following attributes:
  AIR TRAVEL EXPENSE
  TAXI FARE EXPENSE
  REGISTRATION FEES
  LODGING EXPENSES
  MEAL EXPENSES
TOTAL EXPENSES

Algebraic Notation

TRAVEL EXPENSE VOUCHER =
  EMPLOYEE ID NUMBER +
  EMPLOYEE NAME +
  DATE TRIP STARTED +
  DATE TRIP COMPLETED +
  PURPOSE OF TRIP +
  MILES TRAVELED +
  MILEAGE CHARGE +
  < **AIR TRAVEL EXPENSE,**
    TAXI FARE EXPENSE,
    REGISTRATION EXPENSE,
    LODGING EXPENSES,
    MEAL EXPENSES > +
  TOTAL EXPENSES

TM–116

© Richard D. Irwin, Inc., 1994

A Common Misuse of the Selection Data Structure

These data structures demonstrate a common mistake: using the selection structure to document values of data attributes instead of data attributes themselves. Part B fixes the mistake.

English Notation

A. Incorrect

A STUDENT consists of the following data attributes:
- STUDENT ID NUMBER
- STUDENT NAME
- **Only one of the following attributes:**
  - **FRESHMAN**
  - **SOPHOMORE**
  - **JUNIOR**
  - **SENIOR**

B. Correct

A STUDENT consists of the following data attributes:
- STUDENT ID NUMBER
- STUDENT NAME
- **STUDENT CLASSIFICATION**

Algebraic Notation

STUDENT =
STUDENT ID NUMBER +
STUDENT NAME +
[**FRESHMAN,**
  SOPHOMORE,
  JUNIOR,
  SENIOR]

STUDENT =
STUDENT ID NUMBER +
STUDENT NAME +
STUDENT CLASSIFICATION

© Richard D. Irwin, Inc., 1994

The Repetition Data Structure

The repetition data structure consists of a group of data attributes that repeat as a group for each occurrence of the main data structure.

English Notation

An ORDER consists of the following data attributes:
  ORDER NUMBER
  ORDER DATE
Only one of the following attributes:
  SOCIAL SECURITY NUMBER
  CUSTOMER ACCOUNT NUMBER
SHIPPING ADDRESS
1 to 20 occurrences of:
  PRODUCT NUMBER
  PRODUCT DESCRIPTION
  QUANTITY ORDERED
  PRODUCT PRICE
  EXTENDED PRICE
TOTAL ORDER COST

Algebraic Notation

ORDER =
  ORDER NUMBER +
  ORDER DATE +
  [SOCIAL SECURITY NUMBER,
  CUSTOMER ACCOUNT NUMBER] +
  SHIPPING ADDRESS
  1{ **PRODUCT NUMBER** +
     PRODUCT DESCRIPTION +
     QUANTITY ORDERED +
     PRODUCT PRICE +
     EXTENDED PRICE }20 +
  TOTAL ORDER COST

A Nested Repeating Data Structure

A nested repeating data structure contains a group of data attributes that repeat inside another group, which itself repeats.

English Notation

A TIME WORKED RECORD consists of the following data attributes:
EMPLOYEE IDENTIFICATION NUMBER
EMPLOYEE NAME
1 to 4 occurrences of the following:
   START DATE FOR PAY PERIOD
   END DATE FOR PAY PERIOD
   1 to 7 occurrences of the following:
      HOURS WORKED

Algebraic Notation

TIME WORKED RECORD =
  EMPLOYEE IDENTIFICATION NUMBER +
  EMPLOYEE NAME +
  1{   START DATE FOR PAY PERIOD +
      END DATE FOR PAY PERIOD +
      1{   HOURS WORKED   }7   }4

Optional Data Attributes in a Data Structure

This figure demonstrates how to indicate that an attribute does not have to take on a value.

English Notation

A CLAIM consists of the following data attributes:
  POLICY NUMBER
  POLICYHOLDER NAME
  POLICYHOLDER ADDRESS
  SPOUSE NAME (optional)
  0 to 15 occurrences of the following:
    DEPENDENT NAME
    RELATIONSHIP
  CLAIMANT NAME
  1 or more of the following:
    EXPENSE DESCRIPTION
    NAME OR FIRM PROVIDING SERVICE
    TOTAL CHARGE FOR SERVICE

Algebraic Notation

CLAIM =
  POLICY NUMBER +
  POLICYHOLDER NAME +
  POLICYHOLDER ADDRESS +
  (**SPOUSE NAME**)+
  0{ **DEPENDENT NAME** +
     RELATIONSHIP }15 +
  CLAIMANT NAME +
  1{ EXPENSE DESCRIPTION +
     NAME OR FIRM PROVIDING SERVICE +
     TOTAL CHARGE FOR SERVICE }M

TM-120

© Richard D. Irwin, Inc., 1994

Common Data Structures

It is useful to define reusable data structures that can be referenced from within other data structures.

English Notation

A WAGE AND TAX STATEMENT consists of the following data attributes:
SOCIAL SECURITY NUMBER
EMPLOYEE NAME
EMPLOYEE ADDRESS which is defined separately as ADDRESS
EMPLOYER NAME
EMPLOYER ADDRESS which is defined separately as ADDRESS
WAGES, TIPS, COMPENSATION
FEDERAL TAX WITHHELD
STATE TAX WITHHELD
FICA TAX WITHHELD

ADDRESS consists of the following data attributes:
One or both of the following:
   STREET ADDRESS
   POST OFFICE BOX NUMBER

CITY
STATE
ZIPCODE

Algebraic Notation

WAGE AND TAX STATEMENT =
  SOCIAL SECURITY NUMBER +
  EMPLOYEE NAME +
  EMPLOYEE ADDRESS = ADDRESS +
  EMPLOYER NAME +
  EMPLOYER ADDRESS = ADDRESS +
  WAGES, TIPS, COMPENSATION +
  FEDERAL TAX WITHHELD +
  STATE TAX WITHHELD +
  FICA TAX WITHHELD +

ADDRESS =
  < STREET ADDRESS,
    POST OFFICE BOX NUMBER > +
  CITY +
  STATE +
  ZIPCODE

A Decision Table for Specifying a Store's Check-Cashing Policy

Decision tables offer a number of advantages over ordinary English.

TM–122

A.

CHECK-CASHING IDENTIFICATION CARD

Upon presentation person named hereon is entitled to cash personal checks up to $75.00 and payroll checks of accredited companies at Save Super Markets. Card is issued in accordance with terms and conditions of application, remains property of Save Super Markets, Inc., and shall be returned upon request.

Charles C. Parker, Jr

SIGNATURE
ISSUED BY
SAVE SUPER MARKETS, INC.

B.

Check-Cashing Policy

		Rules				
		1	2	3	4	5
Conditions	Type of check	1	2	1	2	2
	Check amount less than or equal to $75	Y	–	N	N	–
	Company accredited by store	–	Y	–	Y	N
Actions	Cash check	X	X			
	Refuse check			X	X	X

©Richard D. Irwin, Inc., 1994

A Decision Table for Solving the Poker Chip Problem

Through the process of elimination, Susan was able to deduce the color of her chip.

Rules

Process Name	1	2	3	4	5	6	7	8
Conditions								
Joe	W	W	W	W	B	B	B	B
Gordon	W	W	B	B	W	W	B	B
Susan	W	Ⓑ	W	Ⓑ	W	Ⓑ	W	Ⓑ
Actions								
Impossible—only two white chips	X							
Joe would have guessed					X			
Gordon would have guessed			X					
Susan knows her chip is black		←		←		←		←

TM–123

© Richard D. Irwin, Inc., 1994

Entering All Possible Rules into a Decision Table
This decision table identifies all possible combinations of conditions.

		Rules																															
		1	2	3	4	5	6	7	8	9	10	11	12	13	14	15	16	17	18	19	20	21	22	23	24	25	26	27	28	29	30	31	32
Conditions	Account type (a)	R	S	R	S	R	S	R	S	R	S	R	S	R	S	R	S	R	S	R	S	R	S	R	S	R	S	R	S	R	S	R	S
	Insurance (b)	Y	Y	Y	Y	Y	Y	Y	Y	Y	Y	Y	Y	Y	Y	Y	Y	N	N	N	N	N	N	N	N	N	N	N	N	N	N	N	N
	Balance dropped below $25 during month (c)	Y	Y	Y	Y	Y	Y	Y	Y	N	N	N	N	N	N	N	N	Y	Y	Y	Y	Y	Y	Y	Y	N	N	N	N	N	N	N	N
	Average daily balance (d)	1	1	1	1	1	1	1	1	2	2	2	2	2	2	2	2	3	3	3	3	3	3	3	3	4	4	4	4	4	4	4	4
Actions	Pay no dividend																																	
	5.750% ÷ 4 as the quarterly dividend on entire balance																																	
	6.000% ÷ 4 as the quarterly dividend on entire balance																																	
	6.000% ÷ 12 as the monthly dividend on balance up to $500																																	
	6.500% ÷ 12 as the monthly dividend on balance between $500.01 and $2,000																																	
	7.000% ÷ 12 as the monthly dividend on balance over $2,000																																	

TM-124

©Richard D. Irwin, Inc., 1994

Defining the Actions for Each Rule in a Decision Table

This decision resulted in some rules (combinations of conditions) that are impossible.

TM–125

Process Name/Dividend Rate

Rules

		1	2	3	4	5	6	7	8	9	10	11	12	13	14	15	16	17	18	19	20	21	22	23	24	25	26	27	28	29	30	31	32
Conditions	Account type	R	S	R	S	R	S	R	S	R	S	R	S	R	S	R	S	R	S	R	S	R	S	R	S	R	S	R	S	R	S	R	S
	Insurance	Y	Y	Y	Y	Y	Y	Y	Y	Y	Y	Y	Y	Y	Y	Y	Y	N	N	N	N	N	N	N	N	N	N	N	N	N	N	N	N
	Balance dropped below $25 during month	Y	Y	Y	Y	Y	Y	Y	Y	N	N	N	N	N	N	N	N	Y	Y	Y	Y	Y	Y	Y	Y	N	N	N	N	N	N	N	N
	Average daily balance	1	1	1	1	1	1	1	1	2	2	2	2	2	2	2	2	3	3	3	3	3	3	3	3	4	4	4	4	4	4	4	4
Actions	Pay no dividend	?	?	?	X								X							X									X				
	5.750% ÷ 4 as the quarterly dividend on entire balance	X	?								X					X			X		X												
	6.000% ÷ 4 as the quarterly dividend on entire balance	?	X												X		X					X		X				X		X		X	
	6.000% ÷ 12 as the monthly dividend on balance up to $500	?										X											X		X								X
	6.500% ÷ 12 as the monthly dividend on balance between $500.01 and $2,000	?												X									X		X		X						X
	7.000% ÷ 12 as the monthly dividend on balance over $2,000	?																				X		X							X		X
	Impossible	?			X	X	X	X	X																	X		X		X		X	

©Richard D. Irwin, Inc., 1994

Simplifying a Decision Table

TM−126

Most decision tables can be simplified by collapsing combinations of certain rules into single rules.

A.

		1	2	3	4	5	6	7	8	9	10	11	12
Conditions	Condition 1	Y	N	Y	N	Y	N	Y	N	Y	N	Y	N
	Condition 2	Y	Y	N	N	Y	Y	N	N	Y	Y	N	N
	Condition 3	L	L	L	L	M	M	M	M	H	H	H	H
Actions	Action 1	X				X				X			
	Action 2		X						X		X	X	X
	Action 3				X	X							
	Action 4			X				X					

B.

		1, 5, 9	2	3	4	6	7	8	10	11, 12
Conditions	Condition 1	Y	N	Y	N	N	Y	N	N	−
	Condition 2	Y	Y	N	N	Y	N	N	Y	N
	Condition 3	−	L	L	L	M	M	M	H	H
Actions	Action 1	X								
	Action 2		X					X	X	X
	Action 3				X	X				
	Action 4			X			X			

© Richard D. Irwin, Inc., 1994

Simplified Decision Table for the Credit Union Dividend Policy TM-127

Notice that conditions 3 and 4 are indifferent to regular accounts. Thus, more than one condition can be indifferent to a single action.

	Process Name/Dividend Rate	Rules					
		1	2	3	4	5	6
Conditions	Account type	R	R	S	S	S	S
	Insurance	Y	N	–	N	N	N
	Balance dropped below $25 during month	–	–	Y	N	N	N
	Average daily balance	–	–	–	2	3	4
Actions	Pay no dividend				X		
	5.750% ÷ 4 as the quarterly dividend on entire balance	X					
	6.000% ÷ 4 as the quarterly dividend on entire balance		X				
	6.000% ÷ 12 as the monthly dividend on balance up to $500				X	X	X
	6.500% ÷ 12 as the monthly dividend on balance between $500.01 and $2,000					X	X
	7.000% ÷ 12 as the monthly dividend on balance over $2,000						X

Account type: R = Regular rate
S = Split rate

Insurance: Y = Yes
N = No

Balance dropped below
$25 during month: Y = Yes
N = No

Average daily balance: 1 = $0.00–$24.99
2 = $25.00–$500.00
3 = $500.01–$2,000.00
4 = More than $2,000.00

©Richard D. Irwin, Inc., 1994

A Sample Structured English Description of a Business Procedure

For each LOAN ACCOUNT NUMBER in the LOAN ACCOUNT FILE do the following steps:
 If the AMOUNT PAST DUE is greater than $0.00 then:
  While there are LOAN ACCOUNT NUMBERs for the CUSTOMER NAME do the following steps:
   Sum the OUTSTANDING LOAN BALANCES.
   Sum the MINIMUM PAYMENTs.
   Sum the PAST DUE AMOUNTs.
  Report the CUSTOMER NAME, LOAN ACCOUNTs on OVERDUE CUSTOMER LOAN ANALYSIS.

A Sample Action Diagram Description of a Business Procedure
This action diagram is equivalent to the Structured English.

```
┌─ For each LOAN ACCOUNT NUMBER in the LOAN ACCOUNT FILE
│  ┌─ If the AMOUNT PAST DUE is greater than $0.00
│  │  ┌─ Do while there are LOAN ACCOUNT NUMBERs for CUSTOMER NAME
│  │  │     Sum the OUTSTANDING LOAN BALANCE
│  │  │     Sum the MINIMUM PAYMENTS
│  │  └─    Sum the PAST DUE AMOUNTs
│  └─
└─    Report the CUSTOMER NAME and LOAN ACCOUNTs on OVERDUE CUSTOMER
      LOAN ANALYSIS
```

TM–129

A Sample Tight English Description of a Business Procedure
This Tight English sample is equivalent to the Structured English.

To complete an overdue customer loan analysis for each loan account:
- Step 1: Identify loan accounts that are past due.
- Step 2: Summarize past due loan accounts by customer as follows:
  - Step 2.1   Sum the outstanding loan balances for each overdue loan account belonging to a given customer.
  - Step 2.2   Sum the minimum required payment balances for each overdue loan account belonging to a given customer.
  - Step 2.3   Sum the current past due amounts for each overdue loan account belonging to a given customer.
- Step 3: Report the name of each customer, the loan account, and loan account sums.

The Case and If-Then-Otherwise Constructs in Structured English

Find the MATERIAL NUMBER in the INVENTORY FILE.
Select the appropriate case:
   Case 1: MATERIAL CLASS = 'stock,' then:
     If the QUANTITY ON HAND is greater than or equal to the QUANTITY REQUISITIONED then:
       Calculate new QUANTITY ON HAND using the formula:
        QUANTITY ON HAND − QUANTITY REQUISITIONED
       Record QUANTITY ON HAND in the INVENTORY FILE.
       Issue a STORES TICKET.
     Otherwise (QUANTITY ON HAND is not greater then the QUANTITY REQUISITIONED) then:
       Issue a STORES STOCKOUT TICKET.
   Case 2: MATERIAL CLASS = 'seasonal,' then:
     Calculate QUANTITY NEEDED using the formula:
       REQUISITIONED QUANTITY × SEASONAL ADJUST RATE
     Issue a PURCHASE REQUISITION.
   Case 3: MATERIAL CLASS = 'requisition,' then:
     Issue a PURCHASE REQUISITION.

© Richard D. Irwin, Inc., 1994

The Repetition Construct of Structured English

For each CUSTOMER NUMBER in the CUSTOMER ACCOUNT file, do the following:
Repeat the following steps for each ACCOUNT NUMBER:
    For each ACCOUNT TRANSACTION for the ACCOUNT NUMBER, do the following:
        Report each ACCOUNT TRANSACTION.
        Sum the following account totals:
            NUMBER OF DEBIT TRANSACTIONS
            NUMBER OF CREDIT TRANSACTIONS
            TOTAL OF DEBIT TRANSACTIONS
            TOTAL OF CREDIT TRANSACTIONS
            ACCOUNT EXPENSES
    Report the account totals for the ACCOUNT NUMBER.
Until there are no more ACCOUNT NUMBERs for the CUSTOMER NUMBER.

TM-132

©Richard D. Irwin, Inc., 1994

Project Repository Entry for a Data Entity from a Data Model   TM–133

This is a typical repository entry for a data entity. The explosion attribute points to a separate description for a record.

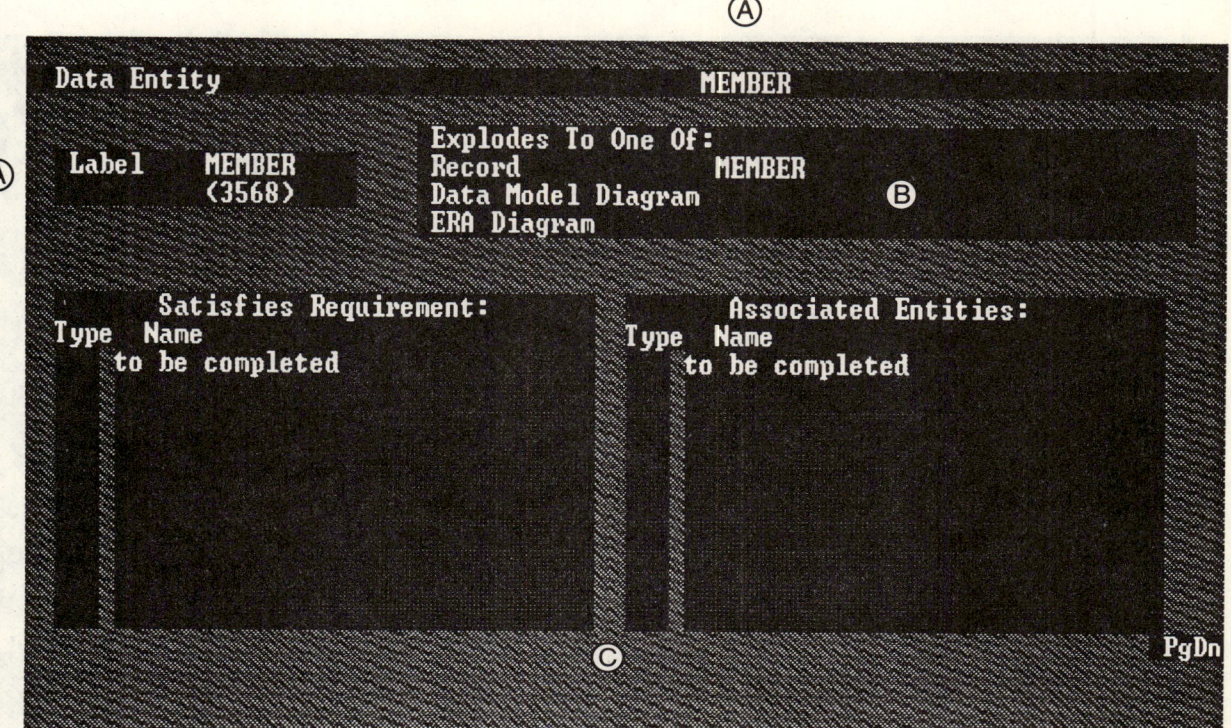
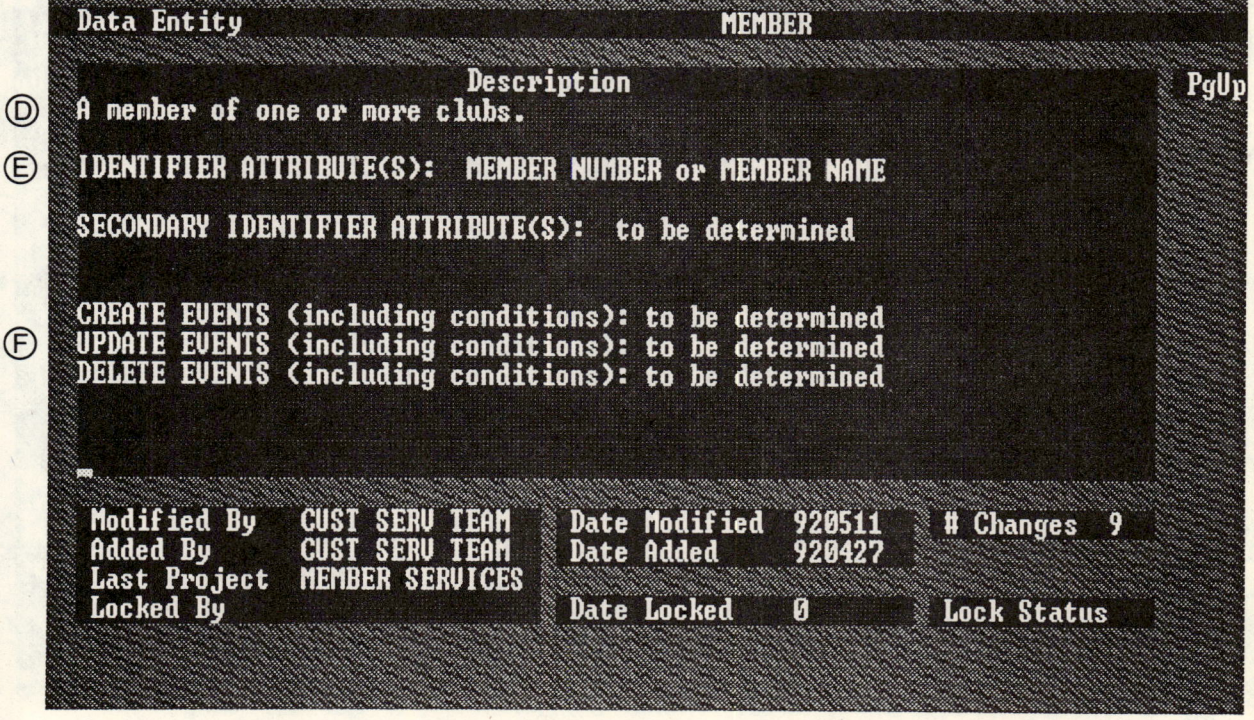

© Richard D. Irwin, Inc., 1994

Project Repository Entry for a Data Flow from a Process Model

TM–134

This is a typical repository entry for a data flow. The explosion attribute points to a separate description for a record.

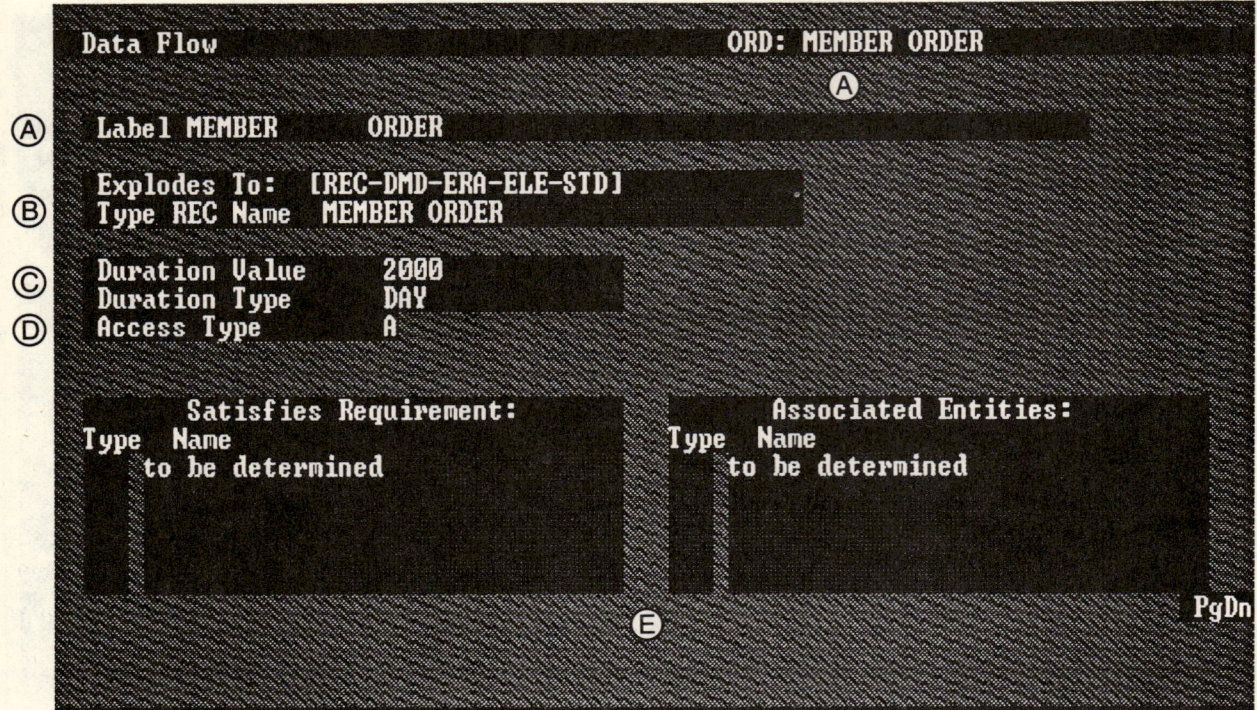

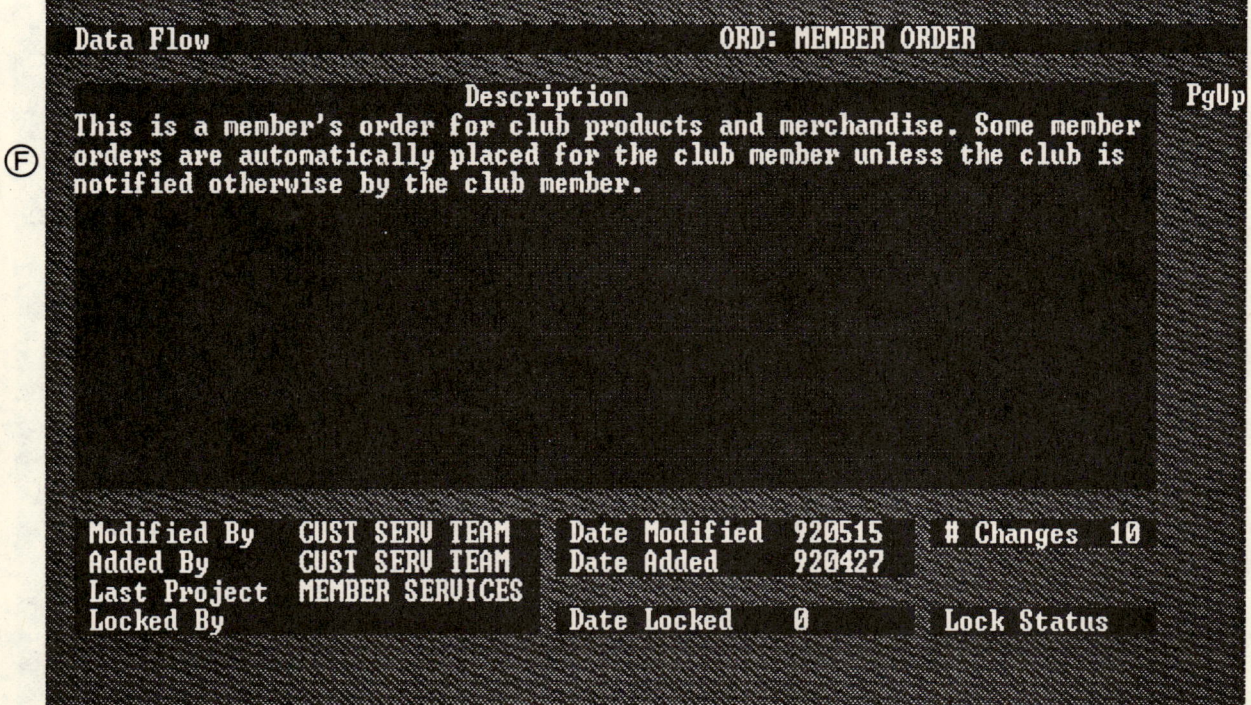

© Richard D. Irwin, Inc., 1994

Project Repository Entry for a Data Store from a Process Model

TM–135

This is a typical repository entry for a data store. The explosion attribute points to a data model diagram.

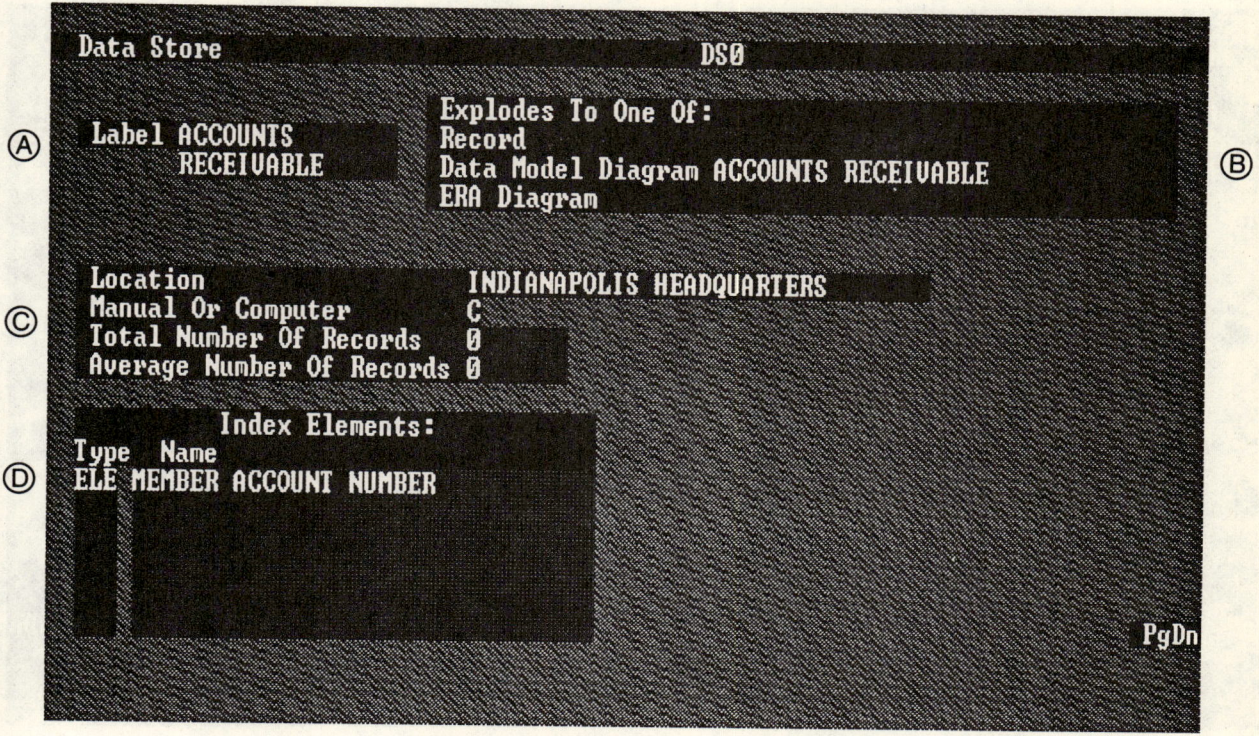

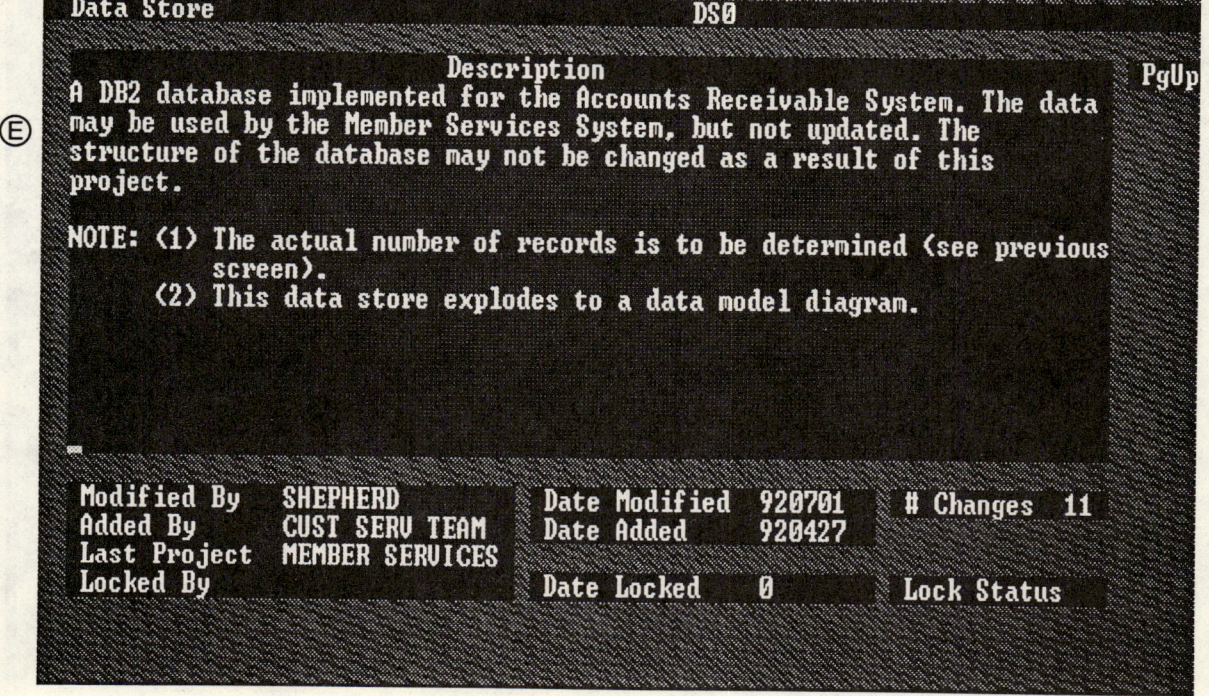

© Richard D. Irwin, Inc., 1994

Project Repository Entry for a Record

This is a typical repository entry for a record. A record describes a data structure.

TM-136

A.

```
Record                                    MEMBER ORDER
Alternate Name  ORDER
Definition      An order placed by a club member.
Normalized      N
                Name of Element or Record   Occ  Seq  Type  Sec-Keys
                ORDER NUMBER                 1    0    E
                ORDER DATE                   1    0    E
                MEMBER NUMBER                1    0    E
                MEMBER NAME                  1    0    E
                AUTO ORDER RESPONSE?         1    0    E
                MEMBER BILLING ADDRESS       1    0    R
                MEMBER SHIPPING ADDRESS      1    0    R
                MEMBER ORDERED PRODUCT      99    0    R
                                             1    0    e
                                             1    0    e
                                             1    0    e
                                             1    0    e
                                             1    0    e
                                                              PgDn
```

B.

```
Record                                    MEMBER ORDERED PRODUCT
Alternate Name
Definition      Refers to a single product appearing on a member's order.
Normalized      N
                Name of Element or Record   Occ  Seq  Type  Sec-Keys
                PRODUCT NUMBER               1    0    E
                MEDIA CODE                   1    0    E
                QUANTITY ORDERED             1    0    E
                                             1    0    e
                                             1    0    e
                                             1    0    e
                                             1    0    e
                                             1    0    e
                                             1    0    e
                                             1    0    e
                                             1    0    e
                                                              PgDn
```

© Richard D. Irwin, Inc., 1994

Project Repository Entry for a Data Attribute　　　　　　　　　　　　　　TM–137

Ⓐ

Element　　　　　　　QUANTITY ORDERED

Ⓑ Alternate Names　QUANTITY SOLD
　　　　　　　　　　　QTY ORDERED

Ⓒ Definition　Quantity ordered for a product on a specific member's order

Ⓓ Input Format　9999
　 Output Format　9999
Ⓔ Edit Rules　　0 thru 2000
　 Storage Type　C
Ⓕ Characters left of decimal 4　Characters right of decimal 0

　 Default
　 Prompt　　　　　QUANTITY ORDERED
　 Column Header　QTY ORD
　 Short Header　　QTY ORD
　 Base or Derived B
　 Data Class
　 Source　　　　　to be determined

PgDn

© Richard D. Irwin, Inc., 1994

Project Repository Entry for a Table of Codes

TM-138

Table of Codes   MEDIA CODE

Alternate Name FORMAT
Definition   THE MEDIA OR FORMAT FOR A MUSIC OR VIDEO PRODUCT

    Next Table of Codes:
Type Name
TAB1

Code	Meaning
L8	8" LASER DISC
LD	STANDARD LASER DISC
LL	LETTERBOX LASER DISC
CD	CDV LASER DISC
VH	VHS
8M	8MM
DC	DIGITAL CASSETTE
CA	CASSETTE
CD	COMPACT DISC
CM	COMPACT MINI DISC

PgDn

© Richard D. Irwin, Inc., 1994

Project Repository Entry for a Process Appearing on a Process Model

TM–139

Note that this sample screen includes a reference to a decision table and the use of a numbering convention within the procedure.

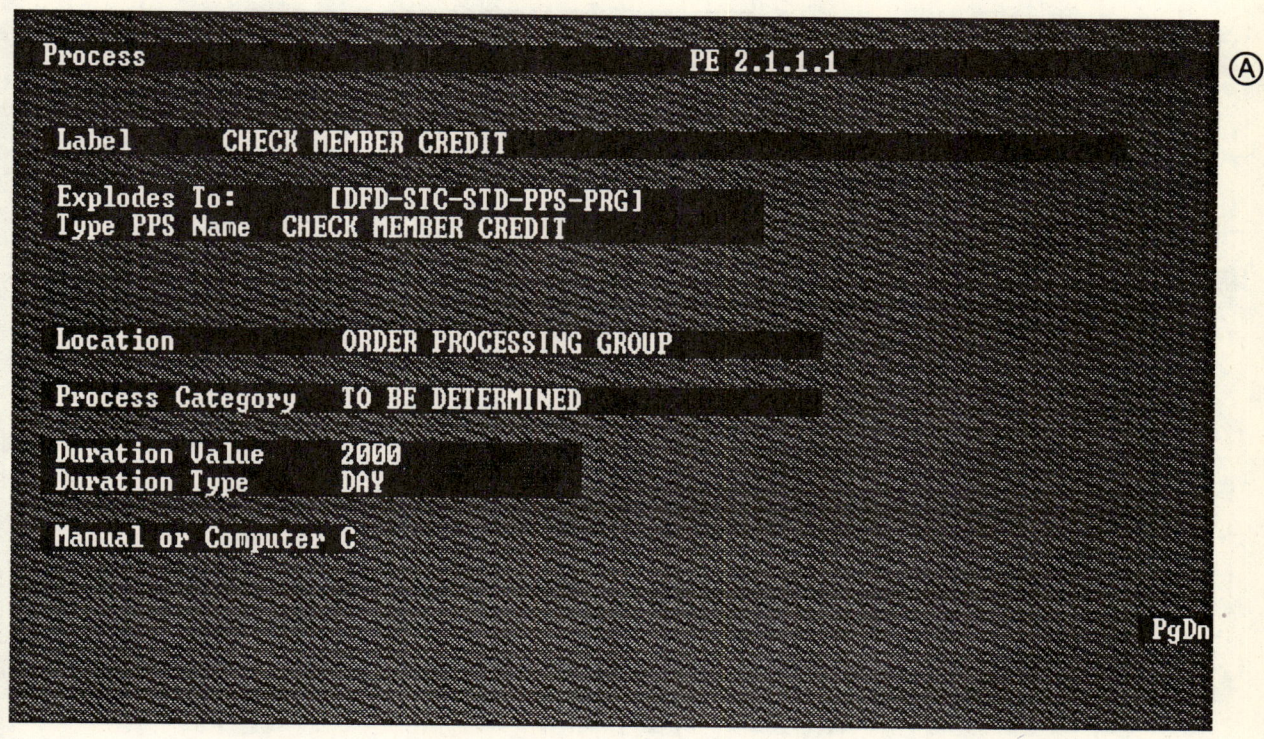

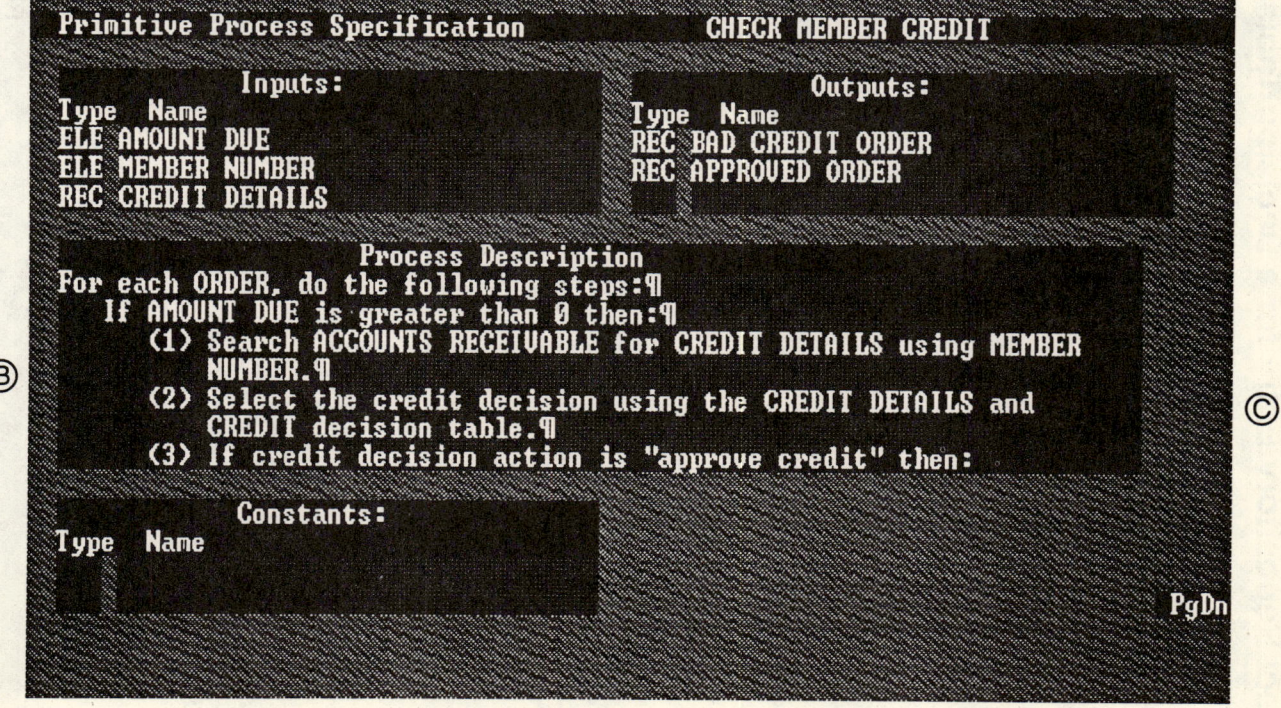

© Richard D. Irwin, Inc., 1994

Project Repository Entry for a Decision Table

(A) CREDIT DECISION TABLE

(B) This decision table defines the rules for approving or rejecting member credit for an order.

Cond/Act	Description	1	2	3
C	AMOUNT DUE > MEMBER CREDIT LIMIT (C)	N	Y	Y
C	CREDIT RATING = "A" OR "B"	–	Y	N
A	APPROVE CREDIT	X		
A	APPROVE CREDIT BUT SEND REMINDER (D)		X (E)	
A	REJECT CREDIT			X

© Richard D. Irwin, Inc., 1994

Project Repository Entry for a Location TM–141

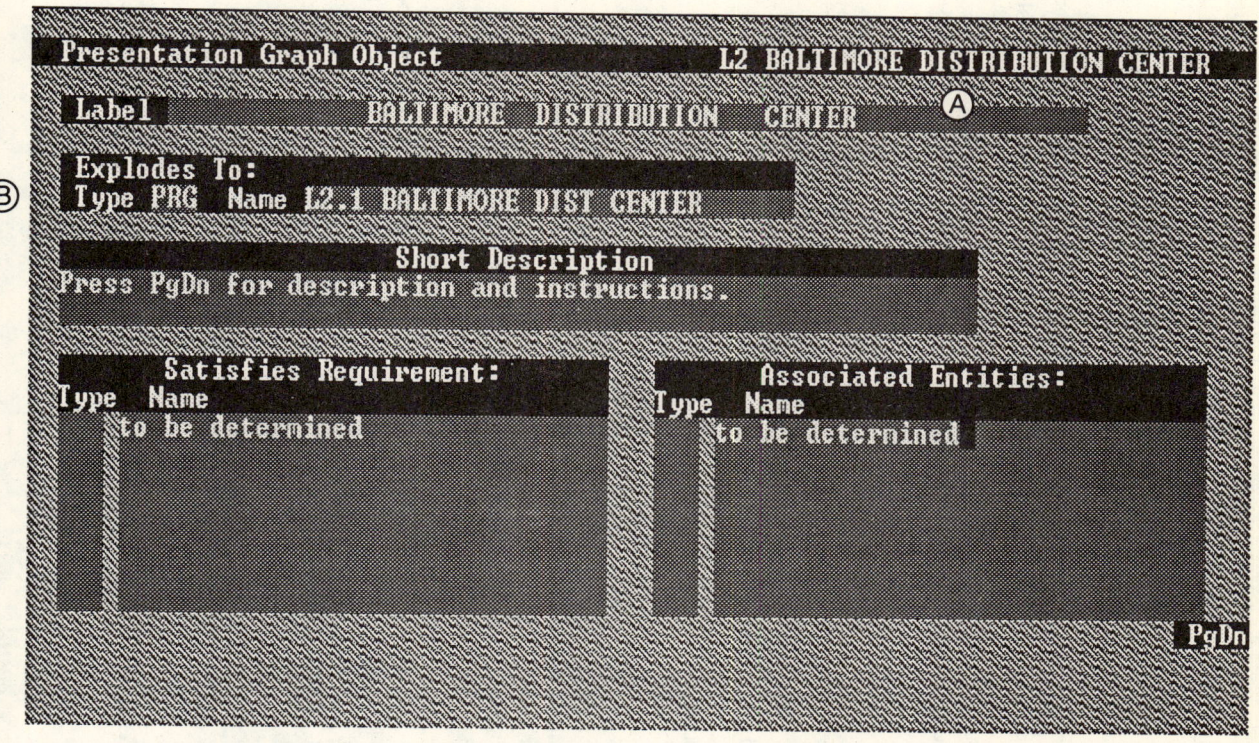
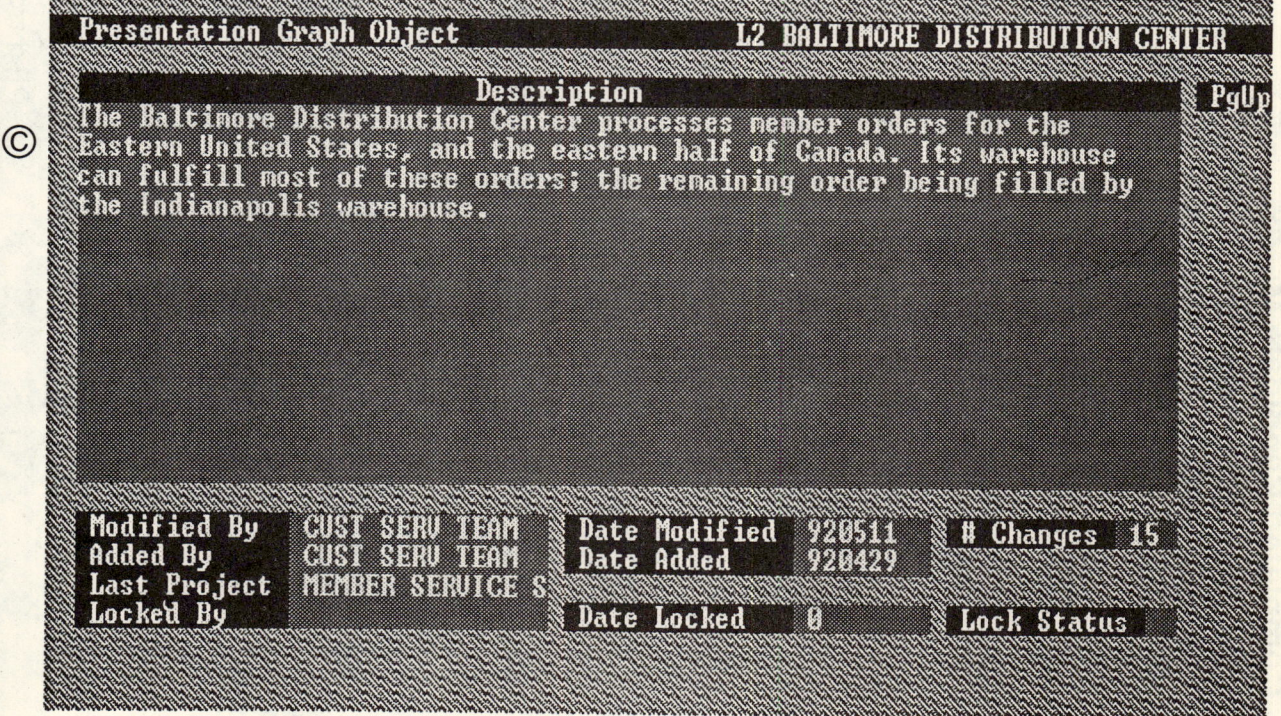

© Richard D. Irwin, Inc., 1994

Partially Completed Candidate Matrix

A matrix is a very useful tool for specifying characteristics for alternative candidate solutions.

TM-142

Characteristics	Candidate 1	Candidate 2	Candidate 3
Portion of System Computerized Brief description of that portion of the system that would be computerized in this candidate.	The scheduling and reporting subsystems would both be computerized.	Same as Candidate 1.	Same as Candidate 1.
Benefits Brief description of that portion of the system that would be computerized in this candidate.	Scheduling: This candidate will allow the schedules of all social workers to be consolidated. This will allow for easy identification of available meeting times. Schedules could be consolidated based on a number of options including, by day, week, or month. Reporting: Case/meeting information would be made readily available for each social worker. Thus, government and internal reporting requirements would be more easily fulfilled.	Scheduling: Same as Candidate 1. However, this candidate will also allow adhoc social worker schedule inquiries based upon a number of "subjects." Reporting: Same as Candidate 1.	Scheduling: Same as Candidate 2. Reporting: Same as Candidate 1.
Software Tools/Applications Needed Software tools needed to design or build the candidate (e.g., database management system, spreadsheet, word processor, terminal emulators, programming languages, etc.). Also, a brief description of software to be purchased, built, accessed, or some combination of these techniques.	This candidate would require that the scheduling subsystem be "purchased" in-house. The reporting subsystem would be built using spreadsheet template(s).	Same as Candidate 1 except: the scheduling subsystem would also be "built" in-house. The scheduling subsystem would be built using a database management system.	Both the scheduling and reporting subsystems would be "purchased."

Page 1 of 3

©Richard D. Irwin, Inc., 1994

Partially Completed Feasibility Matrix

A matrix is a very useful tool for specifying feasibility analyses for alternative candidate solutions.

Feasibility Criteria	Candidate 1	Candidate 2	Candidate 3
Operational Feasibility Brief description of the functionality: to what degree the candidate would benefit the organization and how well the system will work. Also, a brief description of the political feasibility: how well-received the solution would be from the owner's and user's perspectives.	A brief survey of scheduling packages revealed that such packages can provide the users with improved accessibility to information concerning social workers and cases/meetings. This solution should decrease the amount of time needed to schedule social workers. It is felt that management would be satisfied with this candidate only if the direct system users find the packaged application to their satisfaction.	Same as Candidate 1, except a few users will find the capability to do adhoc inquiries according to "subjects" of particular benefit.	Same as Candidate 2.
Technical Feasibility Brief assessment of the maturity, availability, and desirability of the computer technology needed to support the candidate. Also, an assessment of the technical expertise needed to develop, operate, and maintain the candidate.	There are numerous, highly rated scheduling packages available to date. Once the system users have been properly trained in the application, expertise requirements would be minimal. The same is true for spreadsheet reporting software and application.	The technology and expertise to build the scheduling and reporting subsystems are readily available.	Same as Candidate 1. There is also the added concern that no existing packages provides needed support for the reporting subsystem.
Economic Feasibility Cost to develop: Payback period (discounted): Net present value: Detailed calculations:	Approximately $1,000. Approximately 6 months. Approximately $8,300. See Attachment A.	Approximately $2,700. Approximately 2.5 years. Approximately $5,500. See Attachment B.	Approximately $1,500. Approximately 7 months. Approximately $9,000. See Attachment C.
Schedule Feasibility An assessment of how long the solution will take to design and implement.	Approximately 3 months.	Approximately 9 months.	Approximately 4 months.

©Richard D. Irwin, Inc., 1994

Sample Rankings Matrix

A matrix is a very useful tool for specifying the candidate that offers the "best" overall combination of feasibilities.

Feasibility Criteria	Candidate 1	Candidate 2	Candidate 3
Operational Feasibility	85	90	87
Technical Feasibility	90	90	87
Economic Feasibility	86	75	92
Scheduling Feasibility	90	82	90

©Richard D. Irwin, Inc., 1994

Request for Proposals (RFP)

This is an outline for a typical request for proposals.

Request for Proposals

I. Introduction.
   A. Background.
   B. Brief summary of needs.
   C. Explanation of RFP document.
   D. Call for action on part of vendor.

II. Standards and instructions.
   A. Schedule of events leading to contract.
   B. Ground rules that will govern selection decision.
      1. Who may talk with whom and when.
      2. Who pays for what.
      3. Required format for a proposal.
      4. Demonstration expectations.
      5. Contractual expectations.
      6. References expected.
      7. Documentation expectations.

III. Requirements and features.
   A. Hardware.
      1. Mandatory requirements, features, and criteria.
      2. Essential requirements, features, and criteria.
      3. Desirable requirements, features, and criteria.
   B. Software.
      1. Mandatory requirements, features, and criteria.
      2. Essential requirements, features, and criteria.
      3. Desirable requirements, features, and criteria.
   C. Service.
      1. Mandatory requirements.
      2. Essential requirements.
      3. Desirable requirements.

IV. Technical questionnaires.

V. Conclusion.

Data Entities and Attributes for SoundStage Entertainment Club

TM−146

CLUB:
    <u>CLUB NAME</u>
    NUMBER OF MEMBERS ENROLLED
    NUMBER CANCELED YTD
    CURRENT PROMOTION
    TOTAL UNITS SOLD FOR CLUB
    MAXIMUM PERIOD OF OBLIGATION

MEMBER:
    <u>MEMBER NUMBER</u> or <u>MEMBER NAME</u>
    MEMBER ADDRESS consisting of:
        STREET
        P.O. BOX
        CITY
        STATE
        ZIP CODE
    MEMBER PHONE
    DATE ENROLLED
    BALANCE PAST DUE
    BONUS CREDITS NOT USED
    CLUB GROUP (repeats 1-n times)
    consisting of:
        CLUB NAME
        MUSICAL/MOVIE PREFERENCE
        NUMBER OF PURCHASES REQUIRED
        NUMBER OF PURCHASES TO DATE
        AGREEMENT NUMBER SUFFIX
        AGREEMENT ENROLLMENT DATE
        AGREEMENT EXPIRATION DATE

AGREEMENT:
    <u>AGREEMENT NUMBER SUFFIX</u>
    CLUB NAME
    AGREEMENT EXPIRATION DATE
    AGREEMENT PLAN CREATION DATE
    MAXIMUM PERIOD OF OBLIGATION
    BONUS CREDITS AFTER OBLIGATION
    NUMBER OF MEMBERS ENROLLED
    NO. MEMBERS WHO HAVE FULFILLED
    NO. MEMBERS HAVE NOT FULFILLED

BACKORDER:
    <u>ORDERED NUMBER + BACKORDER DATE</u>
    BACKORDERED ITEM (repeats 1-n times)
    consisting of:
        PRODUCT NUMBER
        MEDIA CODE
        PRODUCT DESCRIPTION
        QUANTITY BACKORDERED

PROMOTION:
    <u>CLUB NAME + PROMOTION DATE</u>
    PROMOTION TYPE
    SELECTION OF MONTH NUMBER
    SELECTION OF MONTH TITLE
    AUTOMATIC RELEASE DATE
    AUTOMATIC FILL DATE

ORDER:
    <u>ORDER NUMBER</u>
    ORDER DATE
    ORDER STATUS
    PROMOTION NAME
    PROMOTION DATE
    AUTOMATIC FILL DATE
    MEMBER NUMBER
    MEMBER NAME
    FORMER MEMBER?
    MEMBER ADDRESS consisting of:
        STREET
        P.O. BOX
        CITY
        STATE
        ZIP CODE
    ORDERED PRODUCT (repeats 1-n times)
    consisting of:
        PRODUCT NUMBER
        MEDIA CODE
        PRODUCT DESCRIPTION
        QUANTITY ORDERED
        ORDERED PRODUCT STATUS
        QUANTITY SHIPPED
        ORDER PRICE
        EXTENDED PRICE
    AMOUNT DUE:

PRODUCT:
    <u>PRODUCT NUMBER + MEDIA CODE</u>
    PRODUCT DESCRIPTION
    TITLE OF WORK
    COPYRIGHT DATE
    CURRENT RETAIL PRICE
    CURRENT LIST PRICE
    SUPPLIER NAME
    SUPPLIER ADDRESS consisting of:
        STREET
        P.O. BOX
        CITY
        STATE
        ZIP CODE
    QUANTITY ON HAND
    UNITS SOLD
    VALUE OF UNITS SOLD

© Richard D. Irwin, Inc., 1994

Transformation of the MEMBER Entity into 1NF

TM–147

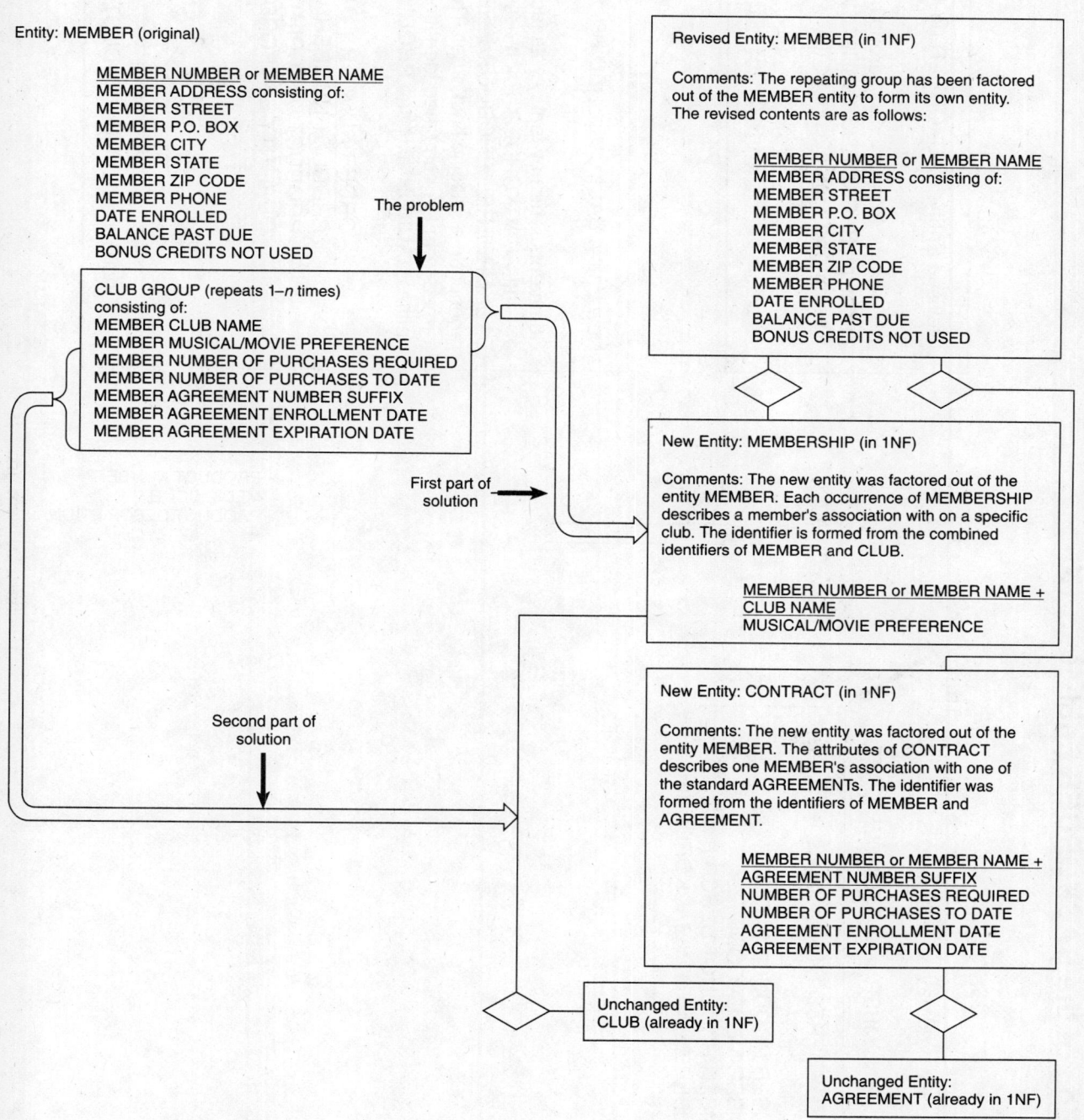

©Richard D. Irwin, Inc., 1994

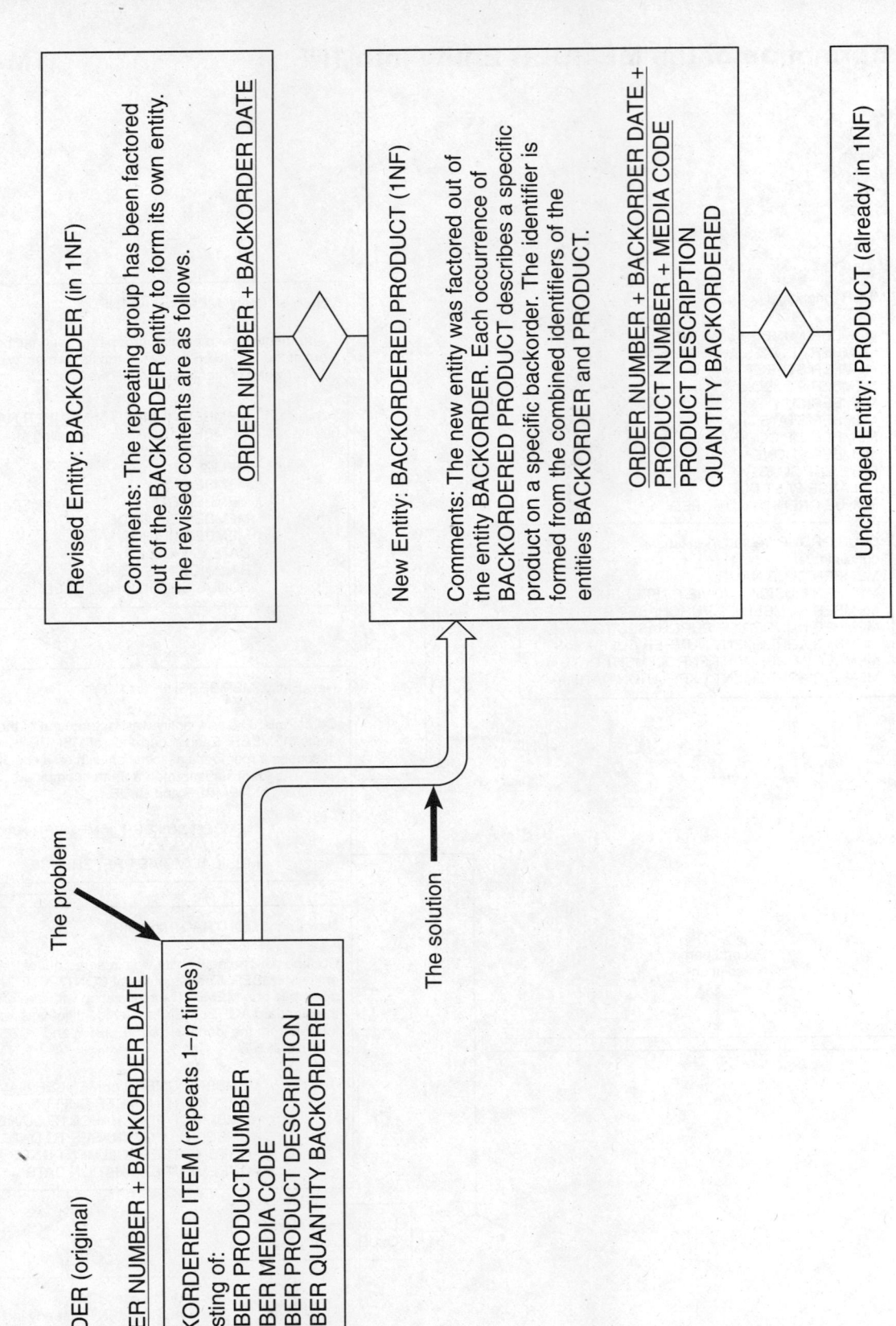

Analysis and Transformation of the ORDERED PRODUCT Entity into 2NF

This revision of our initial mapping shows how certain elements were moved from this concatenated key entity to the entity that they really describe.

Entity: ORDERED PRODUCT (in 1NF)

ORDER NUMBER +
PRODUCT NUMBER +
MEDIA CODE +
PRODUCT DESCRIPTION
QUANTITY ORDERED
ORDERED PRODUCT STATUS
QUANTITY SHIPPED
ORDER PRICE
EXTENDED PRICE

Revised Entity: ORDERED PRODUCT (in 2NF)

Comments: Several attributes in ORDERED PRODUCT have been removed since they did not describe a PRODUCT on an ORDER. Instead, they described PRODUCTs independent of any ORDER. The revised contents are as follows:

ORDER NUMBER +
PRODUCT NUMBER +
MEDIA CODE +
QUANTITY ORDERED
ORDERED PRODUCT STATUS
QUANTITY SHIPPED
EXTENDED PRICE

Unchanged Entity: PRODUCT (in 1NF)

Comments: The attribute PRODUCT DESCRIPTION was already part of the PRODUCT entity; therefore, the entity PRODUCT does not change as a result of the change to ORDERED PRODUCT.

Attributes that truly describe PRODUCT

TM–149

© Richard D. Irwin, Inc., 1994

Analysis and Transformation of Entities into 3NF

Attributes that can be derived from other attributes in the same entity have either been deleted or removed (or merged) into a separate entity that they really describe.

Entity: ORDERED PRODUCT (in 2NF)

ORDER NUMBER +
PRODUCT NUMBER +
MEDIA CODE +
QUANTITY ORDERED
ORDERED PRODUCT STATUS
QUANTITY SHIPPED
ORDER PRICE
EXTENDED PRICE

Revised Entity: ORDERED PRODUCT (in 3NF)

Comments: The attribute EXTENDED PRICE was deleted since it can be calculated from the attributes QUANTITY ORDERED and ORDER PRICE.

ORDER NUMBER +
PRODUCT NUMBER +
MEDIA CODE +
QUANTITY ORDERED
ORDERED PRODUCT STATUS
QUANTITY SHIPPED
ORDER PRICE

Entity: AGREEMENT (in 2NF)

AGREEMENT NUMBER SUFFIX
CLUB NAME
AGREEMENT EXPIRATION DATE
AGREEMENT PLAN CREATION DATE
MAXIMUM PERIOD OF OBLIGATION
BONUS CREDITS AFTER OBLIGATION
NUMBER OF MEMBERS ENROLLED
NO. MEMBERS WHO HAVE FULFILLED
NO. MEMBERS HAVE NOT FULFILLED

Entity: AGREEMENT (in 3NF)

Comments: NO. MEMBERS HAVE NOT FULFILLED was deleted since it could be calculated from NO. MEMBERS WHO HAVE FULFILLED and NUMBER OF MEMBERS ENROLLED.

AGREEMENT NUMBER SUFFIX
CLUB NAME
AGREEMENT EXPIRATION DATE
AGREEMENT PLAN CREATION DATE
MAXIMUM PERIOD OF OBLIGATION
BONUS CREDITS AFTER OBLIGATION
NUMBER OF MEMBERS ENROLLED
NO. MEMBERS WHO HAVE FULFILLED

TM-150

© Richard D. Irwin, Inc., 1994

Further Simplification through Inspection
Attributes that are synonyms represent implied redundancy and must be removed.

Entity: PROMOTION (last seen in 1NF, but also in 2NF and 3NF)

<u>CLUB NAME + PROMOTION DATE</u>
PROMOTION TYPE
SELECTION OF MONTH NUMBER
SELECTION OF MONTH TITLE
SELECTION OF MONTH MEDIA CODE
AUTOMATIC RELEASE DATE
AUTOMATIC FILL DATE

Revised Entity: PROMOTION (in 3NF)

Comments: The synonyms SELECTION OF MONTH NUMBER (= PRODUCT NUMBER in the TITLE entity) and SELECTION OF MONTH TITLE (= TITLE OF WORK in the TITLE entity) have been deleted and replaced with a new relationship back to the TITLE entity. The AUTOMATIC FILL DATE appeared as a non-identifier attribute in ORDER and PROMOTION. This attribute differs; thus, it was renamed within the PROMOTION entity.

<u>CLUB NAME + PROMOTION DATE</u>
PROMOTION TYPE
AUTOMATIC RELEASE DATE
PROMO AUTOMATIC FILL DATE

Unchanged Entity: TITLE (already in 3NF)

©Richard D. Irwin, Inc., 1994

TM–151

Final Entity Relationship Data Model

TM-152

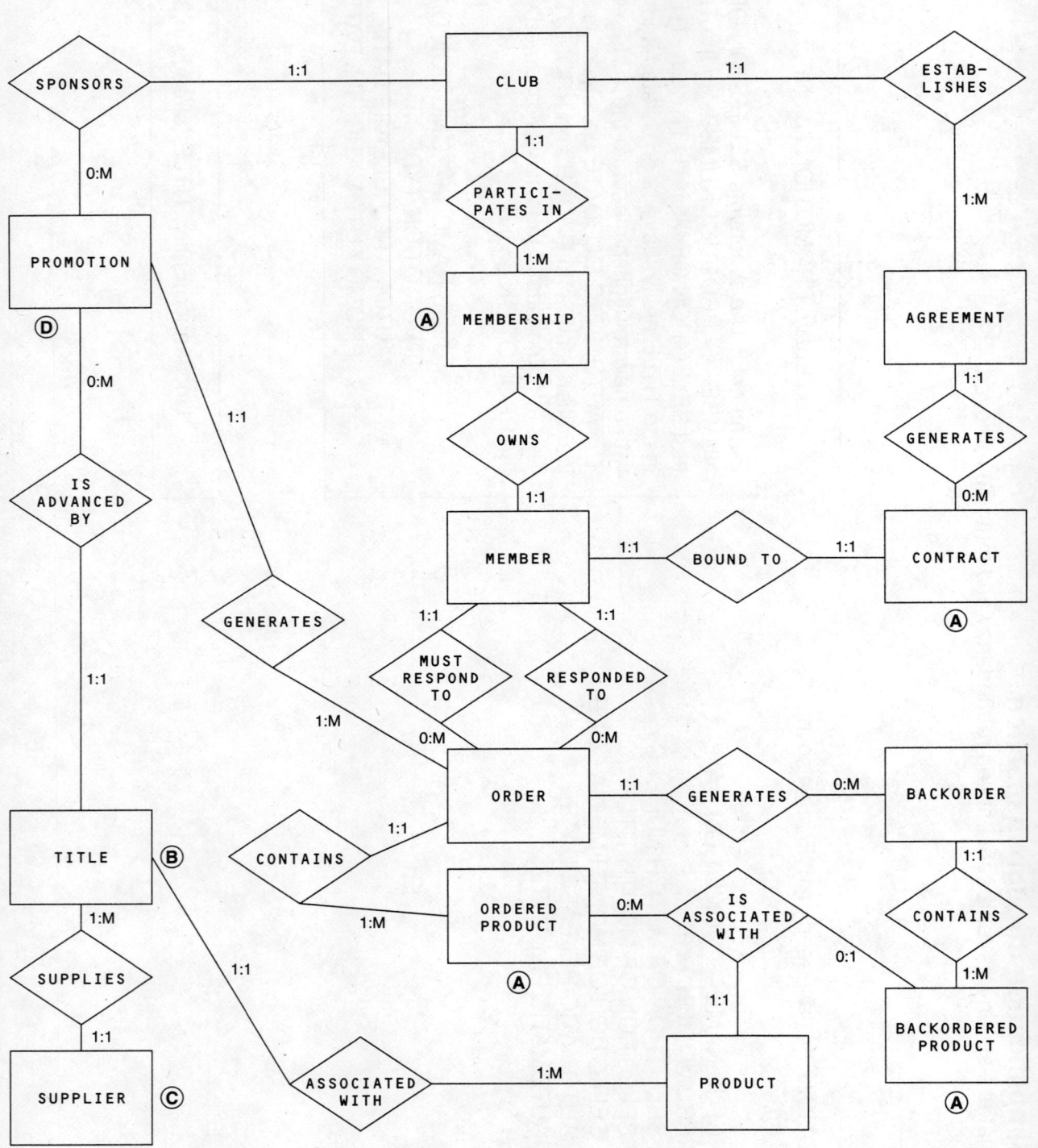

©Richard D. Irwin, Inc., 1994

Final Mapping of Data Attributes to Data Entities

TM–153

Entity: MEMBER

    <u>MEMBER NUMBER</u> or <u>MEMBER NAME</u>
    MEMBER ADDRESS consisting of:
        STREET
        P.O. BOX
        CITY
        STATE
        ZIP CODE
    MEMBER PHONE
    DATE ENROLLED
    BALANCE PAST DUE
    BONUS CREDITS NOT USED
    FORMER MEMBER?

Entity: ORDER

    <u>ORDER NUMBER</u>
    ORDER DATE
    ORDER STATUS
    AUTOMATIC FILL DATE
    AMOUNT DUE

Entity: ORDERED PRODUCT

    <u>ORDER NUMBER +</u>
    <u>PRODUCT NUMBER +</u>
    <u>MEDIA CODE</u>
    QUANTITY ORDERED
    ORDERED PRODUCT STATUS
    QUANTITY SHIPPED
    ORDER PRICE

Entity: PRODUCT

    <u>PRODUCT NUMBER + MEDIA CODE</u>
    PRODUCT DESCRIPTION
    CURRENT RETAIL PRICE
    CURRENT LIST PRICE
    QUANTITY ON HAND
    UNITS SOLD
    VALUE OF UNITS SOLD

Entity: BACKORDER

    <u>ORDER NUMBER + BACKORDER DATE</u>

Entity: BACKORDERED PRODUCT

    <u>ORDER NUMBER + BACKORDER DATE +</u>
    <u>PRODUCT NUMBER + MEDIA CODE</u>
    QUANTITY BACKORDERED

Entity: PROMOTION

    <u>CLUB NAME + PROMOTION DATE</u>
    PROMOTION TYPE
    AUTOMATIC RELEASE DATE
    PROMO AUTOMATIC FILL DATE

Entity: CLUB

    <u>CLUB NAME</u>
    NUMBER OF MEMBERS ENROLLED
    NUMBER CANCELED YTD
    CURRENT PROMOTION
    TOTAL UNITS SOLD FOR CLUB
    MAXIMUM PERIOD OF OBLIGATION

Entity: MEMBERSHIP

    <u>MEMBER NUMBER</u> or <u>MEMBER NAME +</u>
    <u>CLUB NAME</u>
    MUSICAL/MOVIE PREFERENCE

Entity: AGREEMENT

    <u>AGREEMENT NUMBER SUFFIX</u>
    AGREEMENT EXPIRATION DATE
    AGREEMENT PLAN CREATION DATE
    MAXIMUM PERIOD OF OBLIGATION
    BONUS CREDITS AFTER OBLIGATION
    NUMBER OF MEMBERS ENROLLED
    NO. MEMBERS WHO HAVE FULFILLED

Entity: CONTRACT

    <u>MEMBER NUMBER</u> or <u>MEMBER NAME +</u>
    <u>AGREEMENT NUMBER SUFFIX</u>
    NUMBER OF PURCHASES REQUIRED
    NUMBER OF PURCHASES TO DATE
    CONTRACT ENROLLMENT DATE
    CONTRACT EXPIRATION DATE

Entity: SUPPLIER

    <u>SUPPLIER NUMBER</u>
    SUPPLIER NAME
    SUPPLIER ADDRESS consisting of:
        STREET
        P.O. BOX
        CITY
        STATE
        ZIP CODE

Entity: BACKORDERED PRODUCT

    <u>PRODUCT NUMBER</u>
    TITLE OF WORK
    COPYRIGHT DATE

© Richard D. Irwin, Inc., 1994

Sample Table for Recording Event Analysis

TM-154

Ⓐ Entity Name	Ⓑ Event Description	Ⓒ Event Name	Ⓓ CRUD	Ⓔ Condition(s)

© Richard D. Irwin, Inc., 1994

Partially Completed Event Analysis Table

This table contains the event analysis of the data entity PROMOTION and a portion of the event analysis for the entity ORDERS.

Entity Name	Event Description	Event Name	CRUD	Condition(s)
PROMOTION	1. The Marketing Department submits promotion cancellations.	PROMOTION CANCELLATION	D	1. There must be no existing, corresponding occurrences of the entity ORDER.
	2. The Marketing Department provides information about new promotions for the month.	NEW MONTHLY PROMOTION Ⓐ	A	1. A corresponding occurrence of the entity TITLE must already exist. 2. A corresponding occurrence of the entity CLUB must already exist.
	3. The Marketing Department notifies Customer Services of changes to existing promotions.	PROMOTION CHANGES	U	1. None Note: Modifications/updates can affect either of the following attributes: Ⓒ AUTOMATIC RELEASE DATE PROMO AUTOMATIC FILL DATE Ⓑ
ORDERS	1. The Marketing Department notifies Customer Services of promotions for the next month.	NEW MONTHLY PROMOTION	A	1. A corresponding occurrence of the entity MEMBER must already exist. 2. A corresponding occurrence of the entity PROMOTION must already exist.

TM–155

©Richard D. Irwin, Inc., 1994

Sample CASE Tool Entry for Event Analysis

TM-156

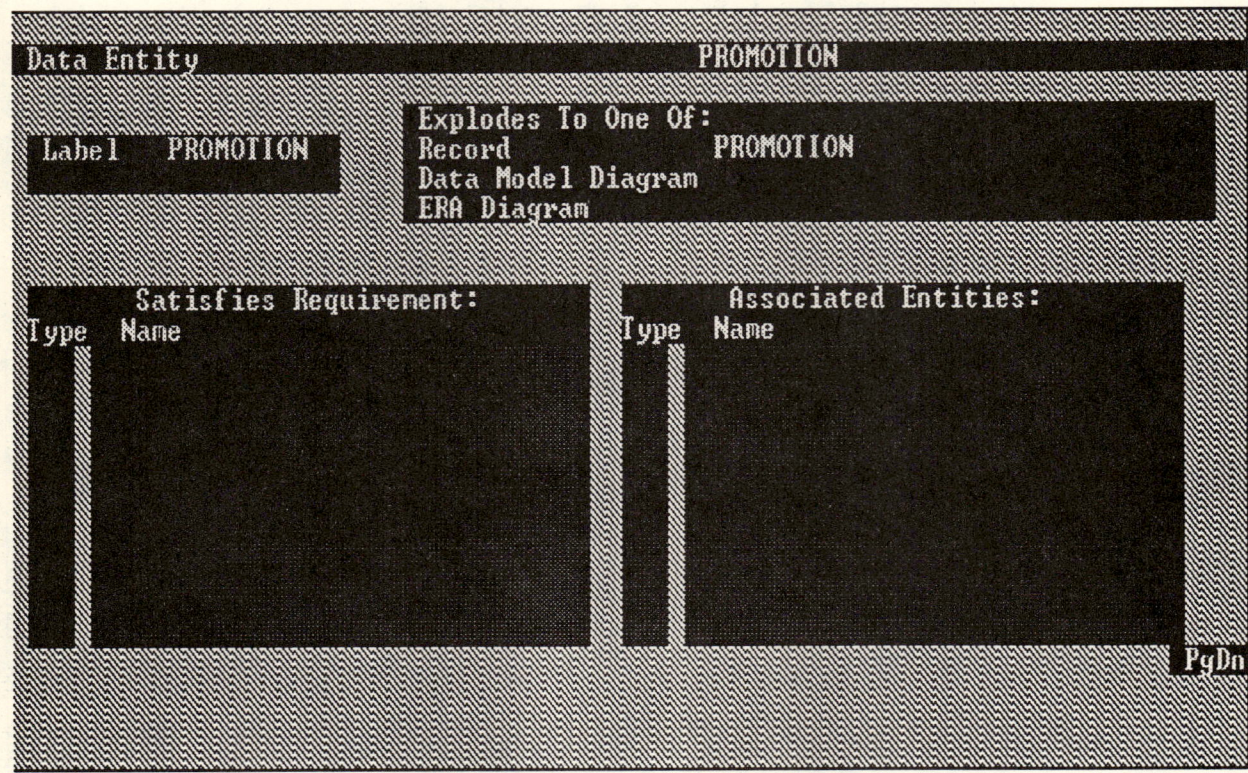

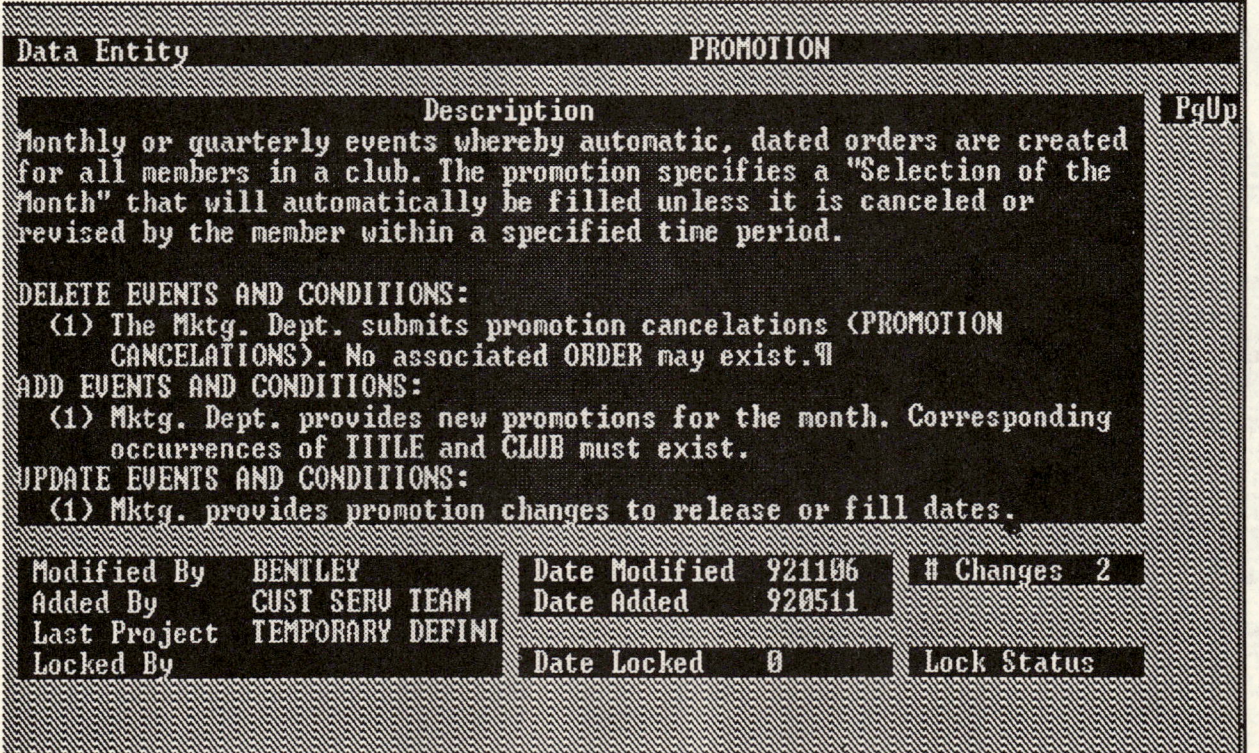

© Richard D. Irwin, Inc., 1994

Revised DFD for PROMOTION Subsystem

TM-157

This DFD, initially developed in the survey phase, has been revised to reflect implications of data and event analysis.

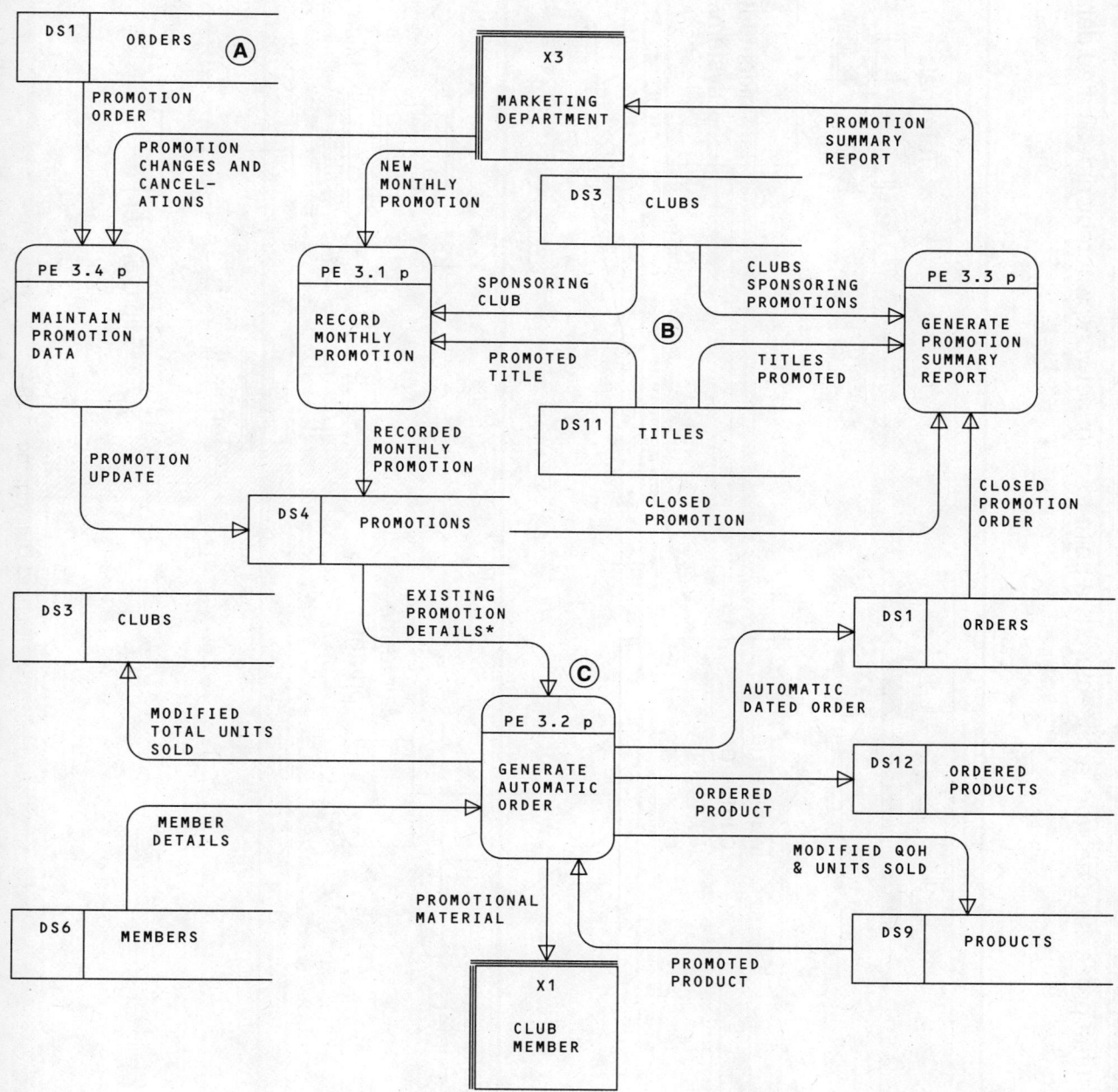

© Richard D. Irwin, Inc., 1994

Point-to-Point Network

The simplest distributed processing network architecture is a point-to-point network, whereby a dedicated data path is placed between two devices.

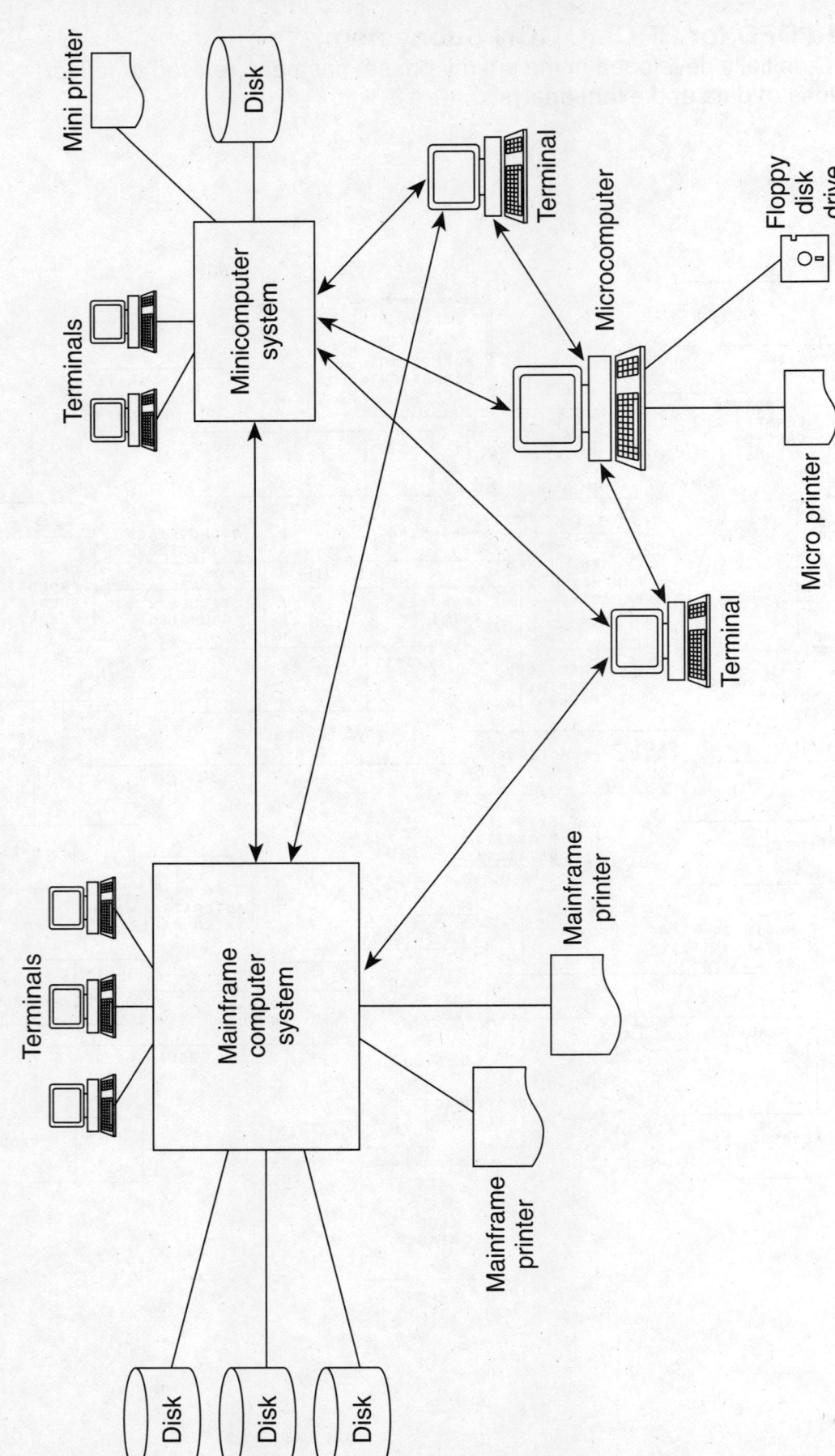

Bus Network

A bus network is similar to point-to-point networks except that multiple devices share a single point-to-point pathway.

TM-159

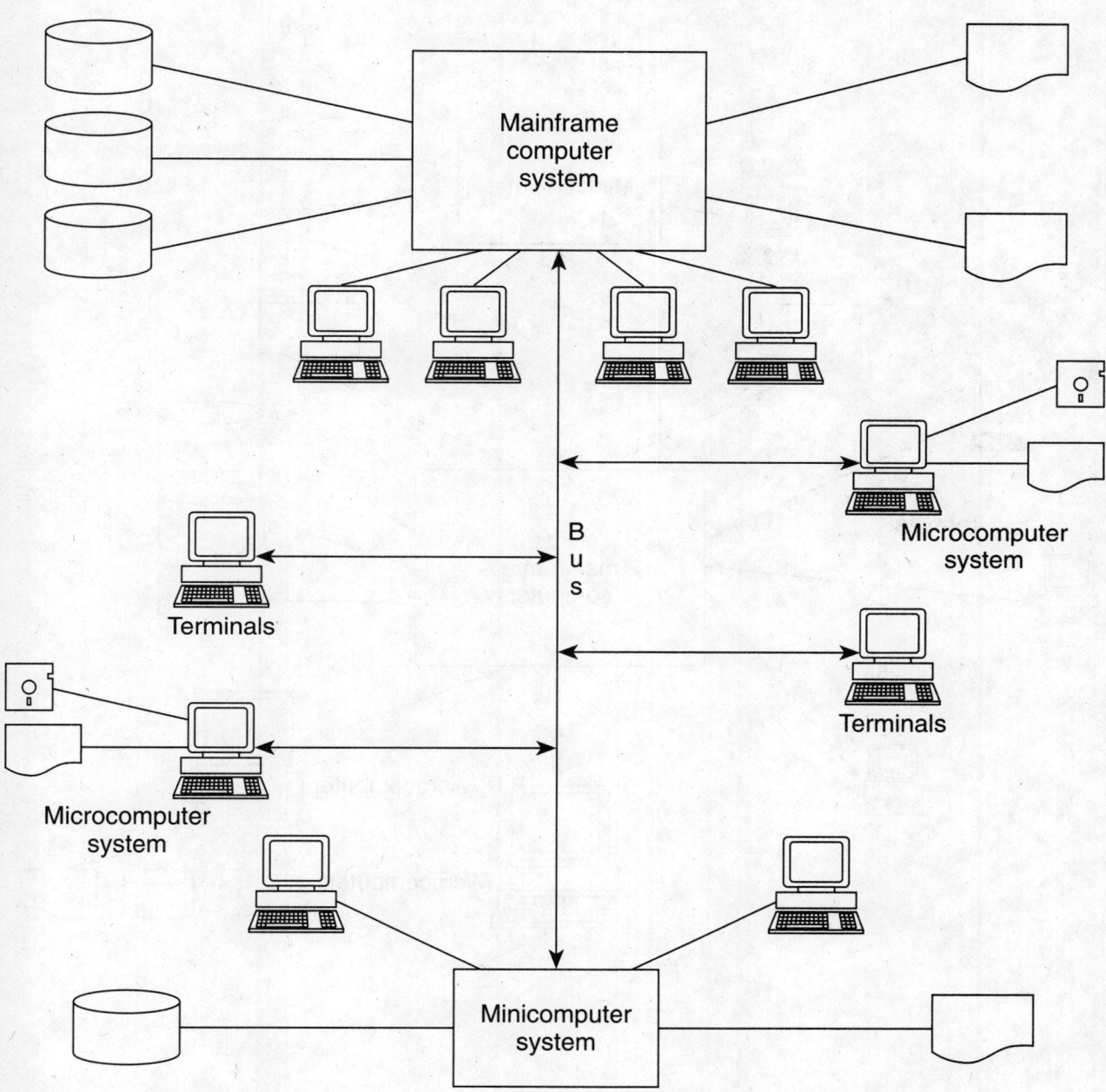

©Richard D. Irwin, Inc., 1994

Star Network
In a star network, a central computer plays traffic cop to satellite processors and devices that are trying to communicate with each other and with the central computer.

TM-160

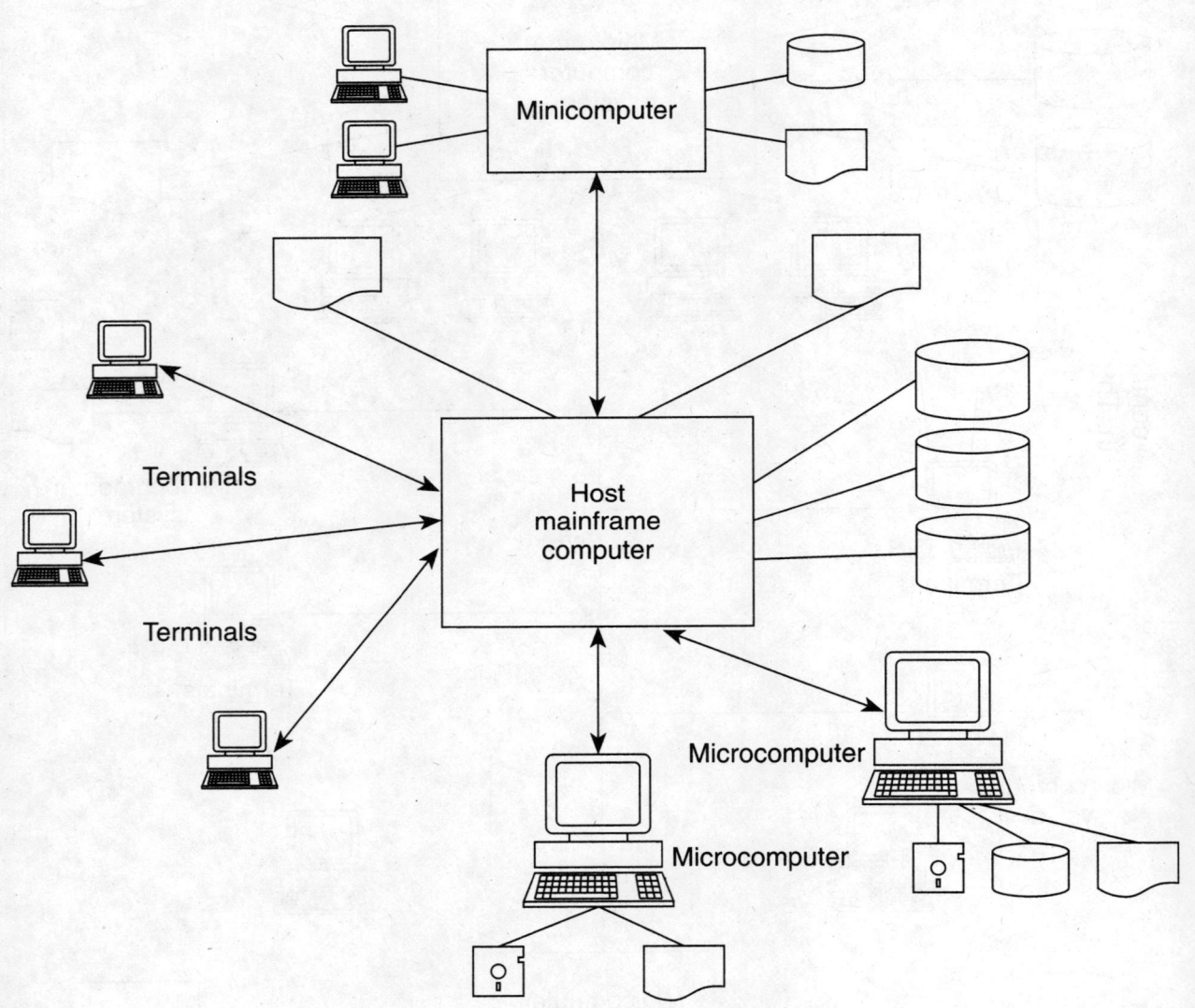

Hierarchical Network

Hierarchical networks, such as IBM's SNA, use a host computer to control satellite processors and devices, which in turn may control other satellite processors and devices, and so forth. The host computer supervises the entire network.

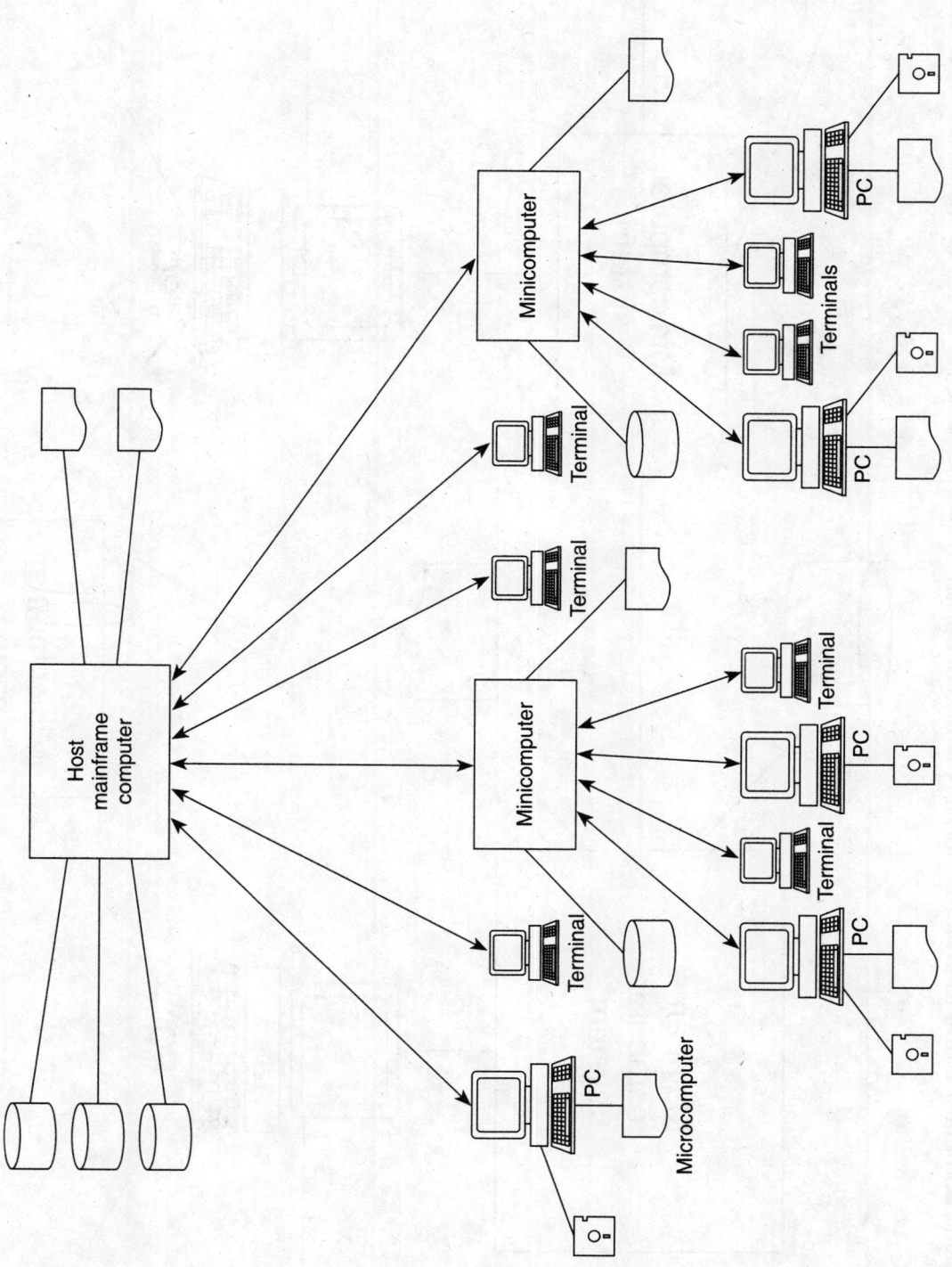

© Richard D. Irwin, Inc., 1994

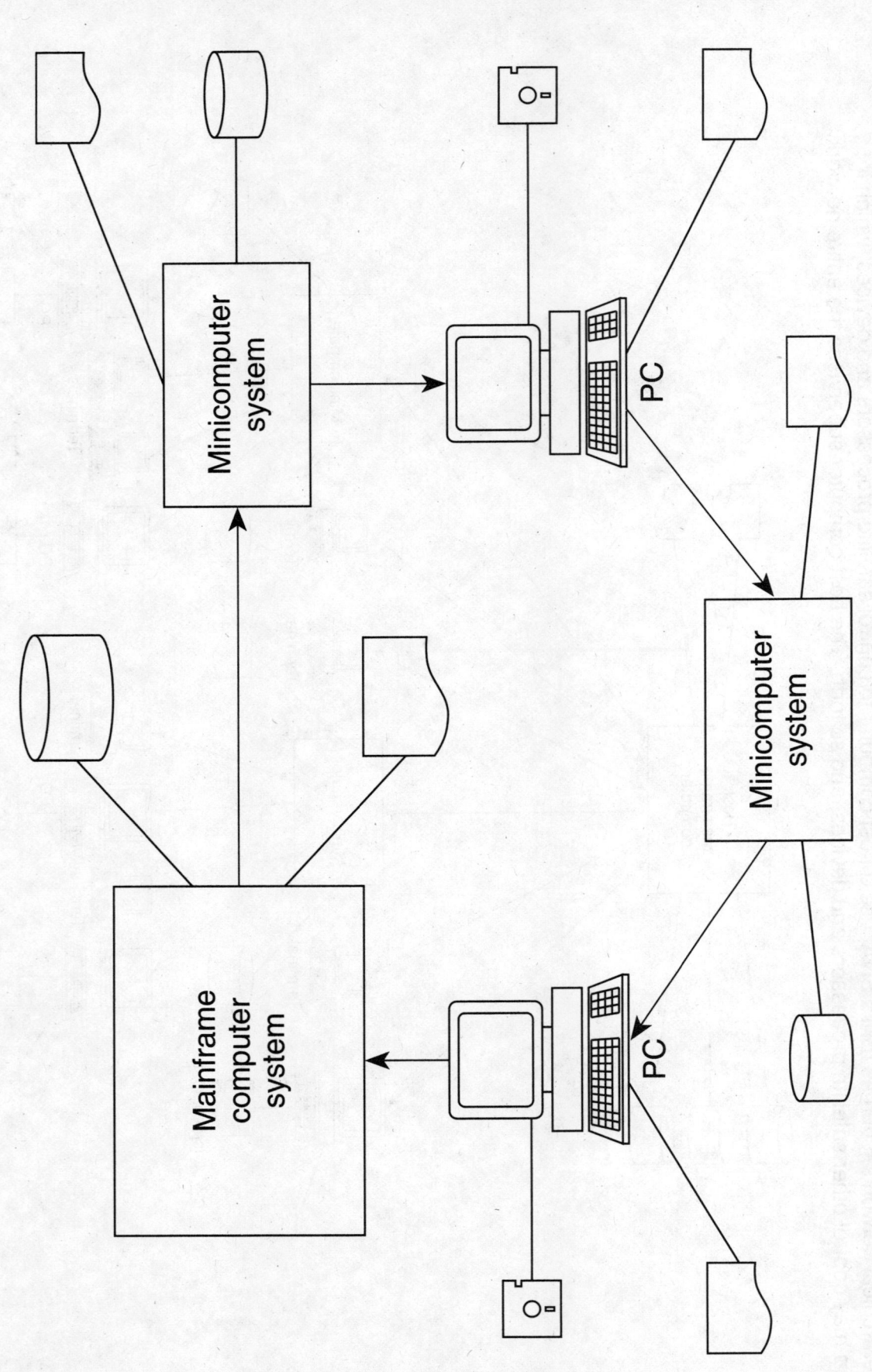

Ring Network
Ring networks link computers, one to another, but only in one direction.

Diverging Data Flows
Diverging data flows on implementation DFDs indicate the common design decision to use multipart forms.

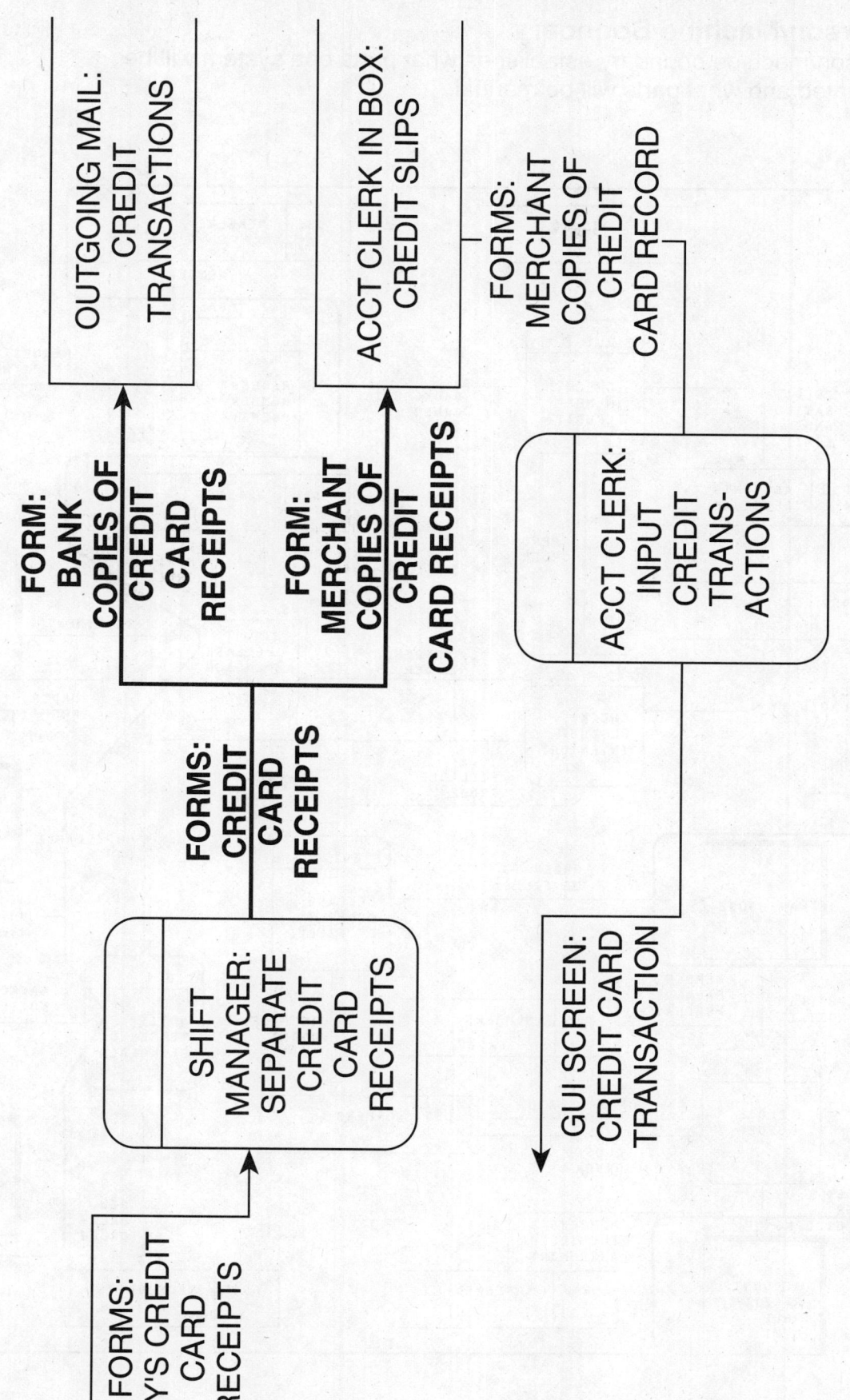

TM–163

©Richard D. Irwin, Inc., 1994

A Person/Machine Boundary

A person/machine boundary establishes what parts of a system will be automated and what parts will be manual.

TM-164

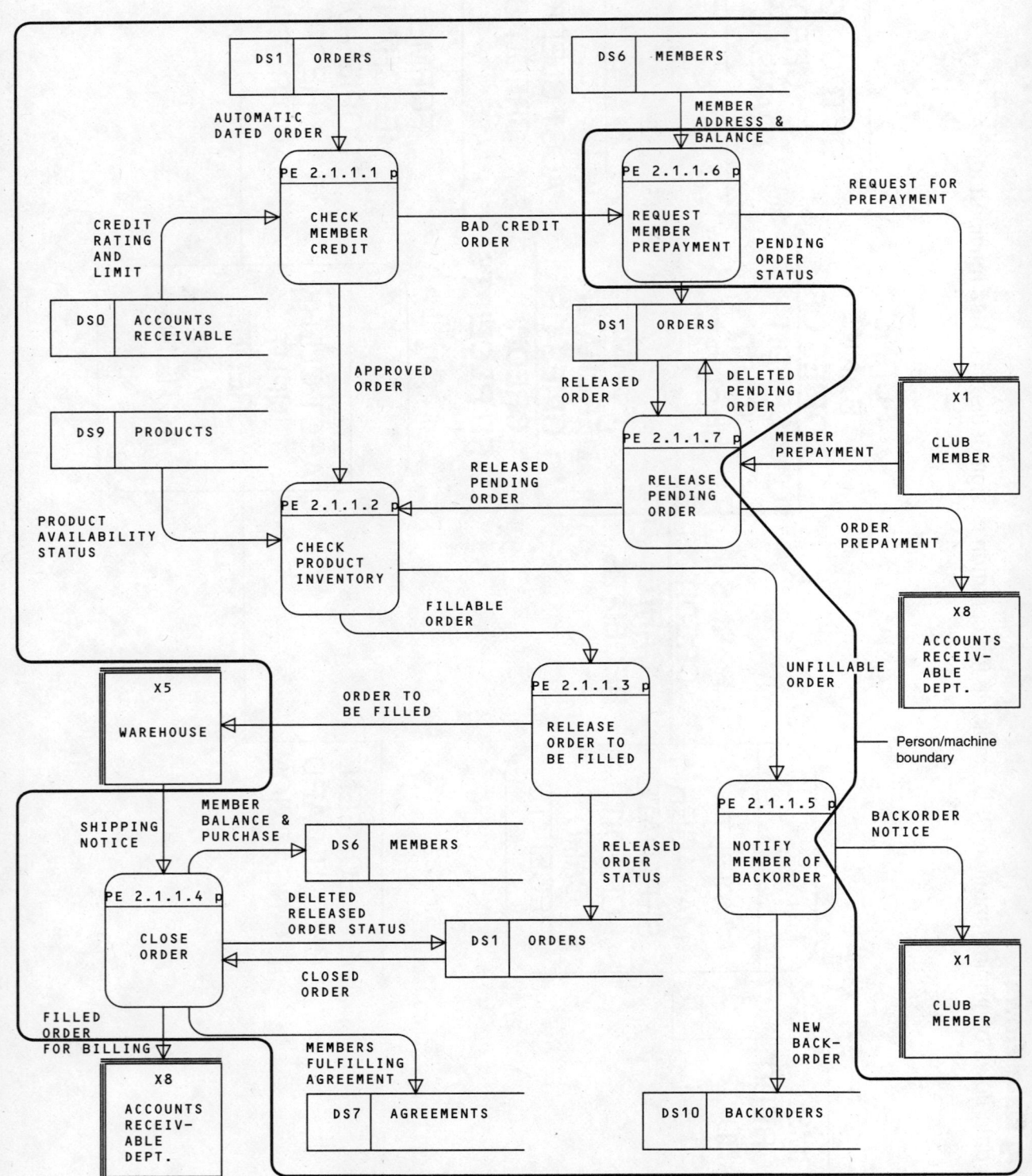

©Richard D. Irwin, Inc., 1994

A Manual Design Unit

This implementation DFD documents a manual design unit factored out of an essential DFD.

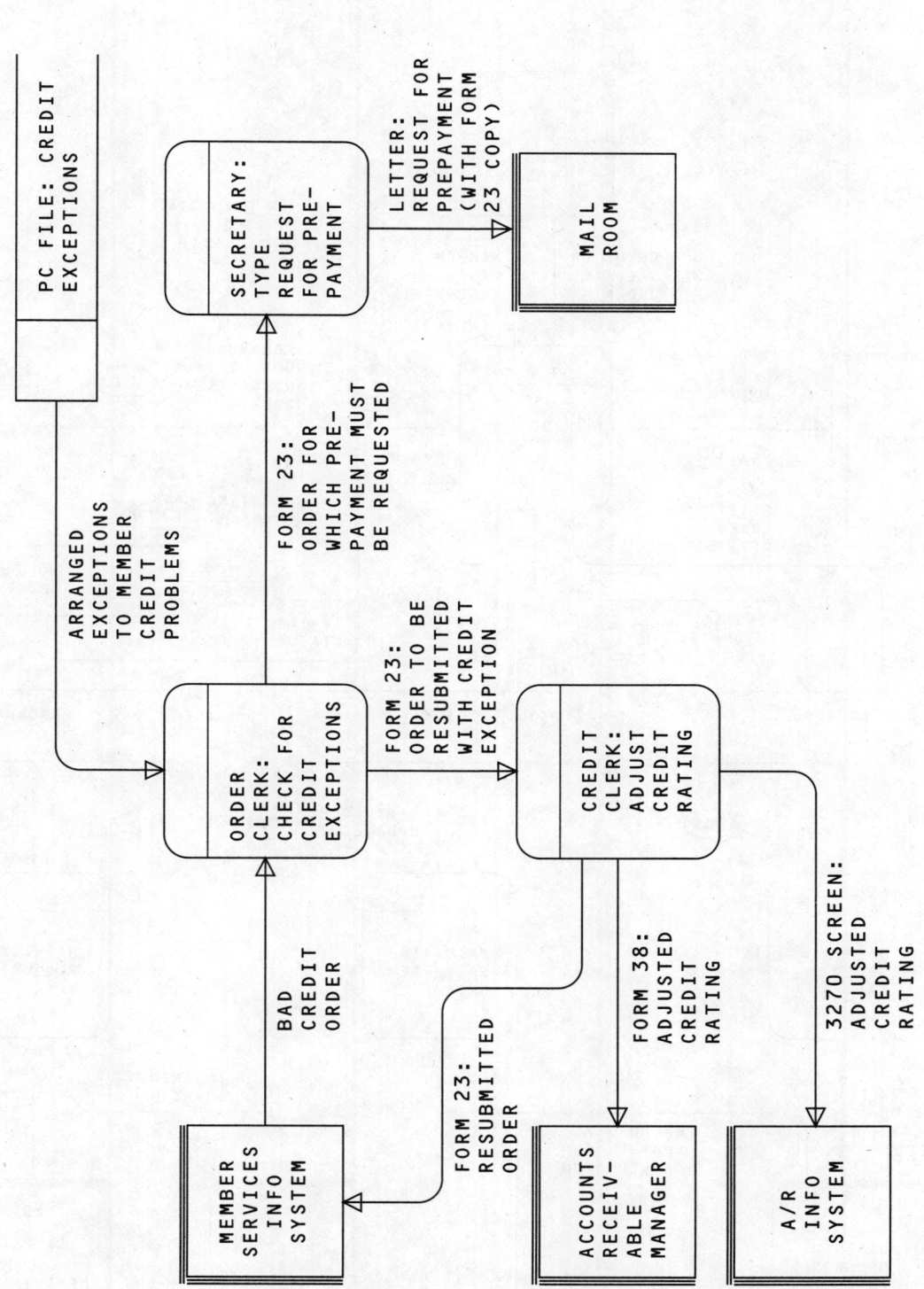

TM-165

Analyzing Response-Time Requirements

This essential DFD has been annotated to indicate which data flows must be made available immediately on demand (IOD) and which may be made available as soon as possible (ASAP).

TM-166

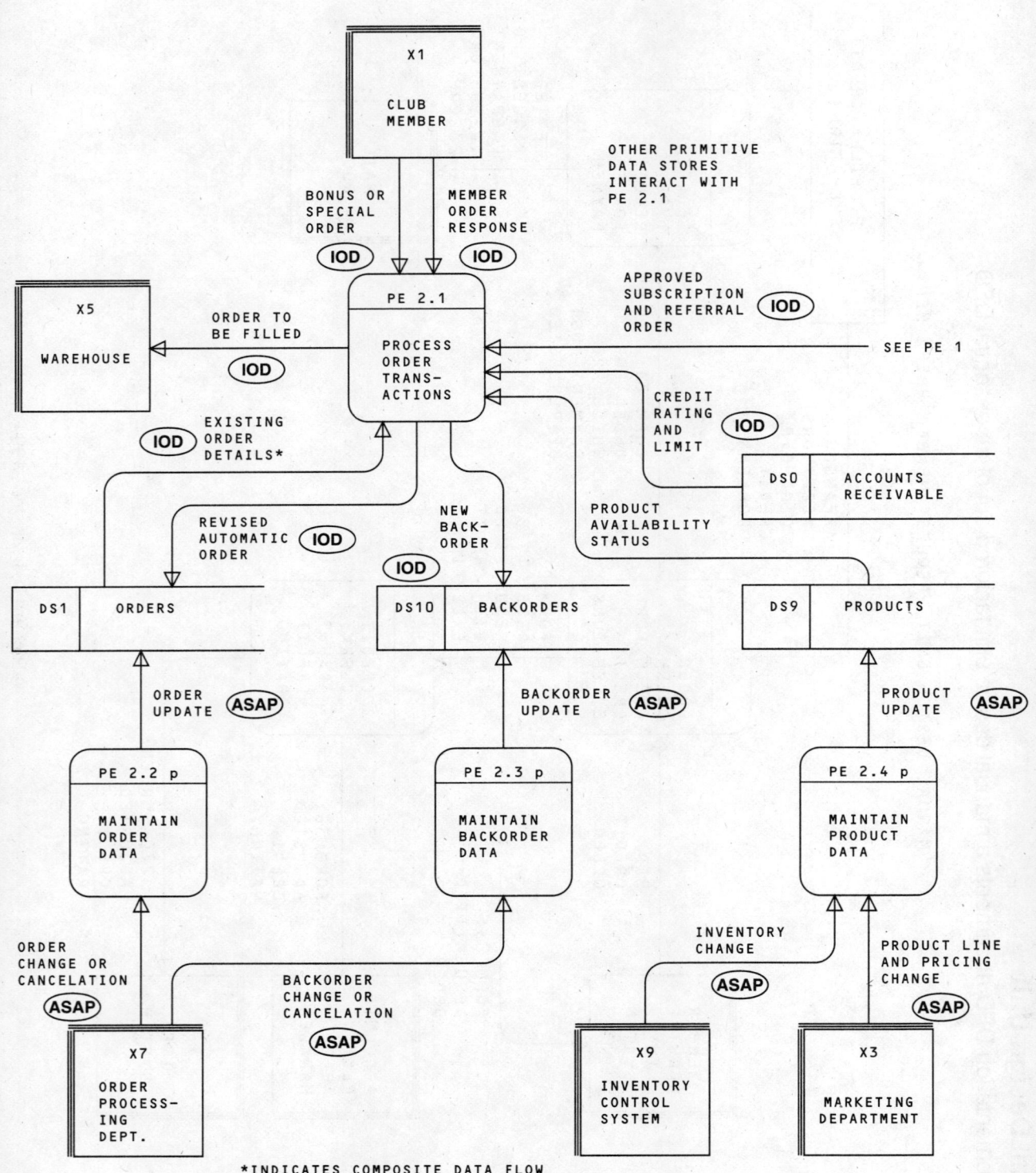

An On-Line Design Unit

This on-line design unit (implementation DFD) was factored out of the annotated DFD in Figure 14.12.

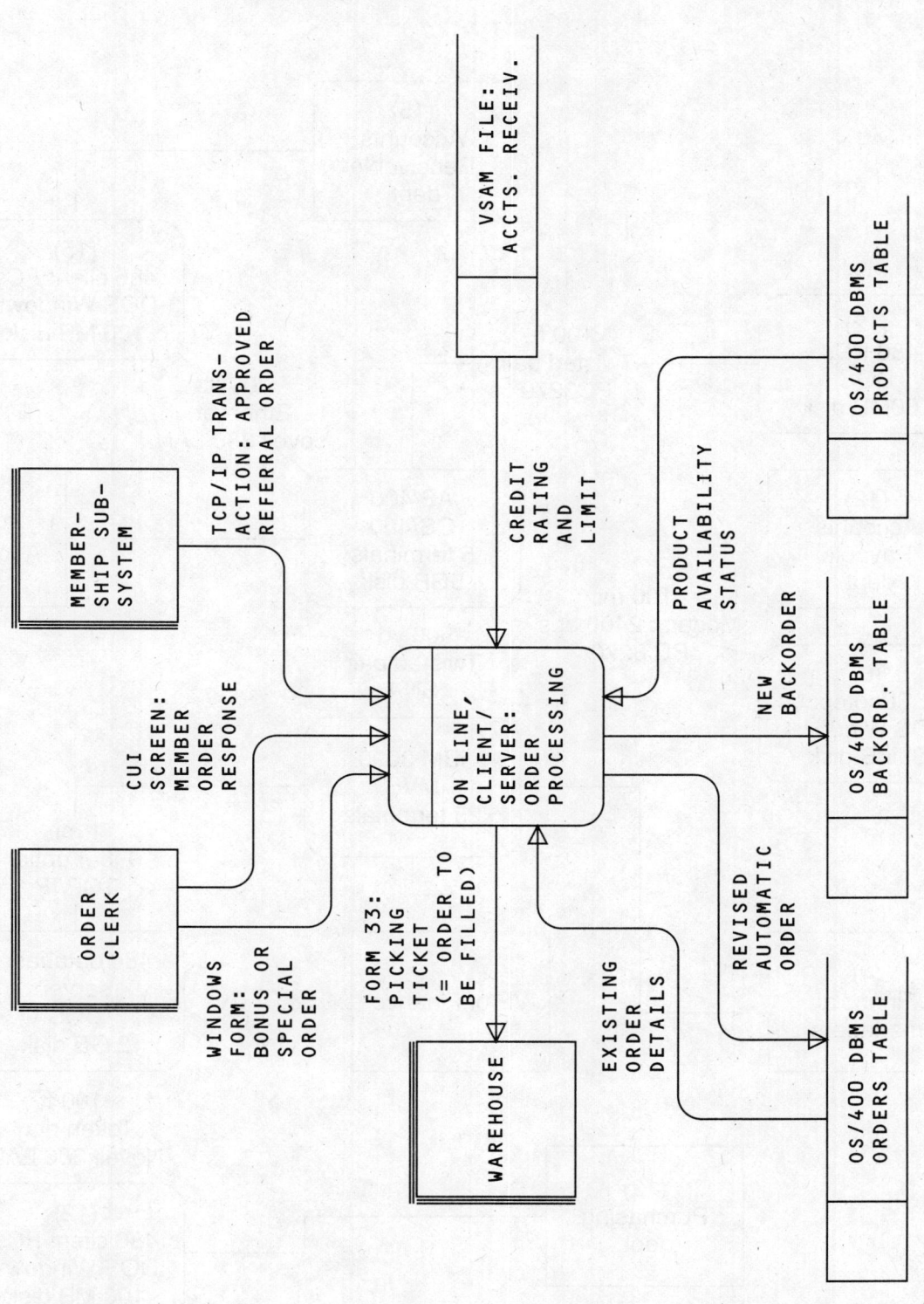

A Network Topology DFD
This figure demonstrates the use of a DFD to document a network topology.

TM–168

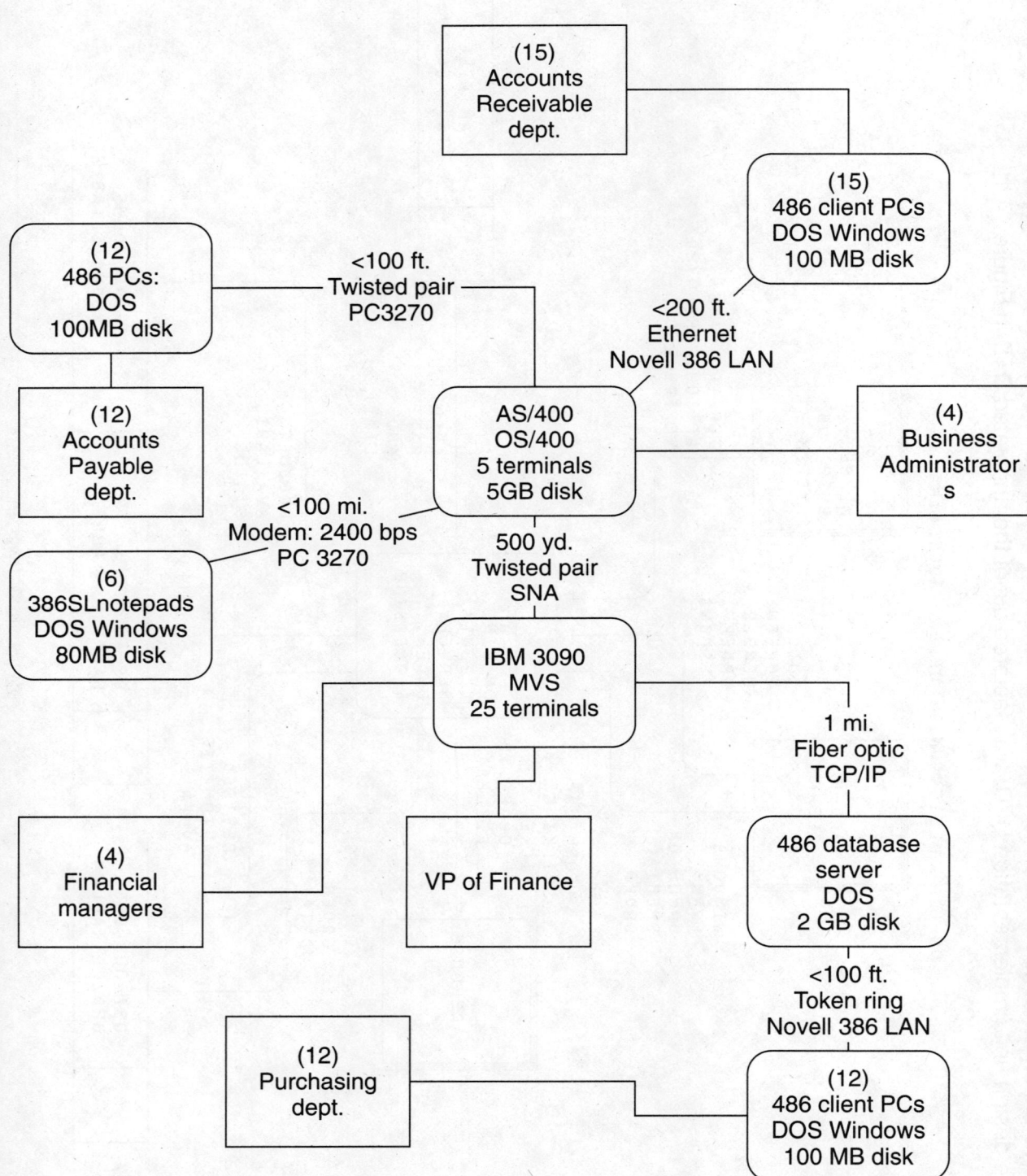

©Richard D. Irwin, Inc., 1994

A Network Topology DFD
This figure documents the topology of the SoundStage network.

TM-169

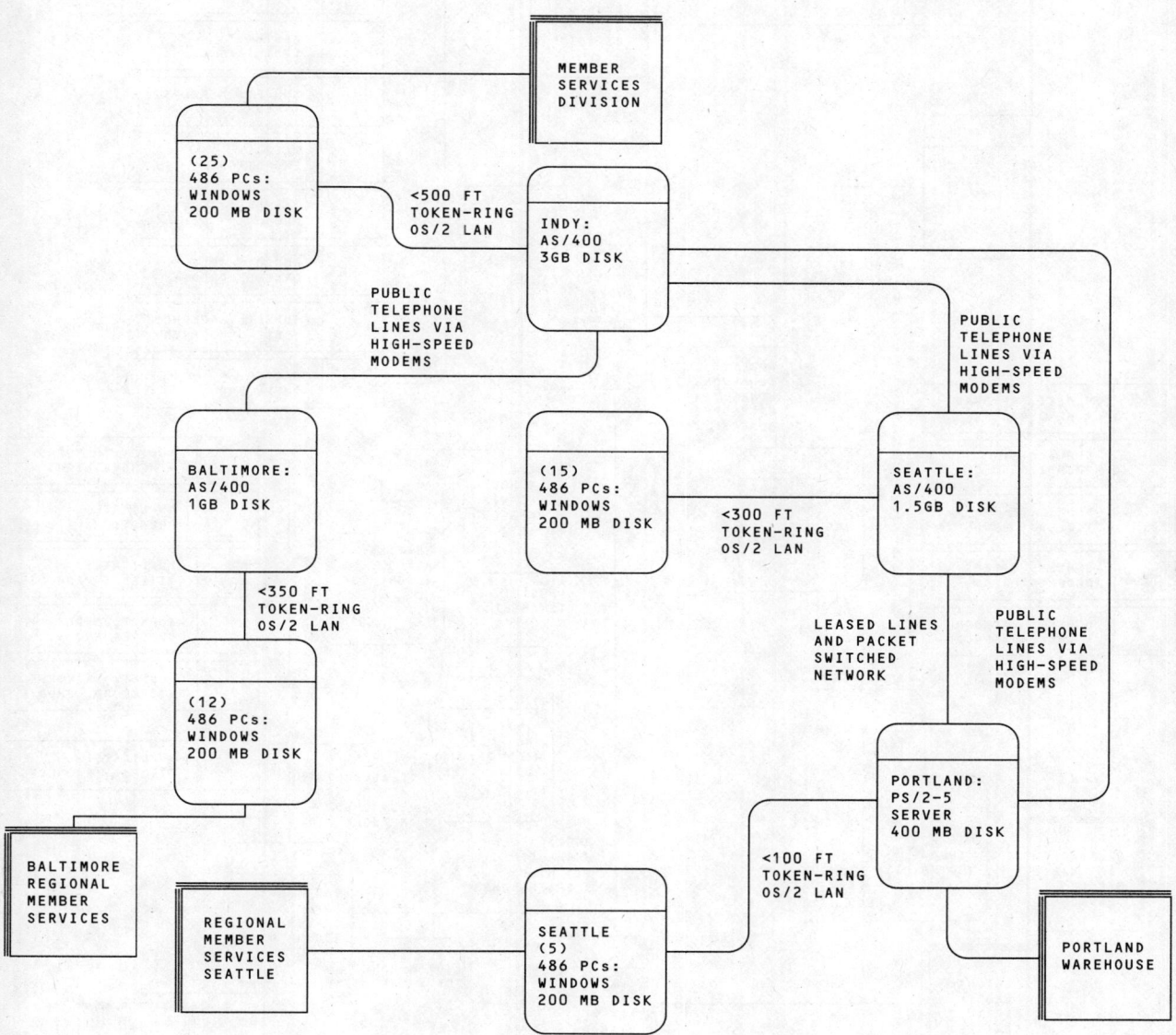

© Richard D. Irwin, Inc., 1994

Distributed Data Stores

This figure documents the data store distribution for the SoundStage application.

TM-170

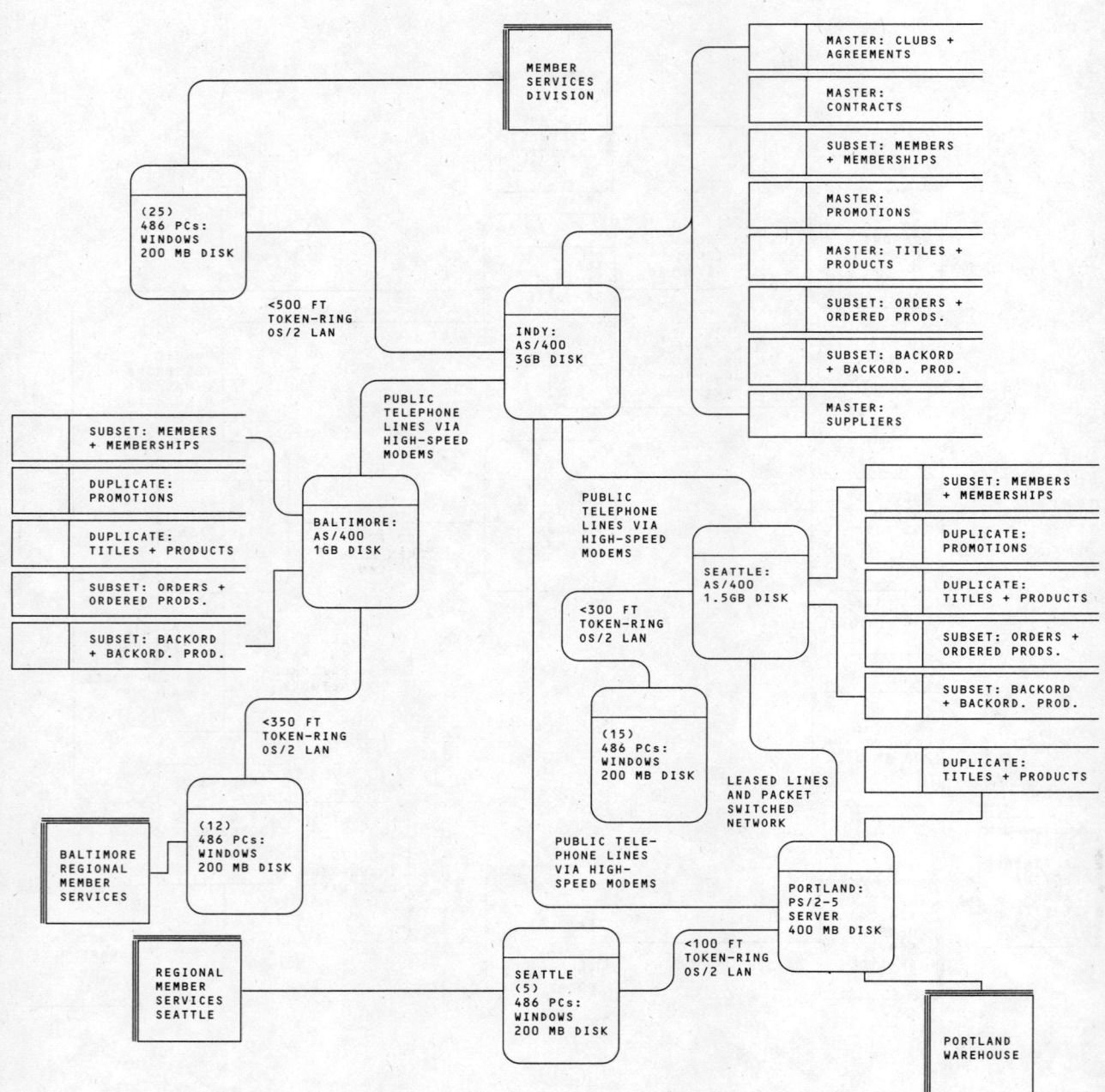

©Richard D. Irwin, Inc., 1994

Distributed Processes

This figure documents the process distribution for the SoundStage application.

TM-171

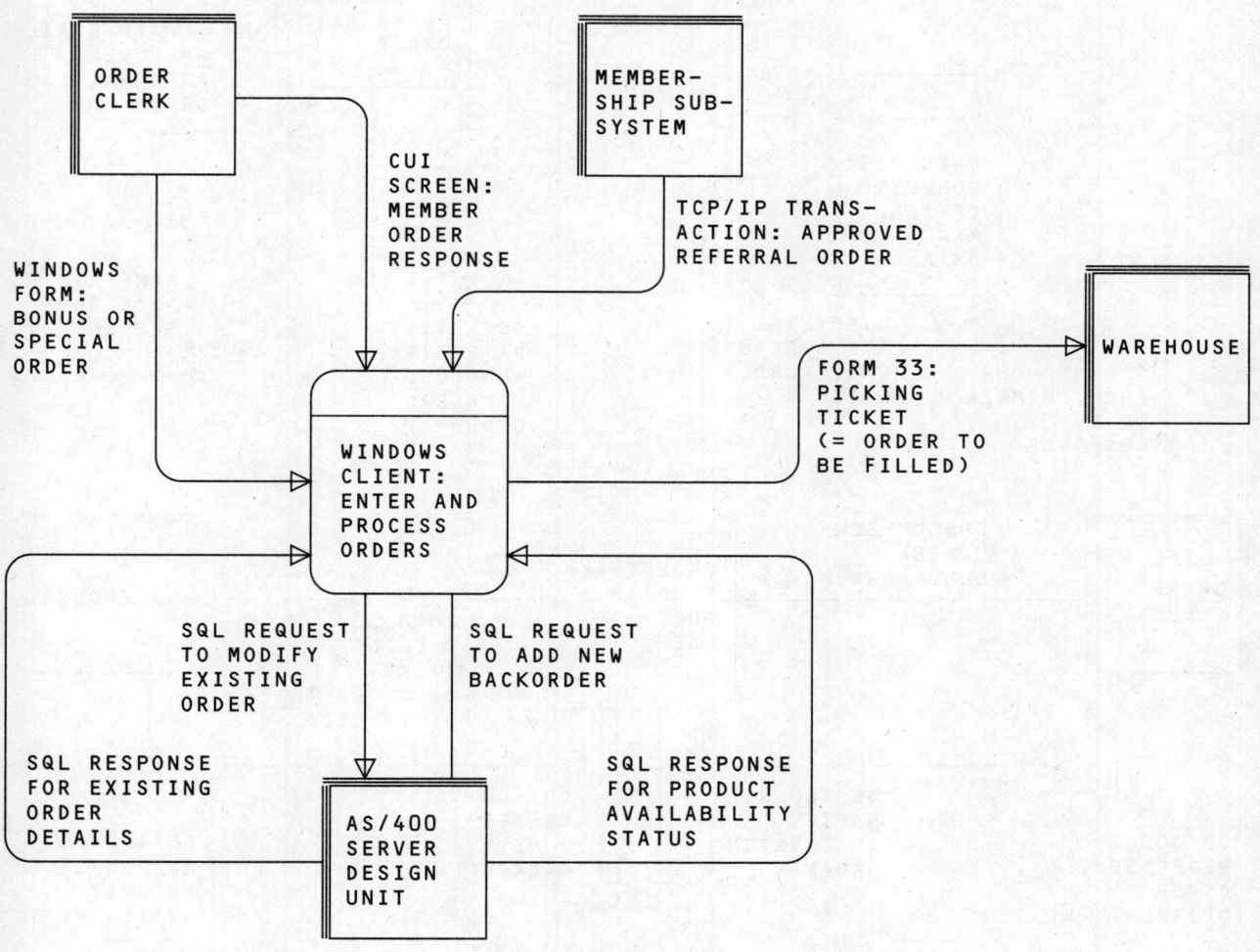

© Richard D. Irwin, Inc., 1994

A Final Design Unit DFD
This figure documents one of many final design unit DFDs.

TM-172

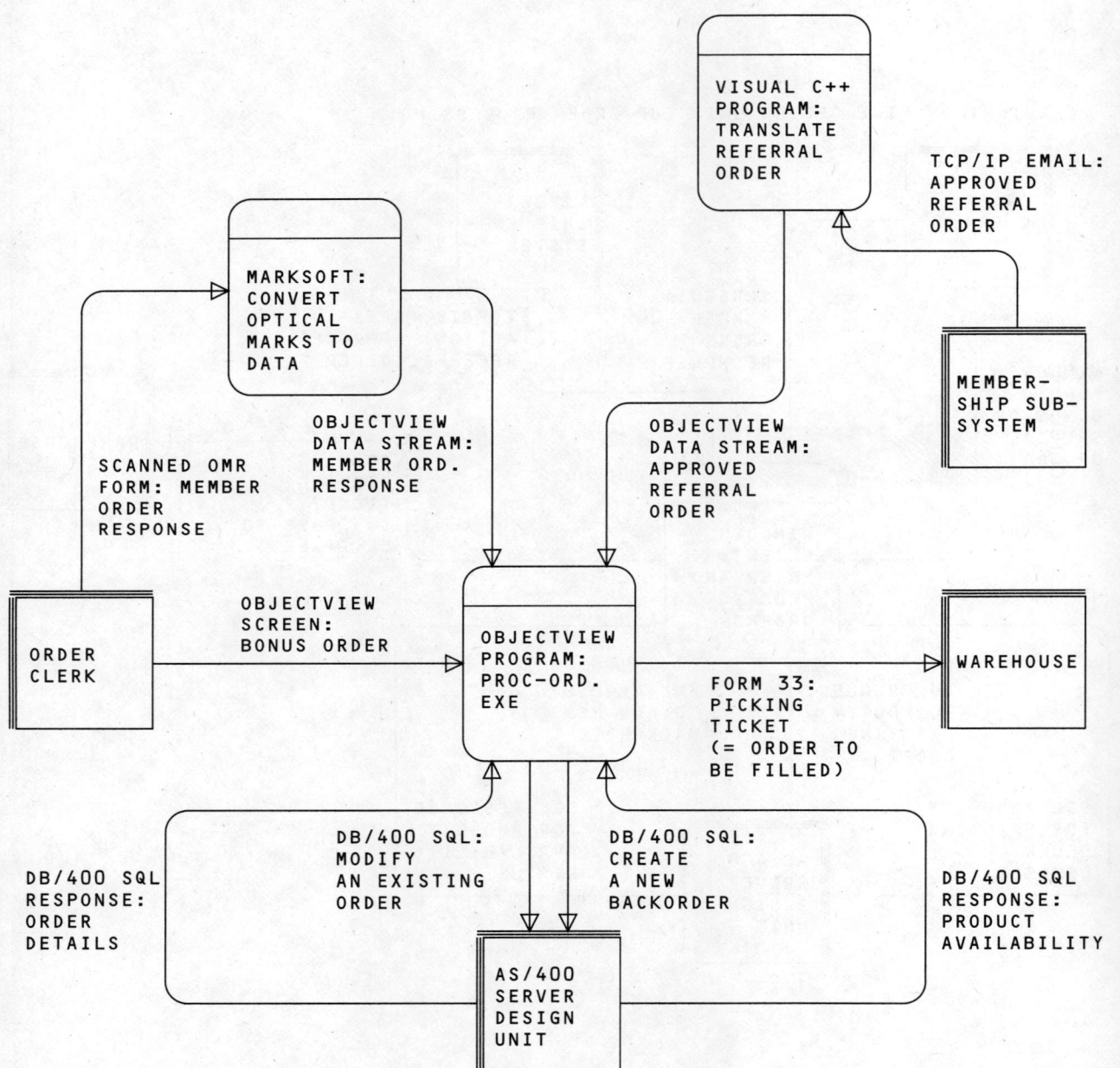

Sample Attribute Repository Description
As attributes are defined, their associated descriptions in the project repository must be updated.

Element	ORDER NUMBER
Alternate Names	MEMBER ORDER NUMBER ORDER NO. ORDER #
Definition	A SIX DIGIT NUMBER THAT UNIQUELY IDENTIFIES AN ORDER.
Input Format	999999
Output Format	ZZZZZ9
Edit Rules	MUST BE UNIQUE FOR AN ORDER; VALUE 1 THRU 999999
Storage Type	C
Characters left of decimal	6
Characters right of decimal	0
Default	
Prompt	ORDER NUMBER
Column Header	ORDER NUMBER
Short Header	ORDER NO.
Base or Derived	B
Data Class	
Source	

TM–173

© Richard D. Irwin, Inc., 1994

Fixed-Length versus Variable-Length Records TM–174
All occurrences of a fixed-length record will be the same size and contain the same fields.

A. Fixed-length records

| Record 1 |
| Record 2 |
| Record 3 |
| Record 4 |
| Record 5 |

B. Variable-length records

FLU: Rec 1	RGU
FLU: Rec 2	RGU	RGU	RGU	RGU
FLU: Rec 3	RGU	RGU
FLU: Rec 4	RGU	RGU	RGU	RGU	RGU
FLU: Rec 5	RGU	RGU

FLU = Fixed-length unit
RGU = Repeating-group unit

©Richard D. Irwin, Inc., 1994

Sample Repository Entry for the ORDERS FILE

TM-175

Fields (attributes) must be organized into records for a computer file.

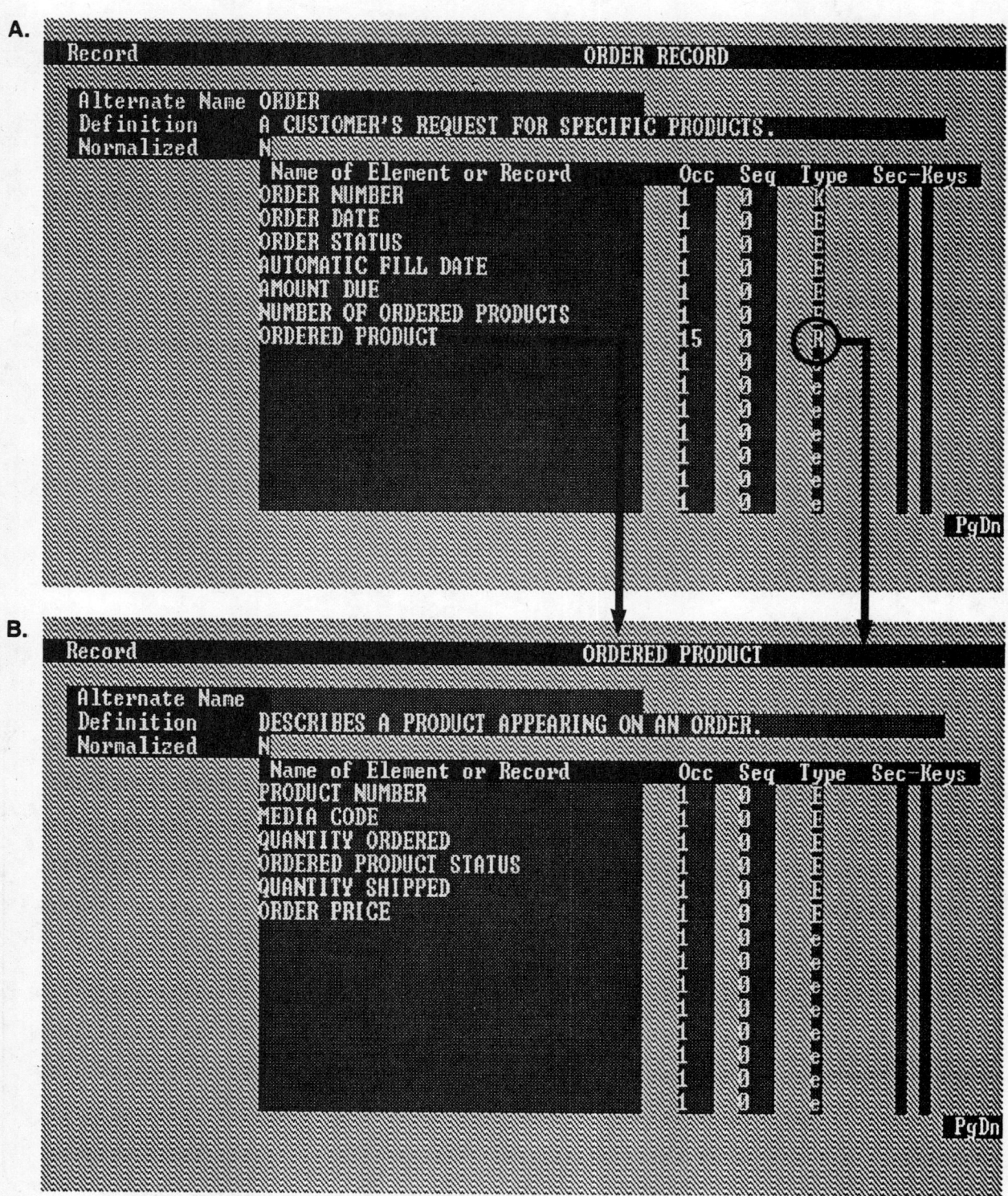

©Richard D. Irwin, Inc., 1994

Alternative Sequential File Organizations of Records

There are two ways to store records in a sequential file.

TM-176

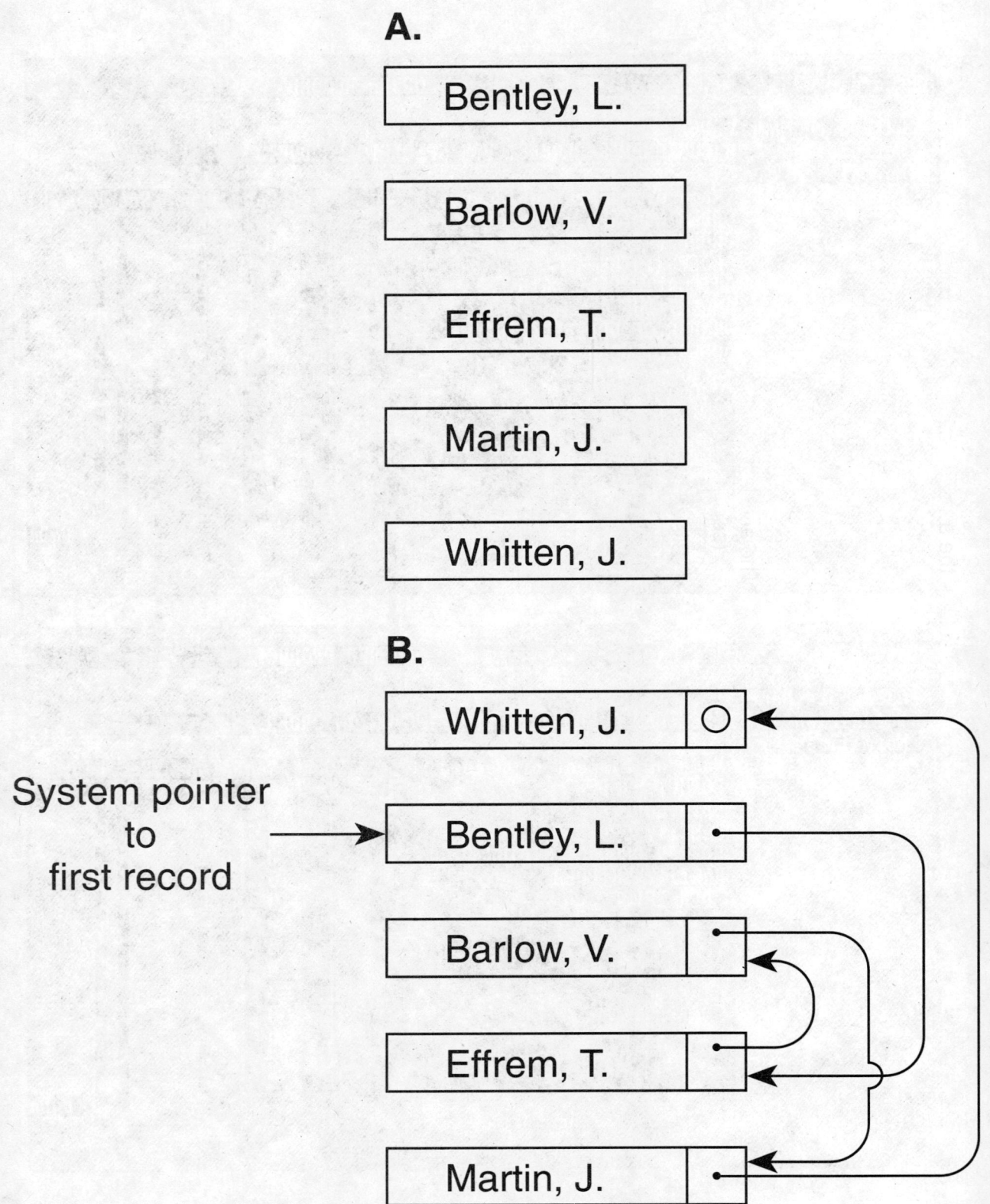

Indexed File Organization

This employee file is organized as an indexed file. In indexed files, the actual records—shown in the middle of the figure—are usually stored sequentially.

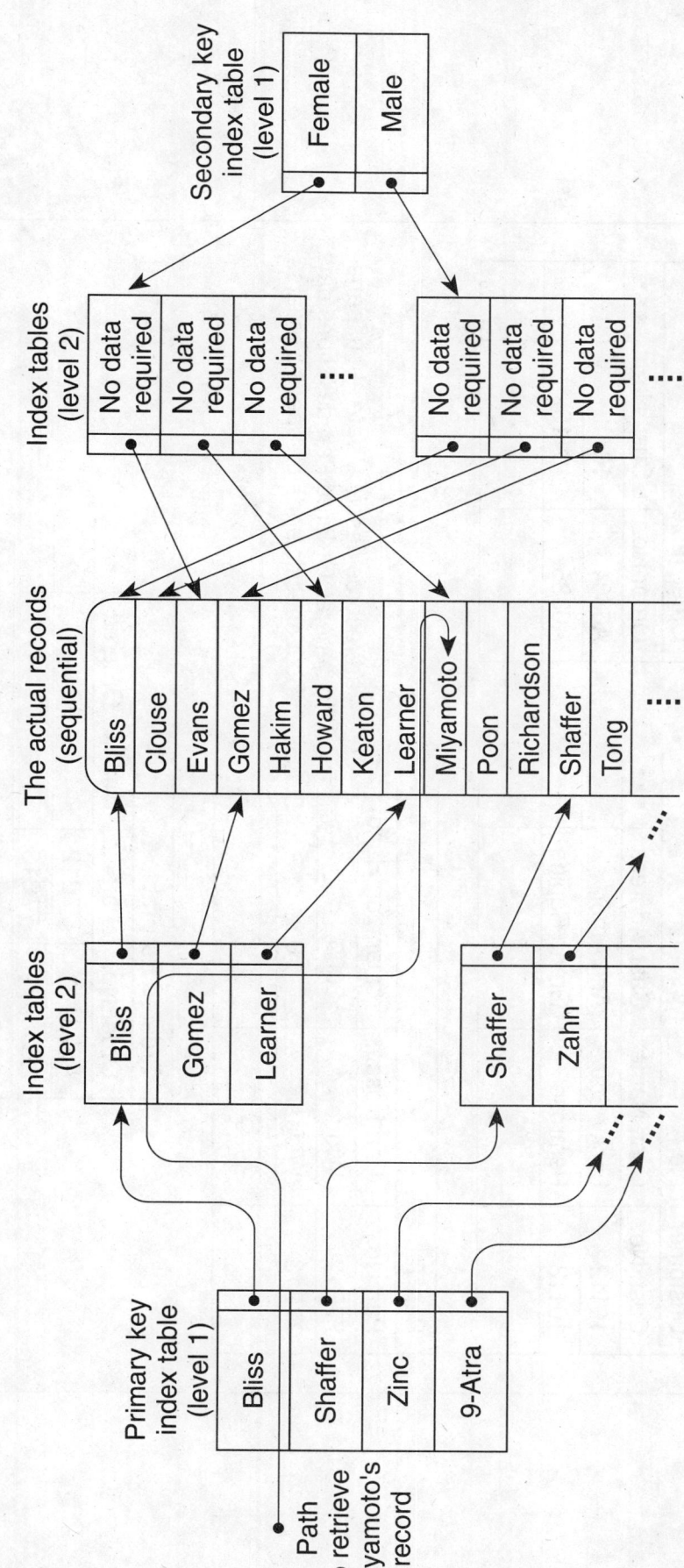

TM–177

©Richard D. Irwin, Inc., 1994

Relational Data Structures

A relational DBMS stores records as simple tables, similar to those seen in some spreadsheets that exhibit relational-like qualities.

Customer Table

Cust. No.	Cust. Name	Cust. Address	...
10112	Lucky Star	Ann Arbor	
10113	Pemrose	Grand Rapids	
...			

Order Table

Order No.	Cust. No.	...
A6334	10112	
A6335	10113	
...		

Part Table

Part No.	Part Desc.	Quant. on Hand
77B12	Widget	8000
77B13	Widget	0
...		

Part records describe data about parts in general. Ordered Part describes data about specific parts on specific orders.

Ordered Part Table

Order No.	Part No.	Quantity Ordered
A6334	77B12	50
A6334	77B13	100
A6335	77B13	25
A6335	77B12	4
	...	

TM–178

©Richard D. Irwin, Inc., 1994

Partitioned Entity Relationship Data Model for SoundStage
The partitioned area represents the scope of implementation for the ORDERS FILE.

TM-179

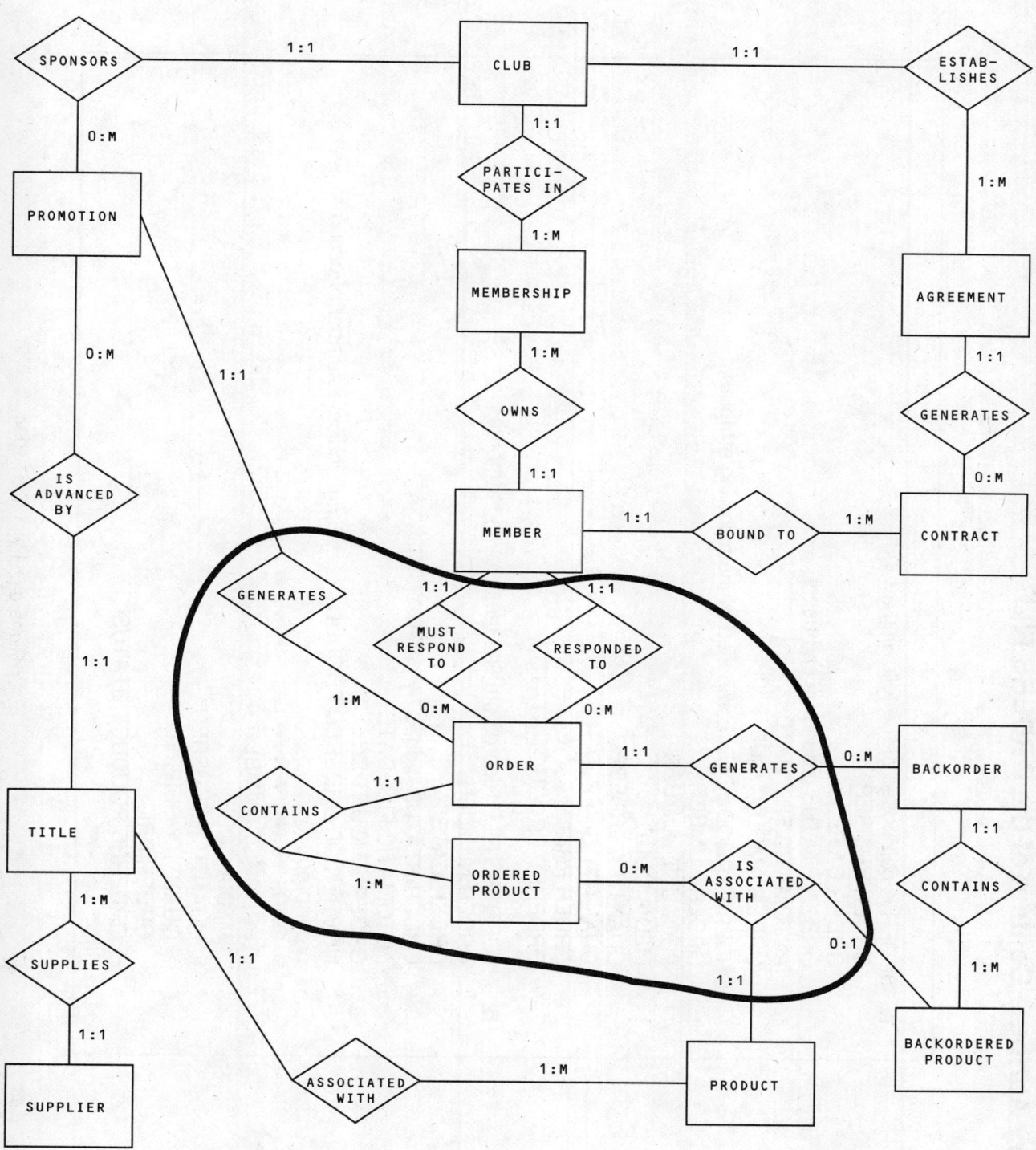

©Richard D. Irwin, Inc., 1994

Preliminary Attribute Content of the ORDERS FILE

A. ORDER is composed of the following attributes:
   ORDER NUMBER
   ORDER DATE
   ORDER STATUS (added by end-users)
   AUTOMATIC FILL DATE
   ORDER AMOUNT DUE

   ORDERED PRODUCT is composed of the following attributes:
   ORDER NUMBER
   PRODUCT NUMBER
   MEDIA CODE
   QUANTITY ORDERED
   QUANTITY SHIPPED
   ORDER PRICE
   ORDERED PRODUCT STATUS

B. An ORDERS FILE record contains the following attributes:
   ORDER NUMBER
   ORDER DATE
   ORDER STATUS (added by end-users)
   AUTOMATIC FILL DATE
   ORDER AMOUNT DUE
   NUMBER OF ORDERED PRODUCTS (added to indicate number of occurrences of order product)
   ~~ORDER NUMBER~~
   PRODUCT NUMBER
   MEDIA CODE
   QUANTITY ORDERED
   QUANTITY SHIPPED
   ORDER PRICE
   ORDERED PRODUCT STATUS

© Richard D. Irwin, Inc., 1994

TM-180

Implementing Relationships through Attributes

Relationships between the ORDERS FILE and other entities appearing in separate files are implemented by redundantly storing the keys of those other entities.

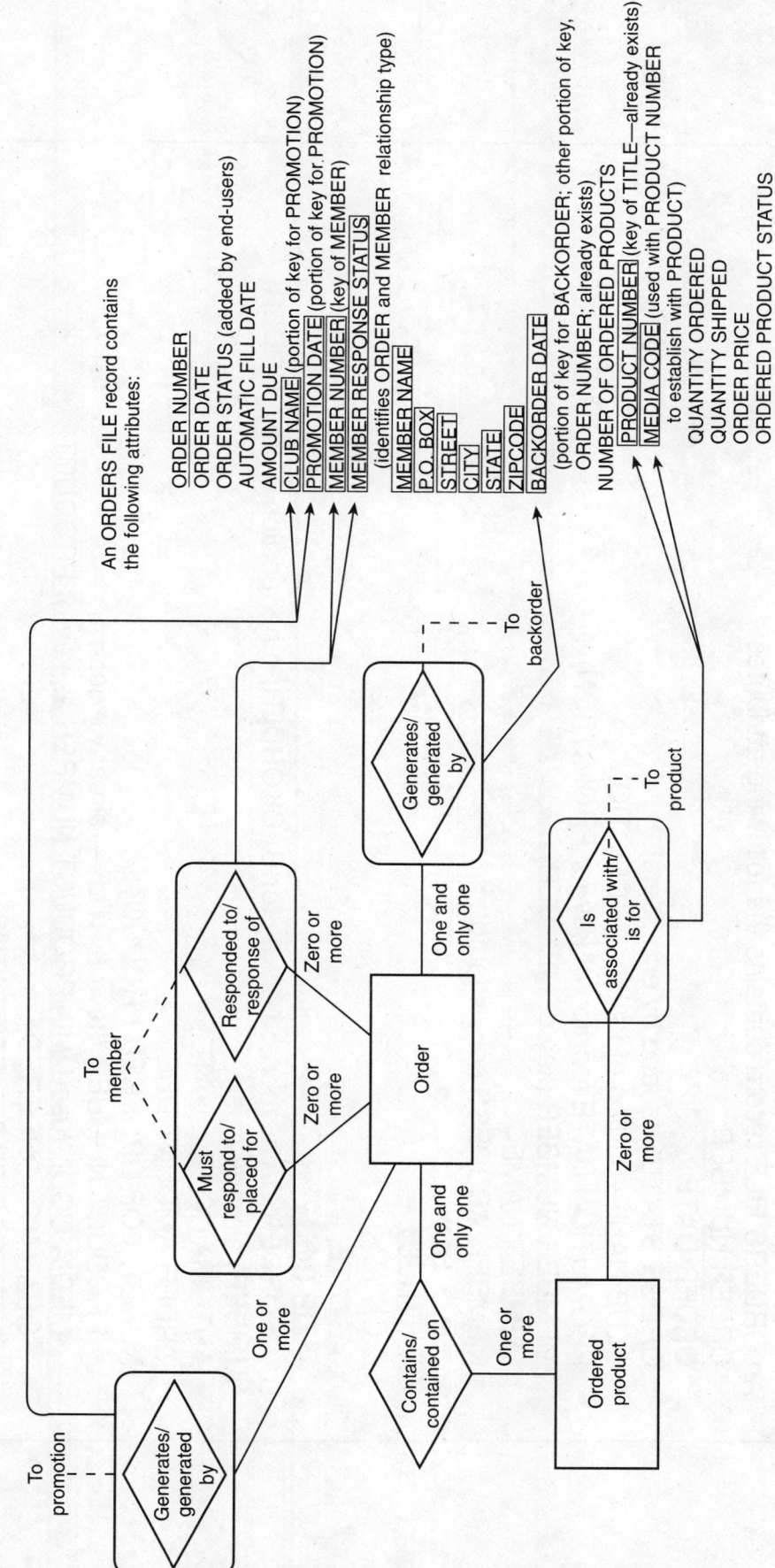

TM–181

© Richard D. Irwin, Inc., 1994

Final Attribute Contents of the ORDERS FILE

The final contents of the ORDERS FILE contains attributes describing entities and relationships.

An ORDERS FILE record contains the following attributes:
ORDER NUMBER
ORDER DATE
ORDER STATUS (added by end-users)
CLUB NAME (portion of key for PROMOTION)
PROMOTION DATE (portion of key for PROMOTION)
MEMBER NUMBER (key of MEMBER)
MEMBER NAME
MEMBER ADDRESS consisting of:
   P.O. BOX
   STREET
   CITY
   STATE
   ZIP CODE
BACKORDER DATE (portion of key for BACKORDER; other portion of key, ORDER NUMBER; already exists
AUTOMATIC FILL DATE
ORDER AMOUNT DUE
NUMBER OF ORDERED PRODUCTS
   PRODUCT NUMBER (key of TITLE—already exists)
   MEDIA CODE (used with PRODUCT NUMBER as key of PRODUCT)
   QUANTITY ORDERED
   ORDERED PRODUCT STATUS
   QUANTITY SHIPPED
   ORDER PRICE

Typical CASE Repository Report

TM–183

This report describes the ORDERS FILE record structure (including sub-records, which are indented) and key field attributes.

```
DATE: 15-DEC-92           RECORD - EXPLOSION
TIME: 00:08               NAME: ORDER RECORD

NAME:          ORDER RECORD
ALIAS:         ORDER

ELEMENT/RECORD                          OFF   OCC   TYPE   LEN
--------------------------------        ---   ---   ----   ---

ORDER NUMBER                            000   001   K      006

ORDER DATE                              006   001   E      002

ORDER STATUS                            008   001   E      001

CLUB NAME                               009   001   E      015

PROMOTION DATE                          024   001   E      002

MEMBER NUMBER                           026   001   E      006

MEMBER NAME                             032   001   E      025

P.O.BOX                                 057   001   E      010

STREET                                  067   001   E      015

CITY                                    082   001   E      015

STATE                                   097   001   E      002

ZIPCODE                                 099   001   E      009

BACKORDER DATE                          108   001   E      002

AUTOMATIC FILL DATE                     110   001   E      002

ORDER AMOUNT DUE                        112   001   E      006

DATE ORDER CREATED                      118   001   E      002

ORDER CREATED BY ID                     120   001   E      004

DATE ORDER LAST MODIFIED                124   001   E      002

ORDER LAST MODIFIED BY ID               126   001   E      004

NUMBER OF ORDERED PRODUCTS              130   001   E      002

ORDERED PRODUCT                         132   015   R
   PRODUCT NUMBER                       132   001   E      008
   MEDIA CODE                           140   001   E      001
   QUANTITY ORDERED                     141   001   E      005
   ORDERED PRODUCT STATUS               146   001   E      001
   QUANTITY SHIPPED                     147   001   E      005
   ORDER PRICE                          152   001   E      005

Record length is 507.
```

© Richard D. Irwin, Inc., 1994

Detailed Logical Requirements and File Design Specifications for the ORDERS FILE

TM–184

DATA STORE - OUTPUT
NAME: ORDERS FILE

TYPE Data Store   NAME ORDERS FILE

Label ORDERS FILE
                               Explodes To One Of:
                               Record   ORDER RECORD
                               Data Model Diagram
                               ERA Diagram

Location   ORDER PROCESSING
Manual Or Computer   C
Total Number Of Records   20034
Average Number Of Records   17300

Index Elements: ORDER NUMBER
                   ORDER STATUS
                   CLUB NAME + PROMOTION DATE
                   MEMBER NUMBER

            Description
AN AUTOMATIC, DATED ORDER GENERATED IN RESPONSE TO A PROMOTION. IT MAY BE REVISED, APPROVED, OR CANCELLED VIA A MEMBER RESPONSE.

LOGICAL, IMPLEMENTATION-INDEPENDENT ATTRIBUTES OF THIS DATA STORE

  VOLUME
    AVERAGE: 17,300   GROWTH RATE (PER TIME PERIOD): 5% PER YEAR
    PEAK: 20,034   WHEN: NOVEMBER THROUGH CHRISTMAS (DECEMBER)

  USER REFERENCES: ORDER PROCESSING STAFF

  CONSTRAINTS: NONE

PHYSICAL, IMPLEMENTATION-DEPENDENT ATTRIBUTES OF THIS DATA STORE

(A) IMPLEMENTED AS: VARIABLE-LENGTH, VSAM
    COMPUTER NAMES OR IDs: ORDER.DAT
    MAXIMUM PHYSICAL RECORD SIZE: 507 (B)
    BLOCKING CONSTRAINTS: 1/3 TRACK BLOCKING
    BLOCKING FACTOR: 5 (C) BLOCK SIZE: 2603
    FILE SIZE (IN BYTES): 10,430,221 (D)
    FILE SIZE (IN TRACKS OR INCHES): 1336 (E)
    FILE SIZE (IN CYLINDERS): 149 (F)
    AVERAGE RECORD LIFETIME UNTIL ARCHIVE: 2 MONTHS
    BACKUP AND RECOVERY
      BACKUP TIMING: DAILY 8:00 PM   BACKUP MEDIA: TAPE
      BACKUP RETENTION: 1 MONTH
      AUDIT TRAIL METHOD: UPDATES LOGGED TO DISK, PRINTED AT END OF DAY
    SECURITY: ONLY ORDER PROCESSING STAFF MAY UPDATE

© Richard D. Irwin, Inc., 1994

Distributed Data Model for SoundStage
This version of the original data model reflects the approved design decisions.

TM–185

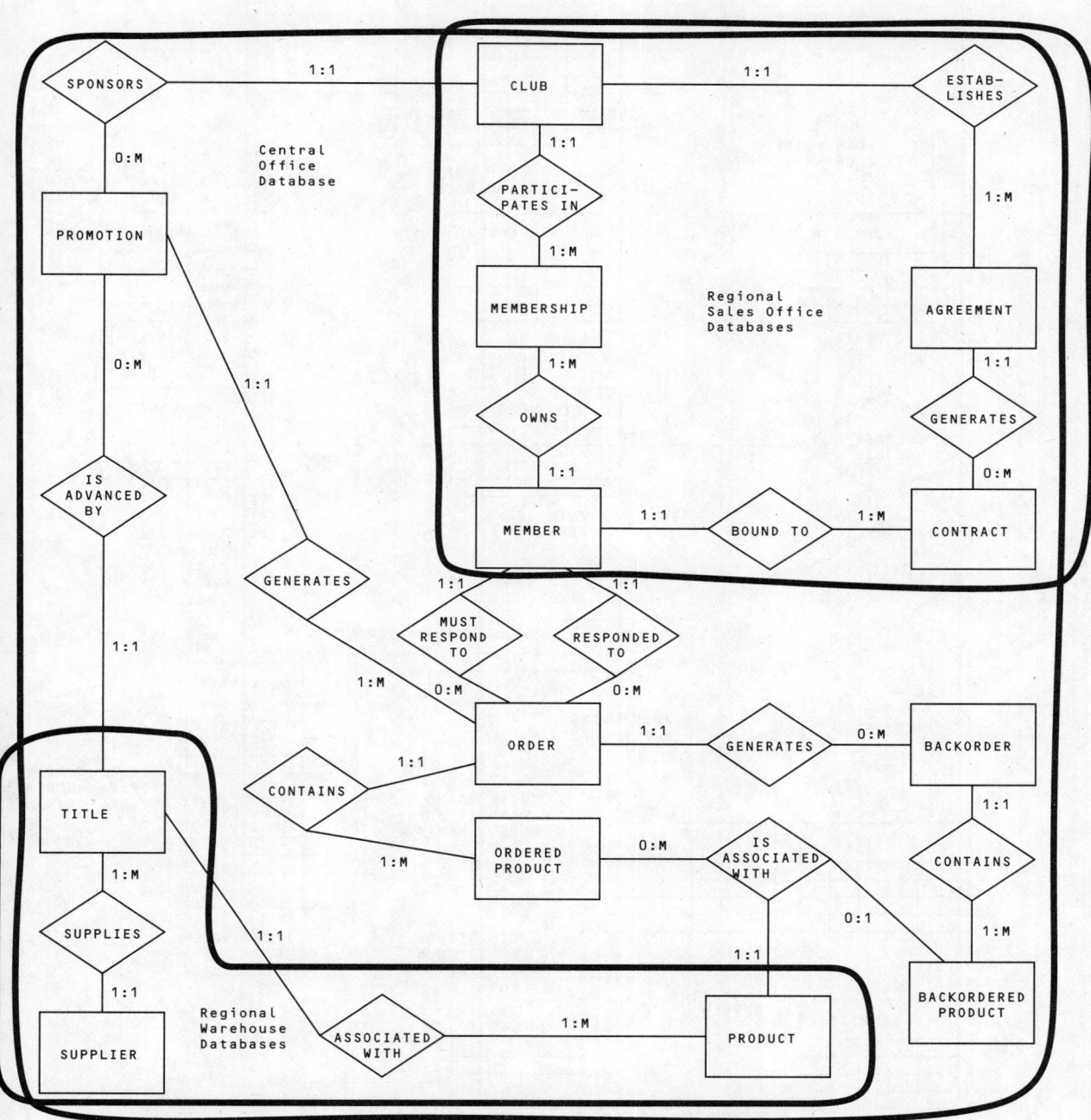

© Richard D. Irwin, Inc., 1994

A Relational Database Schema for SoundStage
TM-186
This database schema illustrates how the SoundStage data model would be implemented as a relational database.

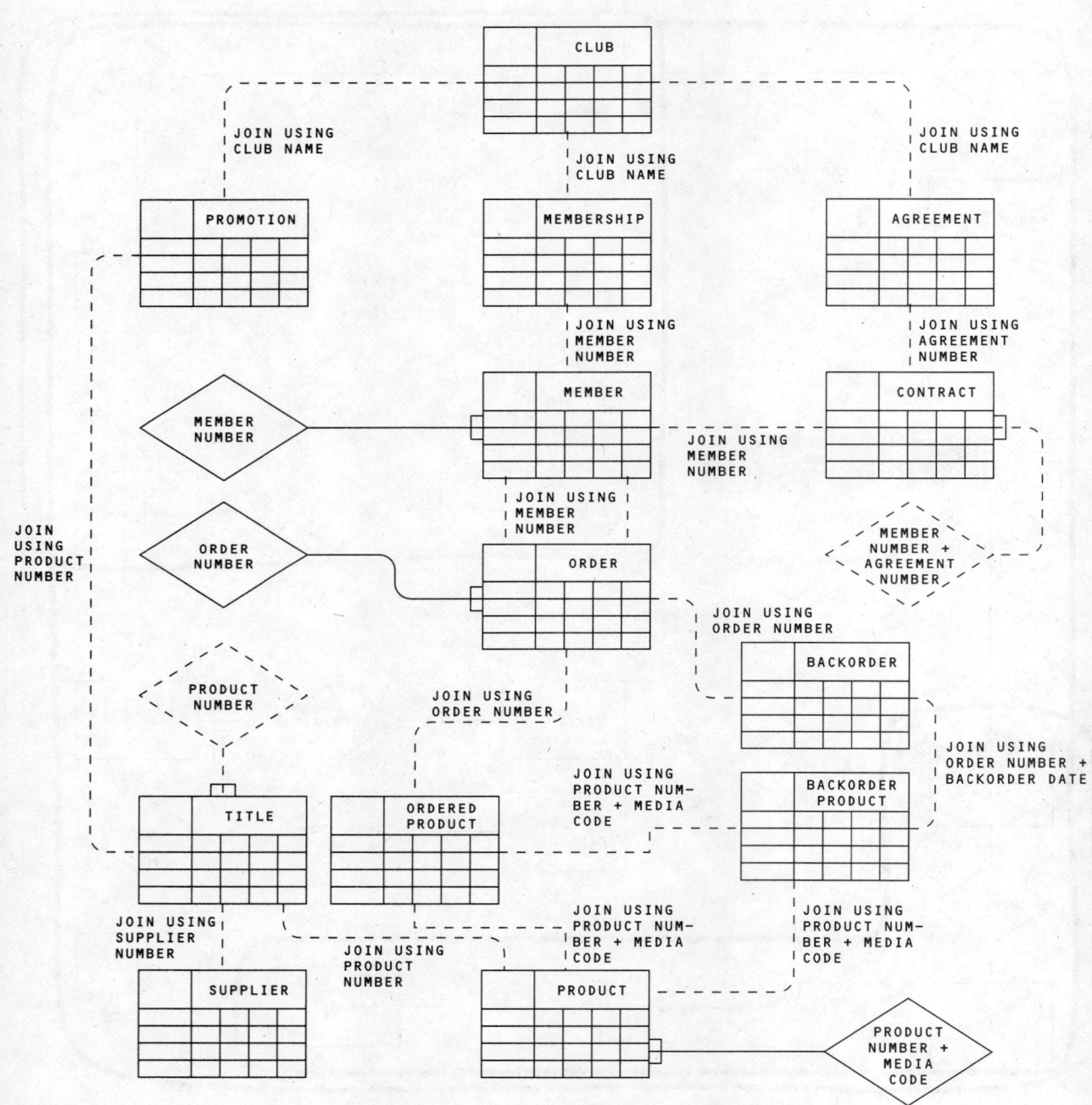

© Richard D. Irwin, Inc., 1994

Project Repository Entry for a Table (Part 1)
Each table in a relational database represents its own data store that should be described in the project repository.

```
Data Store                                                              PgUp
┌─────────────────────────────────────────────────────────────────────────┐
│ AGREEMENT                                                               │
│                    Description                                          │
│ THE DATA STORE AGREEMENT WILL BE IMPLEMENTED AS A DB2 RELATIONAL        │
│ DATABASE TABLE.  THE TABLE IS FURTHER DESCRIBED IN THIS REPOSITORY BY   │
│ THE RECORD TO WHICH IT EXPLODES.  THAT RECORD DESCRIBES THE TABLE'S     │
│ CONTENT.                                                                │
│                                                                         │
└─────────────────────────────────────────────────────────────────────────┘

Modified By    BARLOW             Date Modified  921214    # Changes  0
Added By       BARLOW             Date Added     921214
Last Project   MEMBER SERVICE S
Locked By                         Date Locked    0         Lock Status
```

TM–187

© Richard D. Irwin, Inc., 1994

Project Repository Entry for a Table (Part 2)
The contents of a typical record in a relational table should be described in the project repository.

TM-188

```
NAME:       AGREEMENT RECORD                    RECORD - EXPLOSION
ALIAS:      AGREEMENT                           NAME: AGREEMENT RECORD

ELEMENT/RECORD                       OFF  OCC  TYPE  LENGTH
-------------                        ---  ---  ----  ------
AGREEMENT NUMBER SUFFIX              000  001   K     003
CLUB NAME                            000  001   E     015
AGREEMENT EXPIRATION DATE            003  001   E     002
AGREEMENT PLAN CREATION DATE         005  001   E     002
MAXIMUM PERIOD OF OBLIGATION         007  001   E     004
BONUS CREDITS AFTER OBLIGATION       011  001   E     002
NUMBER OF MEMBERS ENROLLED           013  001   E     006
NO. MEMBERS WHO HAVE FULFILLED       019  001   E     006

Record length is 25.
```

© Richard D. Irwin, Inc., 1994

Typical External Turnaround Document

This output is external because it leaves the system and goes to the customer to initiate a transaction (a payment).

TM-189

```
                    5574831011  0044445  96486803829900055
```

ACCOUNT NUMBER	CLOSING DATE	NEW BALANCE	MINIMUM PAYMENT DUE
55-748-3101-1	03-05-89	88.80	88.80

MAKE CHECK PAYABLE TO WESTERN OIL CO.
RETURN THIS PORTION WITH CHECK.
INDICATE ACCOUNT NUMBER ON CHECK.

▲ PAYMENT IS DUE UPON RECEIPT OF STATEMENT. PAY EITHER AMOUNT. ▲

PLEASE INDICATE AMOUNT PAID

DOLLARS	CENTS

P. O. BOX 3576
SAN FRANCISCO, CA
94123-2300

MICHAEL WINTERS
1414 LINDBERGH DRIVE
MEDFORD, OR 97504

NEW ADDRESS
PLEASE PRINT _____ STREET _____
CITY _____ STATE _____ ZIP CODE _____

PLEASE PLACE YOUR ACCOUNT NUMBER 55-748-3101-1 ON ALL CORRESPONDENCE AND INDICATE THE DATE AND REFERENCE NUMBER SHOWN BELOW, IF APPLICABLE

CLOSING DATE 03-05-89

SEND INQUIRIES TO: WESTERN OIL CO.
P.O. BOX 4400
DENVER, CO 80203
(303) 550-2600

TRAN DATE	REFERENCE NUMBER	PRODUCT CODE	TRANSACTION LOCATION/DESCRIPTION	AMOUNT (CR—CREDIT)
02 05	045762212662	1	534 COUNTRY FM RD MEDFORD OR	11.20

PREVIOUS BALANCE	PAYMENTS/CREDITS	CHARGES	FINANCE CHARGE	NEW BALANCE
76.45		11.20	1.15	88.80

TO AVOID ADDITIONAL FINANCE CHARGE PAYMENT OF NEW BALANCE MUST BE RECEIVED BY 03-30-89

MINIMUM PAYMENT DUE 88.80

SCHEDULE OF FINANCE CHARGES

BALANCE RANGE	PERIODIC RATE (MONTHLY)	ANNUAL PERCENTAGE RATE	BALANCE SUBJECT TO FINANCE CHARGE SEE REVERSE SIDE
TO $ OVER $ 000	1.50 %	18.00 %	76.45 A

NOTICE: SEE REVERSE SIDE FOR IMPORTANT INFORMATION.

PLEASE KEEP THIS PORTION FOR YOUR RECORDS

DO 54495-B

© Richard D. Irwin, Inc., 1994

Sample Internal Outputs
Internal outputs include detailed, summary, and exception reports.

TM–190

```
                                        SUMMARY OF MONTHLY                                              PAGE 01
                                     BANK MACHINE TRANSACTIONS
                                   FOR THE PERIOD 03/01/89 TO 03/31/89

MACHINE    BRANCH     NUMBER OF   AMOUNT OF    NUMBER OF    AMOUNT OF    NUMBER OF   AMOUNT OF    NUMBER OF       AMOUNT OF
NUMBER     NUMBER     DEPOSITS    DEPOSITS     WITHDRAWALS  WITHDRAWALS  TRANSFERS   TRANSFERS    LOAN PAYMENTS   LOAN PAYMENTS
  01         01         192       57,600.32       672        31,213.50      140      14,025.33         23           1,725.86
  02         03         134       43,756.45       478        23,144.75       63       6,192.88         11           1,545.38
  03         05         112       47,650.44       462        24,897.26       43       5,023.61         13           1,195.76
  05         07         155       49,864.04       567        27,875.00       97      11,729.58         15           2,304.42
  06         08         234       61,768.34       748        37,563.73      153      17,688.93         26           2,112.45

TOTAL DOLLARS DEPOSITED         $260,639.59
TOTAL DOLLARS WITHDRAWN         $144,694.24
TOTAL DOLLARS PAID ON LOANS     $  8,883.87
TOTAL DOLLARS TRANSFERRED       $ 54,660.33
```

```
10/02/89                          INTERNATIONAL MANUFACTURING COMPANY                               PAGE 1
                                             BONUS REPORT

   CLOCK                      CLOCK          INCENTIVE        DOWN           BONUS            BONUS
   NUMBER       SHIFT         HOURS            HOURS          TIME          PERCENT           HOURS
    1000          1            35.5             30.0          05.5            150              15.0
    1010          1            40.0             32.0          08.0            110              03.2
    1020          2            40.0             31.5          08.5            142              13.2
    1030          2            36.5             20.3          16.2            113              02.6
    1040          3            09.4             08.2          01.2            144              03.6
    1050          3            10.2             02.8          07.4            107              00.2
    2000          1            55.0             45.3          09.7            134              15.4
    2010          1            50.0             33.2          16.8            139              12.9
    2020          3            12.1             03.4          08.7            132              01.1
    2030          2            20.4             17.9          02.5            125              04.5
    3000          1            16.8             12.6          04.2            127              03.4
    3010          2            40.5             30.1          10.4            104              01.2
    3020          3            40.0             29.0          11.0            143              12.5
    3040          3            32.0             29.5          02.5            147              13.9
    3050          1            07.0             03.8          03.2            141              01.6
    4000          2            60.2             47.8          12.4            150              23.9
    4010          1            61.4             50.3          11.1            117              08.6
    4020          3            14.7             08.5          06.2            121              01.8
    5000          1            50.0             44.1          05.9            100              00.0
    5010          1            52.5             40.0          12.5            133              13.2

   TOTALS:                    684.2            520.3         163.9                            151.8
```

© Richard D. Irwin, Inc., 1994

Alternative Input Procedures for Batch Input Media

These illustrations show the similarities and differences between the most typical batch input methods.

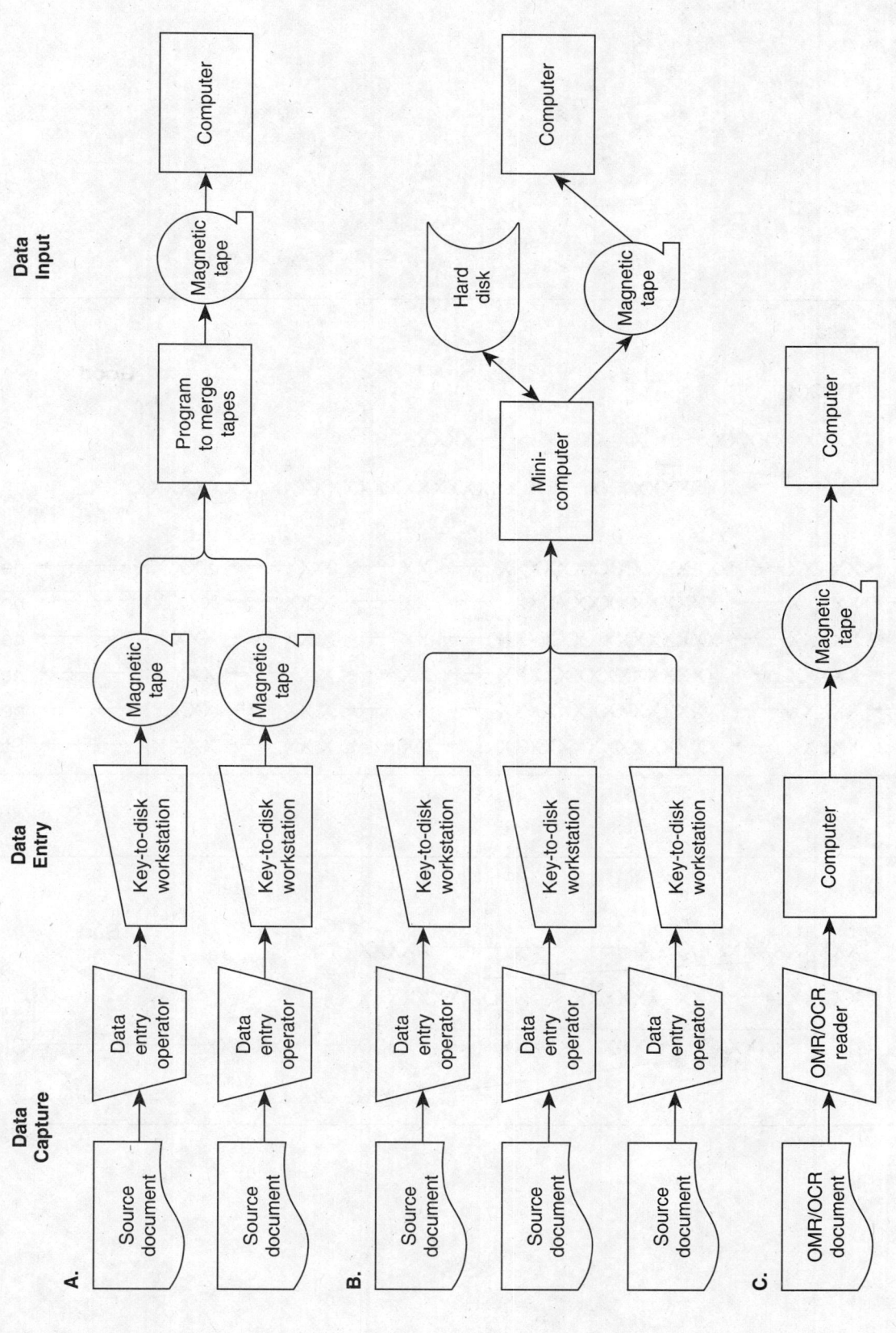

TM–191

© Richard D. Irwin, Inc., 1994

Keying from Source Documents
Source documents should be designed to aid in rapid data entry.

TM–192

A.

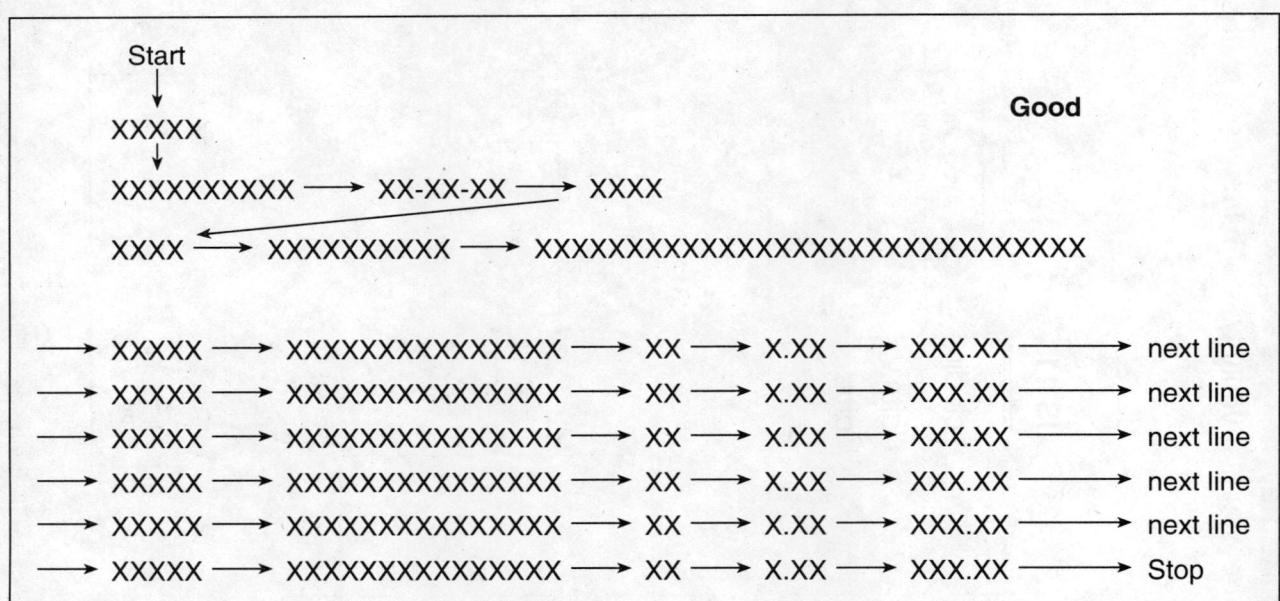

B.

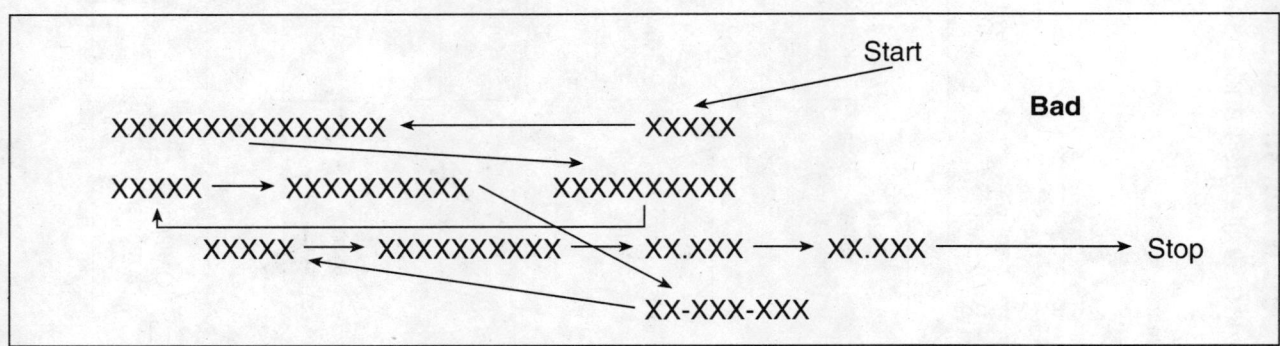

©Richard D. Irwin, Inc., 1994

Modulus 11 Self-Checking-Digit Technique

Modulus 11 is a very common self-checking-digit technique used to verify that the original/source data has been correctly transcribed into machine-processable form.

MODULUS 11

The following procedure is used to assign a check digit to a key field:

STEP 1: Determine the size of the key field in digits.

$$2\ 4\ 1\ 3\ 5 = 5\ \text{digits}$$

STEP 2: Number each digit location from *right* or *left* beginning with the number "2."

$$2\ 4\ 1\ 3\ 5$$
$$6\ 5\ 4\ 3\ 2$$

STEP 3: Multiply each digit in the key field by its assigned location number.

$$2 \times 6 = 12$$
$$4 \times 5 = 20$$
$$1 \times 4 = 4$$
$$3 \times 3 = 9$$
$$5 \times 2 = 10$$

STEP 4: Sum the products from step 3.

$$12 + 20 + 4 + 9 + 10 = 55$$

STEP 5: Divide the sum from step 4 by 11.

$$55/11 = 5\ \text{Remainder}\ 0$$

STEP 6: If the remainder is less than 10, append the remainder digit to the key field. If the remainder is equal to 10, append the character "X" to the key field.

$$2\ 4\ 1\ 3\ 5\ 0$$

© Richard D. Irwin, Inc., 1994

A Design Unit Data Flow Diagram for SoundStage Inputs

TM−194

Those data flows entering the design unit data flow diagram shows inputs that must be designed.

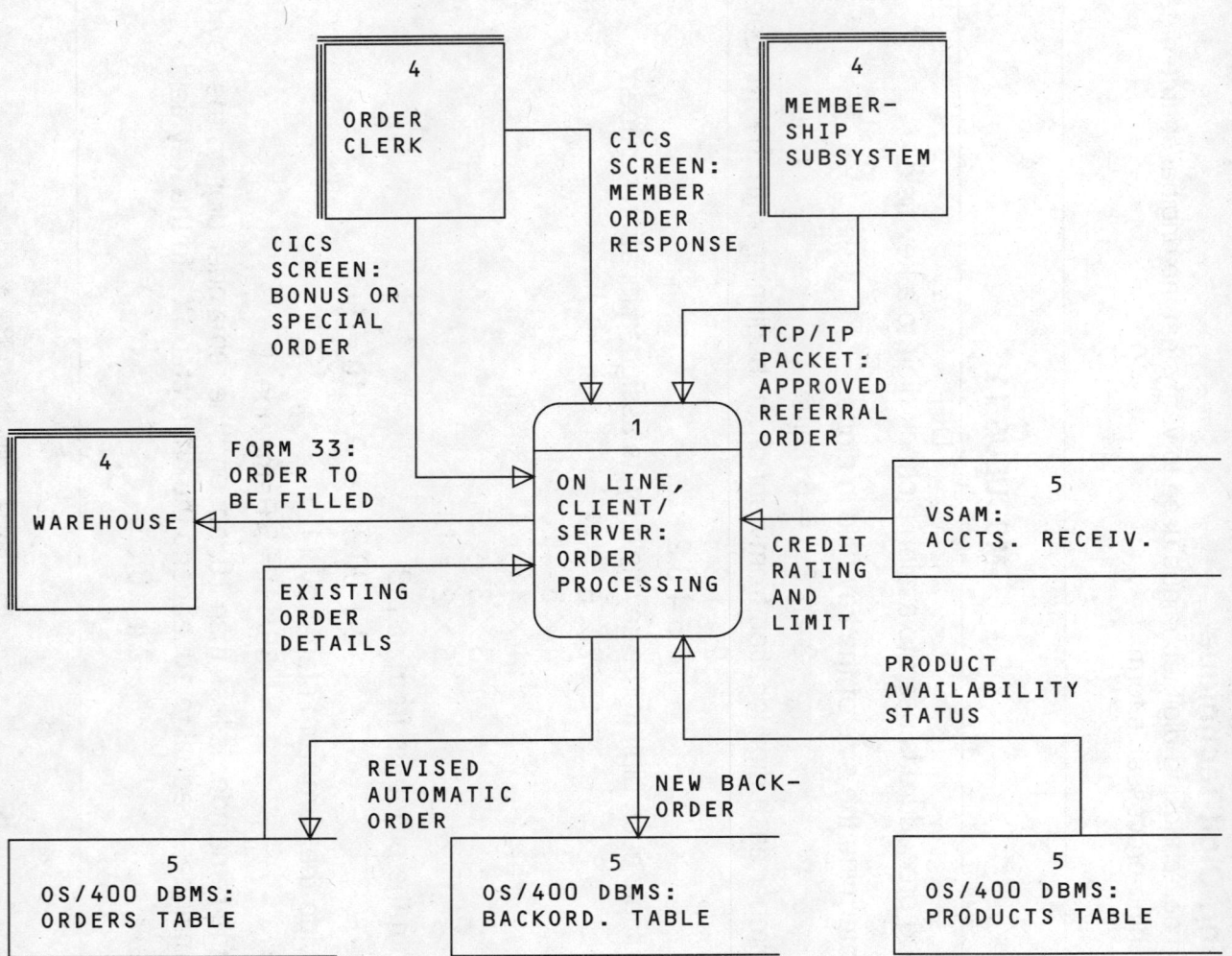

Description of a Typical Input

The input design specifications are recorded in the project repository.

DATA FLOW - INPUT
NAME: MEMBER ORDER RESPONSE

TYPE Data Flow   NAME MEMBER ORDER RESPONSE

Label MEMBER ORDER RESPONSE

Explodes To:
Type REC Name   MEMBER ORDER RESPONSE

Duration Value   5,000
Duration Type   DAY
Access Type   U

Description
SOURCE DOCUMENT: MEMBER ORDER (FORM 40), A TURNAROUND DOCUMENT
INPUT METHOD: ON-LINE
INPUT MEDIUM: DISPLAY
TIMING (frequency prepared):   ON DEMAND WEEKDAYS FROM 8 A.M. TO 5 P.M.
AVERAGE VOLUME (in records):   5,000 PER DAY
PEAK VOLUME AND TIMING: 5,800/DAY FROM NOVEMBER THROUGH DECEMBER
CONTROLS AND SPECIAL INSTRUCTIONS:
  THE INPUT WILL INITIALLY BE DESIGNED AS A TURNAROUND SOURCE
  DOCUMENT. IT WILL BE OUTPUT AND MAILED TO THE MEMBER WHO WILL
  RESPOND BY COMPLETING THE ORDER AND RETURNING IT FOR INPUT BY
  ORDER PROCESSING. AN AUDIT TRAIL FILE SHOULD BE CREATED AND ALL
  RETURNED SOURCE DOCUMENTS MUST BE RETAINED.

©Richard D. Irwin, Inc., 1994

Attribute Repository Entry for the Contents of MEMBER ORDER RESPONSE

This repository printout shows details about the attributes to be input from a MEMBER ORDER RESPONSE.

REPORT OF ATTRIBUTES CONTAINED IN
MEMBER ORDER RESPONSE RECORD

ATTRIBUTE NAME	TYPE	OCC	CHARACTERS LEFT	CHARACTERS RIGHT	INPUT PICTURE	VALUE RANGE
MEMBER NUMBER	C	1	7	0	9999999	MUST BE UNIQUE FOR A MEMBER; VALUE 000001 THRU 9999999
ORDER NUMBER	C	1	6	0	ZZZZZ9	MUST BE UNIQUE FOR AN ORDER; VALUE 1 THRU 999999
MEMBER NAME	C	1	30	0	X(30)	OPTIONAL
ORDER DATE	C	1	8	0	MM/DD/YY	MUST BE VALID MONTH, DAY, AND YEAR (DEFAULT IS TODAY'S DATE)
CLUB NAME	C	1	15	0	X(15)	REQUIRED; MEMBER MUST HOLD AT LEAST 1 CLUB MEMBERSHIP
P.O. BOX	C	1	10	0	X(10)	OPTIONAL
STREET	C	1	15	0	X(15)	
CITY	C	1	15	0	X(15)	
STATE	C	1	2	0	AA	STANDARD STATE CODES
ZIPCODE	C	1	9	0	X(9)	
SELECTION OF MONTH ACCEPTED?	C	1	1	0	A	Y=YES (default) N=NO
PRODUCT NUMBER	C	1-15	7	0	9999999	MUST BE UNIQUE; VALUE 00000000 THRU 9999999
MEDIA CODE	C	1-15	1	0	X	R=RECORD, C=CASSETTE, D=COMPACT DISC, 8=8 TRACK
QUANTITY ORDERED	C	1-15	4	0	ZZZ9	OPTIONAL; IF PRESENT MUST BE > 0

TM-196

© Richard D. Irwin, Inc., 1994

Source Document Design Zones
A source document for input may be designed in zones such as those indicated on this template.

TM-197

Identification Zone Company Name, Form Name, Official Form Number, Date of Last Revision	Sequence Number, Date
Instruction Zone	
Body Zone (Transaction Details)	
	Totals Zone
Authorization Zone	

© Richard D. Irwin, Inc., 1994

Display Layout Chart for On-Line MEMBER ORDER RESPONSE

TM-198

The initial screen seen by the system user is a blank order form to be filled in.

TERMINAL SCREEN DISPLAY LAYOUT FORM

APPLICATION: _____

☑ INPUT MEMBER ORDER RESPONSE   SCREEN NO.: _____   SEQUENCE: _____
☐ OUTPUT

Row 01: `** MEMBER ORDER **`
Row 02: `ENTER THE FOLLOWING ITEMS FROM A MEMBER ORDER (FORM 40). USE TAB OR`
Row 03: `ARROW KEYS TO MOVE FROM ITEM TO ITEM. PRESS ENTER KEY WHEN DONE.`
Row 05: `MEMBER NUMBER: C                              ORDER NUMBER:`
Row 06: `MEMBER NAME:                                  ORDER DATE:`
Row 07: `CLUB NAME:`
Row 08: `MEMBER ADDRESS:`
Row 09: `  P.O. BOX:`
Row 10: `  STREET:`
Row 11: `  CITY:`
Row 12: `  STATE:     ZIPCODE:`
Row 14: `     SELECTION OF      PRODUCT   MEDIA    QUANTITY`
Row 15: `     MONTH ACCEPTED?   NUMBER    CODE     ORDERED`
Row 24: `** PRESS F2 FOR HELP. PRESS F3 TO RETURN TO ORDER PROCESSING OPTIONS MENU **`

FUNCTION KEY ASSIGNMENTS

Key	Assignment	Key	Assignment	Key	Assignment
PF1		PF9		PF17	
PF2	HELP FOR ANY ITEM	PF10		PF18	
PF3	RETURN TO ORDER PROCESSING MENU	PF11		PF19	
PF4		PF12		PF20	
PF5		PF13		PF21	
PF6		PF14		PF22	
PF7		PF15		PF23	
PF8		PF16		PF24	

© Richard D. Irwin, Inc., 1994

Display Layout Chart for On-Line MEMBER ORDER RESPONSE Fields to be Input

TM-199

This screen design shows the proper edit masks for the fields to be entered by the system user.

TERMINAL SCREEN DISPLAY LAYOUT FORM

- ☑ INPUT MEMBER ORDER
- ☐ OUTPUT

APPLICATION _____
SCREEN NO. _____ SEQUENCE _____

```
01                              ** MEMBER ORDER **
02        ENTER THE FOLLOWING ITEMS FROM A MEMBER ORDER (FORM 40). USE TAB OR
03        ARROW KEYS TO MOVE FROM ITEM TO ITEM. PRESS ENTER KEY WHEN DONE.
04
05  MEMBER NUMBER:  9999999                              ORDER NUMBER:  999999
06  MEMBER NAME:    XXXXXXXXXXXXXXXXXXXXXXXXXXX          ORDER DATE:    99/99/99
07  CLUB NAME:      XXXXXXXXXXXXXXX
08  MEMBER ADDRESS:
09    P.O. BOX:    XXXXXXXXXX
10    STREET:      XXXXXXXXXXXXXXXX
11    CITY:        XXXXXXXXXXXXXXXX
12    STATE: AA  ZIPCODE: XXXXXXXXX
13
14              SELECTION OF     PRODUCT    MEDIA    QUANTITY
15              MONTH ACCEPTED?  NUMBER     CODE     ORDERED
16                   X           9999999     X        9999
17                                 (A)
...
23              XXXXXXXXXXXXXXXXXXXXXXXXXXXXXXXXXXXXXXXXXXXXXXXXXXXXX     (B)
24        ** PRESS F2 FOR HELP. PRESS F3 TO RETURN TO ORDER PROCESSING OPTIONS MENU **
```

FUNCTION KEY ASSIGNMENTS

Key	Assignment	Key	Assignment	Key	Assignment
PF1		PF9		PF17	
PF2	HELP FOR ANY ITEM	PF10		PF18	
PF3	RETURN TO ORDER PROCESSING MENU	PF11		PF19	
PF4		PF12		PF20	
PF5		PF13		PF21	
PF6		PF14		PF22	
PF7		PF15		PF23	
PF8		PF16		PF24	

© Richard D. Irwin, Inc., 1994

Specifications for Display Attributes and Error Messages for MEMBER ORDER RESPONSE Input Screen

TM-200

These notes are used to describe attributes — such as blinking fields — and error messages.

MEMO FOR MEMBER ORDER INPUT SCREEN

Message

Ref. No.

a This field is used to provide the end-user with a descriptive error message when invalid commands or data have been entered otherwise the field is not printed. When the message is displayed, it should "blink" to grab the end-user's attention. As a reminder, the editing criteria were explained in the report titled "Report of Data Attributes Contained in Member Order Record." The following specifies the conditions and types of messages to be displayed to the end-user.

Select the appropriate case:

Case 1: **MEMBER NUMBER is invalid**
If the MEMBER NUMBER is not equivalent to a MEMBER NUMBER of an existing MEMBER then:
error message = "MEMBER does not exist, please reenter."

Case 2: **ORDER NUMBER is invalid**
If the ORDER NUMBER is equivalent to the ORDER NUMBER of any previous MEMBER ORDER then:
error message = "ORDER NUMBER was assigned to previously entered MEMBER ORDER, please reenter."

Case 3: **ORDER DATE is invalid**
Select appropriate case:
  Case 2.1 ORDER DATE contains no values, then:
    error message = "The order date must be provided on all orders, please enter."
  Case 2.2 ORDER DATE contains invalid values for month, day, year, then:
    error message = "The order date is not valid, please reenter."

Case 4: **PRODUCT NUMBER is not valid product number, then:**
error message = "Entered an incorrect part number (does not exist), please reenter."

Case 5: **MEDIA CODE is invalid, then:**
error message = "media code is invalid, please reenter or press F2 key for list of valid codes and meanings."

Case 6: **QUANTITY ORDERED is not greater than 0, then:**
error message = "Quantity ordered must be greater than 0, please reenter."

© Richard D. Irwin, Inc., 1994

Alternative Graphic Design for On-Line MEMBER ORDER RESPONSE

TM–201

A.

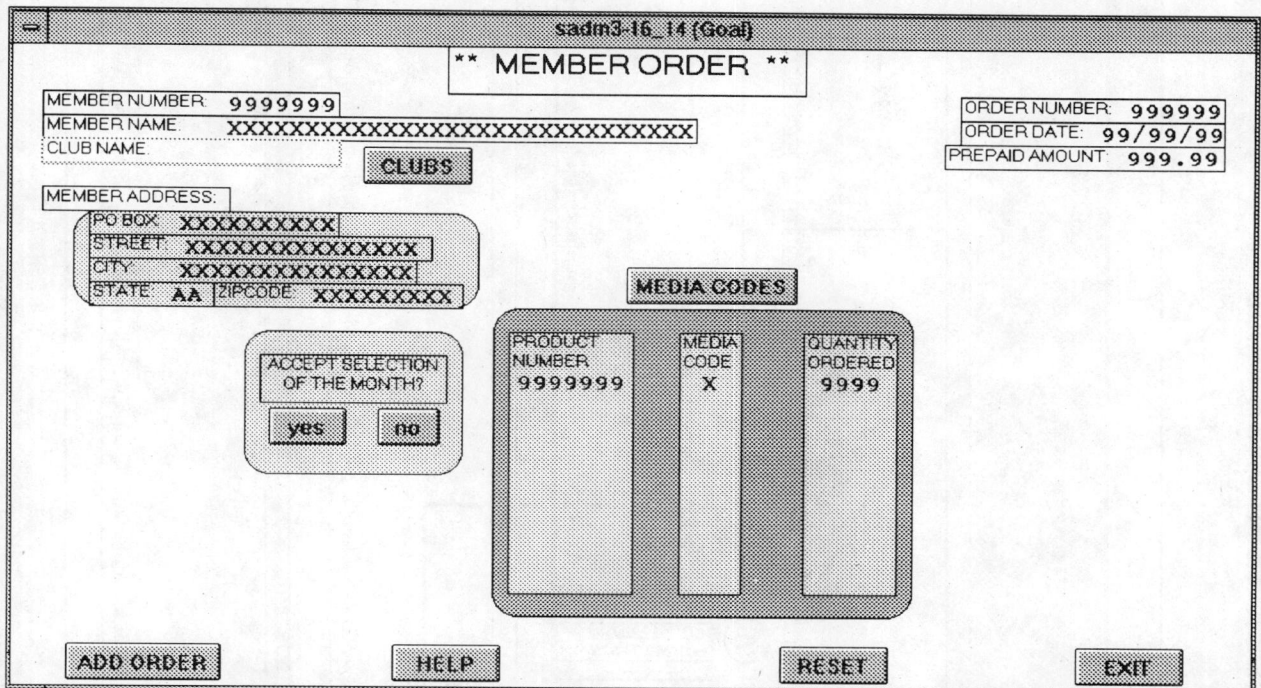

B.

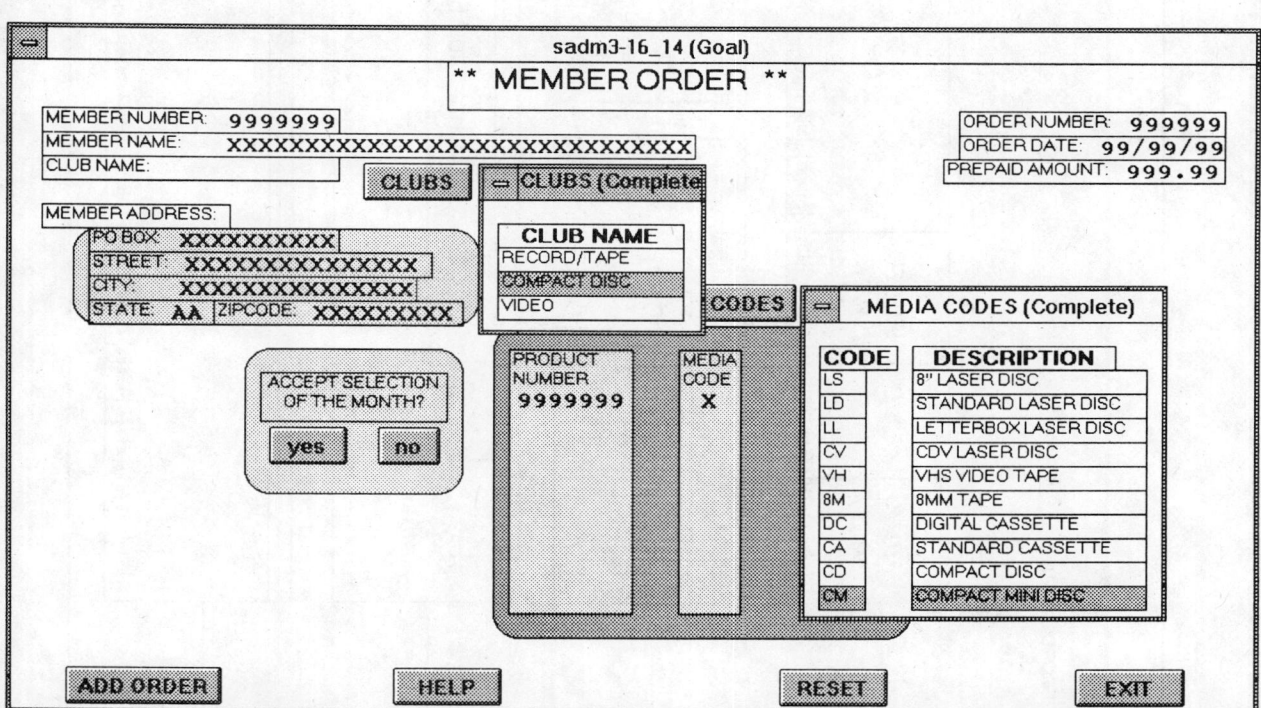

© Richard D. Irwin, Inc., 1994

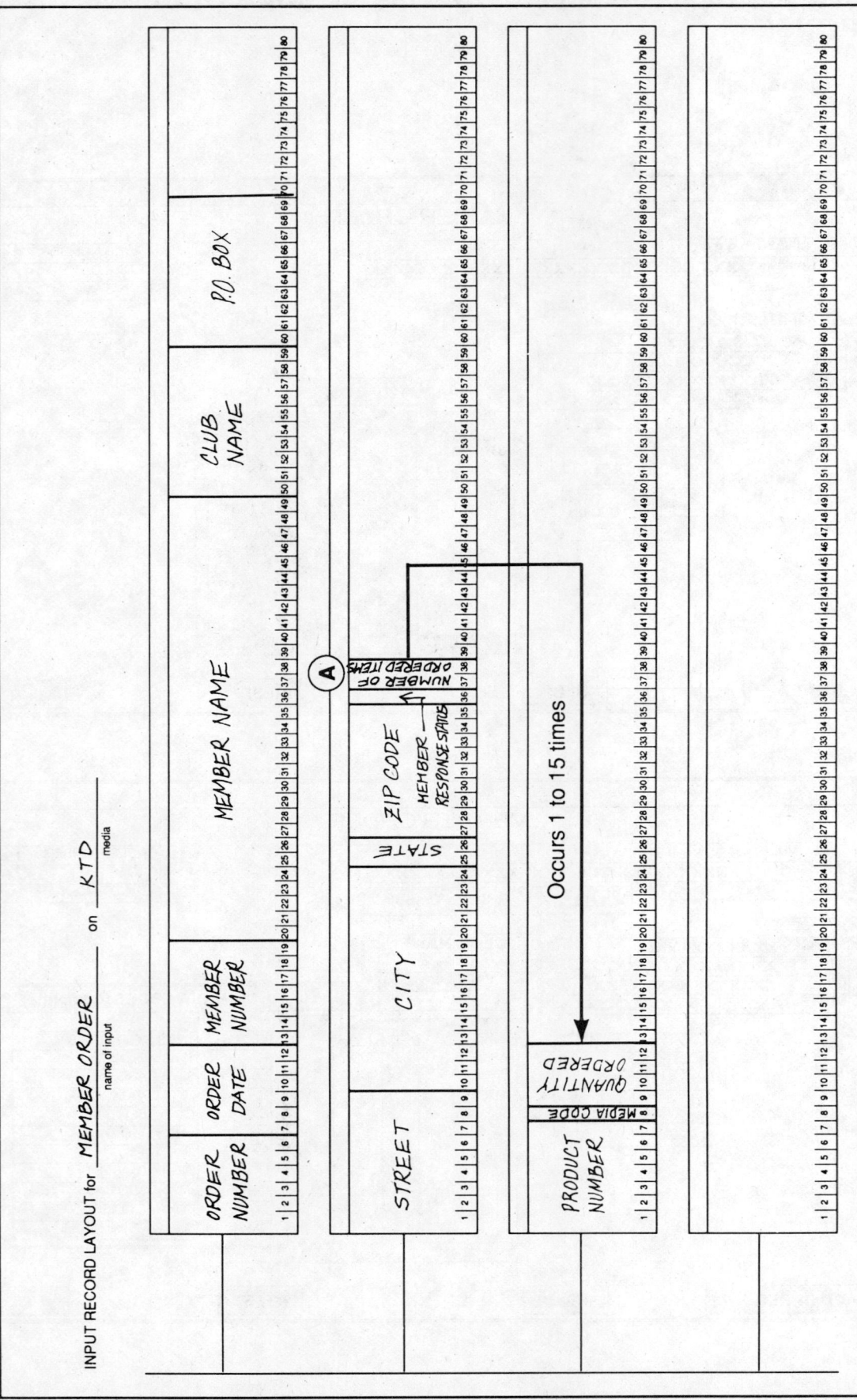

Sample Input Record Layout for Multiple Input Records

TM-203

INPUT RECORD LAYOUT for **PRODUCT UPDATE** on **KTT**
name of input   media

Record 1 (B):
- Transaction Code (col 1)
- Part Number (cols 2–7)
- Part Description (cols 8–21)
- Quantity on Hand (cols 22–25)
- Quantity on Order (cols 26–28)
- Reorder Quantity (cols 29–31)
- Unit Price (cols 32–38)
- Unit of Measure (cols 39–44) (A)

TRANSACTION CODE = A
REPRESENTS ADDITION OF NEW PRODUCT.

Record 2 (C):
- Transaction Code (col 1)
- Part Number (cols 2–7)

TRANSACTION CODE = D
REPRESENTS DELETION OR DISCONTINUATION OF A PRODUCT.

Record 3:
- Transaction Code (col 1)
- Part Number (cols 2–7)
- Unit Price (cols 8–12)
- Unit of Measure (cols 13–17) (D)

TRANSACTION CODE = C
REPRESENTS CHANGE OF PRICE OR MEASUREMENT FOR A PRODUCT.

© Richard D. Irwin, Inc., 1994

Design Specifications for ORDER TO BE FILLED

After the design is approved by system users, the output design decisions are recorded in the project repository.

TM-204

```
                    DATA FLOW - OUTPUT
                    NAME: ORDER TO BE FILLED


TYPE  Data Flow         NAME  ORDER TO BE FILLED

Label  ORDER TO BE FILLED

Explodes To:
Type REC  Name  ORDER TO BE FILLED

Duration Value    5,000
Duration Type     DAY

              Description
DESCRIPTION: A FOUR-PART DOCUMENT DESCRIBING A SALES ORDER
MEDIUM: PAPER                    OUTPUT TYPE: EXTERNAL/FORM
VOLUME: 5,000 PER DAY            NUMBER OF COPIES: 3
COPYING METHOD: SELECTIVE CARBON
FREQUENCY PREPARED: DAILY AT 8 A.M. AND 1:00 P.M.
OUTPUT CHARACTERISTICS: PREPRINTED 8 1/2" x 8 1/2", DESIGNED
OUTPUT CHARACTERISTICS: FOR MAILING. THE 3 COPIES SHOULD HAVE
OUTPUT CHARACTERISTICS: DIFFERENT COLORS:
         ORIGINAL/MASTER = WHITE      PICKING COPY = YELLOW
         PACKING COPY = PINK          SHIPPING COPY = GREEN
OUTPUT RECIPIENT(S): ALL COPIES WILL BE PICKED UP BY ORDER ENTRY
SPECIAL INSTRUCTION(S): QUANTITY SHIPPED IS HAND ENTERED
SPECIAL INSTRUCTION(S): QUANTITY BACKORDERED MAY BE MODIFIED BY HAND
```

© Richard D. Irwin, Inc., 1994

Attribute Details of ORDER TO BE FILLED Output

This report details the attributes to appear on the output.

TM-205

REPORT OF ATTRIBUTES CONTAINED IN ORDER TO BE FILLED RECORD

ATTRIBUTE NAME	TYPE	OCC	CHARACTERS LEFT	CHARACTERS RIGHT	INPUT PICTURE
MEMBER NUMBER	C	1	7	0	9999999
ORDER NUMBER	C	1	6	0	ZZZZZ9
MEMBER NAME	C	1	30	0	X(30)
ORDER DATE	C	1	8	0	MM/DD/YY
ORDER STATUS	C	1	15	0	X(15)
P.O.BOX	C	1	10	0	X(10)
STREET	C	1	15	0	X(15)
CITY	C	1	15	0	X(15)
STATE	C	1	2	0	AA
ZIPCODE	C	1	9	0	X(9)
PRODUCT NUMBER	C	1-15	7	0	9999999
MEDIA CODE	C	1-15	1	0	X
QUANTITY ORDERED	C	1-15	4	0	ZZZ9
QUANTITY SHIPPED	C	1-15	4	0	ZZZ9
ORDER PRICE	C	1-15	3	2	ZZZ.99
EXTENDED PRICE	C	1-15	4	2	ZZZZ.99
TOTAL ORDER PRICE	C	1	5	2	ZZZZ9.99

Ⓐ Ⓑ Ⓑ Ⓒ

© Richard D. Irwin, Inc., 1994

Sample Attribute Screen
This is a sample Excelerator screen for defining the details of an attribute.

TM–206

```
Element                    ORDER NUMBER

Alternate Names   MEMBER ORDER NUMBER
                  ORDER NO.
                  ORDER #

Definition        A SIX DIGIT NUMBER THAT UNIQUELY IDENTIFIES AN ORDER.

Input Format      999999
Output Format     ZZZZZ9
Edit Rules        MUST BE UNIQUE FOR AN ORDER; VALUE 1 THRU 999999
Storage Type      C
Characters left of decimal 6   Characters right of decimal 0

Default
Prompt            ORDER NUMBER
Column Header     ORDER NUMBER
Short Header      ORDER NO.
Base or Derived   B
Data Class
Source
```

© Richard D. Irwin, Inc., 1994

Sample Prototypes Generated from a Spreadsheet

The summary report prototypes were generated using Microsoft's Excel.

TM−207

A.

Member Response to Selection of Month by Club Category
September, 1994

Category	Potential Orders	Selection of Month	Alternate Selection	Selection of Month + Alternates	No Order
Pop/Rock	6342	2410	824	241	2867
Country	3577	1538	644	154	1241
Easy Listening	954	181	38	18	716
Classical	1486	877	45	88	477
Jazz	540	389	54	39	58
Show/Comedy	104	9	54	1	40

LEGEND

Category: Club to which members belong
Potential Orders: Number of members in club who received Selection of the Month promotion
Selection of Month: Number of members who selected ONLY the Selection of the Month
Alternate Selections: Number of members who selected titles other than the Selection of the Month
Selection of Month + Alternates: Number of members who selected both Selection of Month plus alternates
No Order: Number of members who rejected Selection of Month and ordered no alternates

B.

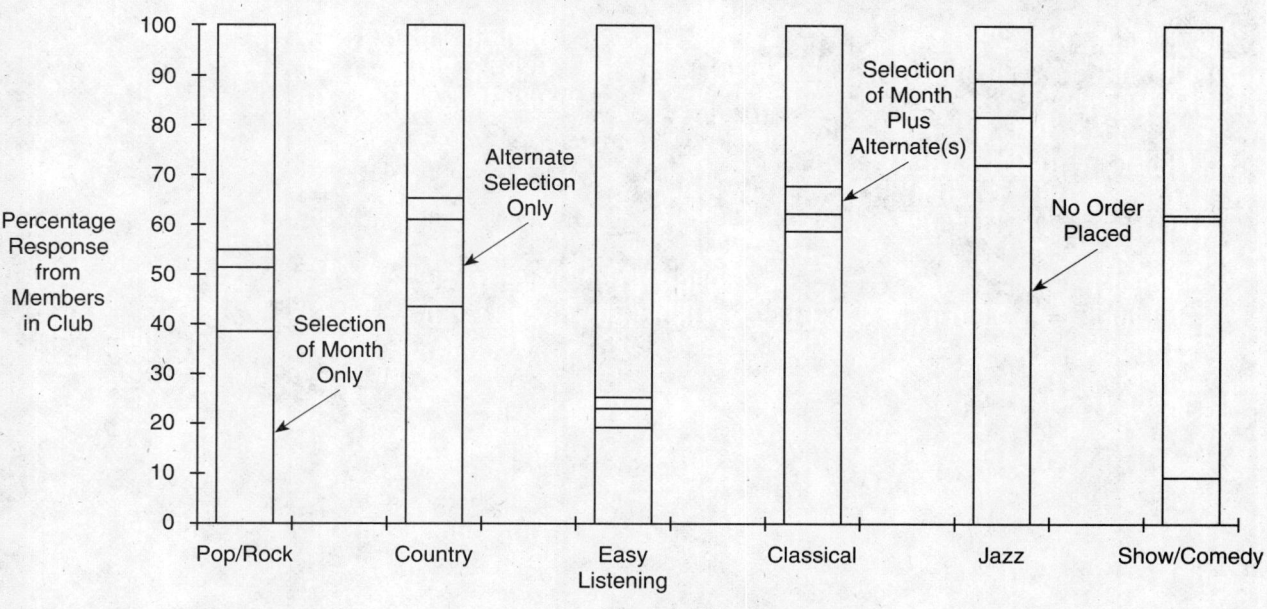

© Richard D. Irwin, Inc., 1994

Prototyped Output Screen from a CASE Tool   TM−208

A.

```
                    *** MEMBER ORDER INQUIRY ***
MEMBER NUMBER:                          ORDER NUMBER:
MEMBER NAME:                            ORDER DATE: 00/00/00
MEMBER ADDRESS:                         ORDER STATUS:
   P.O. BOX:
   STREET:
   CITY:
   STATE:         ZIPCODE:

                                QUANTITY   QUANTITY            EXTENDED
   PRODUCT                      ORDERED    SHIPPED             PRICE
   NUMBER     MEDIA    CREDIT                         PRICE


                        *FIELD DEFINITION SCREEN*
Field name:      MEDIA              Related ELE: MEDIA CODE
Length: 1    I/O/T:I   Required:N  Skip:Y  Bright:N  Reverse:Y Blink:N Underline:N
Storage type: C  Characters left of decimal: 1   Characters right of decimal: 0
Dflt:D
Input format:    X                          Output format:  X
Edit rules:      "R","D","C","8"
Help:ENTER THE MEDIA OF THE ORDERED PRODUCT.
```

B.

```
                    *** MEMBER ORDER INQUIRY ***
MEMBER NUMBER: 230118                   ORDER NUMBER: 172402
MEMBER NAME:   CLAUDIA M. ANDERSON      ORDER DATE: 12/22/92
MEMBER ADDRESS:                         ORDER STATUS: O
   P.O. BOX: 101-A
   STREET:   MAIN STREET
   CITY:     WEST LAFAYETTE
   STATE:    IN ZIPCODE: 47906

                                QUANTITY   QUANTITY            EXTENDED
   PRODUCT                      ORDERED    SHIPPED             PRICE
   NUMBER     MEDIA    CREDIT                         PRICE
   1120015      D        2         1          0       12.99    12.99
   1304599      C        1         2          0        8.99    17.98
   3089031      R        1         1          0        7.45     7.45


                                        TOTAL ORDER PRICE:    38.42


         ** PRESS ARROW KEYS TO SEE ADDITIONAL PRODUCTS **
         ** PRESS F3 TO RETURN TO ORDER INQUIRY OPTIONS MENU **
```

© Richard D. Irwin, Inc., 1994

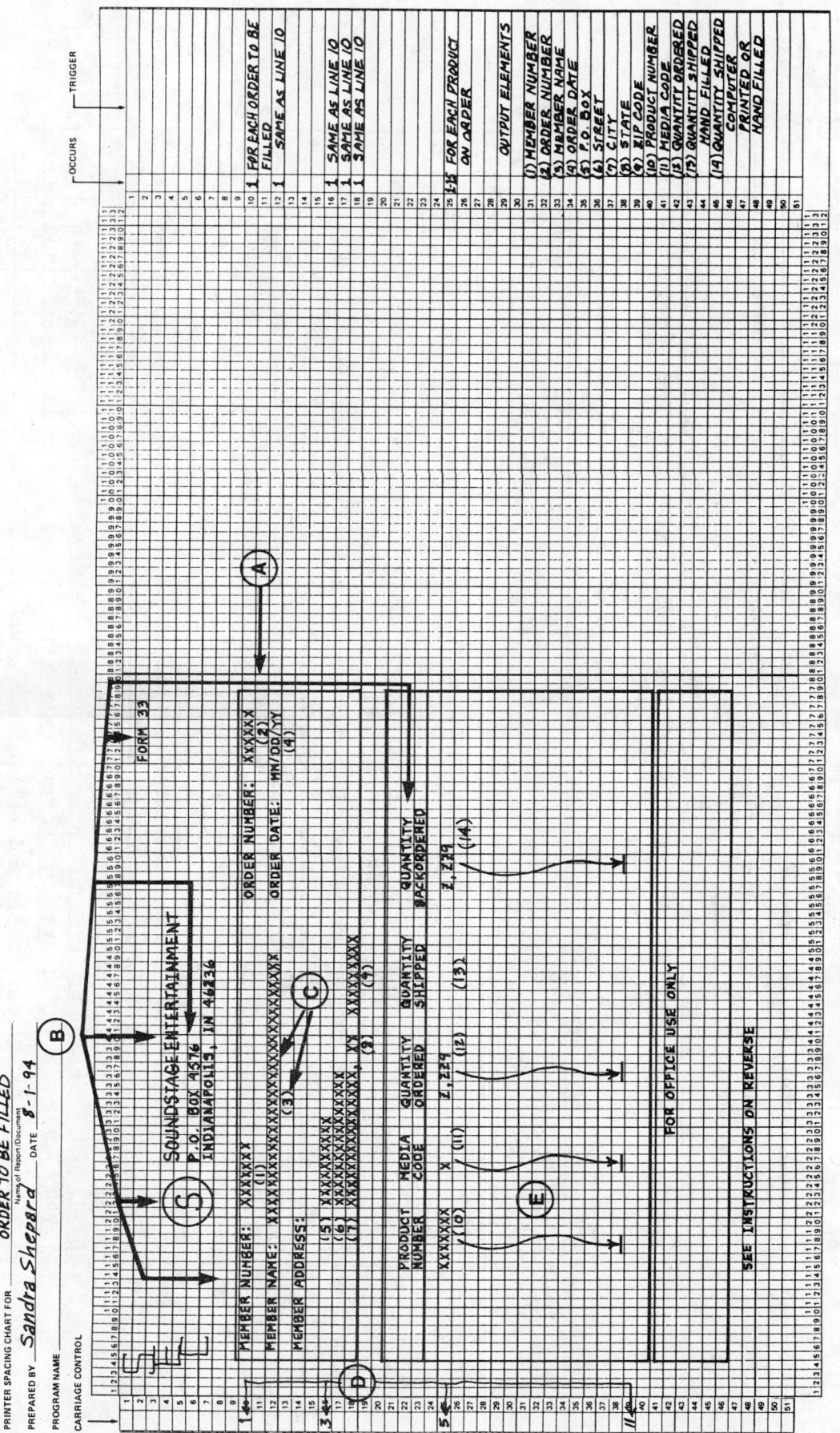

TM-210 (cont)

TERMINAL SCREEN DISPLAY LAYOUT FORM

☐ INPUT
☑ OUTPUT

APPLICATION _CUSTOMER SERVICES_
SCREEN NO. _4_ **SEQUENCE** _4_

```
            1-10        11-20       21-30       31-40       41-50       51-60       61-70       71-80
01                                       *** MEMBER ORDER INQUIRY ***
02
03  MEMBER NUMBER:  XXXXXXXX                                    ORDER NUMBER:  XXXXXXX
04  MEMBER NAME:    XXXXXXXXXX                          X       ORDER DATE:    MM/DD/YY
05  CLUB MEMBERSHIP: XXXXXXXXXXX                                ORDER STATUS:  XXXXXXXX
06  MEMBER ADDRESS:
07   P.O. BOX   XXXXXXXXXX
08   STREET:    XXXXXXXXXXXXXXXX
09   CITY:      XXXXXXXXXXXXXXXX
10   STATE: XX  ZIPCODE: XXXXXXXXXX
11
12  PRODUCT                       QUANTITY   QUANTITY                EXTENDED
13  NUMBER    MEDIA               ORDERED    SHIPPED      PRICE       PRICE
14  XXXXXXX     X                  Z,ZZ9      Z,ZZ9     ZZZ.99     Z,ZZZ.99
15
16
17
18
19
20  TOTAL ORDER CREDITS:  Z9                     TOTAL ORDER PRICE: ZZ,ZZZ.99
21  UNUSED BONUS CREDITS: Z9
22
23          *** PRESS ARROW KEYS TO SEE ADDITIONAL PRODUCTS ***
24          *** PRESS F3 TO RETURN TO ORDER INQUIRY OPTIONS MENU ***
```

© Richard D. Irwin, Inc., 1994

Display Layout Chart

A display layout chart is used to design the layout of displayed outputs.

TM–210
(concl)

FUNCTION KEY ASSIGNMENTS

PF1	
PF2	
PF3	RETURN TO ORDER INQUIRY OPTIONS MENU
PF4	
PF5	
PF6	
PF7	
PF8	
PF9	
PF10	
PF12	
PF13	
PF14	
PF15	
PF16	
PF17	
PF18	
PF19	
PF20	
PF21	
PF22	
PF23	
PF24	

© Richard D. Irwin, Inc., 1994

TM-211

A Typical Example of a Graphical User Interface from Microsoft Windows
Note the pull-down menu, the pop-up window, the scroll bars, and the icons.

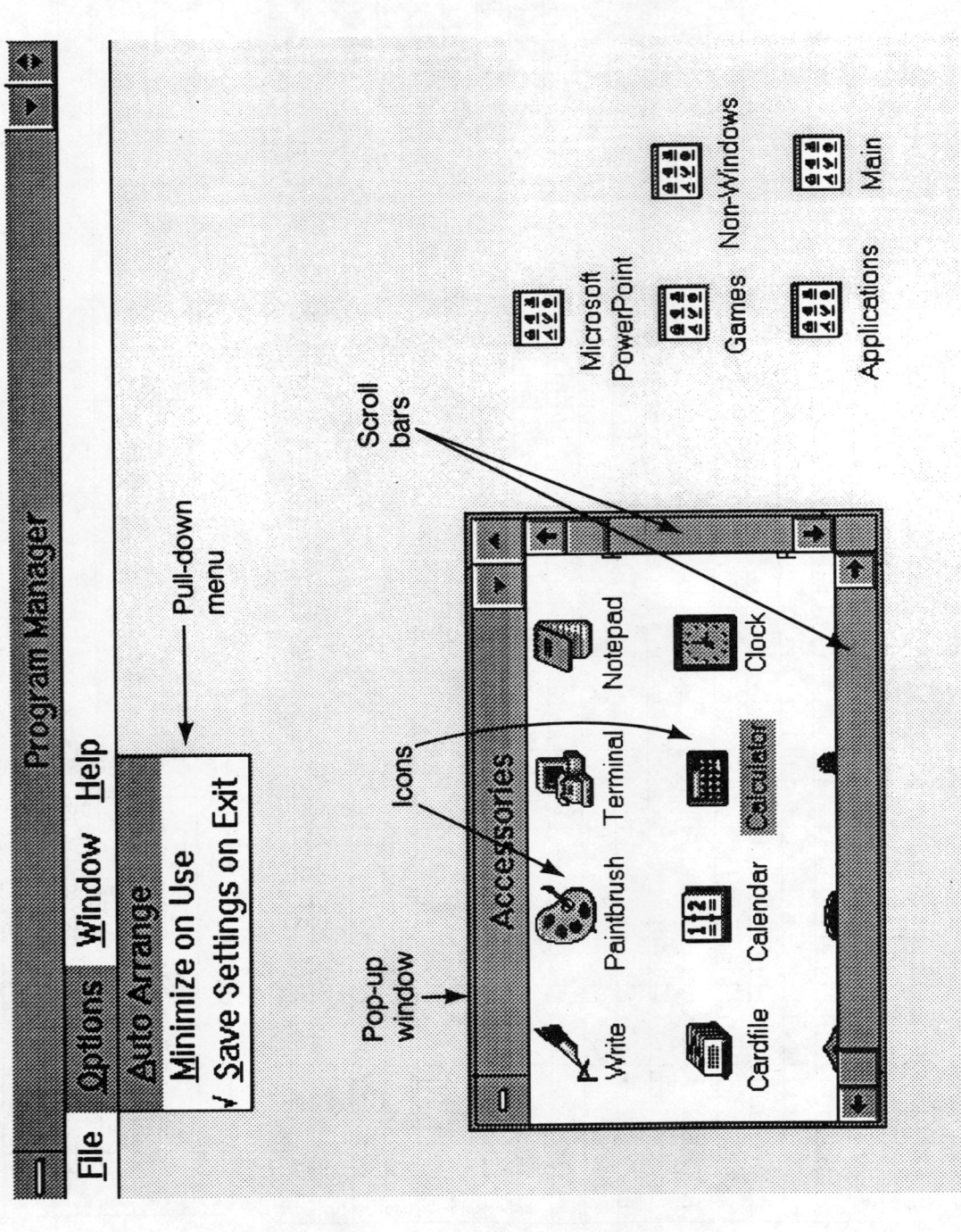

© Richard D. Irwin, Inc., 1994

Radio Buttons and Check Boxes in a Graphical User Interface
Radio buttons and check boxes are a standard part of a CUA compliant graphical user interface (GUI).

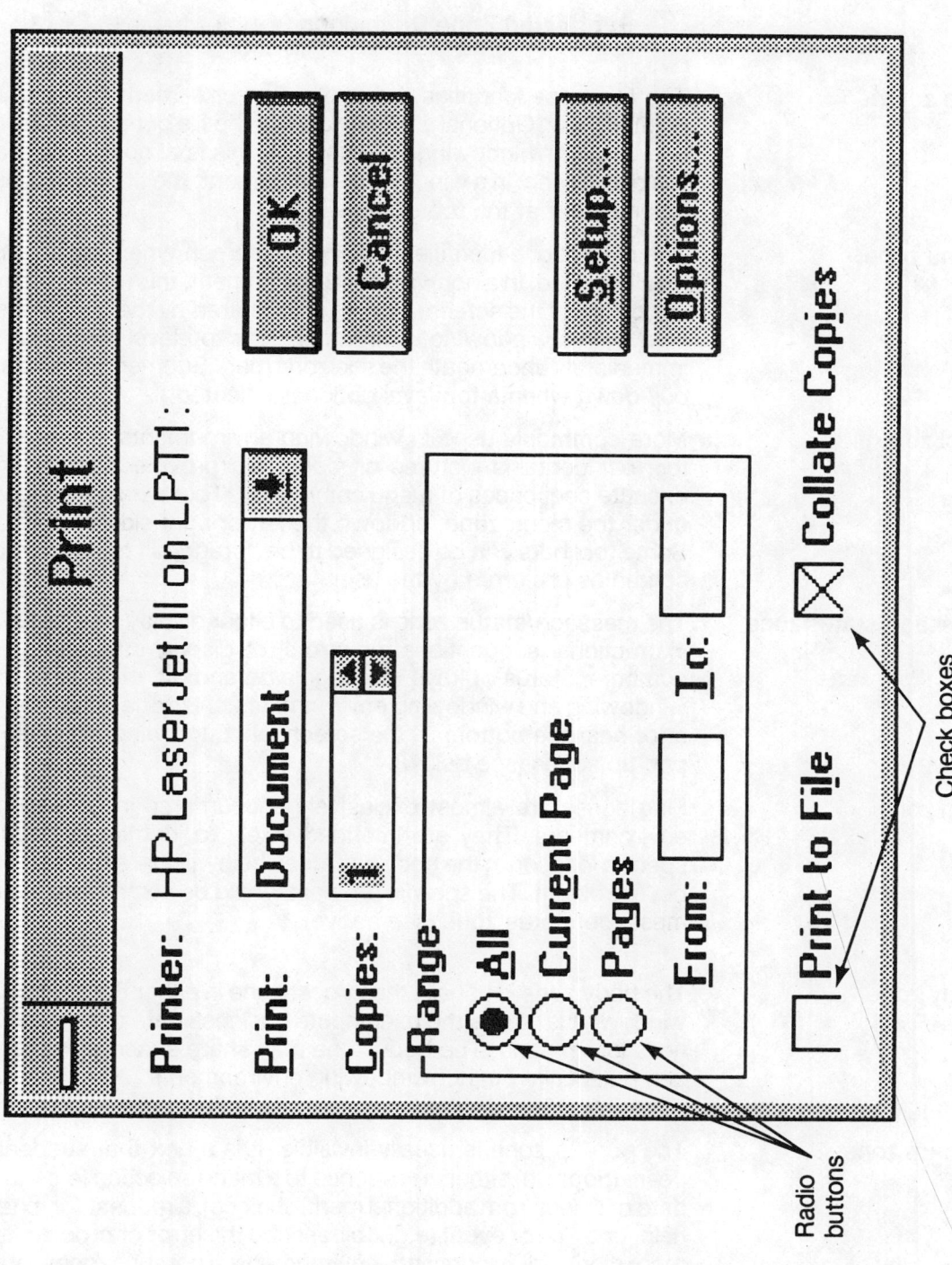

© Richard D. Irwin, Inc., 1994

Screen Zones

TM-213

Screens are easier to read if the similar data, information, and messages are consistently presented in the same areas or zones on the screens.

Suggested Zone Definitions

Title zone	The title zone identifies the application or screen from the user's point of view. Optionally, it may identify the file or record currently in use. In a nonwindowing environment, this is almost always at the top of a screen. In a windowing environment, the title zone is usually a named bar at the top of the window.
Menu zone	The menu zone identifies the area of screen where menu choices may be found. In a nonwindows environment, this may be at the top or bottom of the screen, or in an area shared by the body zone (see below). In a windowing environment, the top-level menu is in a bar immediately underneath the title zone (bar). Submenus may *drop-* or *pull-down* when a top-level option is selected.
Tool zone	More commonly used in windowing environments, a tool zone or *tool bar* contains pictures or *icons* that provide a faster way to execute sequences of menu commands. Tool bars may be located under the menu zone, or down the left or right side of the screen. Some tool bars can be designed to be "dragged" to any part of the screen as preferred by the user.
Message/status zone	The message/status zone is used to either display messages (e.g., instructions, suggestions, or errors) or display status (e.g., page numbers, status of keys that toggle on and off, etc.). In both non-windowing and windowing environments, this zone usually appears at or near the bottom of the screen, although windowing also use pop-up zones (see below).
Flag zone	Flag zones are almost exclusively encountered in nonwindowing environments. They are intended solely to identify or point to a specific location in the body zone (see below) where there is, or may be, a problem. The specific problem would be communicated in the message/status zone (see above).
Body zone	The body zone is usually the largest zone in either the screen or the window. It is where the user inputs business data or receives business information. The body zone may share space with the menu zone, especially in nonwindowing environments.
Pop-up zone	The pop-up zone is usually invisible. It is a box that suddenly appears (pops up) either in response to a menu selection (e.g., to enter data or select from additional menu choices), a request for extended help, or an error event (e.g., to describe the error or problem and its resolution). In windowing environments, pop-up zones are frequently called *dialog boxes* (e.g., Microsoft Windows) or *notebooks* (e.g., IBM Presentation Manager).

© Richard D. Irwin, Inc., 1994

Sample Zones for a Screen

This is one possible zone design for a screen.

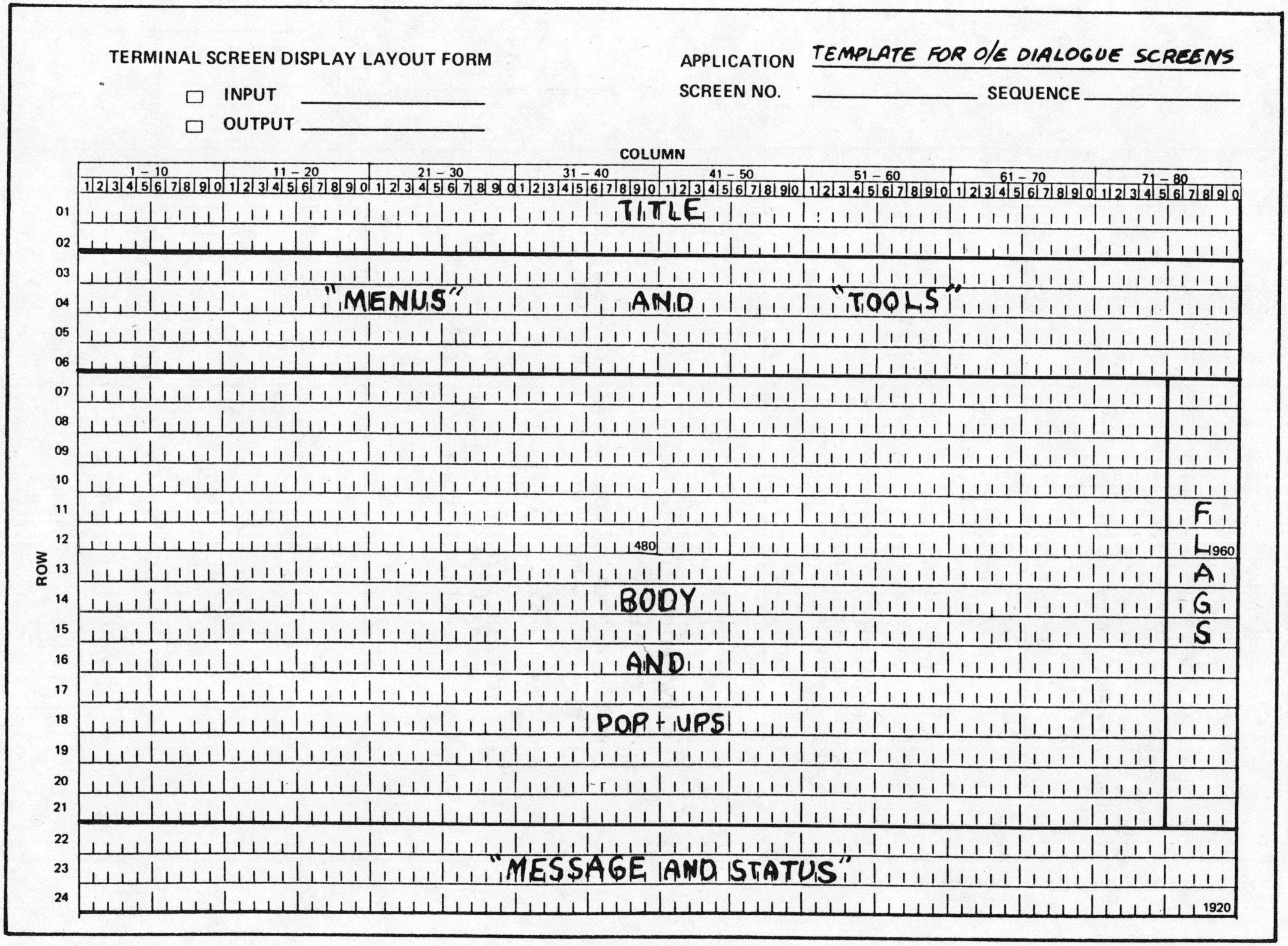
TERMINAL SCREEN DISPLAY LAYOUT FORM
INPUT
OUTPUT
APPLICATION
TEMPLATE FOR O/E DIALOGUE SCREENS
SCREEN NO.
SEQUENCE
COLUMN
1 – 10
11 – 20
21 – 30
31 – 40
41 – 50
51 – 60
61 – 70
71 – 80
ROW
TITLE
"MENUS" AND "TOOLS"
BODY
AND
POP-UPS
FLAGS
480
960
1920
"MESSAGE AND STATUS"

© Richard D. Irwin, Inc., 1994

Classic Hierarchical Menu Dialogue

Classic menu selection is the most common dialogue strategy in use today.

TM-215

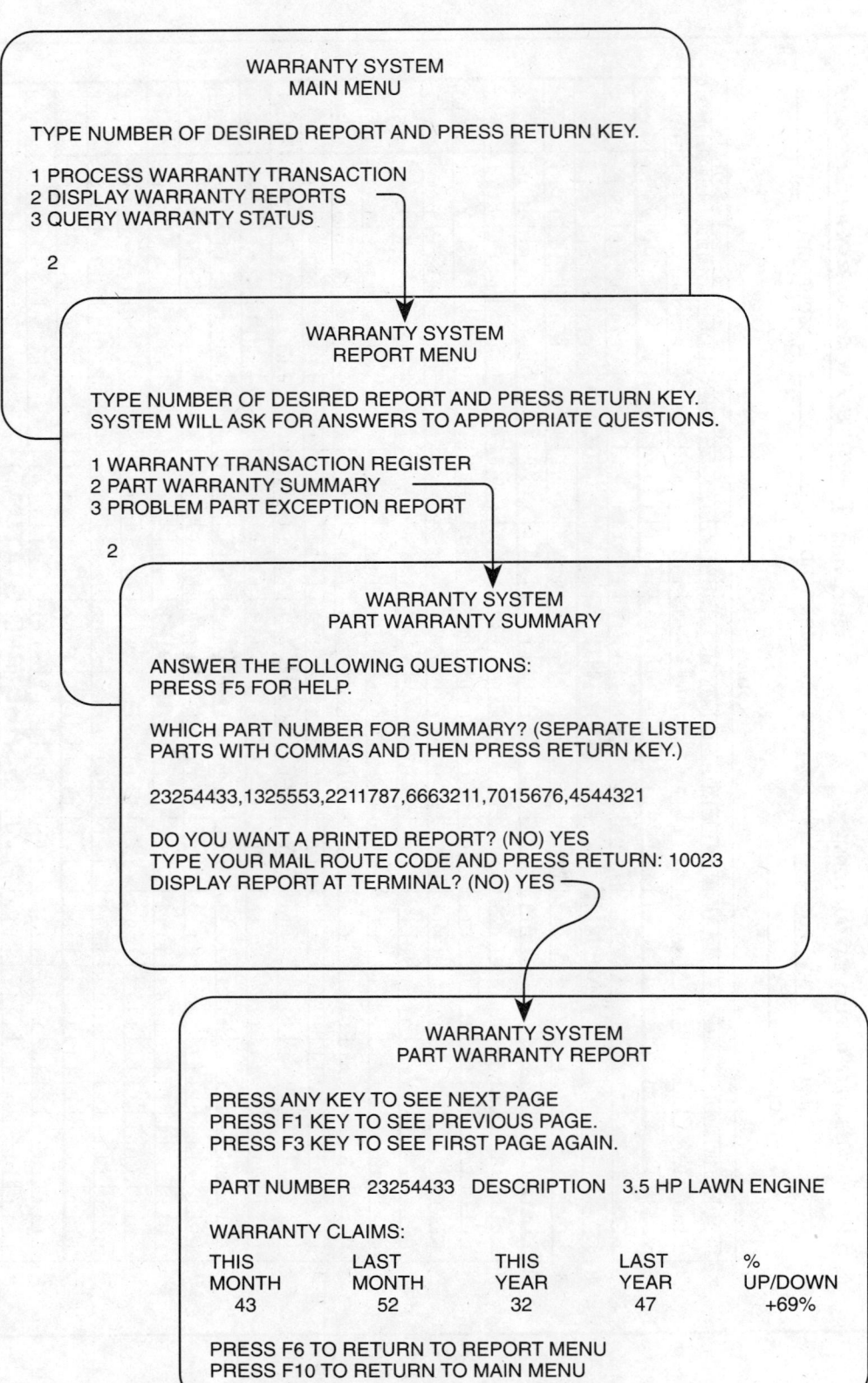

©Richard D. Irwin, Inc., 1994

Alternative Pull-Down and Pop-Up Menu Dialogue   TM−216

A. Pull-down menus are submenus that pull down from a main menu option.
B. Pop-up menus may be activated by function keys and temporarily overlay whatever is located on the screen.

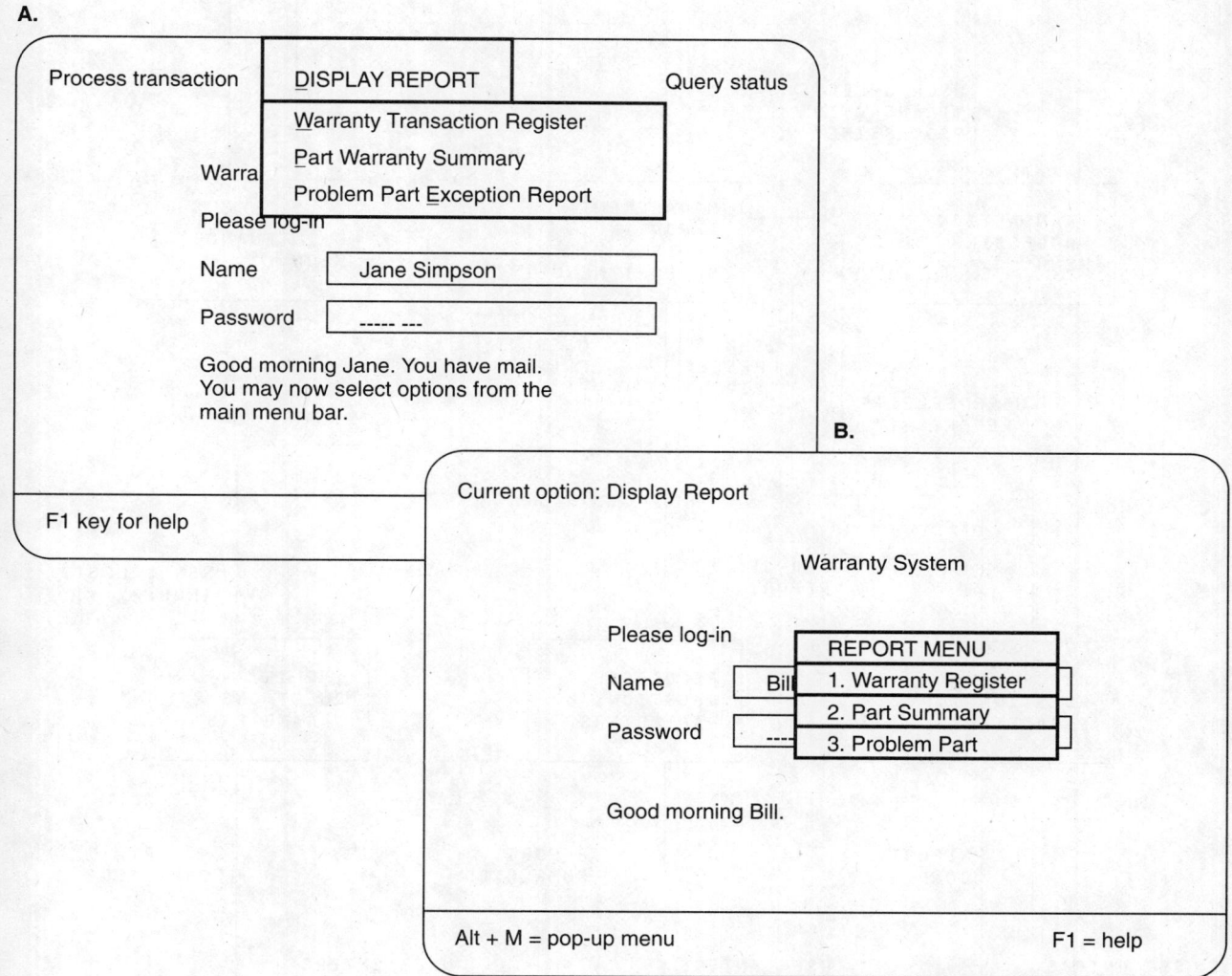

Sample State Transition Diagram for Documenting Dialogue   TM-217
State transition diagrams can be used to design and document user interface screens.

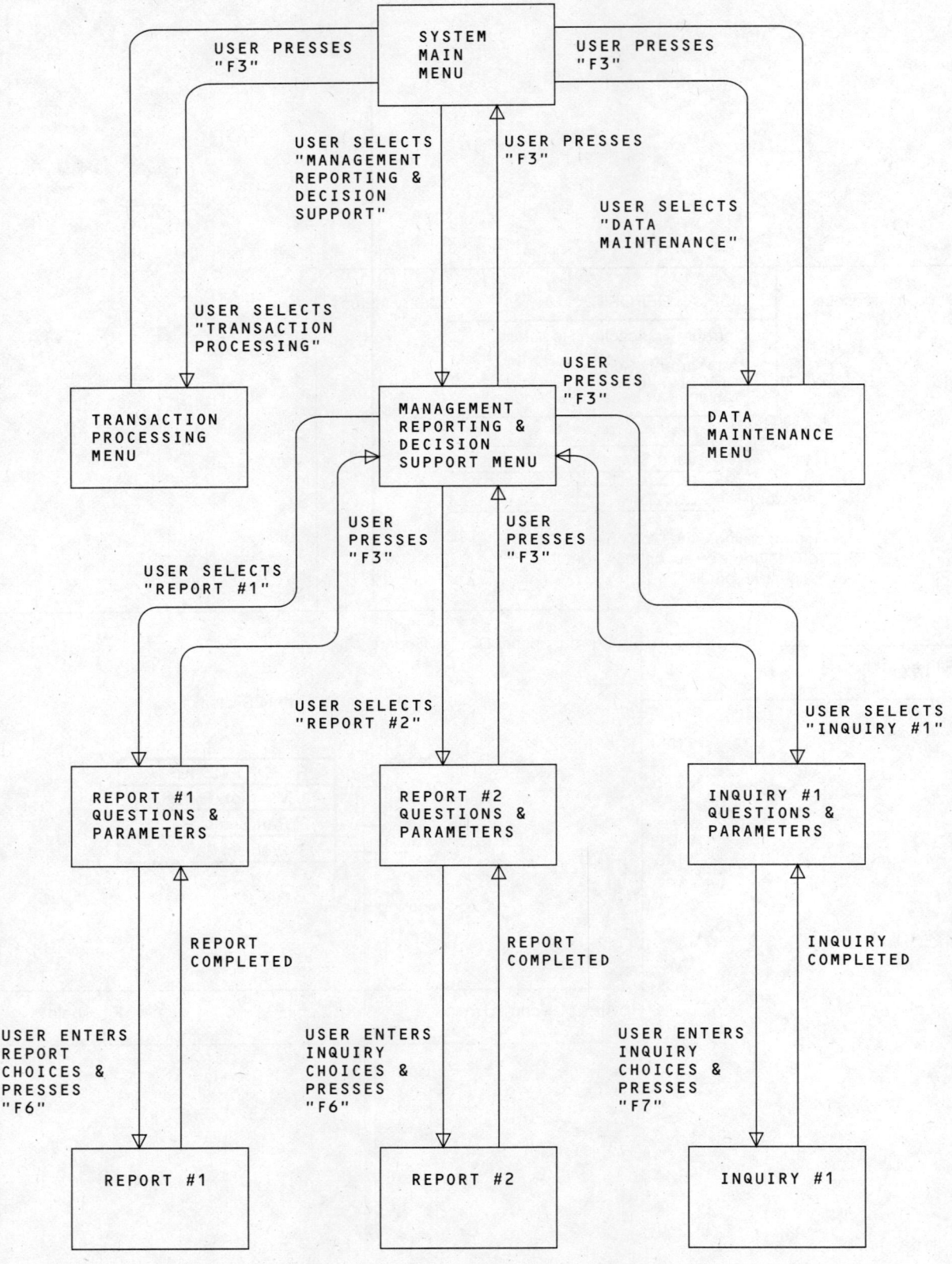

©Richard D. Irwin, Inc., 1994

State Transition Diagram Conventions

A state transition diagram consists of rectangles that represent display screens and arrows that represent the flow of control through various display screens.

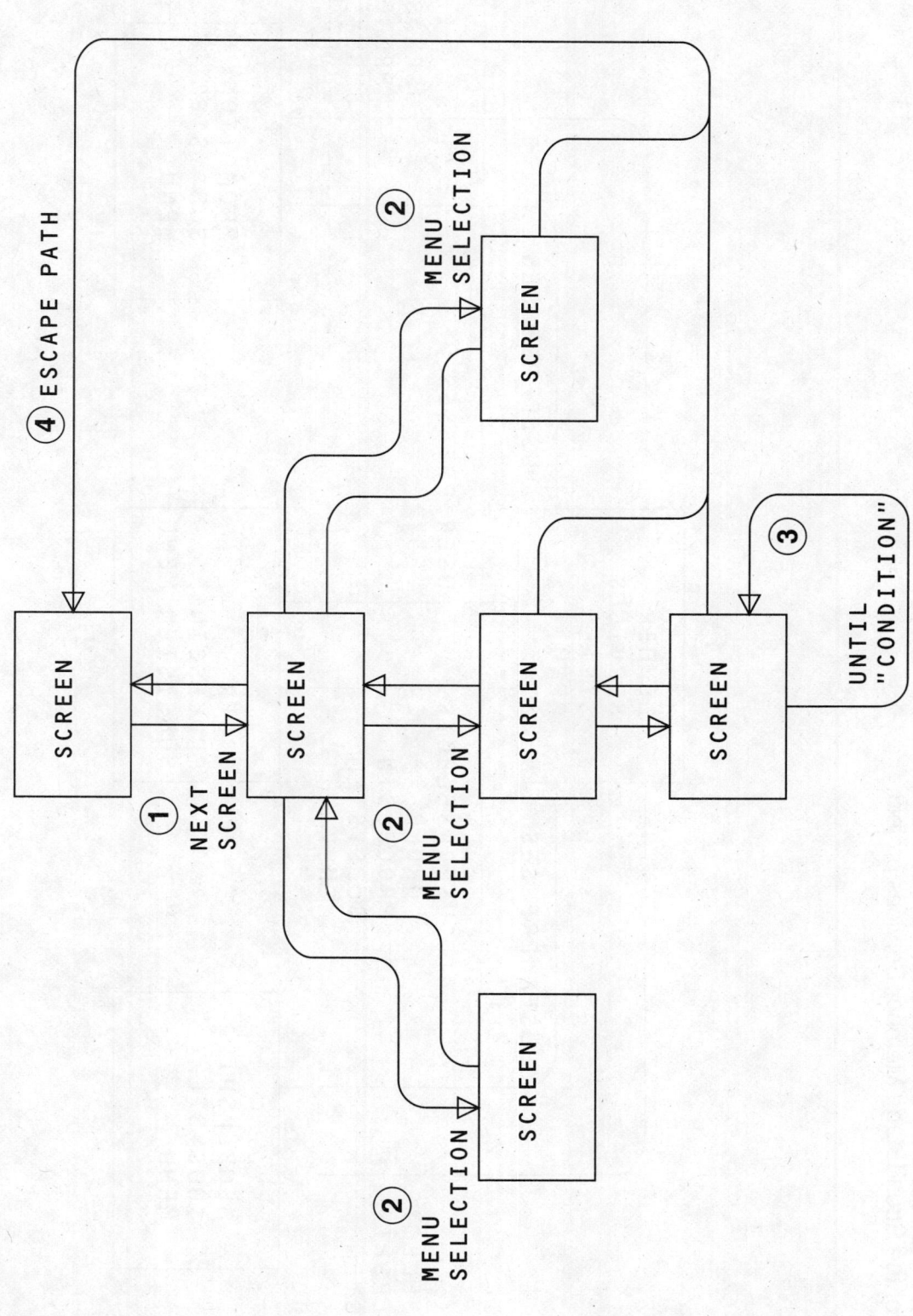

TM-218

© Richard D. Irwin, Inc., 1994

State Transition Diagram for SoundStage Member Services Project

TM-219
(cont)

This state transition diagram shows the relationship between the many display screens needed to describe the dialogue of the SoundStage Member Services project.

A.

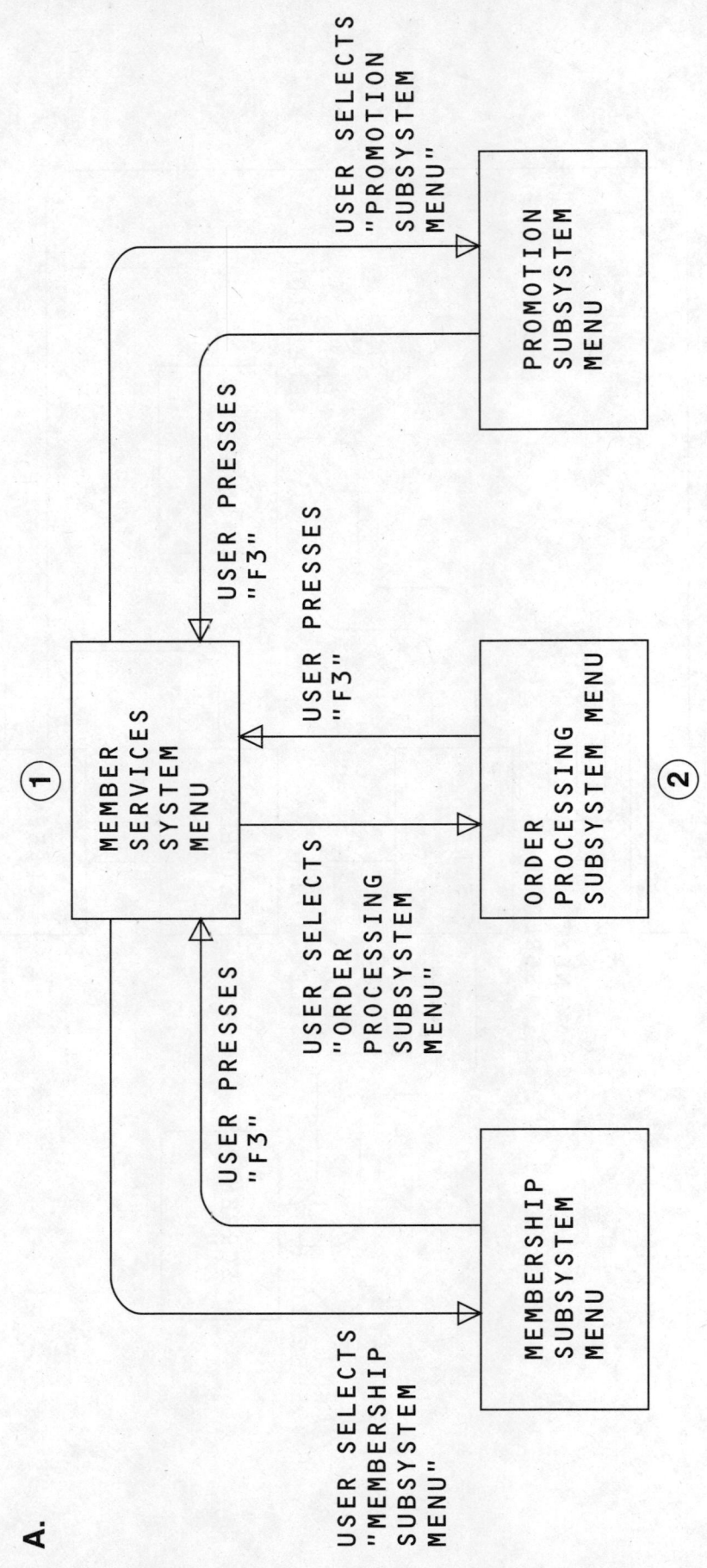

© Richard D. Irwin, Inc., 1994

TM-219
(concl)

B.

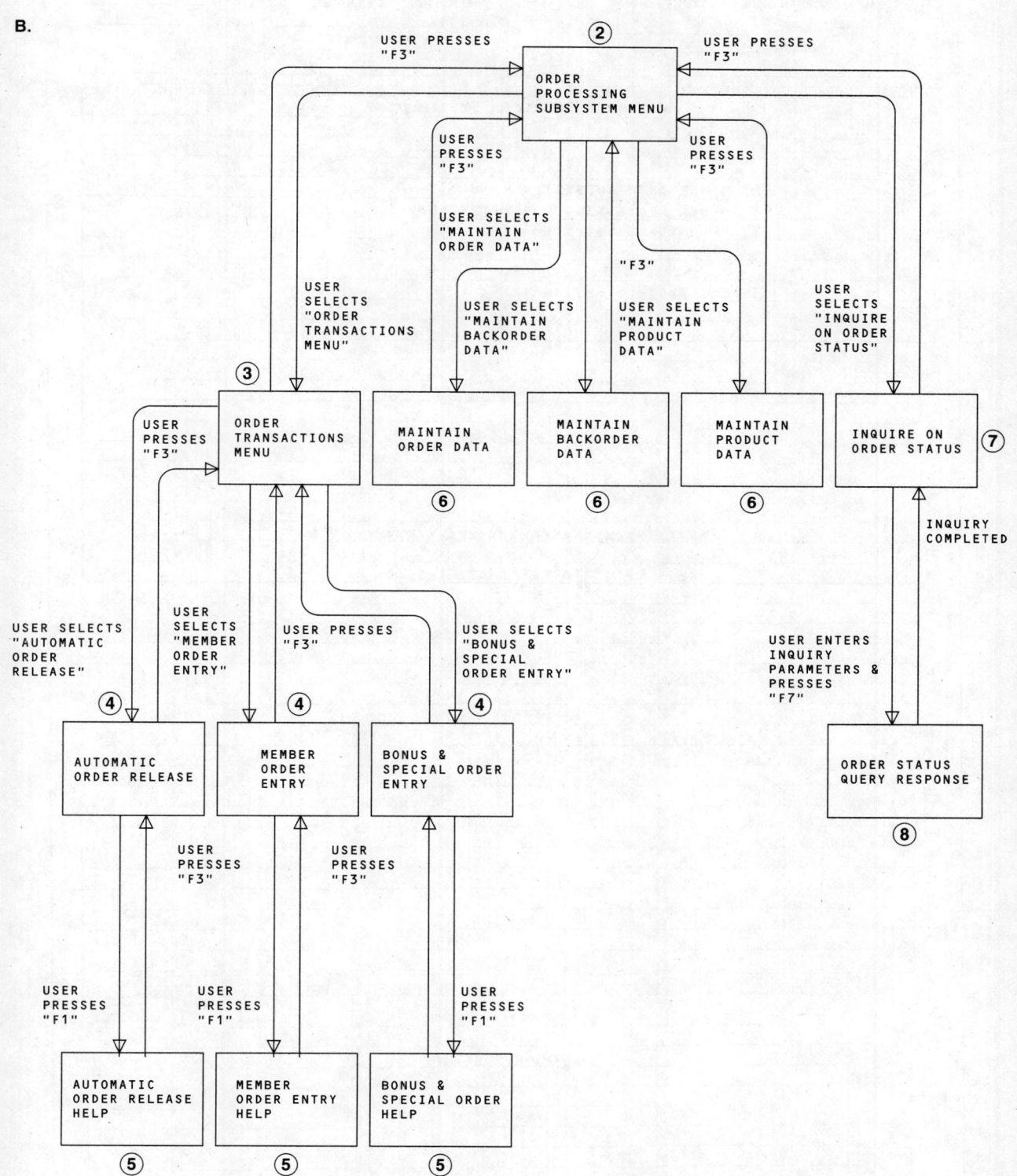

©Richard D. Irwin, Inc., 1994

Display Layout Chart for the MEMBER SERVICES SYSTEM MENU Screen

TM-220

TERMINAL SCREEN DISPLAY LAYOUT FORM

APPLICATION: MEMBER SERVICES
SCREEN NO. _____ SEQUENCE _____

☐ INPUT _____
☐ OUTPUT _____

Row 01: MEMBER SERVICES SYSTEM MENU
Row 05: [1] MEMBERSHIP SUBSYSTEM MENU
Row 06: [2] ORDER PROCESSING SUBSYSTEM MENU
Row 07: [3] PROMOTION SUBSYSTEM MENU
Row 10: SELECT DESIRED OPTION ==> X
Row 22: XXXXXXXXXXXXXXXXXXXXXXXXXXXXXXXXXX (a)
Row 24: PRESS "F10" TO TERMINATE SESSION

FUNCTION KEY ASSIGNMENTS

PF1	PF9	PF17
PF2	PF10 TERMINATE SESSION	PF18
PF3	PF11	PF19
PF4	PF12	PF20
PF5	PF13	PF21
PF6	PF14	PF22
PF7	PF15	PF23
PF8	PF16	PF24

© Richard D. Irwin, Inc., 1994

Display Layout Chart for the ORDER PROCESSING SUBSYSTEM MENU Screen

TM-221

TERMINAL SCREEN DISPLAY LAYOUT FORM

- ☐ INPUT
- ☐ OUTPUT

APPLICATION: MEMBER SERVICES
SCREEN NO: _____ SEQUENCE: _____

Row 01: ORDER PROCESSING SUBSYSTEM MENU
Row 05: [1] ORDER TRANSACTIONS MENU
Row 06: [2] MAINTAIN ORDER DATA
Row 07: [3] MAINTAIN BACKORDER DATA
Row 08: [4] MAINTAIN PRODUCT DATA
Row 09: [5] INQUIRE ON ORDER STATUS
Row 12: SELECT DESIRED OPTION ==> X
Row 22: XXXXXXXXXXXXXXXXXXXXXXXXXXXXXXXXX (a)
Row 24: PRESS "F3" TO RETURN TO THE SYSTEM MENU

FUNCTION KEY ASSIGNMENTS

Key	Assignment	Key	Assignment	Key	Assignment
PF1		PF9		PF17	
PF2		PF10		PF18	
PF3	MEMBER SERVICES SYSTEM MENU	PF11		PF19	
PF4		PF12		PF20	
PF5		PF13		PF21	
PF6		PF14		PF22	
PF7		PF15		PF23	
PF8		PF16		PF24	

© Richard D. Irwin, Inc., 1994

Display Layout Chart for the ORDER TRANSACTIONS MENU Screen — TM-222

TERMINAL SCREEN DISPLAY LAYOUT FORM

APPLICATION: MEMBER SERVICES
☑ INPUT: MEMBER ORDER ENTRY
☐ OUTPUT: _____
SCREEN NO. _____ SEQUENCE _____

```
01                        ** MEMBER ORDER ENTRY **
02    ENTER THE FOLLOWING ITEMS FROM A MEMBER ORDER (FORM MO). USE TAB OR
03    ARROW KEYS TO MOVE FROM ITEM TO ITEM. PRESS THE ENTER KEY WHEN DONE.
04
05  MEMBER NUMBER: 9999999                      ORDER NUMBER: 999999
06  MEMBER NAME:   XXXXXXXXXXXXXXXXXXXXXXXXXXX   ORDER DATE:   99/99/99
07  CLUB NAME:     XXXXXXXXXXXXXXXXX             PREPAID AMOUNT: 999.99
08  MEMBER ADDRESS=
09    P.O. BOX: XXXXXXXXX
10    STREET:   XXXXXXXXXXXXXXXX
11    CITY:     XXXXXXXXXXXXXXX
12    STATE: AA  ZIPCODE: XXXXXXXXX
13
14          SELECTION OF       PRODUCT    MEDIA    QUANTITY
15          MONTH ACCEPTED?    NUMBER     CODE     ORDERED
16                X            9999999    X        9999
...
23    XXXXXXXXXXXXXXXXXXXXXXXXXXXXXXXXXXXXXXXXXXXXXXXXXXXXXXXXXXX
24    PRESS "F1" FOR HELP. PRESS "F3" TO RETURN TO THE ORDER TRANSACTIONS MENU.
```

FUNCTION KEY ASSIGNMENTS

Key	Assignment	Key	Assignment	Key	Assignment
PF1	HELP SCREEN (FOR THAT ITEM)	PF9		PF17	
PF2		PF10		PF18	
PF3	RETURN TO ORDER TRANSACTIONS MENU	PF11		PF19	
PF4		PF12		PF20	
PF5		PF13		PF21	
PF6		PF14		PF22	
PF7		PF15		PF23	
PF8		PF16		PF24	

© Richard D. Irwin, Inc., 1994

Display Layout Chart for the MEMBER ORDER ENTRY HELP Screen — TM-223

TERMINAL SCREEN DISPLAY LAYOUT FORM

APPLICATION: MEMBER SERVICES
SCREEN NO.: _____ SEQUENCE: _____

☐ INPUT _____
☐ OUTPUT _____

Row 01: `** MEMBER ORDER ENTRY **`
Row 02: `HELP SCREEN`
Rows 06–10: (block of X's representing help text)
Row 13: `PRESS "F3" TO RETURN TO THE MEMBER ORDER ENTRY SCREEN`

FUNCTION KEY ASSIGNMENTS: PF1–PF24 (blank)

Sample Help Messages for the Member Order Help Screen

A typical help message includes a brief description of the field, its format, and a valid example.

The MEMBER NUMBER is a right justified, 7-character, positive numeric field in the form of 9999999. Leading zeros should not be entered. For example, MEMBER NUMBER 1473 would be entered as 1473.

The ORDER NUMBER is a right justified, 6-character, positive numeric field in the form of 999999. Leading zeros should not be entered. For example, ORDER NUMBER 531 would be entered as 531.

The ORDER DATE is an 8-character field in the format of MM/DD/YY. The default value is today's date. The slashes must be entered, but leading zeros should not be entered. For example, February 15, 1993 would be entered as 2/15/93.

The PRODUCT NUMBER is a right justified, 7-character, positive numeric field in the format of 9999999. Leading zeros should not be entered. For example, product number 72947 would be entered as 72947.

The MEDIA CODE is a 1-character, alphanumeric field. The valid values for this field are: VH, VHS; 8M, 8MM: DC, Digital Cassette; CA, Cassette; CD, Compact Disc; LD, Laser Disc. For example, if a compact disc was ordered, enter CD.

The QUANTITY ORDERED is a right justified, 4-character, positive numeric field in the format of 9999. Leading zeros should not be entered. The default value is 1. For example, quantity of 45 should be entered as 45.

TM-224

©Richard D. Irwin, Inc., 1994

Warnier/Orr Notation

Warnier/Orr brackets are a popular and simple-to-use modular design tool.

TM-225

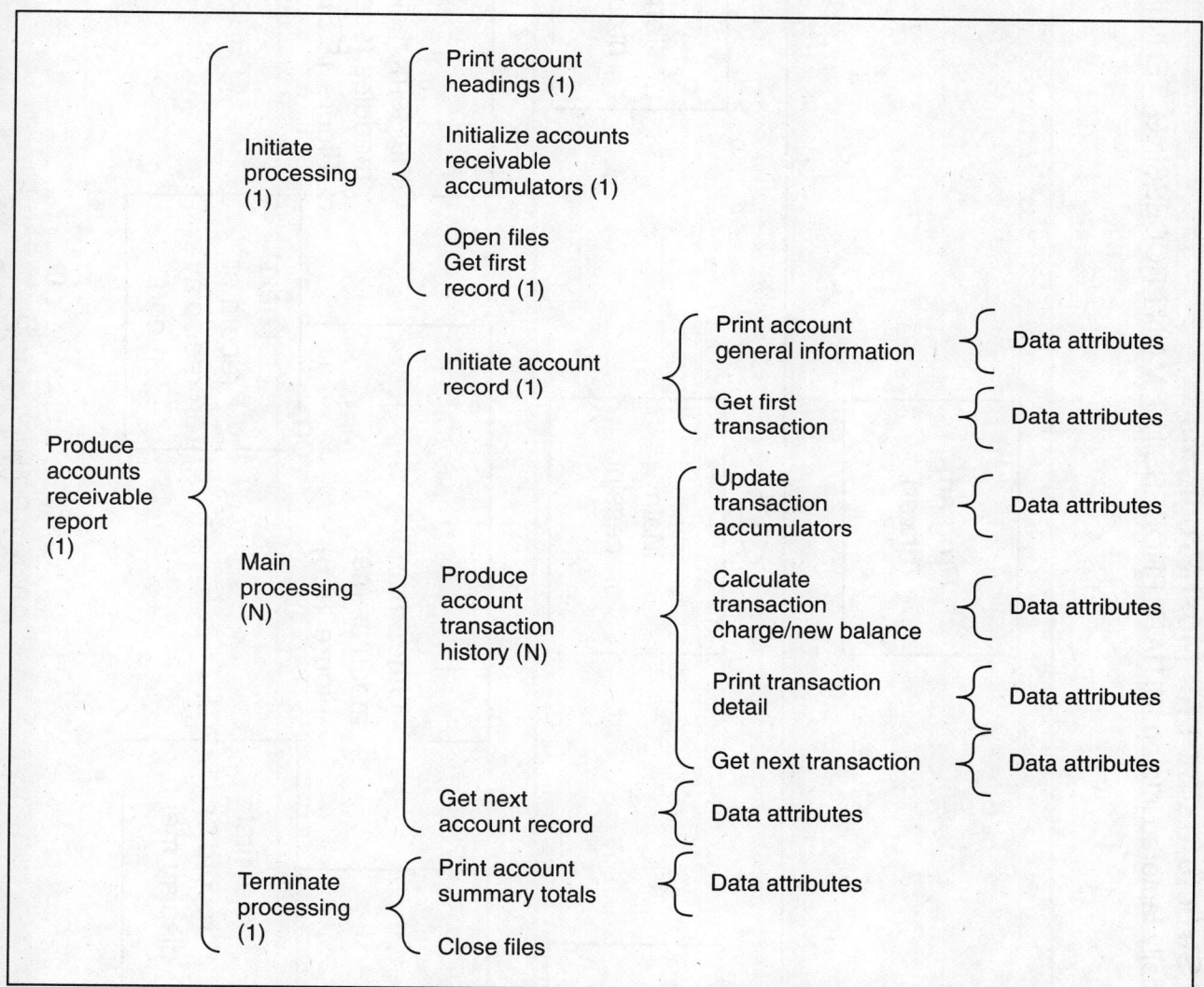

©Richard D. Irwin, Inc., 1994

A De Facto Standard Structure Chart for Most Programs

Most programs can be initially factored into an INITIATE PROCESSING, MAIN PROCESSING, TERMINATE PROCESSING structure.

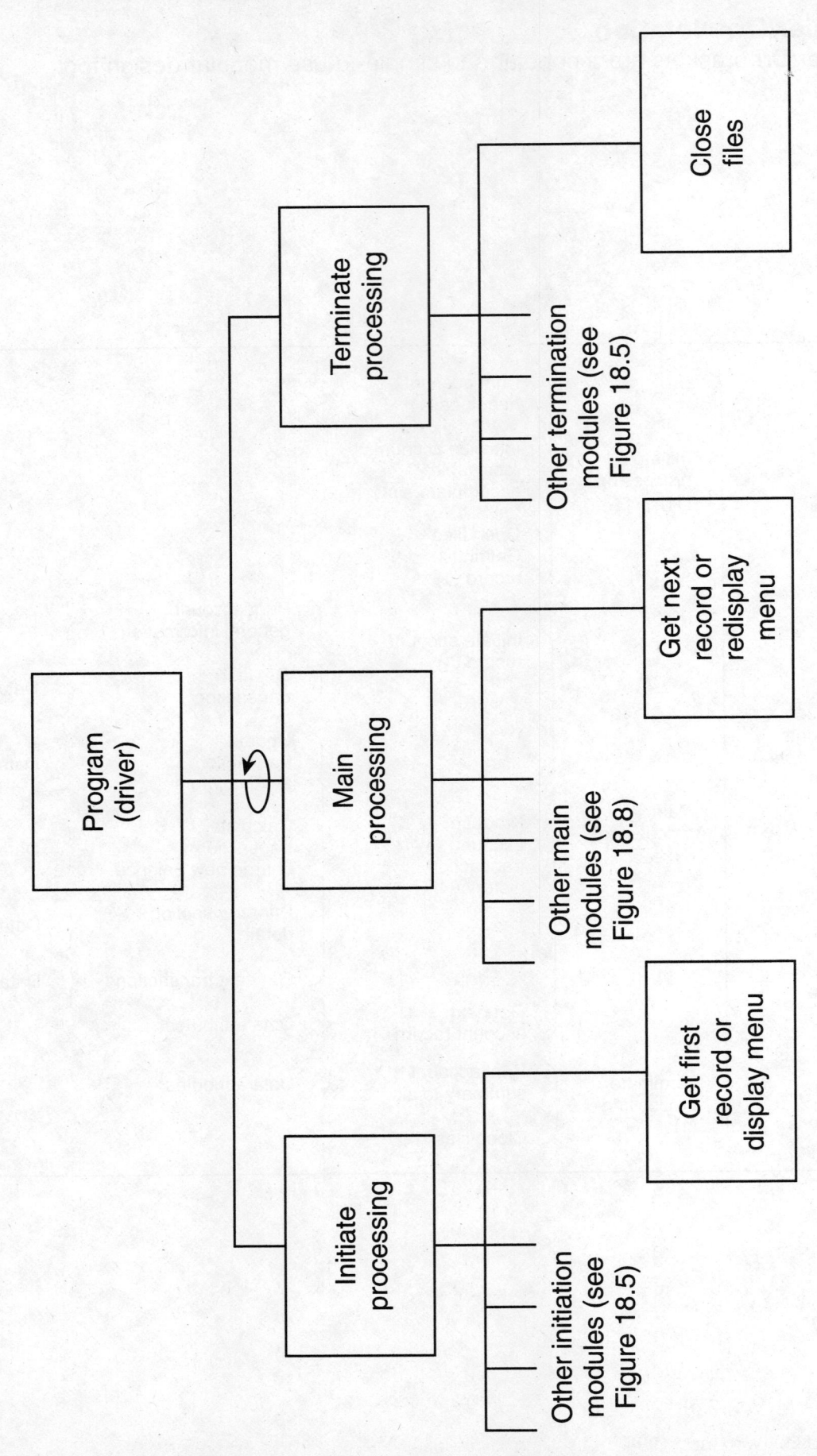

Primitive Functions Performed by INITIATE and TERMINATE PROCESSING Modules

This table suggests highly cohesive primitive modules that are typically controlled by an INITIATE or TERMINATE PROCESSING module.

INITIATE PROCESSING Functions:

BUILDING AND LOADING TABLES: Creating arrays to store tables, such as tax tables, actuary tables, and the like, and loading the data into those tables.

DEFINING CONSTANTS AND ACCUMULATORS: Constants are set in a dedicated module so those constants can be easily located if they need to be changed (for instance, SALES TAX PERCENT). Accumulators are used to count records and control totals during main processing.

OPENING FILES: Files must be opened before they can be read from or written to. It should be noted that some systems limit the number of files that can be open at any one time. If more files are needed than can be opened, then the program must be rewritten as multiple programs that pass intermediate results through temporary (scratch) files (which count as one open file).

FILE MERGING OR SORTING: This must be done before main processing can be done.

PRINTING REPORT HEADINGS: Why relegate report headings to a separate module? So they can be easily located if report headings need to be modified.

DISPLAYING (MAIN) MENU: For on-line systems, displaying the first menu and accepting the first choice from that menu are usually an initiation function.

GET FIRST INPUT RECORD: Read the first input record or file record to be processed.

TERMINATE PROCESSING Functions:

CALCULATING CONTROL TOTALS: Performing arithmetic and statistical operations on totals accumulated during main processing functions.

PRINTING CONTROL TOTALS: Printing the accumulators and control totals maintained and calculated during main processing.

CLOSING FILES: The reverse of opening files. Disconnects the file from the program, thereby allowing other programs, which may have been locked out, to use those files.

Source: Adapted from David R. Adams, Gerald E. Wagner, and Terrence J. Boyer, *Computer Information Systems: An Introduction* (Cincinnati: South-Western Publishing, 1983).

TM–227

Transaction Centers for a Simple Program
Generally, it is useful to factor a module into distinct submodules that act on single transactions.

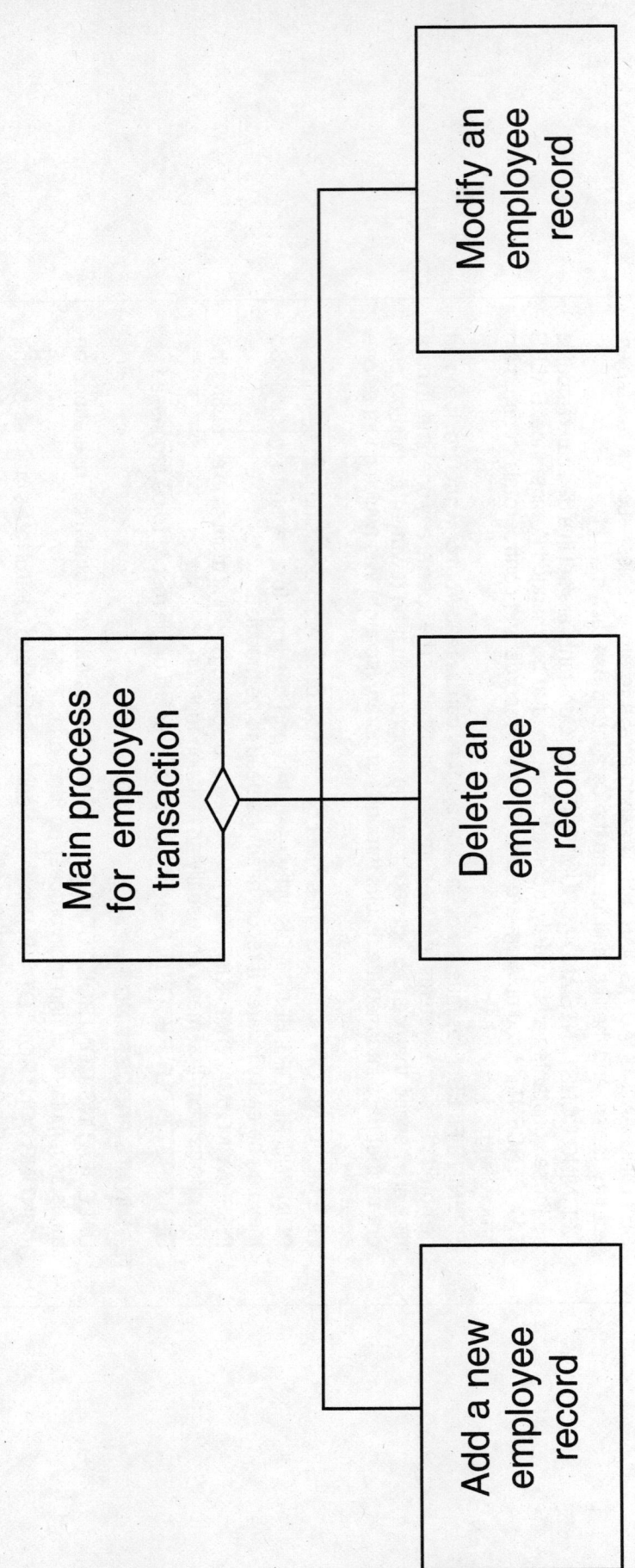

TM-228

© Richard D. Irwin, Inc., 1994

On-Line Transaction Centers

On-line systems are particularly suited to transaction analysis since their capabilities are called on demand and integrated through a high-level control program.

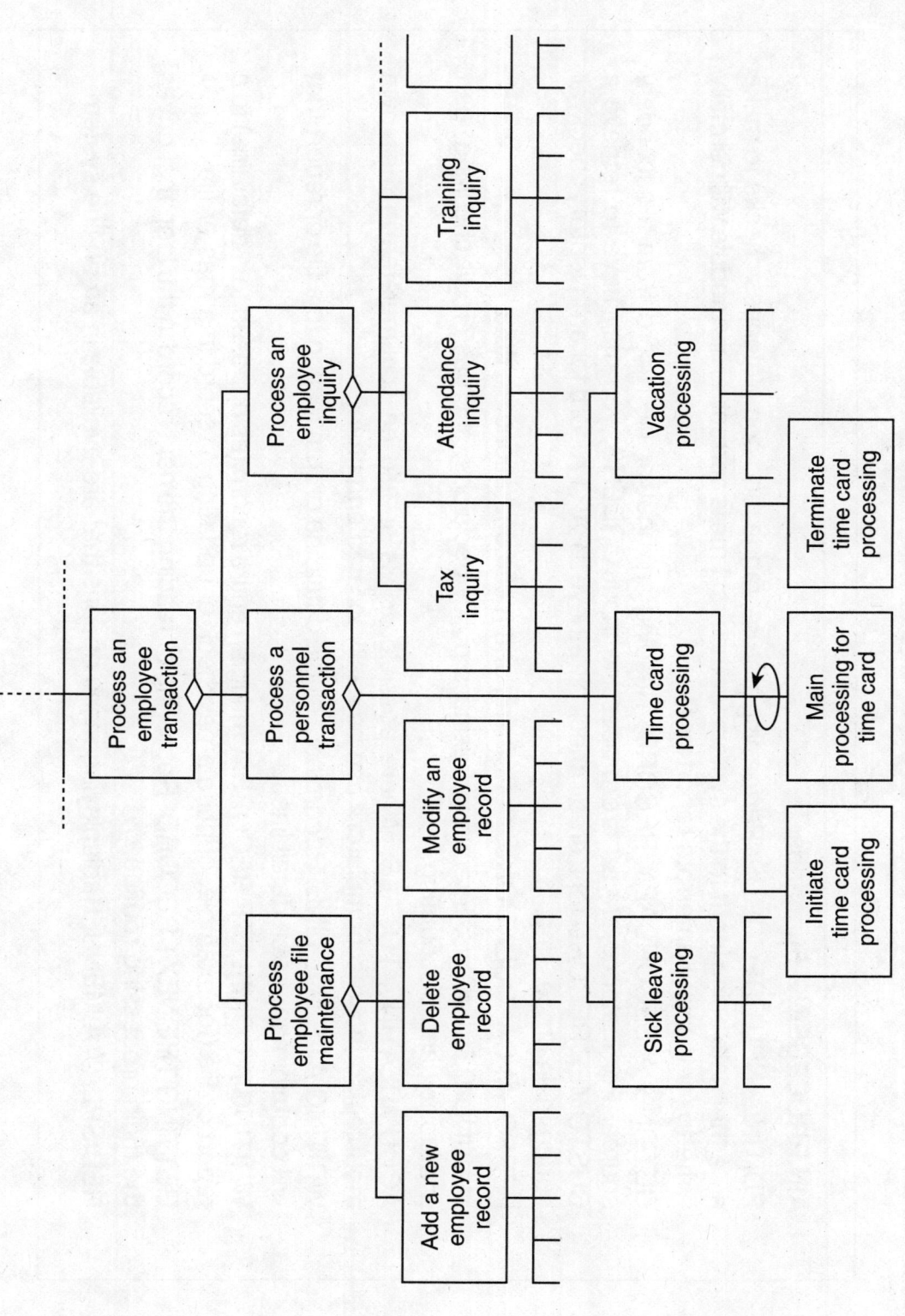

TM–229

©Richard D. Irwin, Inc., 1994

Primitive Process

This list suggests primitive cohesive MAIN PROCESSING functions.

MAIN PROCESSING Functions:

EDITING INPUT RECORDS: Performing picture, range, and completeness checks to make sure that data being input to the system for the first time is correct. (This module will normally write to (or display) an errors report or file.)

GETTING A SECONDARY RECORD: Reading an input or file record from a secondary source. For instance, if you are processing input ORDERS, you may have to retrieve a CUSTOMER RECORD for a credit check or retrieve a PART record for an inventory check, all during main processing.

PERFORM CALCULATIONS: Performing arithmetic operations on data.

MAKING DECISIONS: Executing business policy decisions, such as credit checking, part availability, and discounting.

ACCUMULATING TOTALS: Where possible, totals should be accumulated in their own modules so those accumulators can be easily located and changed.

WRITING A DETAIL LINE: Recording a single detail line or transaction to a file or report that will contain many such detail lines.

WRITING A COMPLETE RECORD: Writing an entire record (as opposed to a detail line) to a report or file (for example, printing a paycheck or updating a record in a master file).

GETTING THE NEXT RECORD: Retrieving or reading the next record in the loop that drives the main processing routine.

REDISPLAY A MENU: Redisplaying menu options that are available in an on-line system.

Source: Adapted from David R. Adams, Gerald E. Wagner, and Terrence J. Boyer, *Computer Information Systems: An Introduction* (Cincinnati: South-Western Publishing, 1983).

Factoring MAIN PROCESSING into Cohesive Primitives

MAIN PROCESSING must eventually be factored down to loosely coupled, highly cohesive primitive modules.

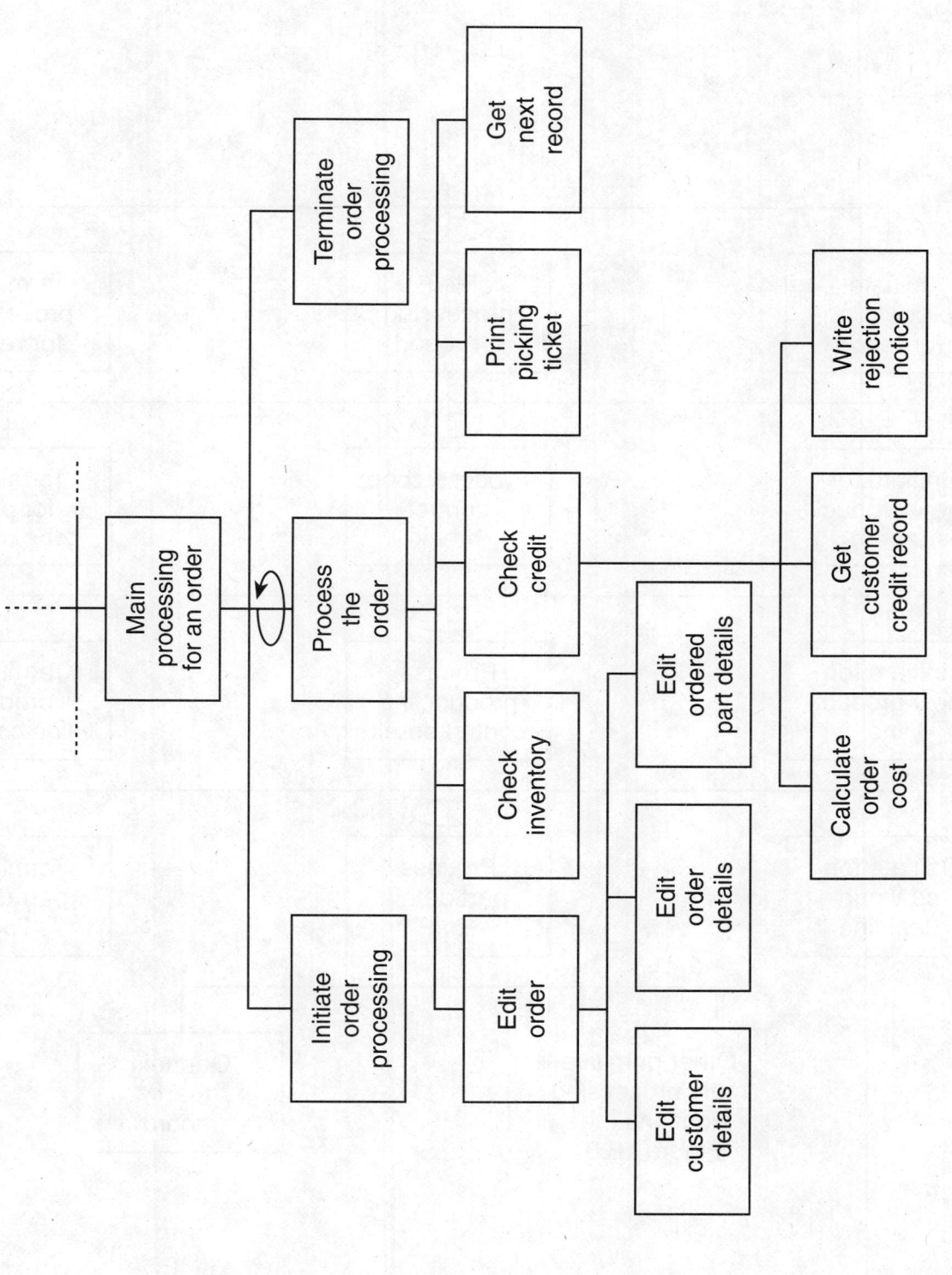

© Richard D. Irwin, Inc., 1994

TM–231

Data Structure Factoring

For programs that produce outputs whose data structure is hierarchical, the MAIN PROCESSING can be factored according to the hierarchy (control breaks).

TM–232

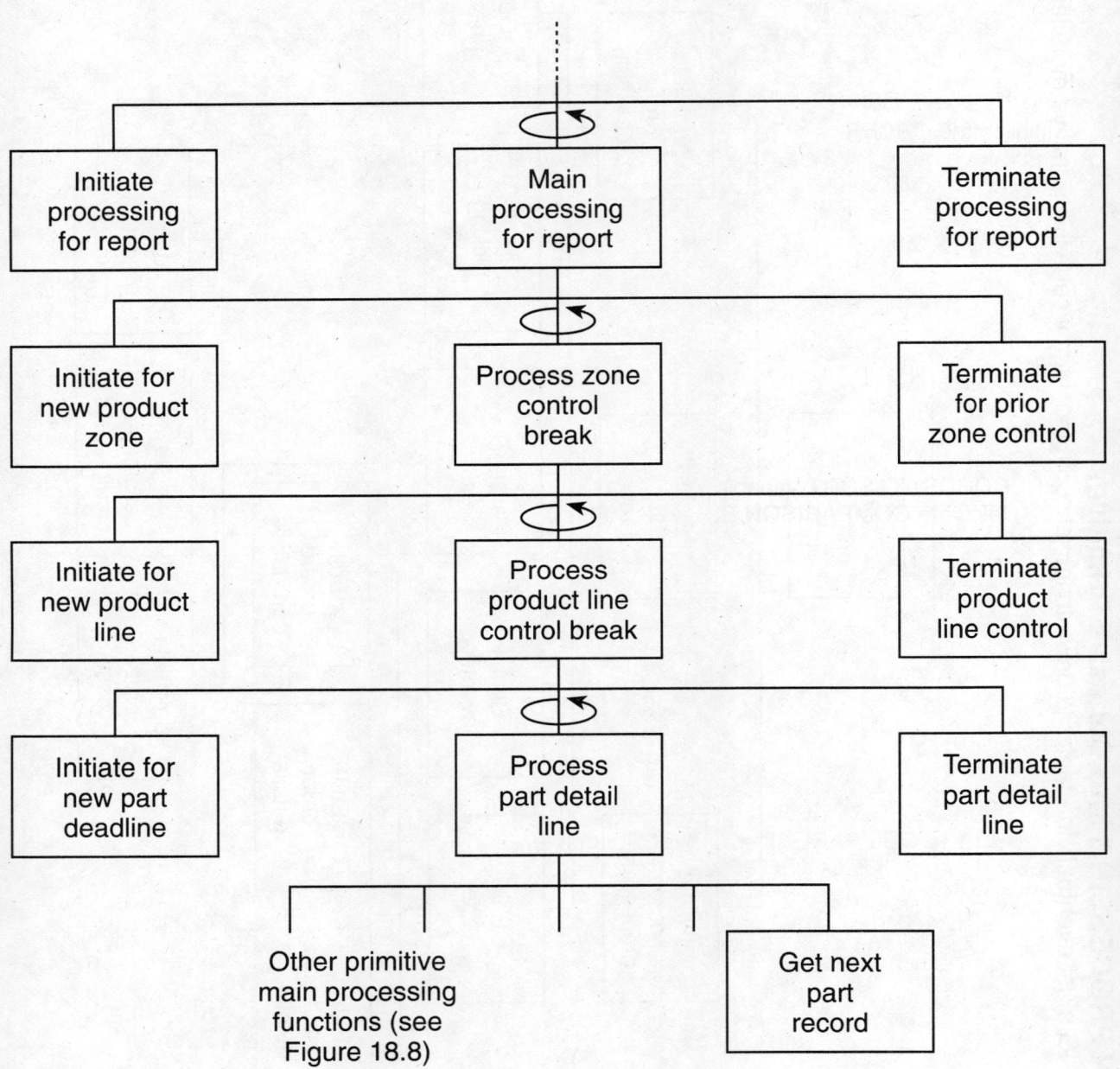

© Richard D. Irwin, Inc., 1994

Pseudocode

TM−233

This is an example of pseudocode for a sorting requirement. The analyst should avoid this level of detail unless systems design standards call for it.

>   Initialize the ORDER SORT array subscript X to 1.
>   For each record in the DAILY ORDER FILE, do the following:
>   Store DAILY ORDER FILE record in ORDER SORT array at subscript X location.
>   Add 1 to subscript X.
>   Initialize the IS SORT COMPLETE FLAG to "NO".
>   Initialize the RECORDS TO SORT variable equal to the subscript X.
>   Repeat the following steps until the SORT COUNTER variable equals X − 1 or the SORT COMPLETE FLAG equals "YES":
>   Initialize SORT COMPLETE FLAG to "YES".
>   Subtract 1 from the RECORDS TO SORT variable.
>   Initialize the COMPARISON COUNTER to 1.
>   Repeat the following steps until the COMPARISON COUNTER is greater than the RECORDS TO SORT variable:
>   Calculate COMPARISON SUBSCRIPT using the following formula:
>   COMPARISON COUNTER + 1
>   If the CUSTOMER ORDER NUMBER for ORDER SORT array record at COMPARISON COUNTER location is less than the CUSTOMER ORDER NUMBER for ORDER SORT array record at COMPARISON SUBSCRIPT location, then:
>   Store ORDER SORT array record at location COMPARISON COUNTER in TEMPORARY STORAGE variable.
>   Store the ORDER SORT array record at location TEMPORARY STORAGE in ORDER SORT array at the COMPARISON COUNTER location.
>   Store the TEMPORARY STORAGE record in the ORDER SORT array at location COMPARISON COUNTER.
>   Set the IS SORT COMPLETED FLAG equal to "NO".
>   Add 1 to COMPARISON COUNTER variable.
>   Add 1 to SORT COUNTER variable.
>   Initialize the SORTED ORDER FINE COUNTER to 0.
>   For each record in the SORT ORDER array, do the following:
>   Store the SORT ORDER array record at the SORTED ORDER FILE COUNTER location in the SORTED ORDER FILE.

© Richard D. Irwin, Inc., 1994

Data Flow Diagram for PROCESS MEMBER ORDERS   TM-234

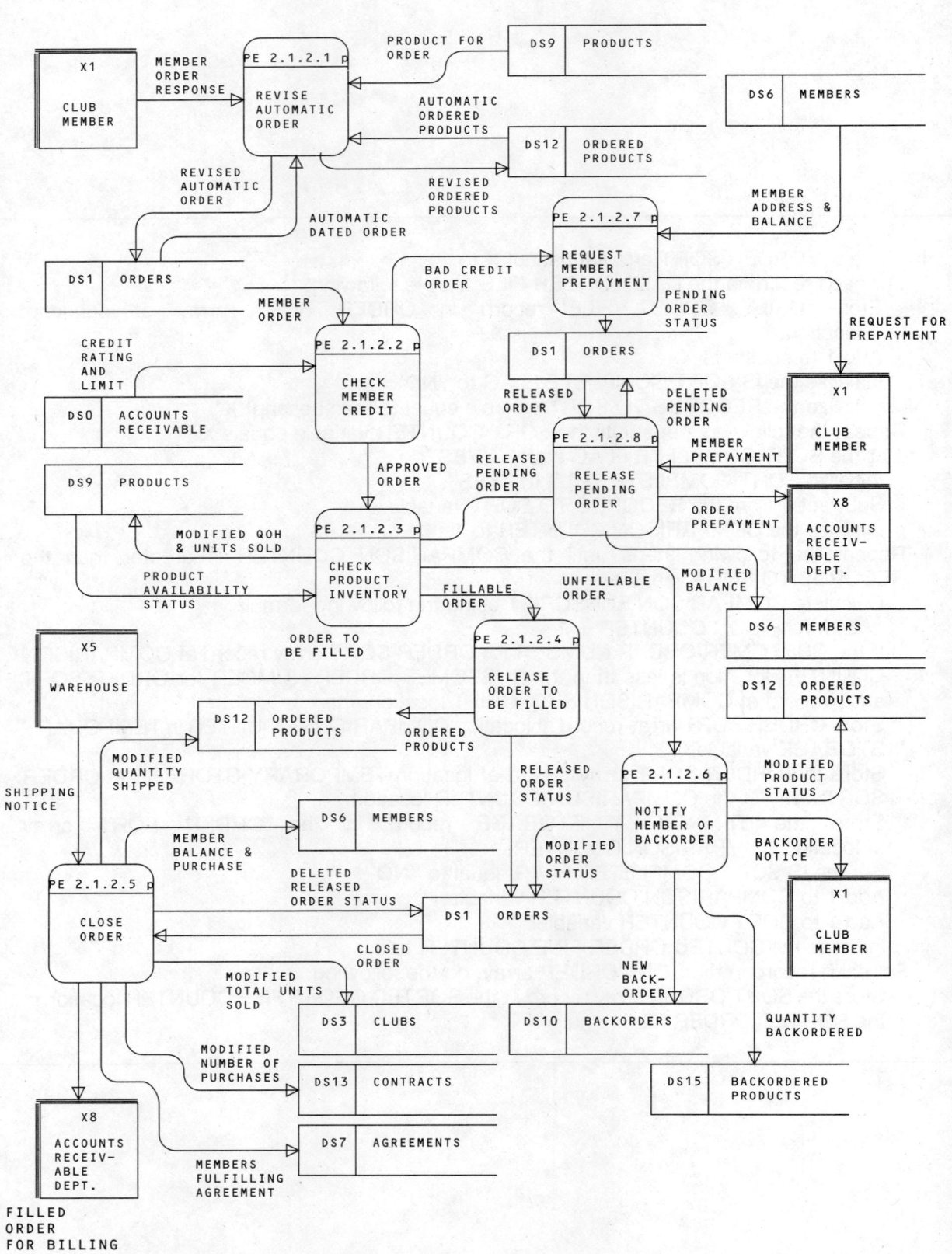

© Richard D. Irwin, Inc., 1994

Structure Chart for PROCESS MEMBER ORDERS

TM-235

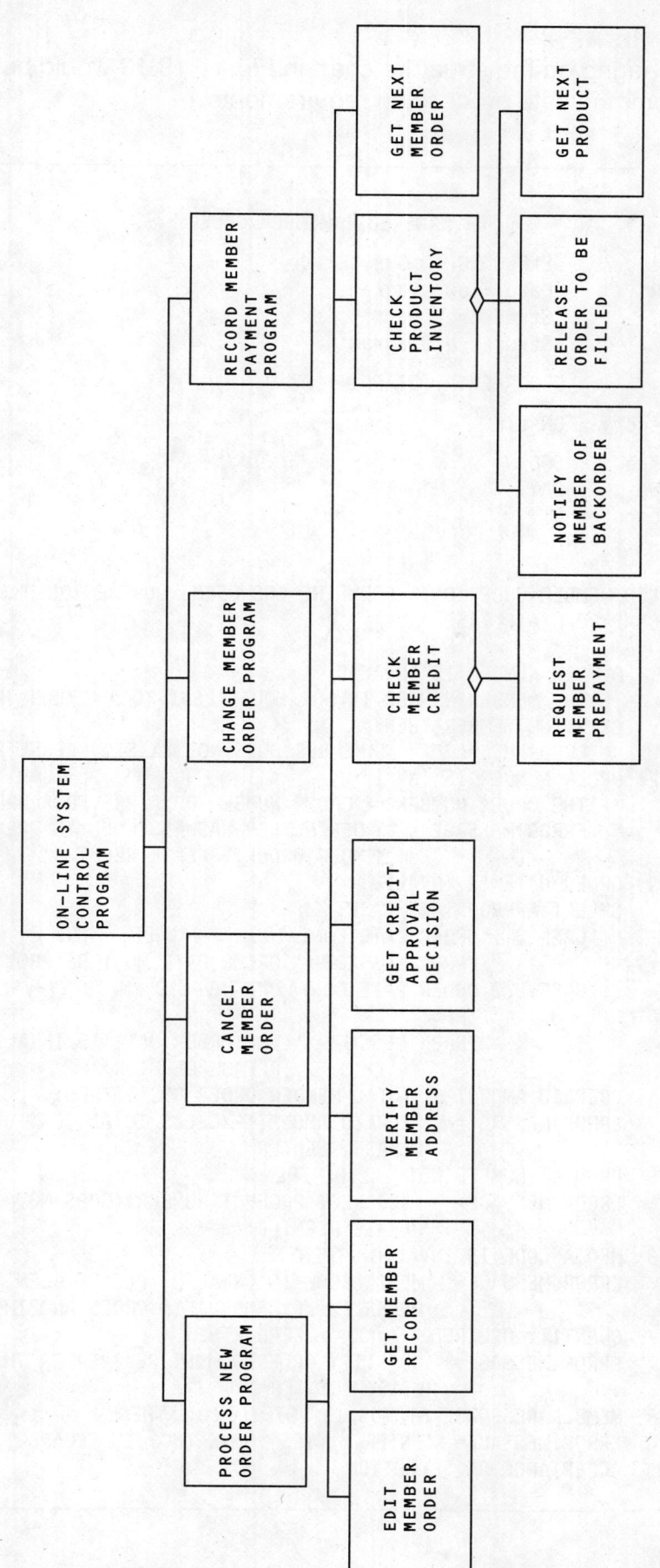

© Richard D. Irwin, Inc., 1994

Structured English

Each module appearing on the structure chart in Figure 18.13 would be documented to communicate processing requirements.

TM-236

```
TYPE Process              NAME EDIT MEMBER ORDER
   Label EDIT             EXPLODES TO ONE OF:
         MEMBER           Data Flow Diagram
         ORDER            Structure Chart
                          Structure Diagram

   Location               ORDER-ENTRY STAFF

   Process Category       ON-LINE

   Duration Value         500
   Duration Type          DAY
   Manual or Computer     C

Description
FOR ALL INVALID MEMBER ORDER DATA FROM THE END-USER, DO THE FOLLOWING:
   SELECT THE APPROPRIATE CASE:

      CASE 1: MEMBER NUMBER IS INVALID
            IF THE MEMBER NUMBER IS NOT EQUIVALENT TO A MEMBER NUMBER OF AN
            EXISTING MEMBER THEN:
               ERROR MESSAGE = ''MEMBER DOES NOT EXIST, PLEASE REENTER''
      CASE 2: ORDER NUMBER IS INVALID
            IF THE ORDER NUMBER = ORDER NUMBER OF A PREVIOUS ORDER THEN:
               ERROR MESSAGE=''ORDER NUMBER WAS ASSIGNED TO PREVIOUSLY ENTERED
                              MEMBER ORDER, PLEASE REENTER''
      CASE 3: ORDER DATE IS INVALID
            SELECT APPROPRIATE CASE:
               CASE 2.1 ORDER DATE CONTAINS NO VALUES. THEN:
                     ERROR MESSAGE=''ORDER DATE MUST BE PROVIDED''
               CASE 2.2 ORDER DATE CONTAINS INVALID MM/DD/YY VALUES,
                     THEN:
                     ERROR MESSAGE=''THE ORDER DATE IS INVALID.
                                    PLEASE REENTER''
      CASE 4: PREPAID AMOUNT > TOTAL MEMBER ORDER COST, THEN:
            ERROR MESSAGE=''PREPAID AMOUNT EXCEEDS TOTAL COST OF MEMBER ORDER.
                           PLEASE REENTER''
      CASE 5: PRODUCT NUMBER NOT VALID, THEN:
            ERROR MESSAGE=''INCORRECT PRODUCT NUMBER (DOES NOT EXIST).
                           PLEASE REENTER''
      CASE 6: MEDIA CODE IS INVALID. THEN:
            ERROR MESSAGE=''MEDIA CODE IS INVALID, PLEASE REENTER OR
                           PRESS F2 KEY FOR VALID CODES AND THEIR MEANINGS''
      CASE 7: QUANTITY ORDERED IS NOT > ZERO, THEN:
            ERROR MESSAGE=''QUANTITY ORDERED MUST BE GREATER THAN ZERO.
                           PLEASE REENTER''
      CASE 8: MEMBER RESPONSE STATUS IS NOT Y OR N. THEN:
            ERROR MESSAGE=''ENTER Y (YES) OR N (NO) IN REGARD TO MEMBER'S
            ACCEPTANCE OF SELECTION
```

© Richard D. Irwin, Inc., 1994

A Program Development Life Cycle

Like the systems development life cycle, there are many version of a program development life cycle.

TM-237

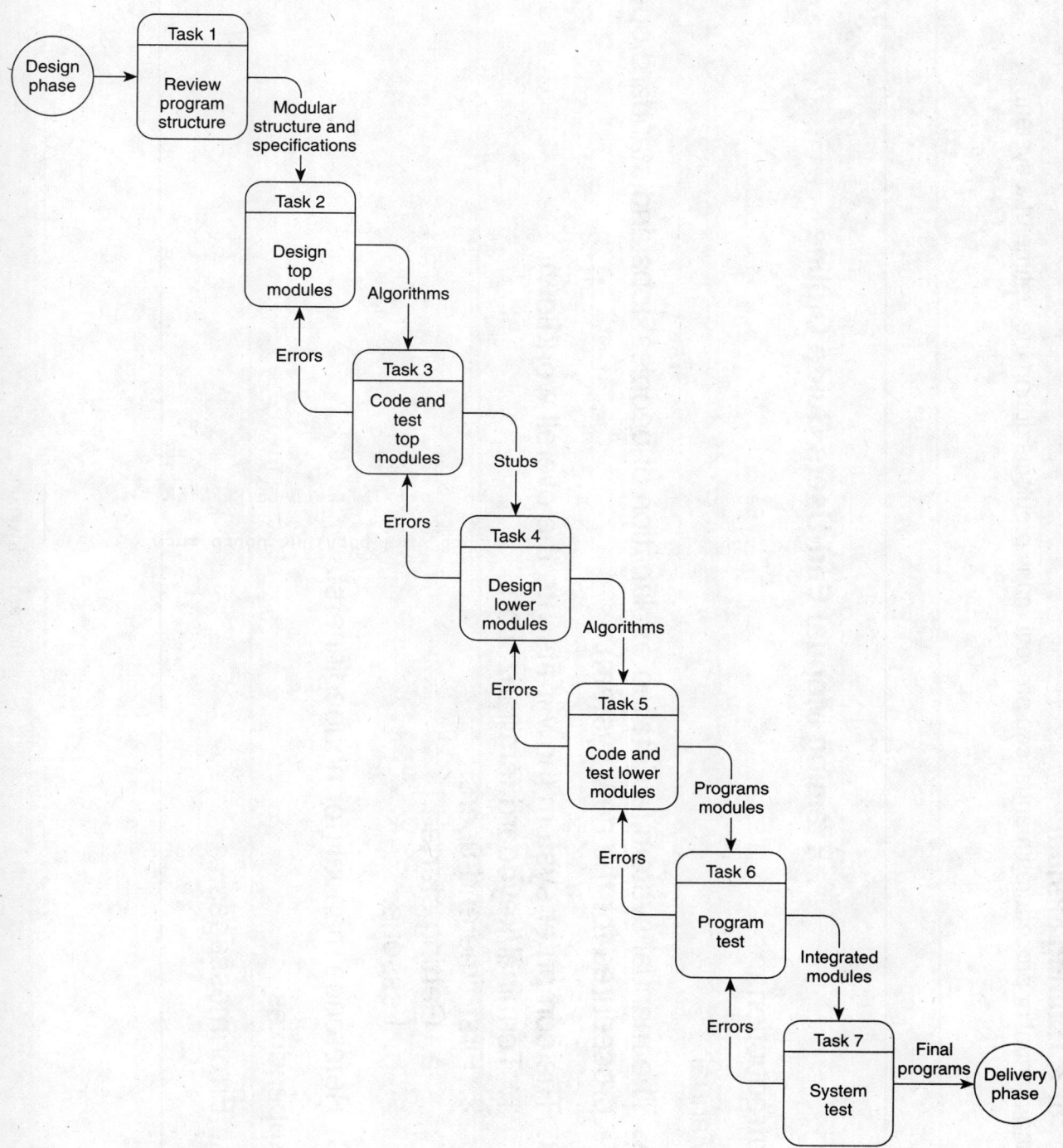

© Richard D. Irwin, Inc., 1994

An Outline for a Training Manual

A good training manual or procedures manual can prevent many problems during the lifetime of a system.

Training Manual End-Users Guide Outline

I. Introduction.

II. Manual.

   A. The manual system (a detailed explanation of peoples' jobs and standard operating procedures for the new system).

   B. The computer system (how it fits into the overall workflow).
      1. Terminal/keyboard familiarization.
      2. First-time end-users.
         a. Getting started.
         b. Lessons.

   C. Reference manual (for nonbeginners).

III. Appendixes.

   A. Error messages.

PERT Notation

A PERT chart depicts events and tasks. Nodes represent events.

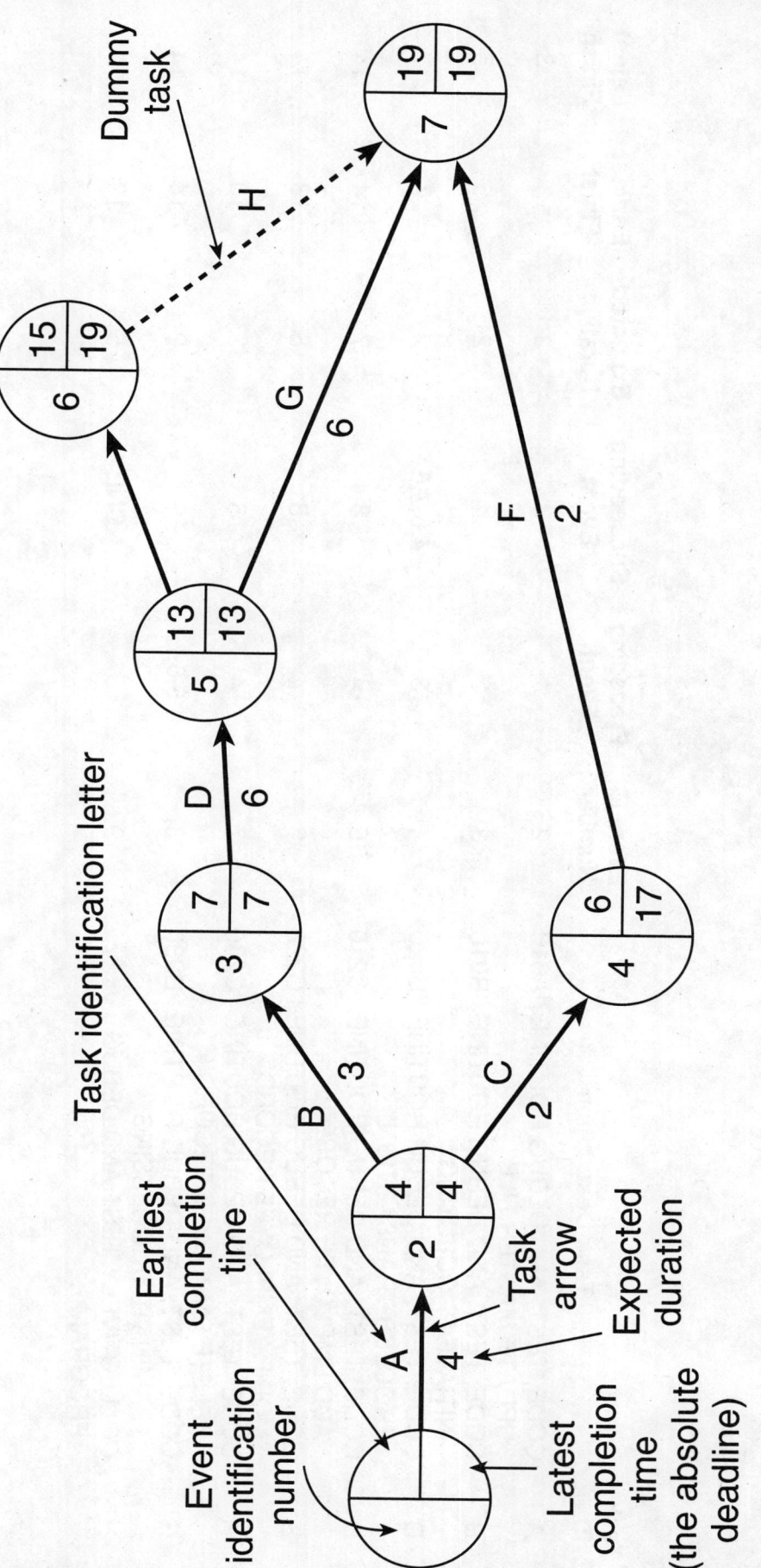

Project Planning Table

A project planning table is used to prepare data for drawing a PERT chart.

TM-240

Task ID	Task Description	Event ID Number	Preceding Event	Succeeding Event	Expected Duration	Earliest Finish	Latest Finish
A	CODE, TEST, AND DEBUG ROUTINE "A010" UPDATE MASTER FILE	2	1	3	3	3	3
B	CODE, TEST, AND DEBUG ROUTINE "B010" INITIATE PROCESSING	3	2	4	2	5	5
C	CODE, TEST, AND DEBUG ROUTINE "B020" PROCESS TRANSACTION	4	3	4,6,7,8	2	7	7
D	CODE, TEST, AND DEBUG ROUTINE "C210" ADD EMPLOYEE RECORD	5	4	8	7	14	14
E	CODE, TEST, AND DEBUG ROUTINE "C220" MODIFY EMPLOYEE RECORD	6	4	8	6	13	14
F	CODE, TEST, AND DEBUG ROUTINE "C230" DELETE EMPLOYEE RECORD	7	4	8	3	10	14
G	CODE, TEST, AND DEBUG ROUTINE "B030" TERMINATE PROCESSING	8	4,5,6,7	9	2	14	14
H	COLLECTIVELY TEST AND DEBUG PROGRAM	9	8	NONE	5	19	19

©Richard D. Irwin, Inc., 1994

Completed PERT Chart

This is the PERT chart for the project planning table completed in Figure A.2.

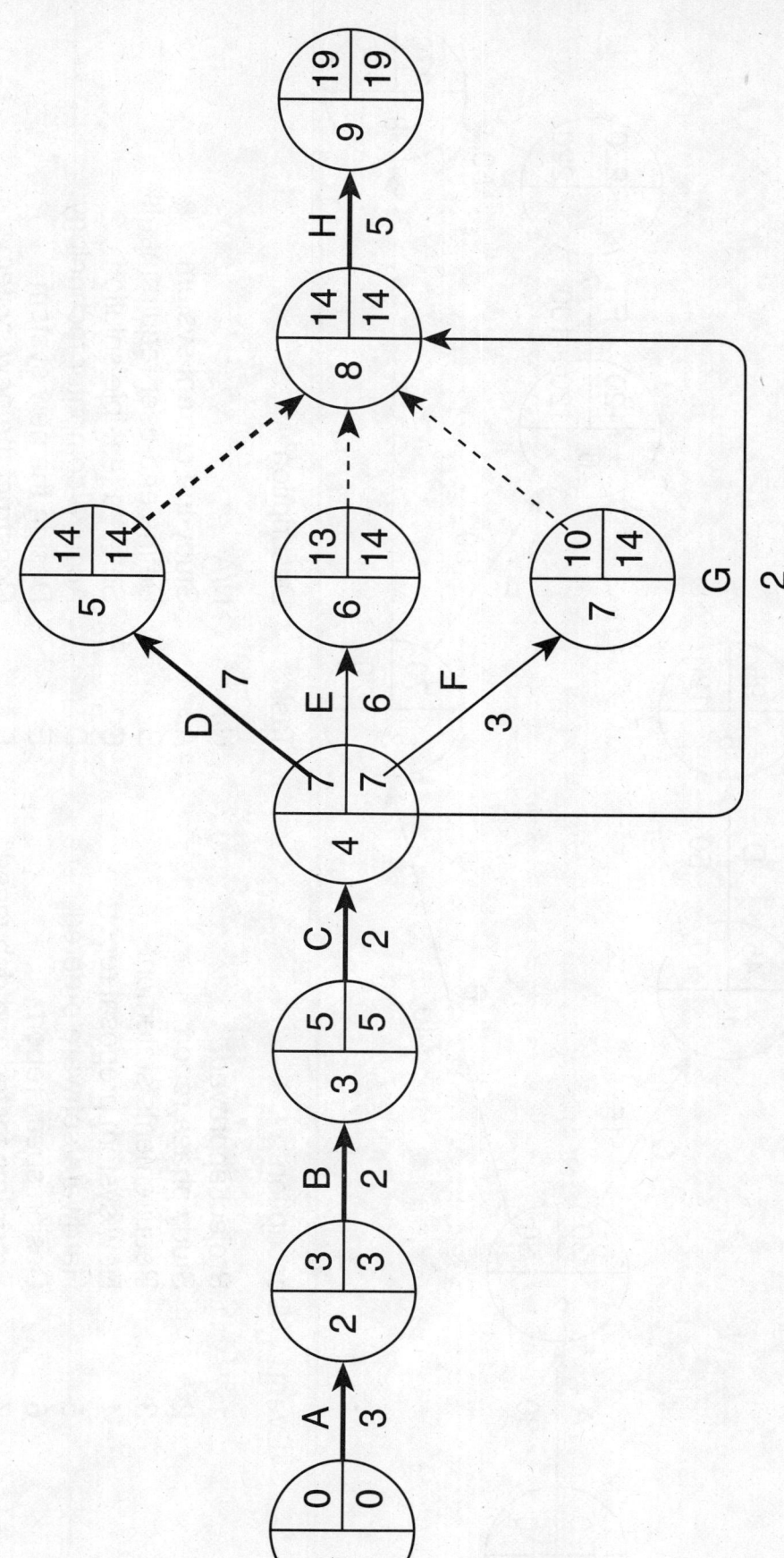

Sample PERT Chart for an SDLC
This simple PERT chart depicts interphase dependencies between deliverables in a systems development life cycle.

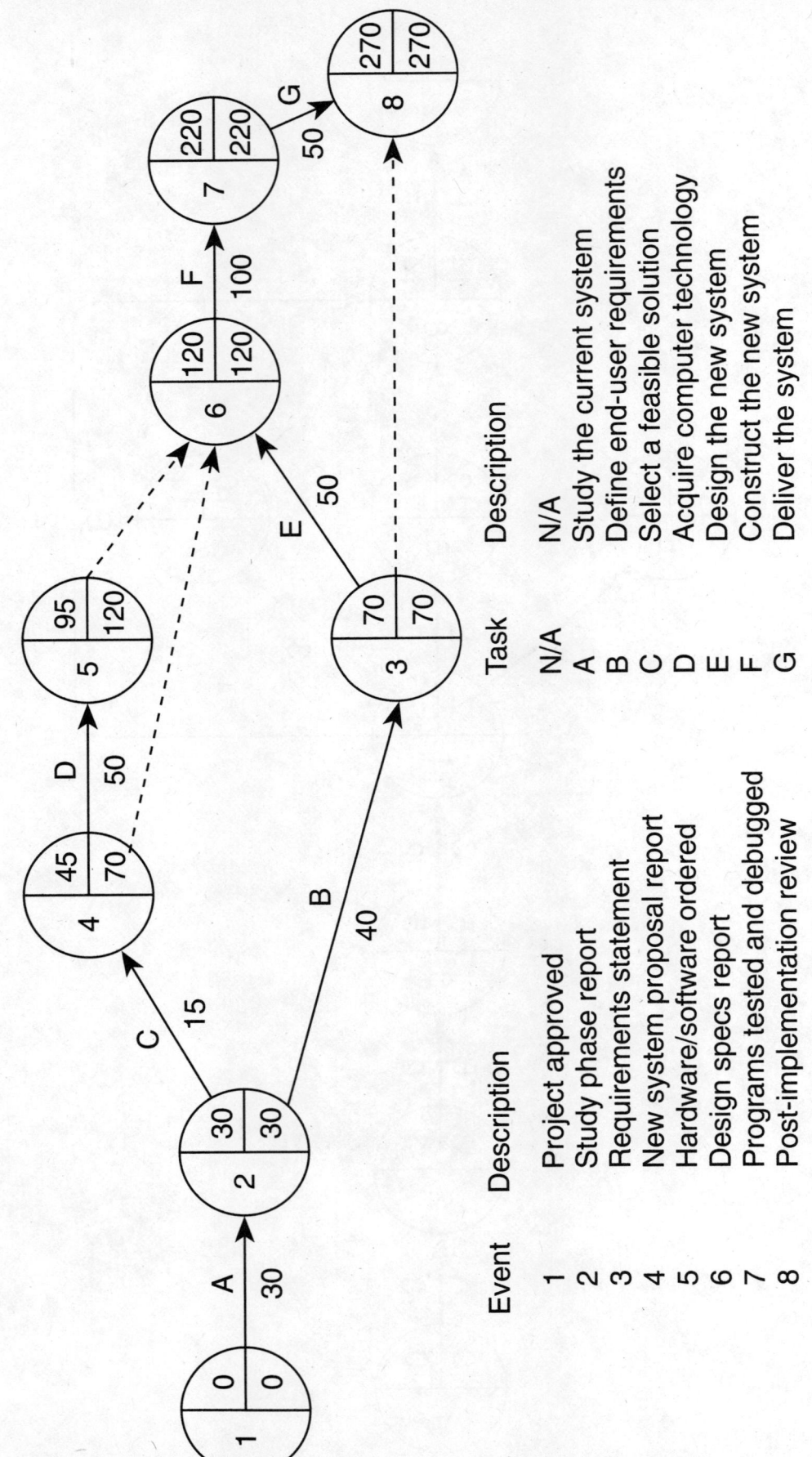

Event	Description
1	Project approved
2	Study phase report
3	Requirements statement
4	New system proposal report
5	Hardware/software ordered
6	Design specs report
7	Programs tested and debugged
8	Post-implementation review

Task	Description
N/A	N/A
A	Study the current system
B	Define end-user requirements
C	Select a feasible solution
D	Acquire computer technology
E	Design the new system
F	Construct the new system
G	Deliver the system

©Richard D. Irwin, Inc., 1994

TM-242

Simple Gantt Chart for an SDLC

This simple Gantt chart represents the systems development life cycle.

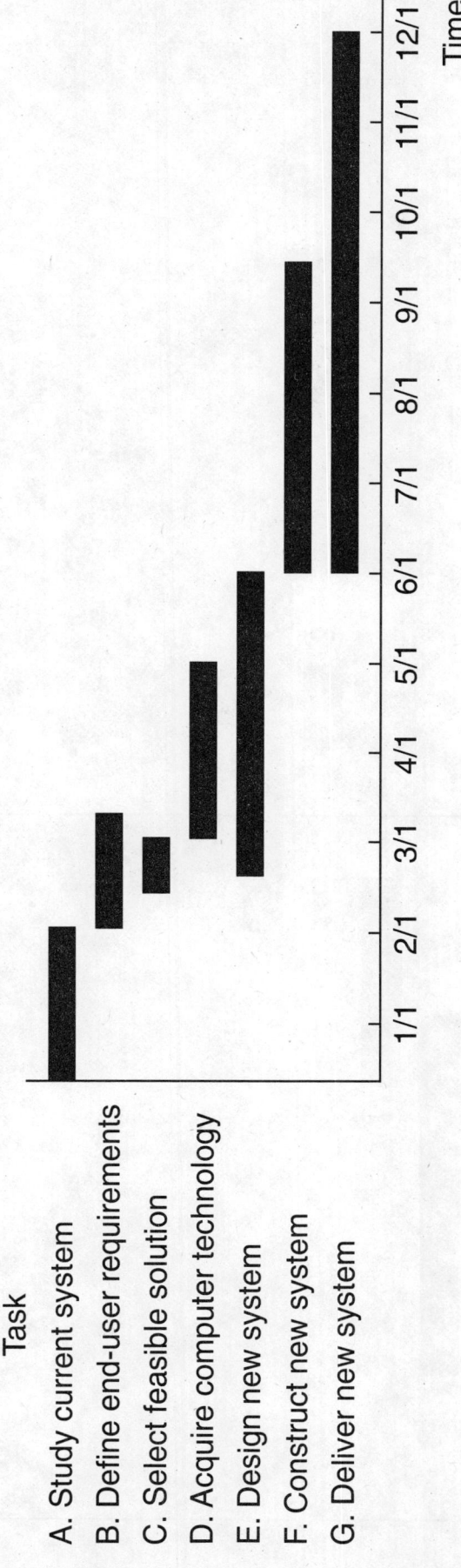

© Richard D. Irwin, Inc., 1994

TM-243

Progress Reporting with Gantt Charts
Gantt charts can be annotated to clearly depict project progress.

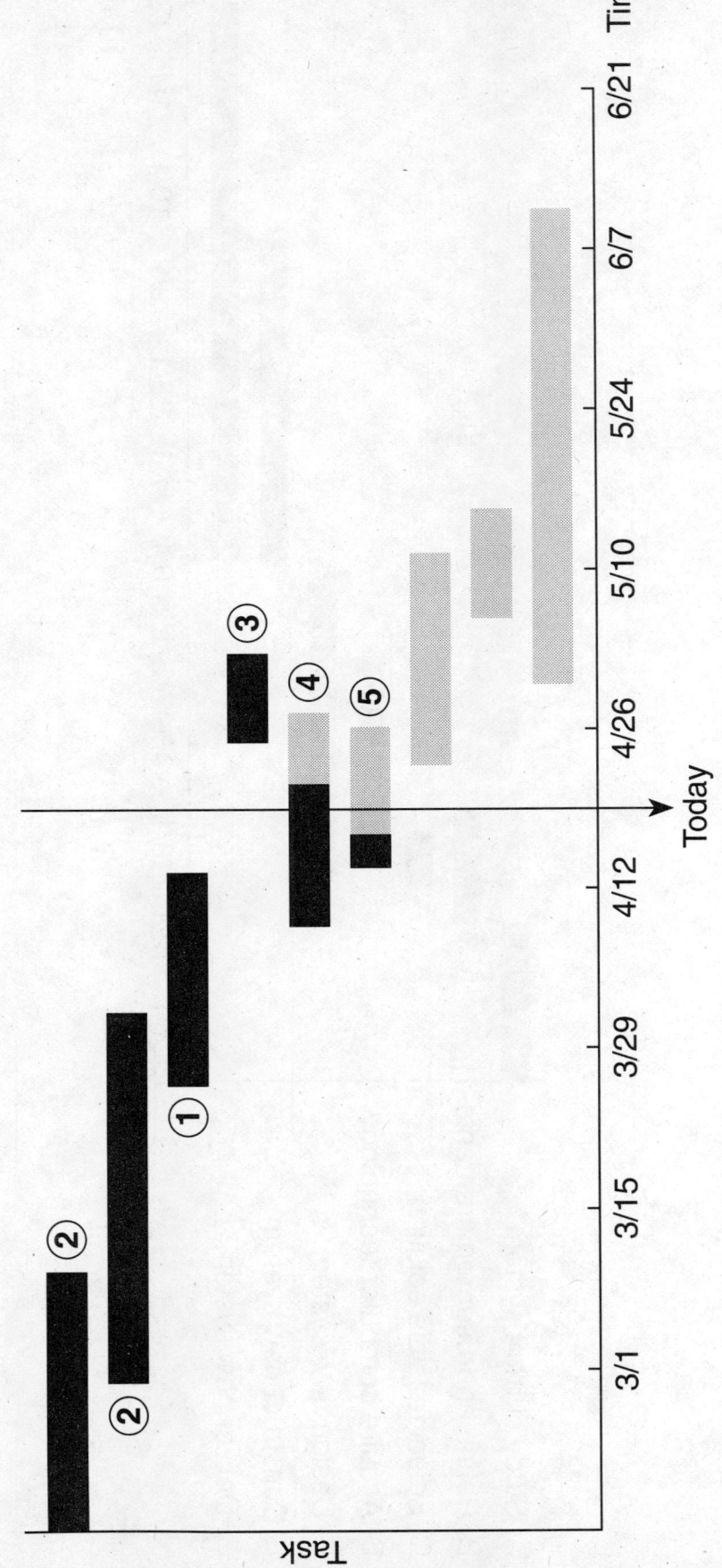

TM-244

© Richard D. Irwin, Inc., 1994

Management Expectations Matrix

This incomplete matrix is used to help project managers and system owners develop realistic expectations for a project.

Priorities Measures of Success	Max or Min	Constrain	Accept
Cost			
Schedule			
Scope and/or Quality			

TM–245

© Richard D. Irwin, Inc., 1994

Management Expectations for the American Moon Landing Project

This complete and valid matrix demonstrates how the government managed the public's expectations in its project to be the first country to land a man on the moon and return him safely.

Priorities Measures of Success	Max or Min	Constrain	Accept
Cost Estimated at $20 billion			X
Schedule Deadline = December 31, 1969		X	
Scope and/or Quality 1. Land a man on the moon. 2. Get him back safely.	X		

TM-246

© Richard D. Irwin, Inc., 1994

An Initial Management Expectations Matrix
This initial matrix is based on a hypothetical situation described in the text.

Priorities / Measures of Success	Max or Min	Constrain	Accept
Cost		X	
Schedule			X
Scope and/or Quality	X		

TM–247

© Richard D. Irwin, Inc., 1994

Adjusting Resources in a Management Expectations Matrix
Adjusted resources are indicated with plus and minus signs. Any comment can be written in a cell.

Priorities Measures of Success	Max or Min	Constrain	Accept
Cost (Record New Budget)		X+ Increase budget	
Schedule (Record New Deadlines)			X− Extend deadline
Scope and/or Quality (Revise attachment that describes scope and quality. Be sure to date all new requirements to distinguish them from original requirements.)	X+ Accept expanded requirements		

TM−248

©Richard D. Irwin, Inc., 1994

Priority Migration in a Management Expectations Matrix
This matrix demonstrates shifting priorities (Step 1) and rebalancing of the matrix (Step 2).

TM-249

Priorities / Measures of Success	Max or Min	Constrain	Accept
Cost		X	
Schedule			X
Scope and/or Quality	X		

Step 1: (Cost) Constrain ↓ Max or Min

Step 2: (Scope and/or Quality) Max or Min ↑ Constrain

© Richard D. Irwin, Inc., 1994

Sample Interview Guide

TM-250

The sample interview guide represents an agenda that a systems analyst will use to obtain facts about a company's existing credit approval policy.

INTERVIEWEE:	Jeff Bentley, Accounts Receivable Manager
DATE:	Tuesday, March 23, 1993
TIME:	1:30 P.M.
PLACE:	Room 223, Admin. Bldg.
SUBJECT:	Current Credit-Checking Policy

1 to 2 min.	Open the interview.
	Introduce ourselves.
	Thank Mr. Bentley for his valuable time.
	State the purpose of the interview — to obtain an understanding of the existing credit-checking policies.
5 min.	What conditions determine whether a customer's order is approved for credit?
5 min.	What are the possible decisions or actions that might be taken once these conditions have been evaluated?
3 min.	How are customers notified when credit is not approved for their order?
1 min.	After a new order is approved for credit and placed in the file containing orders that can be filled, a customer might request that a modification be made to the order. Would the order have to go through credit approval again if the new total order cost exceeds the original cost?
1 min.	Who are the individuals that perform the credit checks?
1 to 3 min.	May I have permission to talk to those individuals to learn specifically how they carry out the credit-checking process?
	If so:
	When would be an appropriate time to meet with each of them?
1 min.	Conclude the interview:
	Thank Mr. Bentley for his cooperation and assure him that he will be receiving a copy of what transpired during the interview.

21 minutes
+9 minutes for follow-up questions and redirection

30 minutes alloted for interview (1:30 P.M. – 2:00 P.M.)

© Richard D. Irwin, Inc., 1994

Costs for a Proposed Systems Solution

TM–251

The costs for a proposed information system should be itemized into development costs and operating costs.

Estimated Costs for the On-Line System Alternative

Development Costs:

Personnel:

2 Systems analysts (400 hours/ea @ $35.00/hr)	$28,000
4 Programmers (250 hours/ea @ $25.00/hr)	25,000
1 Operator (50 hours @ $10.00/hr)	500
1 Secretary (75 hours @ $6.00/hr)	450
3 Data entry clerks (during file conversion — 40 hours/ea @ $5.00/hr)	600

Computer usage:

500 hours @ $25.00	12,500

Supplies and expenses:

Training (database — 3 persons @ $395/person)	1,185
Training users (150 hours @ $10.00/hr)	1,500
Duplication	300

New equipment:

2 Personal computers configured to emulate a terminal — also include printers	14,000
5 CRT terminals	2,500
7 New desks for office personnel	1,400

Annual Operating Costs (not incurred in existing system)

Personnel:

Systems analysts (maintenance — 80 hours/year @ $35.00/hr)	2,800
Programmers (maintenance — 200 hours/year @ $25.00/hr)	5,000
1 additional office clerk — 2,000 hours/year @ $6.00/hr	12,000

Computer usage:

2,000 hours/year @ $45.00/hr — includes overhead	90,000

Supplies and expenses:

Prorated renewal of database software license	1,000
Preprinted forms (15,000/year @ .22/form)	3,300

© Richard D. Irwin, Inc., 1994

Payback Analysis for a Project

TM–252

In payback analysis you determine how much time will pass before the lifetime benefits exceed the lifetime costs. In this example benefits will pass costs between years 4 and 5.

	A	B	C	D	E	F	G	H
1	Payback analysis of on-line conversion				(Numbers rounded to nearest $1)			
2	Alternative for member services system							
3								
4	Cash flow description	Year 0	Year 1	Year 2	Year 3	Year 4	Year 5	Year 6
5								
6	Analysis, design, and implementation cost	$−100,000						
7	Operation and maintenance cost		$−4,000	$−4,500	$−5,000	$−6,000	$−7,000	$−8,000
8	Discount factors for 12%	1.000	0.893	0.797	0.712	0.636	0.567	0.507
9	Time-adjusted costs (adjusted to present value)	−100,000	−3,572	−3,587	−3,560	−3,816	−3,969	−4,056
10	Cumulative time-adjusted costs over lifetime	−100,000	−103,572	−107,159	−110,719	−114,535	−118,504	−122,560
11								
12	Benefits derived from operation of new system	0	25,000	30,000	35,000	50,000	60,000	70,000
13	Discount factors of 12%	1,000	0.893	0.797	0.712	0.636	0.567	0.507
14	Time-adjusted benefits (current or present value)	0	22,325	23,910	24,920	31,800	34,020	35,490
15	Cumulative time-adjusted lifetime benefits	0	22,325	46,235	71,155	102,955	136,975	172,465
16								
17	Cumulative lifetime time-adjusted costs + benefits	−100,000	−81,247	−60,924	−39,564	−11,580	18,472	49,906
18								
19	TIME-ADJUSTED PAYBACK PERIOD			--				4.4 years

© Richard D. Irwin, Inc., 1994

Partial Table for Present Value of a Dollar

This partial table is used to discount a dollar back to present value from the indicated years using the indicated discount rates.

Present Value of a Dollar

Periods	...	8%	10%	12%	14%
1		0.926	0.909	0.893	0.877
2		0.857	0.826	0.797	0.769
3		0.794	0.751	0.712	0.675
4		0.735	0.683	0.636	0.592
5		0.681	0.621	0.567	0.519
6		0.630	0.564	0.507	0.456
7		0.583	0.513	0.452	0.400
8		0.540	0.467	0.404	0.351
...					

© Richard D. Irwin, Inc., 1994

Net Present Value Analysis for a Project

TM-254

Net present value analysis (NPV), determines the profitability, in today's dollars, of any project.

	A	B	C	D	E	F	G	H	I	J
1	Net present value analysis of on-line conversion						(Numbers rounded to nearest $1)			
2	Alternative for member services system									
3										
4	Cash flow description	Year 0	Year 1	Year 2	Year 3	Year 4	Year 5	Year 6	Total	
5										
6	Analysis, design, and implementation cost	−100,000								
7	Operation and maintenance cost		−4,000	−4,500	−5,000	−6,000	−7,000	−8,000		
8	Discount factors for 12%	1.000	0.893	0.797	0.712	0.636	0.567	0.507		
9	Present value of annual costs	−100,000	−3,572	−3,587	−5,560	−3,816	−3,969	−4,056		
10	Total present value of lifetime costs								−122,560	
11										
12	Benefits derived from operation of new system	0	25,000	30,000	35,000	50,000	60,000	70,000		
13	Discount factors for 12%	1,000	0.893	0.797	0.712	0.636	0.567	0.507		
14	Present value of annual benefits	0	22,325	23,910	24,920	31,800	34,020	35,490		
15	Total present value of lifetime benefits								172,465	
16										
17	NET PRESENT VALUE OF THIS ALTERNATIVE								$49,906	

© Richard D. Irwin, Inc., 1994

Sample Blank Feasibility Analysis Matrix

This matrix allows for convenient comparison of candidate solutions characteristics.

TM-255

	Candidate 1 Name	Candidate 2 Name	Candidate *N* Name
TECHNOLOGY			
PEOPLE			
DATA			
PROCESSES			
NETWORKS			

© Richard D. Irwin, Inc., 1994

Sample Candidate System Matrix

A matrix allows for quick and easy side-by-side comparison of candidate solutions and their characteristics.

Characteristics	Candidate 1	Candidate 2	Candidate 3
Portion of System Computerized Brief description of that portion of the system that would be computerized in this candidate.	The scheduling and reporting subsystems would both be computerized.	Same as Candidate 1.	Same as Candidate 1.
Benefits Brief description of the business benefits that would be realized for this candidate.	Scheduling: This candidate will allow the schedules of all social workers to be consolidated. This will allow for easy identification of available meeting times. Schedules could be consolidated based on a number of options including, by day, week, or month. Reporting: Case/meeting information would be made readily available for each social worker. Thus, government and internal reporting requirements would be more easily fulfilled.	Scheduling: Same as Candidate 1. However, this candidate will also allow adhoc social worker schedule inquiries based upon a number of "subjects." Reporting: Same as Candidate 1.	Scheduling: Same as Candidate 2. Reporting: Same as Candidate 1.
Software Tools/Applications Needed Software tools needed to design or build the candidate (e.g., database management system, spreadsheet, word processor, terminal emulators, programming languages, etc.). Also, a brief description of software to be purchased, built, accessed, or some combination of these techniques.	This candidate would require that the scheduling subsystem be "purchased" in-house. The reporting subsystem would be built using spreadsheet template(s).	Same as Candidate 1 except the scheduling subsystem would also be "built" in-house. The scheduling subsystem would be built using a database management system.	Both the scheduling and reporting subsystems would be "purchased."

© Richard D. Irwin, Inc., 1994

Sample Blank Feasibility Comparison Matrix

The matrix allows for convenient comparisons of candidate solutions according to feasibility criteria.

	Candidate 1 Name	**Candidate 2 Name**	**Candidate *N* Name**
Description			
Operational Feasibility			
Technical Feasibility			
Schedule Feasibility			
Economic Feasibility			
Ranking			

© Richard D. Irwin, Inc., 1994

Sample Feasibility Analysis Matrix

The matrix communicates the operational, technical, economic, and schedule feasibility assessments and scores for each candidate. Notice how this matrix allows for convenient comparisons of candidate solutions.

Feasibility Criteria	Candidate 1	Candidate 2	Candidate 3
Operation Feasibility Brief description of the functionality—to what degree the candidate would benefit the organization and how well the system will work. Also, a brief description of the political feasibility—how well-received the solution would be from the owners' and users' perspectives.	A brief survey of scheduling packages revealed that such packages can provide the users with improved accessibility to information concerning social workers and cases/meetings. This solution should decrease the amount of time needed to schedule social workers. It is felt that management would be satisfied with this candidate only if the direct system users find the packaged application to their satisfaction. Score = 85	Same as Candidate 1, except a few users will find the capability to do adhoc inquiries according to "subjects" of particular benefit. Score = 90	Same as Candidate 2. Score = 87
Technical Feasibility Brief assessment of the maturity, availability, and desirability of the computer technology needed to support the candidate. Also, an assessment of the technical expertise needed to develop, operate, and maintain the candidate.	There are numerous, highly rated scheduling packages available to date. Once the system users have been properly trained in the application, expertise requirements would be minimal. The same is true for spreadsheet reporting software and application. Score = 90	The technology and expertise to build the scheduling and reporting subsystems are readily available. Score = 90	Same as Candidate 1. There is also the added concern that no existing packages provides needed support for the reporting subsystem. Score = 87
Economic Feasibility Cost to develop: Payback period (discounted): Net present value: Detailed calculations:	Approximately $1,000. Approximately 6 months. Approximately $8,300. See Attachment A. Score = 86	Approximately $2,700. Approximately 2.5 years. Approximately $5,500. See Attachment B. Score = 75	Approximately $1,500. Approximately 7 months. Approximately $9,000. See Attachment C. Score = 92
Schedule Feasibility An assessment of how long the solution will take to design and implement.	Approximately 3 months. Score = 90	Approximately 9 months. Score = 82	Approximately 4 months. Score = 90

©Richard D. Irwin, Inc., 1994

Typical Outline and Time Allocation for an Oral Presentation
This figure illustrates some of the typical topics of an oral presentation and the amount of time to allow for those topics.

TM-259

I. Introduction (one-sixth of total time available)
   A. Problem statement
   B. Work completed to date

II. Part of the presentation (two-thirds of total time available)
   A. Summary of existing problems and limitations
   B. Summary description of the proposed system
   C. Feasibility analysis
   D. Proposed schedule to complete project

III. Questions and concerns from the audience (time here is not to be included in the time allotted for presentation and conclusion; it is determined by those asking the questions and voicing their concerns)

IV. Conclusion (one-sixth of total time available)
   A. Summary of proposal
   B. Call to action (request for whatever authority you require to continue systems development)

© Richard D. Irwin, Inc., 1994

Guidelines for Visual Aids

Visual aids should both enhance and expedite a presentation.

TM–260

Typical Project Walkthrough Form

This walkthrough form can be completed by the recorder and distributed to all walkthrough participants as a record of the walkthrough.

TM−261 (cont)

WALKTHROUGH REPORT

Coordinator	Project
Segment for Review	

Coordinator's checklist:

1. Confirm with developer that material is ready and stable _____

2. Issue invitations, assign responsibilities, distribute materials

Date _____ Time _____ Duration _____

Place _____

Responsibilities	Participants	Can attend	Received materials?
_____	_____	_____	_____
_____	_____	_____	_____
_____	_____	_____	_____
_____	_____	_____	_____
_____	_____	_____	_____
_____	_____	_____	_____

Agenda

_____ 1. All participants agree to follow the *SAME* set of rules.

_____ 2. New segment: walkthrough of material

_____ 3. Old segment: item-by-item checkoff of previous action list

_____ 4. Group decision

_____ 5. Deliver copy of this form to project management.

Decision: _____ Accept product as is

_____ Revise (no further walkthrough)

_____ Revise and schedule another walkthrough

Signatures

© Richard D. Irwin, Inc., 1994

TM-261
(concl)

WALKTHROUGH ACTION LIST—SCRIBE'S REPORT

Coordinator	Scribe	Date
Project	Segment	

= fixed | Issues raised in review

© Richard D. Irwin, Inc., 1994

Formats for Written Reports

The factual format places emphasis on details. The administrative format places emphasis on conclusions and recommendations.

TM-262

Formats for Written Reports

The factual format places emphasis on details. The administrative format places emphasis on conclusions and recommendations.

Factual Format

I. Introduction
II. Methods and procedures
III. Facts and details
IV. Discussion and analysis of facts and details
V. Recommendations
VI. Conclusion

Administrative Format

I. Introduction
II. Conclusions and recommendations
III. Summary and discussion of facts and details
IV. Methods and procedures
V. Final conclusion
VI. Appendices with facts and details

© Richard D. Irwin, Inc., 1994

Secondary Elements for a Written Report

Secondary elements are used to package a report and are used with both factual and administrative formats.

Letter of transmittal
Title page
Table of contents
List of figures, illustrations, and tables
Abstract or executive summary
 (The primary elements — the body of the report, in either the factual or administrative format —
 are presented in this portion of the report.)
Appendices

Steps in Writing a Report

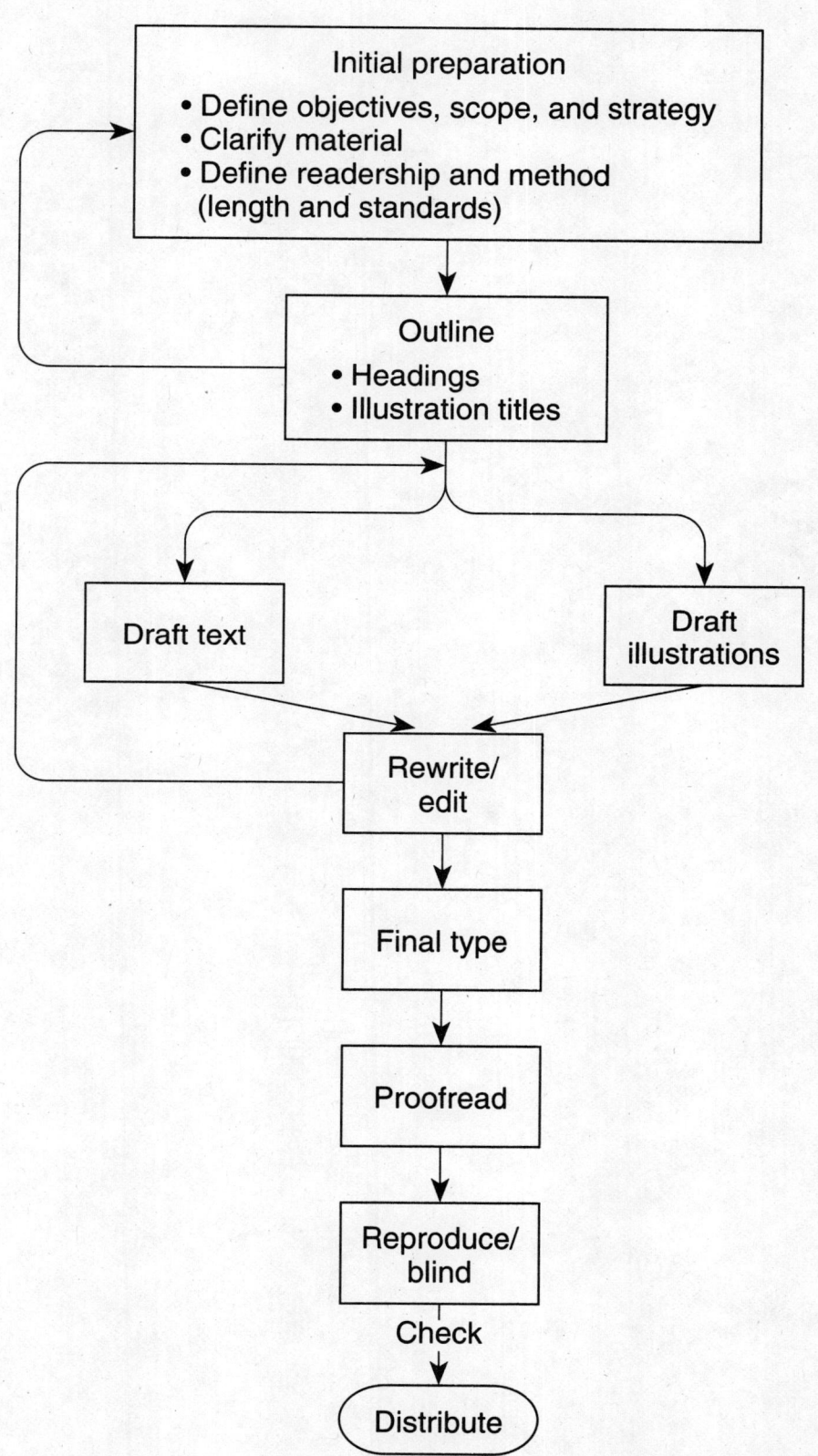